STAR SIGNS
FOR LOVERS

STAR SIGNS FOR LOVERS

LIZ GREENE

STEIN AND DAY/Publishers/New York

First published in the United States of America in 1980

STEIN AND DAY/Publishers
Scarborough House
Briarcliff Manor, N.Y. 10510

Greene, Liz.
    Star signs for lovers.

    1. Astrology. 2. Love—Miscellanea. I. Title.
BF1729.L6G7 1980   133.5'864677   80-5890
ISBN 0-8128-2765-1

Contents

Part One: Sun Signs 11

What a Horoscope Can and Can't Tell You 15
About Mirrors . . . 21
Suns and Rising Signs and Other Things . . . 37
Table of Ascendants 45

Part Two: The Elements of Fire and Earth 109
Vision v. Reality

The Element of Fire 111
Aries 122
Leo 147
Sagittarius 174

The Element of Earth 198
Taurus 207
Virgo 230
Capricorn 255

Some Last Words . . . 281

Part Three: The Elements of Air and Water 291
Harmony v. Truth

The Element of Air 293

Gemini   304
Libra   331
Aquarius   358

The Element of Water   383
Cancer   395
Scorpio   419
Pisces   446

Some Further Last Words . . .   471

Conclusion   477

ACKNOWLEDGEMENT

The illustrations in this book are taken from *Poeticon Astronomicon* by C. J. Hyginus (Venice, 1485) and *De Magnis Copiunctionibus* by Albumasar (Augsburg, 1489) and are reproduced by kind permission of the Victoria and Albert Museum.

Sun Signs

$\mathcal{W}$hy, queries Woody Allen in the film *Annie Hall*, do we bother with such problematic, complicated, tortuous things as relationships? Why make the effort to learn something about, care for, give to, take from, cherish, fight, love other human beings? Woody Allen answers his own question with a joke:

My brother has gone crazy. He thinks he's a
  chicken.
Then why don't you commit him?
Because I need the eggs, says Woody.
Relationships are something like that.

It's certainly fashionable at the moment, in some parts of society, to abandon the often outmoded values of our parents and grandparents. For one thing, it's obvious to a lot of people that they haven't worked; the marriages of the past were no better than the marriages of the present. There were fewer divorces, of course; but then you had two people living side by side until death did them part who filled the house with silent enmity and poison that caused not a few psychological conflicts in their children. Even if you don't 'believe' in psychology, it's sadly apparent that the modern family unit needs a little refurbishing if it's to continue to exist at all. Have a look at a few divorce statistics.

Now, along with the state of the economy, the dangers of nuclear destruction, the energy crisis, the overpopulated and undervalued earth, the endangering of animals (and humans) and the other favourite nightmares of this, the end of the twentieth century and the dawn of what astrology calls the Aquarian Age, we also have a big problem with human relationships. This is attributable to various things, depending on your viewpoint. Morals are collapsing, not enough good old-fashioned discipline, not enough faith in God and the Catholic Church, not enough faith in God and the Anglican Church, sexual repression, capitalism, communism, and any other scapegoat you care to think of that will exonerate you, or me, from taking responsibility for our own messes. In an age of superlative technology where, for the first time, millions can purchase a little leisure, millions of people also, desperate to understand why everything is so damned meaningless and why they're so lonely, turn to disciplines and beliefs so ancient that we can't even fathom their origins. What are now known as esoteric studies are slowly but steadily encroaching on the domain once held tightly in the grip of orthodox religion.

The word 'esoteric' simply means 'inner'. 'Esoteric' can refer to a lot of different things, from the Maharishi and Transcendental Meditation, to the Children of the Temple of God in Guyana. Esoteric studies can range from the ridiculous to the sublime. They can plumb ancient and learned treatises on alchemy, magic, Hermetic philosophy and the kaballah. They can explore mysteries like the Bermuda Triangle. Inner is about parapsychological phenomena, dreams, visions, altered states of consciousness. It's about synchronistic phenomena, precognitive dreams, telepathy, clairvoyance. It's also about depth psychology, the study of the human soul. And it can also be about astrology.

Can astrology – familiar to us all through that silly but irresistible column in the daily newspaper wherein Madame Somebody-or-other tells one that Wednesday will be a rotten day – possibly contribute anything at all to our dilemma of living on an overpopulated planet where we must rub shoulders (and souls) with all those strangers?

Lately, there has been a good deal of public outcry from academia against astrology as well as from the scientific community at large; which has apparently got a little frightened by its popularity. (After all, if there's something mysterious about life which orthodox science can't answer, what sort of world do we live in?) But no matter how strenuously it's proclaimed that astrology is really a load of medieval superstitious nonsense, belief in it is spreading. Once upon a time everyone read those ubiquitous sun-sign columns with tongue-in-cheek, laughing all the while – still secretly wondering whether Wednesday really *would* be a rotten day and heaving a sigh of relief when it wasn't. (Irresistible, that stuff. It touches close to the bone of that favourite of all human pastimes – reading about oneself.) But no one would dare admit – especially a rational person like yourself – that there might be anything in it. Granted, there were some fairly respectable folk like Sir Isaac Newton and Professor Carl Jung who dabbled in it. But for the most part, if you did read a book on astrology, you wrapped it in a plain brown cover so as not to be thought an eccentric. Better you should be caught reading *Playboy*!

Then a persistent Frenchman named Michel Gauquelin arrived, and decided that he would disprove once and for all astrology's ludicrous claims. He launched a massive statistical project, accumulating thousands of horoscopes of people working in various professions to see if the evidence showed any correlation at all between those bits of rock orbiting out in space and our ordinary human lives. And, lo and behold, Monsieur Gauquelin found to his horror and astonishment that, far from proving astrology's definitive irrelevance, he had proved that it worked.

From the time of M. Gauquelin's findings (which he duly published in the form of several very impressive books) astrology has at last begun to earn a modicum of respect from academic quarters. It's also begun to infiltrate some places where you wouldn't have expected to find it, like universities and psychiatrists' offices. It's used by the American and Israeli governments, and possibly a few more – we don't really know. It's used by businesses for employment decisions. It's used by doctors for diagnosis. And at long last it's being used for the real purpose for which it exists: for each person to learn something about themselves because in learning about themselves they no longer vent their own problems and difficulties on the people around them.

Before the temple of the oracle at Delphi, the ancient Greeks – who were by no means fools – had two pieces of advice carved on the portals. One was, 'Nothing in excess.' The other was, 'Know thyself'.

The first instruction is much subtler than it sounds. It doesn't just mean curb excessive behaviour. It also means don't be lopsided. And lopsidedness – the over-emphasis on one way of looking at life and people – is a propensity we all share. Astrology has a lot to say about lopsidedness. By learning something about your own astrological makeup, you can see pretty quickly just how one-sided your own view of reality is.

The second instruction is easy enough to understand. It's much more difficult to follow. On any journey, inner or outer, we need road maps. Outer road maps are plentiful enough. Inner ones aren't. Astrology is an inner road map.

If you really think the solution to the problem of relationships lies in things 'out there' in society, look again. It may just lie in ourselves, in our ways of dealing with our lopsidedness and our lack of self-knowledge. How in the world can you possibly expect to get on with somebody else when you don't even know who you yourself are?

And if you think astrology is a pretty abstruse way of attempting to get insight into one's own behaviour and motives, read on.

What a Horoscope Can and Can't Tell You

*F*irst things first. Please put away that newspaper sun-sign column. Yes, I know that's what you thought astrology was about. But that's like assuming the entire world of music, ranging from Beethoven to Pythagoras' Music of the Spheres, can be encapsulated in an advertising jingle of ten notes. To understand astrology, we must first learn something about its roots and its meaning.

The symbolism of astrology is an attempt to portray – in pictorial rather than conceptual form – the basic energies behind life and behind human beings. It's very ancient; so ancient that we don't know its origins. We know that the ancient Egyptians, Babylonians, Sumerians, Chaldeans, Indians and Chinese used it. Also, a little careful scholarly research has revealed that there are similarities between the 'study of the stars' in every ancient civilization, even when there could have been no conceivable link between these disparate cultures. And we know that this incredibly old portrayal of the forces of life is still as alive and fascinating today as it was five thousand years ago.

Why a pictorial language? A fair question, since we live in a scientific age and are taught that there must be a rational, conceptual answer for every one of life's puzzles. But science is in fact ill-equipped to explain many of life's mysteries, since these mysteries are non-rational in nature. They can be understood, felt, intuited, imagined, glimpsed through the language of image, metaphor, parable, symbol, myth. But to try to define them in easy sentences like a multiple-choice question in an IQ test is downright ridiculous. After all the explanations of the biological processes of conception and birth, do we know any more about where life comes from? Can we comprehend the mystery of death? How about electricity, which we all use, and which has been harnessed for our comfort and convenience. What is it? We still don't know. In fact, we don't really know what 'matter' is. In quantum physics, one of the twentieth century's most sophisticated disciplines, they have begun to observe that in any scientific experiment involving sub-atomic particles, the experimenter and the experiment affect each other. This means – astonishingly enough – that so-called 'objective' matter is no longer objective, since it's intimately bound up with the psyche of the observer. Matter, in the end, is as mysterious to us as spirit. Maybe it's a reasonable idea to learn a little humility in this arrogant age, and recognize that we know precious little about the universe in which we live. Nature is jealous of its mysteries. Just when we think we've explained it, it produces something which baffles the most sophisticated intellect. Like astrology.

Astrology is baffling because it works. So, what, in fact, is a horoscope?

What it's *not* is a way of foretelling the future, or of determining whether that tall dark stranger will turn up next week. Definitions first. A birth horoscope is a map of the heavens – the solar system, to be precise – at the exact moment, day and year of birth. It is a map, pure and simple, relating the positions of the eight known planets, sun and moon to the horizon and meridian of the earth. And it's precise astronomy that can't be faulted from the astronomer's point of view.

The zodiac is a circle or band which is really the apparent path of the sun around the earth. Yes, we know perfectly well the sun doesn't go around the earth. But it appears as though it does, and its path is called the ecliptic. Astrology divides this circle of the ecliptic into twelve equal-sized pie slices. The astrological year begins around the twentieth of March, the occurrence of the vernal equinox. That starts the zodiacal sign of Aries. Your birth sign or sun-sign is the part of the zodiac in which the sun is passing during the thirty days of your sign.

This is where sun-sign columns end. If you're born on 18 April, you're an Aries. If you're born on 4 September, you're a Virgo. But that's just the beginning. We forgot the moon and the eight planets. They too are important, and part of the horoscope. So the astrologer plots where each of these heavenly bodies falls in reference to the zodiacal band. Finally, he needs to know the time of birth, so that he can work out what sign of the zodiac is rising in the east at the moment of birth. Presto. A horoscope. What can it tell us?

A lot. To put it briefly and succinctly, the horoscope is a map of the psyche of the individual. It's a kind of blueprint, a seed plan, a model of the energies and drives which make up any person. Because it's calculated precisely for time and place, it's unique, unlike the sun-sign column. Even identical twins are born at least four minutes apart, and in four minutes the picture has shifted.

Annoyingly, few people in England know the exact moment of their birth. It's not recorded. More often, the astrologer, asking for his client's birth time, gets a reply like, 'Well, it was around tea-time,' or, 'Well, the milkman had just delivered the milk.' An approximate time must serve in these cases. The Scots are a lot smarter, and so are the French and the Americans: they record precise birth times. Perhaps one day British hospitals will as well, when it dawns on the public at large that astrology can be a very important tool for living.

The horoscope maps out the potential pattern of the individual. The operative word here is 'potential'. It's potential in the same way that an apple seed will potentially produce an apple tree. It contains the entire cycle inside it: seed, young plant, tree, flower, fruit, seed. But if you hold it in your hand, it's still only a seed. A lot can happen to a seed. Nurtured, fertilized, watered and given sufficient sunshine, it will produce a splendid tree. Neglected, it will produce far short of its potential, or may not produce at all. That's where free will comes into the picture. We are given certain potentials. What we make of them is our own business. We have the option to become ourselves in full flower, or produce a stunted tree that bears no fruit. And the gardener isn't anybody but oneself.

A lot of people are frightened of astrology because they believe it claims to predict fate. Once upon a time, during the Middle Ages and the Renaissance, it claimed to do precisely that. But astrology has evolved since then, just as medicine has. We in the West – unlike India – don't like to think that there's any factor shaping our lives except ourselves and the tax collector. The social sciences acknowledge a little pressure from environment, psychology from childhood. But for the most part we want to believe we're free to make choices and decisions. Any impingement on our personal freedom is acceptable only if it comes in a recognizable form, like bad weather, or the 'act of God' as it's called in insurance policies. We call those accidents. And when something happens that we can't control, we whinge and moan a lot. Particularly if it's another person that we can't control: the child who grows up differently from our original plan, the husband who leaves, the wife who decides not to be submissive and adoring any more, the mother who interferes, the boss who doesn't appreciate our work. We don't see these unpleasant intrusions as fate, we see them as nuisances, obviously due to the stupidity of others, and we do our best to eradicate the cause, which is naturally the fault of the other person.

But is it really the fault of the other? And how free are we? Astrology offers a humble suggestion. Numerous poets, philosophers, and psychologists have offered the same suggestion in different languages throughout the centuries. Here are Rainer Maria Rilke's words for it:

What is within surrounds us.

Remember that quote. It's crucial to the understanding not only of astrology, but of relationships as well. In fact, we might go so far as to say that it's crucial to understanding life. The inner stuff of which a person is made – the emotions, drives, desires, fantasies, dreams, conflicts, loves, hatreds, talents – is like a magnet, or like the musical note of a tuning fork. It resonates to its pitch outside, attracts substance to itself from the world which is the same kind of substance. Carl Jung puts it another way. He says:

A man's life is characteristic of himself.

So what happens to you – in personal life, that is, since we're not at this point considering what happens to the great collectives like races and nations – is in some way a reflection, a symbolic portrait, of something in yourself.

Now you know why the Greeks carved, 'Know thyself' by the temple at Delphi. A lot of people find this very uncomfortable. It means we must take responsibility for what comes to us, pick up our equal share of the creation of our worlds. And it's so much nicer, so much easier, to blame someone else for the negative things, and praise ourselves for the positive ones.

Only a child expects life to be that easy. A wise person accepts what's given, and expects the rest to become what they create of it.

The horoscope describes a person's inner nature. Their life will run according to this magical (don't be afraid of the word – the law of attraction is one of the basic principles of magic, too, and all of life is magical) process of mutual attraction. The more unaware they are of the stuff of which they're made, the more 'fated' they are by their own inner self. They'll go on attracting things into their life for good or ill whether they care to acknowledge it or not. The more aware (or we might say conscious) they are, the more choices they have. They may not be able to change their basic substance. Remember the apple seed. It can't suddenly leap out of the core of the apple and decide it's going to be a lentil when it grows up. But an awful lot of variations can be made on one apple tree.

This is the meaning of fate in astrology. Not some Old Man in the clouds punishing the sinner and rewarding the righteous. No dark gods lurking in the shadows waiting to dictate, like the Three Grey Ones in ancient Greek myth, the length of the thread that marks a man's life. Only ourselves – our Self, our own deepest and innermost being dictates our Fate. And how much of our Self do we truly know, and how much lies unknown, hidden, unconscious?

About Mirrors...

*A*nyone who has had experience of one of those controversial trials where many witnesses provide their own perceptions of a particular event will know that if you ask twelve witnesses to describe a road accident they will describe twelve different accidents. It isn't that anybody is lying, or even deliberately exaggerating. It's just that any viewpoint or perception is subjective. The so-called 'objectivity' of the rational person who prides themselves on their attentiveness to facts is equally subjective, because their vision doesn't perceive the non-rational factors in the situation that would frighten and perplex them were they to recognize them. In short, we see life and other people through our own eyes, and our own eyes are tinted like a pair of cosmetic contacts with the particular viewpoint of our own personalities.

This sounds very simple. You'd be surprised how antagonistic people become, however, when you present such a basic and fundamental reality. What? No objectivity? Well, yes, I can understand that about my wife, or my mother-in-law, or the blacks, or the Jews, or the Arabs, or the Irish, or the communists, or the capitalists ... But me? Why, *my* viewpoint is objective. I *know* it is. I know it's right because it's mine.

It's all very well to poke fun at the distorted visions of life and reality and relationships that others hold. It's not funny when we have to question the very ground upon which we stand ourselves. Am I really seeing him/her correctly? Does my husband really hold the motives

I attribute to him when he withholds affection? Does my lover really wish to chain me and possess me? Is the world really misunderstanding of my genius? The buck, as Harry Truman once said, stops here.

Now let's go back to astrology. The entire horoscope is a map of the individual. That means that it describes their temperament, their psychological makeup, their inner landscape. All things being equal, they experience life through it, so that the life they know – or what they know to be life – is coloured by their own nature, own needs, own drives, own experiences. But, you may argue, a person's viewpoint is shaped by their experience of life, not the other way around. To say that it's the other way around is very disturbing: it implies that we are responsible for what our lives are. Well, yes. In a way. Or at least responsible for understanding why what happens, happens to me and not to you. Because if we take the standpoint of astrology, the birth horoscope postulates an inherent temperament, an *a priori* subjective nature. We come in like that. Nobody made us that way. And we create our realities, or interpret reality, according to that *a priori* viewpoint.

An example. I had a Capricornian client once who exhibited all the typical characteristics of this complex and difficult-to-understand sign. This was because my client wasn't just a Capricorn; he also had Capricorn on the ascendant, which made the sign particularly strong in his nature. For the first half hour of our session he complained bitterly about how harsh life had been to him. This was in reply to my comment that Capricorn had a tendency to be over-cautious, over-suspicious in human relationships.

'But,' he said, 'I have good reason for not trusting anybody. People always let you down. They always take advantage of you. They're out for what they can get. I'm only being smart if I hit first, if I take advantage before the other bastard can use me.'

'Have you ever tried another approach?' I queried politely. 'Like expecting the better side of a person to show itself? Like trusting? Trust does remarkable things, you know. If you really accept a person, it will often mysteriously bring out the most trustworthy aspects of him.'

'Ridiculous,' my sceptical, pragmatic Capricorn replied. 'I watched my father abuse and take advantage of my mother. Everybody is the same.'

You can guess what happened. My client, given this none-too-friendly attitude toward people, had a tendency to irritate them. Nobody likes to be thought a conniving bastard before they've had a chance to open their mouth. He irritated people so much that they decided to give him a little of his own medicine. Since he only thought of using them, they reasoned, he was good for nothing except being used. So they used him, and he drew his own experiences down on his own head and then blamed other people, and life, for something which he saw as a child and which – like a lot of us – he assumed defined the real nature of life. A tragic but common example of how our particular attitudes influence others to treat us in the manner in which we see things.

People wonder why Sagittarians are so proverbially lucky. It's the same phenomenon. Sagittarius is a fire sign, and the fire signs have a kind of innate trust in life. They are like large overgrown children in a playground, and if something goes wrong, well, it will certainly right itself. Something will happen to get me out of this. Life can't possibly let me down. There must be a lesson in it, a meaning. Result? Something inevitably *does* happen to get the Sagittarian out of his jam. It isn't that he's given the gift of luck by the gods. It's that he's got something innately sorted out: he believes in life, and life vindicates him. Because he thinks he's in a big candy shop, someone always comes up with candy.

Free. And when he does fall down, he doesn't attribute it to other people's nasty natures. He attributes it to bad luck which will soon right itself. How can you argue with that?

These two examples illustrate a profoundly important point. The whole point of astrology is to learn something about what you are. Because if you haven't a clue what is really going on inside you, you're still going to carry around those little bits of magnetic substance which make you attract the people and situations which resonate to your substance. If you know about it, you might just have something to say about the matter. If you don't know about it, then you're fated: but not by your stars. By yourself, mate. Remember Shakespeare? 'The fault, dear Brutus, is not in our stars, but in ourselves.'

Now let's take any horoscope. Or for that matter, any astrological sign. There are facets to each sign which are readily observable. They are in the shop window, so to speak. We can read about these qualities in any newspaper column. Everyone familiar with popular astrology will recognize, for example, the familiar Leo who is warm, confident, magnanimous, loves to entertain, loves to be at the centre of the stage. Or the familiar Virgo who is neat, orderly, tidy, well-organized, efficient, never caught unprepared. Or the typical Cancer who is sensitive, imaginative, moody, fluid, shifting, kaleidoscopic, changeable as the moon, in need of security and a nest into which to retreat. Or the aggressive, ebullient Aries who is always ready for a challenge and loves a good fight.

But there is a secret underside to every sign too. Anything that casts light also casts a shadow. And these secret shadow sides of each sign of the zodiac are rarely talked about because they are embarrassing. But if you walk around never acknowledging that undertow, like the undertow of a tide, it can drag you out to sea. All of a sudden you are caught up in moods or situations or relationships which are not what you bargained for – because your own unconscious behaviour got you there by provoking a whole set of reactions beyond your control. It pays to know something about the shadow trailing behind you, *especially* if you think you have a lot of light.

Let's run through the zodiac quickly and talk about these shadow sides of each sign. They will be elaborated more fully when we get to the signs themselves and their elements. But here's some basic groundwork.

Remember the decisive, aggressive, brave Aries? Who would guess that there lurks beneath that shiny, confident, rash surface a very indecisive streak, and a terrible sensitivity to whether other people like him? Not the image he would like to project. But it tails him like a shadow nonetheless. Sometimes you'll see him overcompensating, because this indecisiveness and dependency on other people's approval nags at him and makes him very uncomfortable. So the Aries leader may wind up a follower, because he just can't stand up for himself when the real bell rings and the fight is on.

And the stable, calm, reliable Taurus? Yes, he's the one who is always reasonable, slow to anger, patient. The beast of burden who will cheerfully take your burdens off your back and never complain. Gentle, peaceable, easy-going. Who would guess that there is a passionate, unreasonable, demanding, possessive side to him that secretly provokes those very crises that he hates so much, and pushes him into the changes and chaotic crises that he would do anything or pay anything to avoid? Taurus loves stability and intensely dislikes change. But the secret theatrical destructive side keeps trying to bring the play to a violent climax. It's so uncomfortable for him to sense those seething currents inside that he will often overdo the patience bit, and nail everything down to the floor, in order to avoid it.

Guess whom he dislikes most? Right. People who constantly stir up emotional trouble and overcomplicate things. But those people he doesn't like are secretly within himself.

Have a look at Gemini. Rational man, clever, witty, intellectual, cool, cerebral. You won't catch him 'believing' gullibly in anything; he likes crystal-clear concepts, logical structures. He may be abstract, but he's rational. A brilliant debater, a skilled critic, a gifted reporter, scrupulously adhering to the logic of the situation. But beneath that sparkling intellect is a naïve, gullible and rather woolly-minded mystic who is ready to believe anything, to distort the truth to prove the intuition, to exaggerate facts to illustrate dramatically the connections. Listen to Gemini get carried away telling a story. At first he's strictly reporting facts. Then he begins to add a little, fill in some here, some more there. Pretty soon you discover that he's longing to believe in something. Out come the ghost stories, the psychic experiences, the mysterious and meaningful coincidences. The reporter has become a novelist. It can make a Gemini so uncomfortable that he becomes scathingly critical of anything non-intellectual, and keeps his conversations to the most banal chit-chat.

And Cancer. Warm, sensitive, changeable. We mentioned Cancer before, fluid, changeable like water (the element to which the sign belongs), tender, nurturing, caring. And the undertow? Yes, of course. Calculating. It's those sensitive, helpless Cancers who manage to extract those enormous maintenance payments, secrete thousands of pounds of stocks in the rafters, manipulate money and material situations to their liking and can, when necessary, use anybody or anything to their own advantage – one of self-protection. This side of Cancer is so disturbing to the gentle, caring Cancerian that he will often recoil violently from more cynical, harder

people. Cancer usually dislikes an insensitive and calculating person. But this secret shadow is inside them.

Ah, Leo. King of the Beasts and of the Zodiac.
Individualistic, self-confident, self-conscious Leo. The
actor, the hero, the knight on the white horse, the
chivalrous prince ready to rescue any damsel in distress
and defend the weak and the poor. He believes in
himself and his unique destiny, and is touched with the
faint gilt edge of natural aristocracy. Of course he's
egocentric. Doesn't the universe really revolve around
him? Doesn't everybody else look to him as example?
The conscious side of him probably feels that way. But
the undertow, the secret shadow doesn't. Watch Leo
closely and you'll see that he can't really make a move
without the approval and love of others. Self-confidence? Why, it's hardly there at all. He's only a cog in
a big machine, a faceless face among a mass, a droplet
in an ocean. And all the while he's compensating madly
by being the most unique person he knows, he's trying
hard to fend off that nagging uncomfortable sense of his
own ordinariness. His belief is in his own heroic myth.
But the secret voice says, No special exemptions for
anybody. A kind of psychic communism.

Let's look at Virgo. Precise, orderly, tidy – in thinking
if not in practical matters. There are generally two
types of Virgo. There are the ones who empty ashtrays
a lot, where everything is spotless and carefully planned.
(That happens more often when Virgo is on the
ascendant.) And there are the congenitally sloppy ones
with, nevertheless, filing-cabinet minds. Objects may
skitter away, but memories and facts and the latest
books don't. Admirable Virgo who, like the boy scout,
is never caught unprepared. And the undertow in Virgo
is? You guessed it, vagueness and chaos. Hard and
businesslike on the surface, Virgos are secretly suckers
for every stray in the world. Sensitive beyond belief,
they defend the secret shadow side by trying to organize

life so that it can't slide around where they can't see it.
Lazy and indolent. Drifting with the current. Day-
dreaming. It's so uncomfortable, that a lot of Virgos
become obsessive about having the blue shirts on the
left side of the cupboard and the yellow shirts on the
right, because if a blue shirt wanders over to the yellow
the forces of chaos might ensue.

By now you can see what we're up to. Yes, every sign
is secretly its opposite. You'll recognize Libran characteristics in the Arian, Scorpionic troublemaking in
the Taurus, Sagittarian gullibility in the Gemini, Capricornian manipulativeness in the Cancer, Aquarian
collectivity in the Leo, Piscean disintegration in the
Virgo. There is more besides, to this secret undertow.
But we'll go on with the last six signs to finish demon-
strating the point.

The Libran may be plagued by an unconscious
aggressiveness, egocentricity and rudeness, just when
he's trying hard to be polite. The Scorpio may be
dogged by a Taurean materialism and dogged tenacity
to what he has outgrown, just when he's trying to
fathom the meaning of a new experience. The Sagittarian may be plagued with nagging scepticism just when
he's trying to experience the divine, the numinous. The
Capricorn may be nagged by an oversensitivity and
moodiness when he has to be most realistic and hard-
headed. The Aquarian may be tailed by his own secret
self-glorification when he's in the middle of a speech on
the rights of man. And the Piscean may find himself
compulsively nitpicking and organizing trivia when he's
trying to be accepting and compassionate and inclusive.

Each person has a dark and a light side. And if we
use astrology to understand someone's dearest dreams
and needs and natural manner of expression, we must
equally well use it to discover the parts of his personality
which are a little more infantile or rough, and which
cause him problems just at a critical moment. And this

takes us to the most important concept in this book. Because what we can't recognize in ourselves we have a tendency to think we see in other people. We may love them or hate them for it, persecute them and make their lives miserable, or feel immense compassion and extend every effort to help them and protect them. But in the end it's very subjective. We don't really know, until a relationship has passed beyond that wonderful initial honeymoon stage, whether the person we're perceiving is really like that at all, or whether we're really falling in love with the hidden part of ourselves.

The Latin American novelist Alejo Carpentier says,

> People never love other people. They love themselves through other people.

While that's a little cynical it applies to a good many relationships that start off hot and furious and sputter out when the other person mysteriously 'changes'. The other person hasn't changed at all. It's just that our image of them has fallen apart, and the real person has peeped out from underneath. The reaction varies, depending upon how well we know ourselves. Most often it's a feeling of being let down and betrayed, as though the beloved has committed a sin by not living up to the ideal image we had and which in fact is something we should be capable of living out ourselves, since it's a piece of our own psyche.

In psychology, this mysterious and horribly common process is known as projection. Remember that word. Because there isn't a human being walking who doesn't project some dark or shadowy part of themselves onto others. And as long as we do that, we're not relating. We're living in a fantasy, which inevitably, like all good films and fairy tales, ends with the rude nudge of the reality of the stranger opposite.

Now we need to go back to the horoscope again. You

can make a rough approximation of your birth chart by
looking at the tables at the back of this book. First
check the ascendant table for the time of your birth.
You should take into account whether there might have
been summer-time or daylight-saving time in effect,
and deduct an hour from the time. Then check the
ascendant. Of course this is only a rough calculation.
For a proper chart, you need to calculate the ascendant
precisely. But for the time being, the table in the back
might be of help.

The ascendant is one of the most important factors
in any person's chart. Most of us can work out the sun-
sign under which we are born. This sign is a symbol of
the person we are striving to become, the kind of
attributes which we need to acquire, the special individual myth which we are living out. The ascendant – the
sign rising in the east at the time of birth – means
something different. It is the way in which we express
ourselves outward into life. How we see life, and how
others in turn see us. An analogy of this pair of points
– sun and ascendant – can be found in mythology. The
sun is the solar hero of myth, the individual on a quest
to become himself. The ascendant is the journey he
uniquely must make – the particular path or task which
will eventually lead him to self-realization, and meaning. So you think meaning is an abstruse word? Think
again. Victor Frankl, a psychiatrist writing about Jewish
concentration camp prisoners during the last war, made
a very important observation. He found that although
the cruelties and hardships to which the Jewish prisoners
were subjected were similar, those that managed to
survive the holocaust were those who had some innate
conviction that their lives had meaning. Those who
died were those who felt their own lives to be meaningless, random bits of flotsam floating on the sea of life.
Meaning has a lot to do not only with personal happiness, but with survival itself.

So: the ascendant is the point on the horoscope which not only describes the manner in which a person expresses himself, but also how he may begin to find some personal, subjective meaning in his own life. Often the ascendant represents an area of difficulty in life. It may be something we have a lot of trouble understanding in ourselves, or in expressing, but which we are drawn to over and over again.

Let's take an example. Enter a sun in Aquarius, male, about thirty-five years old. He is a typical Aquarian (maybe he has a couple of other planets, say Mercury and Venus in Aquarius, and maybe the moon in Libra or some other airy sign which emphasizes his airy temperament). Aquarius: rational, logical, deeply concerned with finding the truth. Interested in people, but not very demonstrative with individual persons. Controlled on the emotional level, and sometimes downright oblivious to the emotional undercurrents in himself and in others. Fair, honest, full of integrity. Anxious to be a 'good' or 'selfless' person. Idealistic. Reasonable. A thinker, scientist, academic, engineer, academic psychologist. But, like the rest of us, our Aquarian is two people: dark and light. Let's say he has, along with an Aquarian sun, a Scorpio ascendant. Like oil and water, Scorpio and Aquarius just don't mix.

My Aquarian client – for he is indeed a real person – couldn't understand why, despite his persistent attempts to run his life according to logical, reasonable patterns, he was always getting entangled in rather exotic relationships which had a powerful emotional current and usually erupted in crises. He also couldn't understand why he kept attracting a certain kind of woman: intense, volatile, possessive, demanding, deeply emotional. In fact, the kind of woman who might be represented by his ascendant. He was 'projecting' this bit of his own nature outside himself, and it kept coming to meet him in all his love affairs. He couldn't come to terms with it. But he also couldn't stay away from it. What was he to do?

I asked if he had ever felt intense, obsessive emotions himself. No, certainly not, he replied. I'm always reasonable. Have you ever felt jealous? 'Never,' he replied. 'I hate possessiveness. It's always my women who try to possess me.'

Now it happened that I had occasion to observe this highly intelligent man in action. I also had the opportunity to talk about his relationship patterns with one of his many women friends. Jealous? God, yes, she replied. Oh, not openly. He would never say, 'You can't go out to lunch with him,' or 'Why were you talking to that man for such a long time?' But he exudes this kind of atmosphere. You know, the sort that makes you feel you could cut it with a knife. A really poisonous atmosphere, like a black cloud. He punishes me that way when I flirt with anybody. And then he cuts off from me for a few days. Goes ice cold. When I ask why, he denies knowing what I'm talking about. I don't think he does know. But how can he not know?

Indeed, how can he not know his own feelings? But Aquarians are masters at remaining utterly and blithely ignorant of their own atmosphere, their own feelings. Everyone else feels it. But not the Aquarian. Busy living in their intellect, they are genuinely surprised and hurt when accused of coldness or unconscious resentment.

Now, taking this Scorpio ascendant on one level means that our friend has a lot of Scorpio qualities. It's just that he isn't aware of some of them, because they don't gel with his image of himself. Also, it's easier to blame somebody else, than to try to reconcile the opposing values of two such diametrically opposite signs.

But if we look at the ascendant as the journey, it

reads something like this: Scorpio is a watery sign, and therefore pertains to the realm of human emotion and relating. It is a sexual sign, in the sense that its meaning is about the conflict between and the union of opposites, male and female. It is a primitive sign, in the sense that its values are not those of civilized twentieth century academic intelligentsia, but more those of the basic life of nature: what I love is mine. What I don't love I choose to stay away from. And if you hurt me, then I will hurt you back, so that you know how it feels.

Scorpio is a sign of immense depth, immense insight. His journey is through the dark mire of human sexuality and emotion, through the struggles of two people trying to pierce the veil of illusions and fantasies so that they may couple as individuals and experience the transformation which comes from the abdication of power over another. It deals with the unconscious: what is hidden, the secret motive behind the mask of behaviour. It is about the secrets of the soul.

My Aquarian friend was very struck when I pointed out to him that the fact that he had a consistent repetitive pattern of difficult relationships in his life meant something. It wasn't chance, or accident. It wasn't rotten luck. It wasn't even a neurosis. I had seen it over and over in those with Scorpio ascendants. Could he possibly give it a chance, take the gamble of exploring his own inner emotional life, and try to find the meaning in this pattern?

The ascendant draws us to what we most need to learn, and what can open up whole new vistas of life. It takes time and work. But this is using astrology as the real tool it is, rather than as a parlour game by which fortunes can be told. For the horoscope tells us about what is most meaningful to us: the path we are on, the reason why we are here, the reason why we meet the people we do and get involved in relationships with them. From astrology's point of view, there are no accidents. As Ralph Waldo Emerson once wrote,

> The secret of the world is the tie between person and event. The soul contains the event that shall befall it . . . the event is the print of your form . . . A man will see his character emitted in the events that seem to meet, but which exude from and accompany him.

By now it should be fairly clear where we are going: birth chart equals character, and character equals fate. And our relationships are our fate because they reflect back to us our own character. We fall in love with ourselves through others; because we are seeking to develop in a relationship that which is incomplete in ourselves. When you compare two horoscopes, you see this in living technicolour. That which is blocked and difficult to see or express in one chart will be mirrored in the other. A wonderful opportunity, as the old alchemists might have said, to develop, to become oneself through the experience of another. But what do we do? We botch it. We dissociate ourselves from the event – the quarrel, the hurt, the misunderstanding, the vanished illusion, the idealization – and we place it firmly on the other person's shoulders, and then yell at him as though we had nothing whatsoever to do with it. The following scenario may be heard at the end of, or in the aftermath of, a broken marriage:

> INJURED PARTY TO FRIEND: Of course it was all his fault. I did everything I could. I was the one who *gave* all the *time*. I never once got anything back. Oh, how much I sacrificed! The bastard . . . it's all his fault. He ran off with another woman. Imagine! After I've taken care of him all these years . . .

There are numerous other scenarios, each reflecting the viewpoint of the injurer and the injured. We can all recognize ourselves in these scenarios; they're classic, you hear them repeated a thousand times. What, oh what, do we do?

Listen. Someone once asked Jung how it was that he seemed to be able to help even the most difficult, the most distraught, of his patients. He replied: 'I listen.' Start off listening to yourself. Who is it you're really accusing? Have you heard that scenario before? Maybe on your mother's lips? Your father's? Is it really in the other person? Or maybe in yourself?

Easy questions. Painful to answer, because any retracting of a psychological projection involves a discovery of something in oneself that one didn't really want to see. Sometimes we do this with positive things too: 'Oh, everyone is so much prettier/smarter/more successful than I am.' 'Oh, he/she has everything.' Oh, really? That's as much of a cop-out as blaming everyone. And just as destructive, because it breeds all sorts of unconscious resentments.

Yes, I know, you thought it was all going to be fun and easy. It can be. Astrology has its humour too; and the humour shows its happiest face when you learn to recognize signs and their habits. And it's part of the humour of life as well – you develop a sense of irony, and a little, maybe just a little, ability to laugh at yourself. But if you really want to find where the sun truly shines, in yourself and in others, you've got to be prepared for the shadow too. Everything in this strange world of ours comes in doubles. Astrology knows that too; everything has its opposite. And sometimes just the process of accepting those doubles in ourselves does wonders. Yes, it's all right to be both gentle and loving and also bitchy and devouring. Yes, it's fine to be intelligent and stupid. Yes, we all have a little male and a little female in us. One of the great lessons astrology teaches is tolerance: tolerance of others, and tolerance of ourselves. Remember the Biblical quote, 'Love thy neighbour as thyself'? Well, the good Christian, and the philanthropist of any persuasion, tries hard to love his neighbour. It's a thing any person who aspires to be loving tries to do. But we forget the 'as thyself' quietly tacked on to the end. How many of us really love ourselves?

Suns and Rising Signs and Other Things...

When people say, 'What's your sign?' they are referring to the sign under which you were born. Which means, essentially, the zodiacal sign through which the sun was travelling on your birthday. The sun takes about a month to clear one sign. Of course we all know (unless we belong to the Flat Earth Society) that it is really the earth travelling around the sun, not the sun travelling around the earth, that gives us the phenomenon of a rising and setting sun that appears to travel across the sky. The Greeks, watching the glory of the eternally moving sun through the heavens, called it Phoebus, and envisioned it as a god in his chariot of gold, drawn by snowy horses, traversing the vault of the sky. In our scientific age, we explain by astronomical terms what once was a mystery. Astrology is not so unsophisticated that it does not recognize the real astronomical phenomenon behind the path of the sun. But, from the symbolic point of view, it is the sun crossing the heavens, following the circle of the zodiac.

So if you are born on the first of June, you are a Gemini, because the sun appeared to be transiting the segment of the zodiac called Gemini on that day. If you were born on November 14, you are a Scorpio. And if you are born on those tricky days which fall between two signs – like 23 December, or 21 May – then you are called a 'cusper', a person born on the cusp of two signs, and said to partake of a little of both. You'll still be one or the other. Sometimes you need a proper astrological chart cast to determine exactly which you are, because the sun might change over on your birthday. But we can generally use the following calendar:

Born between 23 December and 20 January –
   Capricorn
Born between 21 January and 20 February –
   Aquarius
Born between 21 February and 21 March – *Pisces*
Born between 22 March and 21 April – *Aries*
Born between 22 April and 22 May – *Taurus*
Born between 23 May and 22 June – *Gemini*
Born between 23 June and 23 July – *Cancer*
Born between 24 July and 23 August – *Leo*
Born between 24 August and 23 September – *Virgo*
Born between 24 September and 22 October –
   Libra
Born between 23 October and 22 November –
   Scorpio
Born between 23 November and 22 December –
   Sagittarius

Now we've already mentioned that the sun-sign, as well as any other placement in astrology, represents a potential, not a fact. A lot of confusion ensues when you read sun-sign columns because of this. If you are born under Aries, it doesn't automatically mean you are going to behave like the traditional Aries: aggressive, impulsive, self-centred, heroic, and all that other good Don Quixote stuff. It means that your innate motivation is represented by Aries. But you might find it a little difficult to live out, either because your environment and the people in it won't let you, or because you don't like to think of yourself in that way, or because you have simply never had a chance. This is where astrology becomes both complex and terribly important. If all it could tell you was what you already know, what would be the point? But because it maps out potentials, and portrays the natural direction in which the person innately longs to go, it can help us a lot to discover that secret frustrated self that has always longed for expression. Some people are lucky enough, or pushy enough, or healthy enough (and there aren't many of those) to know who they are, and to be unafraid as far as showing that self to the world. Most of us have lots of smokescreens and a good dash of self-doubt to confuse the issue. Some of us even hate ourselves as we are, because we've been brought up to believe we ought to be different – either by parents, church, education, or the general collective pressures of society as we find them in magazines, newspapers, television, films and other media.

So when you read the description of your sun-sign, or the sun-sign of someone close to you, don't just say, 'Oh, he never does that.' Think for a moment. Some of the behaviour patterns may not be obvious. But really think, hard, about what truly motivates you, or your loved one. How honest are you with yourself?

There's more. A proper horoscope is a map of the whole solar system. It takes into account not only the sign through which the sun was passing at your birth, but also the signs in which the moon, Mercury, Venus, Mars, Jupiter, Saturn, Uranus, Neptune and Pluto were placed as well. Now you need a proper astrologer, or have to be able to draw up the map correctly yourself, to find out where all these heavenly bodies were placed at your birth. They all have meaning. The sun is the most important of them, because it describes your basic essence, the person you're trying – knowingly or unknowingly – to become. The other planets all describe different needs and drives. Like how you communicate, and how you relate to others, and where your secret fears lie. But most important is the sun, because that symbolizes the urge to be yourself.

There's another equally important point in the horoscope which we will consider, because although a book like this can't really explore the technicalities of casting a horoscope and interpreting it, we would like to offer more than just a sun-sign reading. Then you can go on to any one of a number of good textbooks which can teach you the mechanics of setting up the horoscope. Or you can get your chart drawn up by someone who is experienced at it. But first, we would like to introduce you to the ascendant, which is also known as the rising sign.

The ascendant is the sign which was rising in the sky due east of your birthplace, at the time of your birth. Now, to cast a proper horoscope, you need a birth time as well as a date and year. You also need to know where you were born, because longitude and latitude for your birthplace are necessary for a proper calculation. The whole wheel of the zodiac revolves once in 24 hours. If you freeze it at any moment – say, your birth, then you'll have one of those twelve signs rising in the east, one setting in the west, one culminating overhead at the zenith, and one beneath your feet at the nadir. The one which is most important is the one rising in the east, for this has traditionally been the point of sunrise, the emergence of life, the dawn of the new day, the meeting of sun and earth after the long night. It looks like this in the diagram on the facing page.

As we have said, the ascendant is a very important point in the horoscope. It shows how you express yourself to the world. It's you showing yourself to the world outside. In many ways the ascendant is more

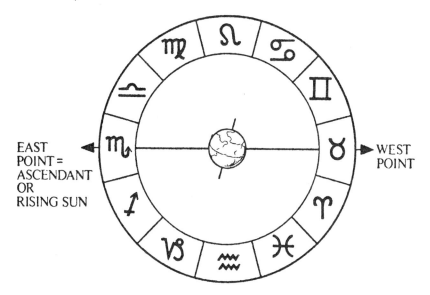

EAST
POINT =
ASCENDANT
OR
RISING SUN

WEST
POINT

obvious in people than the sun. You have to know someone for a while to really see how the sun-sign operates. But if you meet someone at a party, or are just introduced, then you'll see the sign on the ascendant. It's like the doorway to the house. No matter what's going on in that house, the first thing you see is the door. Some doors are open, welcoming, inviting, painted in cheery colours. Other doors are silent, closed, with a little peephole so whoever lives inside can check you out first before you're let in. Some doors are large and grandiose, like palace entrances. Others are small and unobtrusive. The door isn't really any index to the inside of the house. There are houses where you'd never notice that shabby little door, but the inside is beautiful. Others are very flamboyant outside, but small and unobtrusive inside. Never judge a house by its door. But the door reflects how that person wants you to see him. So, we have the sign on the ascendant.

To find out precisely what your ascendant sign is, and what degree of that sign is rising, you need to do a mathematical calculation involving Greenwich Mean

Time, longitude and latitude of the place of birth, birth time, and a lot of other stuff which you would, no doubt, not really want to be subjected to right at this moment. We've compiled a table to make life a little easier. This is a table of simplified ascendants (see pp. 47–107). If you use it correctly, you should be able to come up with a rough idea of the degree and sign of your ascendant.

It should be emphasized that this is only a rough, general idea. It cannot give you an exact ascendant. This is because of factors like time changes unaccounted for, summertime in countries which aren't tabulated, war time, and the little differences in time between cities within the same standard time zone. So bear in mind that your result might be a little off; and if it seems really unsuitable, and you've come up with the very end of a sign as the ascendant, it might well be the next one. So read that section and see how it fits. But from this table you can have a rough idea; and you can also see how the signs for the sun and ascendant sometimes get along, and sometimes don't.

For example: let's take somebody born on 4 September at noon. We know that your sun is in Virgo, if you were born on that day. Now check the table. You'll find that the entries for the dates are given every three days. There happens to be one for 4 September. If you had been born on the third, you should take the closest. So, on 4 September, at 12.00 noon, 27 degrees Scorpio was on the ascendant. So you're a Virgo with Scorpio rising, if anyone asks.

What does that mean? It means that your essence will be Virgo. See how you feel about the description of Virgo given on page 230. But the way you express yourself to others will be Scorpio. Sometimes people might only see the Scorpio side of you. They'll miss the more rational, cooler qualities of your sun-sign. You'll also perhaps notice, if you reflect on it, that in some ways these two signs get along. They're both quiet, introverted signs. Neither is quick to show its heart on its sleeve. But Scorpio is a highly emotional sign, while Virgo is much more controlled and rational. A collision. The sometimes over-sensitive reactions of Scorpio might come out before that Virgo sun has had a chance to assess the situation. Then you have the person who's always saying, 'I'm sorry, I just reacted too quickly.' Or, 'I wish I wasn't so terribly sensitive and emotional.' Virgo is judging Scorpio. We all judge ourselves in just such a way.

Or let's take somebody born on 12 December at 9.00 am. You'll see that the ascendant given for 9.00 am on that date is 13 degrees Capricorn. So this volatile, fiery, fluid, adventure-loving Sagittarian has a rather narrow, unassuming door to his noble house. The inside is freedom-loving; but the expression of a person outward with Capricorn rising is a good deal more self-contained. The nice side of this is that all that fiery exuberance is controlled and disciplined, tempered with a sense of responsibility. But sometimes it can feel pretty constricting, as though you can never totally break loose.

Anyway, you get the idea. You should read both sections, and see how they blend and disagree. In relationships, people are often drawn toward partners who have the same sign on the ascendant as their own suns. This is considered in traditional astrology to indicate a strong tie between two people. Some people don't like their ascendant signs, and are irritated by people whose sun-signs are similar to their own. They don't like themselves, and find themselves annoyed when others remind them of it. It's interesting to work out among the people you're close to how many sun-ascendant crossings there are.

No person is only one thing. We all have many faces, many masks, many voices, many needs. Some get along and emphasize each other; others conflict violently. Get to know yourself. This means not just knowing what you like about yourself, or the obvious attitudes and beliefs you hold. It also means knowing the dark side of yourself, the socially unadapted side which you hide from people, the 'weak' side that you're ashamed of, the secret longings and aspirations which are as much part of you – and as necessary - as the more 'acceptable' traits. So check your ascendant carefully. This marriage of sun and ascendant is like any marriage between two people. In some ways they meet, in others they clash. But they have made a commitment to find a way to harmonize, sometimes with sacrifices on either side. So it is with the different parts of ourselves.

Table
of Ascendants

January 1

AM		PM	
1	21 Libra	1	13 Taurus
2	12 Scorpio	2	3 Gemini
3	14 Scorpio	3	19 Gemini
4	26 Scorpio	4	4 Cancer
5	8 Sagittarius	5	17 Cancer
6	21 Sagittarius	6	29 Cancer
7	4 Capricorn	7	10 Leo
8	19 Capricorn	8	22 Leo
9	7 Aquarius	9	3 Virgo
10	28 Aquarius	10	16 Virgo
11	23 Pisces	11	28 Virgo
12 *noon*	19 Aries	12 *midnight*	10 Libra

January 4

AM		PM	
1	23 Libra	1	17 Taurus
2	5 Scorpio	2	6 Gemini
3	16 Scorpio	3	22 Gemini
4	28 Scorpio	4	6 Cancer
5	11 Sagittarius	5	19 Cancer
6	23 Sagittarius	6	1 Leo
7	7 Capricorn	7	13 Leo
8	22 Capricorn	8	24 Leo
9	11 Aquarius	9	6 Virgo
10	3 Pisces	10	18 Virgo
11	29 Pisces	11	29 Virgo
12 *noon*	25 Aries	12 *midnight*	12 Libra

January 7

AM		PM	
1	25 Libra	1	22 Taurus
2	7 Scorpio	2	9 Gemini
3	18 Scorpio	3	25 Gemini
4	29 Scorpio	4	9 Cancer
5	12 Sagittarius	5	21 Cancer
6	26 Sagittarius	6	3 Leo
7	10 Capricorn	7	15 Leo
8	25 Capricorn	8	26 Leo
9	15 Aquarius	9	8 Virgo
10	7 Pisces	10	20 Virgo
11	4 Aries	11	2 Libra
12 *noon*	29 Aries	12 *midnight*	14 Libra

January 10

AM		PM	
1	28 Libra	1	25 Taurus
2	9 Scorpio	2	12 Gemini
3	21 Scorpio	3	28 Gemini
4	3 Sagittarius	4	11 Cancer
5	15 Sagittarius	5	23 Cancer
6	28 Sagittarius	6	5 Leo
7	13 Capricorn	7	17 Leo
8	29 Capricorn	8	29 Leo
9	20 Aquarius	9	11 Virgo
10	14 Pisces	10	23 Virgo
11	9 Aries	11	4 Libra
12 *noon*	3 Taurus	12 *midnight*	16 Libra

January 13

AM		PM	
1	29 Libra	1	29 Taurus
2	12 Scorpio	2	15 Gemini
3	24 Scorpio	3	29 Gemini
4	5 Sagittarius	4	13 Cancer
5	18 Sagittarius	5	26 Cancer
6	1 Capricorn	6	8 Leo
7	16 Capricorn	7	19 Leo
8	3 Aquarius	8	1 Virgo
9	23 Aquarius	9	13 Virgo
10	18 Pisces	10	24 Virgo
11	14 Aries	11	7 Libra
12 *noon*	8 Taurus	12 *midnight*	18 Libra

January 16

AM		PM	
1	2 Scorpio	1	2 Gemini
2	14 Scorpio	2	18 Gemini
3	26 Scorpio	3	3 Cancer
4	8 Sagittarius	4	16 Cancer
5	20 Sagittarius	5	28 Cancer
6	3 Capricorn	6	10 Leo
7	19 Capricorn	7	22 Leo
8	7 Aquarius	8	3 Virgo
9	28 Aquarius	9	15 Virgo
10	23 Pisces	10	27 Virgo
11	19 Aries	11	9 Libra
12 *noon*	13 Taurus	12 *midnight*	21 Libra

January 19

AM		PM	
1	5 Scorpio	1	6 Gemini
2	16 Scorpio	2	21 Gemini
3	28 Scorpio	3	6 Cancer
4	10 Sagittarius	4	18 Cancer
5	23 Sagittarius	5	1 Leo
6	7 Capricorn	6	13 Leo
7	22 Capricorn	7	24 Leo
8	11 Aquarius	8	6 Virgo
9	3 Pisces	9	18 Virgo
10	29 Pisces	10	29 Virgo
11	24 Aries	11	12 Libra
12 *noon*	17 Taurus	12 *midnight*	23 Libra

January 22

AM		PM	
1	7 Scorpio	1	9 Gemini
2	19 Scorpio	2	24 Gemini
3	29 Scorpio	3	8 Cancer
4	13 Sagittarius	4	21 Cancer
5	26 Sagittarius	5	3 Leo
6	10 Capricorn	6	15 Leo
7	25 Capricorn	7	26 Leo
8	15 Aquarius	8	8 Virgo
9	8 Pisces	9	20 Virgo
10	4 Aries	10	1 Libra
11	28 Aries	11	13 Libra
12 *noon*	20 Taurus	12 *midnight*	25 Libra

January 25

AM		PM	
1	9 Scorpio	1	12 Gemini
2	21 Scorpio	2	28 Gemini
3	3 Sagittarius	3	11 Cancer
4	15 Sagittarius	4	23 Cancer
5	28 Sagittarius	5	5 Leo
6	13 Capricorn	6	17 Leo
7	29 Capricorn	7	29 Leo
8	19 Aquarius	8	10 Virgo
9	13 Pisces	9	22 Virgo
10	8 Aries	10	4 Libra
11	3 Taurus	11	16 Libra
12 *noon*	24 Taurus	12 *midnight*	28 Libra

January 28

AM		PM	
1	12 Scorpio	1	15 Gemini
2	24 Scorpio	2	29 Gemini
3	5 Sagittarius	3	13 Cancer
4	18 Sagittarius	4	26 Cancer
5	1 Capricorn	5	7 Leo
6	16 Capricorn	6	19 Leo
7	3 Aquarius	7	1 Virgo
8	23 Aquarius	8	13 Virgo
9	17 Pisces	9	24 Virgo
10	14 Aries	10	7 Libra
11	8 Taurus	11	18 Libra
12 *noon*	28 Taurus	12 *midnight*	29 Libra

January 31

AM		PM	
1	14 Scorpio	1	18 Gemini
2	26 Scorpio	2	3 Cancer
3	8 Sagittarius	3	16 Cancer
4	20 Sagittarius	4	28 Cancer
5	3 Capricorn	5	10 Leo
6	19 Capricorn	6	22 Leo
7	7 Aquarius	7	3 Virgo
8	28 Aquarius	8	15 Virgo
9	23 Pisces	9	27 Virgo
10	19 Aries	10	9 Libra
11	13 Taurus	11	21 Libra
12 *noon*	2 Gemini	12 *midnight*	2 Scorpio

February 3

AM		PM	
1	16 Scorpio	1	21 Gemini
2	28 Scorpio	2	6 Cancer
3	10 Sagittarius	3	18 Cancer
4	22 Sagittarius	4	1 Leo
5	6 Capricorn	5	13 Leo
6	22 Capricorn	6	24 Leo
7	11 Aquarius	7	6 Virgo
8	3 Pisces	8	18 Virgo
9	29 Pisces	9	29 Virgo
10	23 Aries	10	12 Libra
11	16 Taurus	11	23 Libra
12 *noon*	6 Gemini	12 *midnight*	5 Scorpio

February 6

AM		PM	
1	18 Scorpio	1	24 Gemini
2	29 Scorpio	2	8 Cancer
3	12 Sagittarius	3	21 Cancer
4	26 Sagittarius	4	3 Leo
5	9 Capricorn	5	15 Leo
6	25 Capricorn	6	26 Leo
7	14 Aquarius	7	8 Virgo
8	6 Pisces	8	20 Virgo
9	2 Aries	9	2 Libra
10	28 Aries	10	14 Libra
11	20 Taurus	11	26 Libra
12 *noon*	9 Gemini	12 *midnight*	7 Scorpio

February 9

AM		PM	
1	21 Scorpio	1	27 Gemini
2	3 Sagittarius	2	10 Cancer
3	14 Sagittarius	3	23 Cancer
4	28 Sagittarius	4	5 Leo
5	12 Capricorn	5	17 Leo
6	29 Capricorn	6	29 Leo
7	18 Aquarius	7	11 Virgo
8	12 Pisces	8	23 Virgo
9	8 Aries	9	4 Libra
10	3 Taurus	10	16 Libra
11	24 Taurus	11	28 Libra
12 *noon*	12 Gemini	12 *midnight*	9 Scorpio

February 12

AM		PM	
1	23 Scorpio	1	29 Gemini
2	5 Sagittarius	2	13 Cancer
3	17 Sagittarius	3	26 Cancer
4	1 Capricorn	4	8 Leo
5	15 Capricorn	5	19 Leo
6	2 Aquarius	6	1 Virgo
7	23 Aquarius	7	13 Virgo
8	17 Pisces	8	24 Virgo
9	14 Aries	9	7 Libra
10	8 Taurus	10	18 Libra
11	28 Taurus	11	29 Libra
12 *noon*	15 Gemini	12 *midnight*	12 Scorpio

February 15

AM		PM	
1	25 Scorpio	1	3 Cancer
2	7 Sagittarius	2	16 Cancer
3	20 Sagittarius	3	28 Cancer
4	3 Capricorn	4	10 Leo
5	18 Capricorn	5	22 Leo
6	5 Aquarius	6	3 Virgo
7	28 Aquarius	7	15 Virgo
8	23 Pisces	8	27 Virgo
9	17 Aries	9	9 Libra
10	11 Taurus	10	21 Libra
11	2 Gemini	11	2 Scorpio
12 *noon*	18 Gemini	12 *midnight*	14 Scorpio

February 18

AM		PM	
1	27 Scorpio	1	6 Cancer
2	10 Sagittarius	2	18 Cancer
3	22 Sagittarius	3	1 Leo
4	6 Capricorn	4	13 Leo
5	21 Capricorn	5	24 Leo
6	9 Aquarius	6	6 Virgo
7	1 Pisces	7	18 Virgo
8	27 Pisces	8	29 Virgo
9	23 Aries	9	12 Libra
10	16 Taurus	10	23 Libra
11	6 Gemini	11	5 Scorpio
12 *noon*	21 Gemini	12 *midnight*	17 Scorpio

February 21

AM		PM	
1	29 Scorpio	1	8 Cancer
2	12 Sagittarius	2	22 Cancer
3	25 Sagittarius	3	2 Leo
4	9 Capricorn	4	13 Leo
5	24 Capricorn	5	26 Leo
6	14 Aquarius	6	8 Virgo
7	6 Pisces	7	20 Virgo
8	2 Aries	8	1 Libra
9	28 Aries	9	13 Libra
10	20 Taurus	10	24 Libra
11	9 Gemini	11	6 Scorpio
12 *noon*	24 Gemini	12 *midnight*	18 Scorpio

February 24

AM		PM	
1	3 Sagittarius	1	10 Cancer
2	14 Sagittarius	2	23 Cancer
3	27 Sagittarius	3	5 Leo
4	12 Capricorn	4	17 Leo
5	28 Capricorn	5	29 Leo
6	16 Aquarius	6	10 Virgo
7	10 Pisces	7	22 Virgo
8	9 Aries	8	4 Libra
9	5 Taurus	9	16 Libra
10	27 Taurus	10	28 Libra
11	12 Gemini	11	9 Scorpio
12 *noon*	27 Gemini	12 *midnight*	21 Scorpio

February 27

AM		PM	
1	5 Sagittarius	1	13 Cancer
2	17 Sagittarius	2	26 Cancer
3	1 Capricorn	3	7 Leo
4	15 Capricorn	4	19 Leo
5	2 Aquarius	5	1 Virgo
6	22 Aquarius	6	13 Virgo
7	16 Pisces	7	24 Virgo
8	12 Aries	8	7 Libra
9	7 Taurus	9	18 Libra
10	28 Taurus	10	29 Libra
11	15 Gemini	11	12 Scorpio
12 *noon*	29 Gemini	12 *midnight*	24 Scorpio

March 2

AM		PM	
1	7 Sagittarius	1	16 Cancer
2	20 Sagittarius	2	28 Cancer
3	3 Capricorn	3	10 Leo
4	18 Capricorn	4	22 Leo
5	5 Aquarius	5	3 Virgo
6	26 Aquarius	6	15 Virgo
7	21 Pisces	7	27 Virgo
8	17 Aries	8	9 Libra
9	11 Taurus	9	21 Libra
10	2 Gemini	10	2 Scorpio
11	18 Gemini	11	14 Scorpio
12 *noon*	2 Cancer	12 *midnight*	26 Scorpio

March 5

AM		PM	
1	9 Sagittarius	1	18 Cancer
2	22 Sagittarius	2	29 Cancer
3	6 Capricorn	3	12 Leo
4	22 Capricorn	4	24 Leo
5	9 Aquarius	5	5 Virgo
6	1 Pisces	6	18 Virgo
7	27 Pisces	7	29 Virgo
8	23 Aries	8	11 Libra
9	16 Taurus	9	23 Libra
10	4 Gemini	10	5 Scorpio
11	21 Gemini	11	16 Scorpio
12 *noon*	6 Cancer	12 *midnight*	28 Scorpio

March 8

AM		PM	
1	12 Sagittarius	1	20 Cancer
2	25 Sagittarius	2	2 Leo
3	9 Capricorn	3	14 Leo
4	24 Capricorn	4	26 Leo
5	14 Aquarius	5	8 Virgo
6	6 Pisces	6	19 Virgo
7	2 Aries	7	1 Libra
8	28 Aries	8	13 Libra
9	20 Taurus	9	25 Libra
10	8 Gemini	10	7 Scorpio
11	24 Gemini	11	18 Scorpio
12 *noon*	8 Cancer	12 *midnight*	29 Scorpio

March 11

AM		PM	
1	14 Sagittarius	1	23 Cancer
2	27 Sagittarius	2	5 Leo
3	12 Capricorn	3	16 Leo
4	28 Capricorn	4	29 Leo
5	18 Aquarius	5	10 Virgo
6	12 Pisces	6	22 Virgo
7	6 Aries	7	4 Libra
8	2 Taurus	8	16 Libra
9	24 Taurus	9	28 Libra
10	11 Gemini	10	9 Scorpio
11	27 Gemini	11	21 Scorpio
12 *noon*	10 Cancer	12 *midnight*	3 Sagittarius

March 14

AM		PM	
1	17 Sagittarius	1	25 Cancer
2	29 Sagittarius	2	7 Leo⁻
3	15 Capricorn	3	19 Leo
4	2 Aquarius	4	29 Leo
5	21 Aquarius	5	13 Virgo
6	15 Pisces	6	24 Virgo
7	12 Aries	7	7 Libra
8	7 Taurus	8	18 Libra
9	27 Taurus	9	29 Libra
10	14 Gemini	10	12 Scorpio
11	29 Gemini	11	24 Scorpio
12 *noon*	13 Cancer	12 *midnight*	5 Sagittarius

March 17

AM		PM	
1	19 Sagittarius	1	28 Cancer
2	2 Capricorn	2	10 Leo
3	18 Capricorn	3	21 Leo
4	5 Aquarius	4	3 Virgo
5	26 Aquarius	5	15 Virgo
6	21 Pisces	6	26 Virgo
7	17 Aries	7	8 Libra
8	11 Taurus	8	20 Libra
9	1 Gemini	9	2 Scorpio
10	17 Gemini	10	14 Scorpio
11	2 Cancer	11	26 Scorpio
12 *noon*	15 Cancer	12 *midnight*	8 Sagittarius

March 20

AM		PM	
1	21 Sagittarius	1	29 Cancer
2	5 Capricorn	2	12 Leo
3	21 Capricorn	3	23 Leo
4	8 Aquarius	4	5 Virgo
5	1 Pisces	5	17 Virgo
6	27 Pisces	6	29 Virgo
7	22 Aries	7	11 Libra
8	16 Taurus	8	23 Libra
9	4 Gemini	9	5 Scorpio
10	20 Gemini	10	16 Scorpio
11	5 Cancer	11	28 Scorpio
12 *noon*	18 Cancer	12 *midnight*	10 Sagittarius

March 23

AM		PM	
1	24 Sagittarius	1	2 Leo
2	8 Capricorn	2	14 Leo
3	24 Capricorn	3	26 Leo
4	12 Aquarius	4	8 Virgo
5	5 Pisces	5	19 Virgo
6	1 Aries	6	1 Libra
7	26 Aries	7	13 Libra
8	19 Taurus	8	24 Libra
9	8 Gemini	9	7 Scorpio
10	23 Gemini	10	18 Scorpio
11	7 Cancer	11	29 Scorpio
12 *noon*	20 Cancer	12 *midnight*	12 Sagittarius

March 26

AM		PM	
1	27 Sagittarius	1	4 Leo
2	12 Capricorn	2	16 Leo
3	28 Capricorn	3	28 Leo
4	17 Aquarius	4	10 Virgo
5	10 Pisces	5	22 Virgo
6	6 Aries	6	4 Libra
7	2 Taurus	7	16 Libra
8	23 Taurus	8	28 Libra
9	11 Gemini	9	9 Scorpio
10	26 Gemini	10	21 Scorpio
11	10 Cancer	11	3 Sagittarius
12 *noon*	23 Cancer	12 *midnight*	15 Sagittarius

March 29

AM		PM	
1	29 Sagittarius	1	7 Leo
2	15 Capricorn	2	19 Leo
3	2 Aquarius	3	29 Leo
4	21 Aquarius	4	13 Virgo
5	15 Pisces	5	24 Virgo
6	12 Aries	6	6 Libra
7	7 Taurus	7	18 Libra
8	27 Taurus	8	29 Libra
9	14 Gemini	9	12 Scorpio
10	29 Gemini	10	23 Scorpio
11	13 Cancer	11	5 Sagittarius
12 *noon*	25 Cancer	12 *midnight*	18 Sagittarius

April 1

AM		PM	
1	2 Capricorn	1	10 Leo
2	18 Capricorn	2	21 Leo
3	5 Aquarius	3	3 Virgo
4	26 Aquarius	4	14 Virgo
5	21 Pisces	5	26 Virgo
6	17 Aries	6	8 Libra
7	11 Taurus	7	20 Libra
8	1 Gemini	8	2 Scorpio
9	17 Gemini	9	14 Scorpio
10	2 Cancer	10	25 Scorpio
11	15 Cancer	11	8 Sagittarius
12 *noon*	27 Cancer	12 *midnight*	20 Sagittarius

April 4

AM		PM	
1	5 Capricorn	1	12 Leo
2	21 Capricorn	2	23 Leo
3	9 Aquarius	3	5 Virgo
4	1 Pisces	4	17 Virgo
5	26 Pisces	5	29 Virgo
6	21 Aries	6	11 Libra
7	14 Taurus	7	23 Libra
8	4 Gemini	8	4 Scorpio
9	20 Gemini	9	15 Scorpio
10	5 Cancer	10	28 Scorpio
11	17 Cancer	11	10 Sagittarius
12 *noon*	29 Cancer	12 *midnight*	22 Sagittarius

April 7

AM		PM	
1	8 Capricorn	1	14 Leo
2	24 Capricorn	2	26 Leo
3	12 Aquarius	3	8 Virgo
4	5 Pisces	4	19 Virgo
5	1 Aries	5	1 Libra
6	26 Aries	6	13 Libra
7	19 Taurus	7	25 Libra
8	8 Gemini	8	6 Scorpio
9	23 Gemini	9	18 Scorpio
10	7 Cancer	10	29 Scorpio
11	20 Cancer	11	12 Sagittarius
12 *noon*	2 Leo	12 *midnight*	25 Sagittarius

April 10

AM		PM	
1	11 Capricorn	1	16 Leo
2	28 Capricorn	2	28 Leo
3	17 Aquarius	3	9 Virgo
4	10 Pisces	4	22 Virgo
5	6 Aries	5	3 Libra
6	2 Taurus	6	15 Libra
7	23 Taurus	7	27 Libra
8	11 Gemini	8	9 Scorpio
9	26 Gemini	9	21 Scorpio
10	10 Cancer	10	3 Sagittarius
11	23 Cancer	11	14 Sagittarius
12 *noon*	4 Leo	12 *midnight*	27 Sagittarius

April 13

AM		PM	
1	14 Capricorn	1	19 Leo
2	29 Capricorn	2	29 Leo
3	21 Aquarius	3	12 Virgo
4	15 Pisces	4	24 Virgo
5	12 Aries	5	6 Libra
6	7 Taurus	6	18 Libra
7	27 Taurus	7	29 Libra
8	14 Gemini	8	12 Scorpio
9	29 Gemini	9	23 Scorpio
10	13 Cancer	10	5 Sagittarius
11	25 Cancer	11	17 Sagittarius
12 *noon*	7 Leo	12 *midnight*	1 Capricorn

April 16

AM		PM	
1	17 Capricorn	1	21 Leo
2	4 Aquarius	2	3 Virgo
3	26 Aquarius	3	14 Virgo
4	20 Pisces	4	26 Virgo
5	16 Aries	5	8 Libra
6	10 Taurus	6	20 Libra
7	1 Gemini	7	2 Scorpio
8	17 Gemini	8	13 Scorpio
9	1 Cancer	9	25 Scorpio
10	15 Cancer	10	7 Sagittarius
11	27 Cancer	11	20 Sagittarius
12 *noon*	9 Leo	12 *midnight*	3 Capricorn

April 19

AM		PM	
1	20 Capricorn	1	23 Leo
2	8 Aquarius	2	5 Virgo
3	29 Aquarius	3	17 Virgo
4	25 Pisces	4	29 Virgo
5	21 Aries	5	11 Libra
6	14 Taurus	6	23 Libra
7	4 Gemini	7	4 Scorpio
8	20 Gemini	8	15 Scorpio
9	5 Cancer	9	28 Scorpio
10	17 Cancer	10	10 Sagittarius
11	29 Cancer	11	22 Sagittarius
12 *noon*	11 Leo	12 *midnight*	10 Capricorn

April 22

AM		PM	
1	24 Capricorn	1	26 Leo
2	14 Aquarius	2	7 Virgo
3	5 Pisces	3	19 Virgo
4	1 Aries	4	1 Libra
5	26 Aries	5	13 Libra
6	19 Taurus	6	24 Libra
7	8 Gemini	7	6 Scorpio
8	23 Gemini	8	18 Scorpio
9	7 Cancer	9	29 Scorpio
10	20 Cancer	10	13 Sagittarius
11	2 Leo	11	25 Sagittarius
12 *noon*	14 Leo	12 *midnight*	9 Capricorn

April 25

AM		PM	
1	27 Capricorn	1	28 Leo
2	17 Aquarius	2	9 Virgo
3	10 Pisces	3	21 Virgo
4	6 Aries	4	3 Libra
5	2 Taurus	5	15 Libra
6	23 Taurus	6	27 Libra
7	11 Gemini	7	9 Scorpio
8	26 Gemini	8	20 Scorpio
9	10 Cancer	9	3 Sagittarius
10	22 Cancer	10	14 Sagittarius
11	4 Leo	11	27 Sagittarius
12 *noon*	16 Leo	12 *midnight*	12 Capricorn

April 28

AM		PM	
1	2 Aquarius	1	29 Leo
2	21 Aquarius	2	12 Virgo
3	15 Pisces	3	24 Virgo
4	10 Aries	4	6 Libra
5	5 Taurus	5	18 Libra
6	27 Taurus	6	29 Libra
7	14 Gemini	7	11 Scorpio
8	29 Gemini	8	23 Scorpio
9	12 Cancer	9	5 Sagittarius
10	25 Cancer	10	17 Sagittarius
11	7 Leo	11	29 Sagittarius
12 *noon*	19 Leo	12 *midnight*	15 Capricorn

May 1

AM		PM	
1	4 Aquarius	1	3 Virgo
2	24 Aquarius	2	14 Virgo
3	19 Pisces	3	26 Virgo
4	16 Aries	4	8 Libra
5	10 Taurus	5	20 Libra
6	29 Taurus	6	2 Scorpio
7	17 Gemini	7	13 Scorpio
8	1 Cancer	8	25 Scorpio
9	15 Cancer	9	7 Sagittarius
10	27 Cancer	10	19 Sagittarius
11	9 Leo	11	3 Capricorn
12 *noon*	21 Leo	12 *midnight*	18 Capricorn

May 4

AM		PM	
1	8 Aquarius	1	4 Virgo
2	29 Aquarius	2	17 Virgo
3	25 Pisces	3	28 Virgo
4	21 Aries	4	10 Libra
5	14 Taurus	5	22 Libra
6	3 Gemini	6	4 Scorpio
7	20 Gemini	7	15 Scorpio
8	5 Cancer	8	27 Scorpio
9	17 Cancer	9	9 Sagittarius
10	29 Cancer	10	21 Sagittarius
11	11 Leo	11	5 Capricorn
12 *noon*	23 Leo	12 *midnight*	21 Capricorn

May 7

AM		PM	
1	21 Aquarius	1	7 Virgo
2	5 Pisces	2	18 Virgo
3	1 Aries	3	1 Libra
4	26 Aries	4	13 Libra
5	19 Taurus	5	24 Libra
6	7 Gemini	6	6 Scorpio
7	23 Gemini	7	18 Scorpio
8	7 Cancer	8	29 Scorpio
9	20 Cancer	9	12 Sagittarius
10	1 Leo	10	25 Sagittarius
11	13 Leo	11	9 Capricorn
12 *noon*	25 Leo	12 *midnight*	24 Capricorn

May 10

AM		PM	
1	16 Aquarius	1	9 Virgo
2	9 Pisces	2	21 Virgo
3	4 Aries	3	3 Libra
4	29 Aries	4	15 Libra
5	23 Taurus	5	27 Libra
6	10 Gemini	6	9 Scorpio
7	26 Gemini	7	20 Scorpio
8	10 Cancer	8	2 Sagittarius
9	22 Cancer	9	14 Sagittarius
10	4 Leo	10	27 Sagittarius
11	16 Leo	11	11 Capricorn
12 *noon*	27 Leo	12 *midnight*	28 Capricorn

May 13

AM		PM	
1	20 Aquarius	1	12 Virgo
2	14 Pisces	2	24 Virgo
3	10 Aries	3	6 Libra
4	5 Taurus	4	18 Libra
5	26 Taurus	5	29 Libra
6	13 Gemini	6	11 Scorpio
7	29 Gemini	7	22 Scorpio
8	12 Cancer	8	5 Sagittarius
9	25 Cancer	9	17 Sagittarius
10	7 Leo	10	29 Sagittarius
11	18 Leo	11	15 Capricorn
12 *noon*	29 Leo	12 *midnight*	2 Aquarius

May 16

AM		PM	
1	24 Aquarius	1	14 Virgo
2	19 Pisces	2	25 Virgo
3	16 Aries	3	7 Libra
4	10 Taurus	4	19 Libra
5	29 Taurus	5	2 Scorpio
6	16 Gemini	6	13 Scorpio
7	1 Cancer	7	25 Scorpio
8	14 Cancer	8	7 Sagittarius
9	27 Cancer	9	19 Sagittarius
10	9 Leo	10	2 Capricorn
11	20 Leo	11	18 Capricorn
12 *noon*	2 Virgo	12 *midnight*	5 Aquarius

May 19

AM		PM	
1	29 Aquarius	1	16 Virgo
2	25 Pisces	2	28 Virgo
3	21 Aries	3	10 Libra
4	14 Taurus	4	22 Libra
5	3 Gemini	5	4 Scorpio
6	19 Gemini	6	15 Scorpio
7	4 Cancer	7	27 Scorpio
8	17 Cancer	8	9 Sagittarius
9	29 Cancer	9	21 Sagittarius
10	11 Leo	10	5 Capricorn
11	22 Leo	11	21 Capricorn
12 *noon*	4 Virgo	12 *midnight*	9 Aquarius

May 22

AM		PM	
1	5 Pisces	1	18 Virgo
2	29 Pisces	2	1 Libra
3	25 Aries	3	13 Libra
4	18 Taurus	4	24 Libra
5	7 Gemini	5	5 Scorpio
6	22 Gemini	6	18 Scorpio
7	6 Cancer	7	29 Scorpio
8	20 Cancer	8	12 Sagittarius
9	1 Leo	9	25 Sagittarius
10	13 Leo	10	9 Capricorn
11	25 Leo	11	24 Capricorn
12 *noon*	7 Virgo	12 *midnight*	14 Aquarius

May 25

AM		PM	
1	8 Pisces	1	21 Virgo
2	4 Aries	2	3 Libra
3	29 Aries	3	15 Libra
4	22 Taurus	4	27 Libra
5	10 Gemini	5	9 Scorpio
6	25 Gemini	6	20 Scorpio
7	9 Cancer	7	2 Sagittarius
8	22 Cancer	8	14 Sagittarius
9	4 Leo	9	27 Sagittarius
10	16 Leo	10	11 Capricorn
11	27 Leo	11	28 Capricorn
12 *noon*	9 Virgo	12 *midnight*	17 Aquarius

May 28

AM		PM	
1	14 Pisces	1	23 Virgo
2	10 Aries	2	6 Libra
3	5 Taurus	3	17 Libra
4	26 Taurus	4	29 Libra
5	13 Gemini	5	10 Scorpio
6	29 Gemini	6	22 Scorpio
7	11 Cancer	7	4 Sagittarius
8	24 Cancer	8	17 Sagittarius
9	6 Leo	9	29 Sagittarius
10	18 Leo	10	14 Capricorn
11	29 Leo	11	2 Aquarius
12 *noon*	12 Virgo	12 *midnight*	21 Aquarius

May 31

AM		PM	
1	19 Pisces	1	25 Virgo
2	16 Aries	2	7 Libra
3	10 Taurus	3	19 Libra
4	29 Taurus	4	2 Scorpio
5	16 Gemini	5	13 Scorpio
6	1 Cancer	6	24 Scorpio
7	14 Cancer	7	7 Sagittarius
8	27 Cancer	8	19 Sagittarius
9	8 Leo	9	2 Capricorn
10	20 Leo	10	18 Capricorn
11	2 Virgo	11	5 Aquarius
12 *noon*	13 Virgo	12 *midnight*	26 Aquarius

June 3

AM		PM	
1	25 Pisces	1	28 Virgo
2	19 Aries	2	10 Libra
3	13 Taurus	3	22 Libra
4	3 Gemini	4	3 Scorpio
5	19 Gemini	5	15 Scorpio
6	4 Cancer	6	27 Scorpio
7	17 Cancer	7	9 Sagittarius
8	29 Cancer	8	21 Sagittarius
9	11 Leo	9	5 Capricorn
10	22 Leo	10	21 Capricorn
11	4 Virgo	11	8 Aquarius
12 *noon*	16 Virgo	12 *midnight*	1 Pisces

June 6

AM		PM	
1	29 Pisces	1	1 Libra
2	25 Aries	2	13 Libra
3	17 Taurus	3	24 Libra
4	7 Gemini	4	5 Scorpio
5	22 Gemini	5	18 Scorpio
6	6 Cancer	6	29 Scorpio
7	19 Cancer	7	11 Sagittarius
8	1 Leo	8	24 Sagittarius
9	13 Leo	9	8 Capricorn
10	25 Leo	10	23 Capricorn
11	7 Virgo	11	12 Aquarius
12 *noon*	18 Virgo	12 *midnight*	5 Pisces

June 9

AM		PM	
1	4 Aries	1	3 Libra
2	29 Aries	2	14 Libra
3	22 Taurus	3	27 Libra
4	10 Gemini	4	8 Scorpio
5	25 Gemini	5	20 Scorpio
6	9 Cancer	6	2 Sagittarius
7	21 Cancer	7	14 Sagittarius
8	4 Leo	8	27 Sagittarius
9	16 Leo	9	11 Capricorn
10	27 Leo	10	28 Capricorn
11	9 Virgo	11	17 Aquarius
12 *noon*	21 Virgo	12 *midnight*	10 Pisces

June 12

AM		PM	
1	10 Aries	1	5 Libra
2	3 Taurus	2	17 Libra
3	26 Taurus	3	29 Libra
4	13 Gemini	4	10 Scorpio
5	28 Gemini	5	22 Scorpio
6	11 Cancer	6	4 Sagittarius
7	24 Cancer	7	16 Sagittarius
8	6 Leo	8	29 Sagittarius
9	18 Leo	9	14 Capricorn
10	29 Leo	10	29 Capricorn
11	11 Virgo	11	21 Aquarius
12 *noon*	23 Virgo	12 *midnight*	15 Pisces

June 15

AM		PM	
1	14 Aries	1	7 Libra
2	8 Taurus	2	19 Libra
3	29 Taurus	3	1 Scorpio
4	16 Gemini	4	12 Scorpio
5	29 Gemini	5	24 Scorpio
6	13 Cancer	6	6 Sagittarius
7	26 Cancer	7	19 Sagittarius
8	8 Leo	8	2 Capricorn
9	20 Leo	9	17 Capricorn
10	2 Virgo	10	4 Aquarius
11	13 Virgo	11	26 Aquarius
12 *noon*	25 Virgo	12 *midnight*	20 Pisces

June 18

AM		PM	
1	19 Aries	1	10 Libra
2	13 Taurus	2	22 Libra
3	3 Gemini	3	3 Scorpio
4	19 Gemini	4	15 Scorpio
5	3 Cancer	5	27 Scorpio
6	17 Cancer	6	8 Sagittarius
7	28 Cancer	7	21 Sagittarius
8	10 Leo	8	5 Capricorn
9	22 Leo	9	20 Capricorn
10	4 Virgo	10	8 Aquarius
11	16 Virgo	11	29 Aquarius
12 *noon*	28 Virgo	12 *midnight*	25 Pisces

June 21

AM		PM	
1	25 Aries	1	12 Libra
2	17 Taurus	2	24 Libra
3	7 Gemini	3	5 Scorpio
4	22 Gemini	4	18 Scorpio
5	6 Cancer	5	29 Scorpio
6	19 Cancer	6	11 Sagittarius
7	1 Leo	7	24 Sagittarius
8	13 Leo	8	8 Capricorn
9	25 Leo	9	23 Capricorn
10	6 Virgo	10	12 Aquarius
11	18 Virgo	11	5 Pisces
12 *noon*	1 Libra	12 *midnight*	1 Aries

June 24

AM		PM	
1	29 Aries	1	14 Libra
2	22 Taurus	2	26 Libra
3	10 Gemini	3	8 Scorpio
4	25 Gemini	4	19 Scorpio
5	9 Cancer	5	1 Sagittarius
6	21 Cancer	6	14 Sagittarius
7	4 Leo	7	26 Sagittarius
8	16 Leo	8	11 Capricorn
9	27 Leo	9	27 Capricorn
10	8 Virgo	10	16 Aquarius
11	20 Virgo	11	10 Pisces
12 *noon*	2 Libra	12 *midnight*	5 Aries

June 27

AM		PM	
1	3 Taurus	1	17 Libra
2	25 Taurus	2	28 Libra
3	12 Gemini	3	10 Scorpio
4	28 Gemini	4	22 Scorpio
5	11 Cancer	5	4 Sagittarius
6	24 Cancer	6	16 Sagittarius
7	6 Leo	7	29 Sagittarius
8	18 Leo	8	14 Capricorn
9	29 Leo	9	29 Capricorn
10	11 Virgo	10	21 Aquarius
11	23 Virgo	11	14 Pisces
12 *noon*	5 Libra	12 *midnight*	10 Aries

June 30

AM		PM	
1	8 Taurus	1	19 Libra
2	29 Taurus	2	1 Scorpio
3	16 Gemini	3	12 Scorpio
4	29 Gemini	4	24 Scorpio
5	13 Cancer	5	6 Sagittarius
6	26 Cancer	6	18 Sagittarius
7	8 Leo	7	1 Capricorn
8	20 Leo	8	17 Capricorn
9	2 Virgo	9	4 Aquarius
10	13 Virgo	10	24 Aquarius
11	25 Virgo	11	19 Pisces
12 *noon*	7 Libra	12 *midnight*	16 Aries

July 3

AM		PM	
1	13 Taurus	1	22 Libra
2	2 Gemini	2	3 Scorpio
3	18 Gemini	3	15 Scorpio
4	3 Cancer	4	27 Scorpio
5	17 Cancer	5	8 Sagittarius
6	28 Cancer	6	21 Sagittarius
7	10 Leo	7	5 Capricorn
8	22 Leo	8	20 Capricorn
9	3 Virgo	9	8 Aquarius
10	16 Virgo	10	29 Aquarius
11	28 Virgo	11	25 Pisces
12 *noon*	9 Libra	12 *midnight*	21 Aries

July 6

AM		PM	
1	17 Taurus	1	24 Libra
2	6 Gemini	2	5 Scorpio
3	22 Gemini	3	17 Scorpio
4	6 Cancer	4	29 Scorpio
5	19 Cancer	5	11 Sagittarius
6	1 Leo	6	24 Sagittarius
7	13 Leo	7	8 Capricorn
8	25 Leo	8	23 Capricorn
9	6 Virgo	9	12 Aquarius
10	18 Virgo	10	5 Pisces
11	29 Virgo	11	1 Aries
12 *noon*	12 Libra	12 *midnight*	26 Aries

July 9

AM		PM	
1	22 Taurus	1	26 Libra
2	9 Gemini	2	8 Scorpio
3	25 Gemini	3	19 Scorpio
4	9 Cancer	4	2 Sagittarius
5	21 Cancer	5	14 Sagittarius
6	3 Leo	6	26 Sagittarius
7	15 Leo	7	11 Capricorn
8	26 Leo	8	27 Capricorn
9	8 Virgo	9	17 Aquarius
10	20 Virgo	10	8 Pisces
11	2 Libra	11	5 Aries
12 *noon*	14 Libra	12 *midnight*	29 Aries

July 12

AM		PM	
1	24 Taurus	1	28 Libra
2	12 Gemini	2	10 Scorpio
3	28 Gemini	3	21 Scorpio
4	11 Cancer	4	3 Sagittarius
5	23 Cancer	5	16 Sagittarius
6	6 Leo	6	29 Sagittarius
7	17 Leo	7	14 Capricorn
8	29 Leo	8	29 Capricorn
9	11 Virgo	9	20 Aquarius
10	23 Virgo	10	14 Pisces
11	5 Libra	11	10 Aries
12 *noon*	17 Libra	12 *midnight*	5 Taurus

July 15

AM		PM	
1	28 Taurus	1	1 Scorpio
2	15 Gemini	2	12 Scorpio
3	29 Gemini	3	24 Scorpio
4	13 Cancer	4	6 Sagittarius
5	26 Cancer	5	18 Sagittarius
6	8 Leo	6	1 Capricorn
7	20 Leo	7	16 Capricorn
8	1 Virgo	8	4 Aquarius
9	13 Virgo	9	24 Aquarius
10	25 Virgo	10	19 Pisces
11	7 Libra	11	16 Aries
12 *noon*	19 Libra	12 *midnight*	10 Taurus

July 18

AM		PM	
1	2 Gemini	1	3 Scorpio
2	18 Gemini	2	15 Scorpio
3	3 Cancer	3	27 Scorpio
4	16 Cancer	4	8 Sagittarius
5	28 Cancer	5	21 Sagittarius
6	10 Leo	6	4 Capricorn
7	22 Leo	7	20 Capricorn
8	3 Virgo	8	8 Aquarius
9	15 Virgo	9	29 Aquarius
10	27 Virgo	10	25 Pisces
11	10 Libra	11	19 Aries
12 *noon*	21 Libra	12 *midnight*	13 Taurus

July 21

AM		PM	
1	6 Gemini	1	5 Scorpio
2	21 Gemini	2	17 Scorpio
3	6 Cancer	3	29 Scorpio
4	18 Cancer	4	11 Sagittarius
5	1 Leo	5	24 Sagittarius
6	13 Leo	6	7 Capricorn
7	24 Leo	7	23 Capricorn
8	6 Virgo	8	12 Aquarius
9	18 Virgo	9	3 Pisces
10	29 Virgo	10	29 Pisces
11	12 Libra	11	25 Aries
12 *noon*	23 Libra	12 *midnight*	17 Taurus

July 24

AM		PM	
1	9 Gemini	1	8 Scorpio
2	24 Gemini	2	19 Scorpio
3	8 Cancer	3	1 Sagittarius
4	21 Cancer	4	13 Sagittarius
5	3 Leo	5	26 Sagittarius
6	15 Leo	6	11 Capricorn
7	26 Leo	7	27 Capricorn
8	8 Virgo	8	16 Aquarius
9	20 Virgo	9	8 Pisces
10	2 Libra	10	4 Aries
11	14 Libra	11	29 Aries
12 *noon*	26 Libra	12 *midnight*	22 Taurus

July 27

AM		PM	
1	12 Gemini	1	9 Scorpio
2	27 Gemini	2	21 Scorpio
3	11 Cancer	3	3 Sagittarius
4	23 Cancer	4	16 Sagittarius
5	5 Leo	5	29 Sagittarius
6	17 Leo	6	13 Capricorn
7	29 Leo	7	29 Capricorn
8	11 Virgo	8	20 Aquarius
9	23 Virgo	9	14 Pisces
10	5 Libra	10	10 Aries
11	16 Libra	11	5 Taurus
12 *noon*	28 Libra	12 *midnight*	26 Taurus

July 30

A M		P M	
1	15 Gemini	1	12 Scorpio
2	29 Gemini	2	24 Scorpio
3	13 Cancer	3	5 Sagittarius
4	26 Cancer	4	18 Sagittarius
5	7 Leo	5	1 Capricorn
6	19 Leo	6	16 Capricorn
7	1 Virgo	7	3 Aquarius
8	13 Virgo	8	24 Aquarius
9	24 Virgo	9	19 Pisces
10	7 Libra	10	15 Aries
11	18 Libra	11	8 Taurus
12 *noon*	1 Scorpio	12 *midnight*	29 Taurus

August 2

A M		P M	
1	18 Gemini	1	15 Scorpio
2	3 Cancer	2	26 Scorpio
3	16 Cancer	3	8 Sagittarius
4	28 Cancer	4	21 Sagittarius
5	10 Leo	5	4 Capricorn
6	22 Leo	6	20 Capricorn
7	3 Virgo	7	7 Aquarius
8	15 Virgo	8	29 Aquarius
9	27 Virgo	9	25 Pisces
10	9 Libra	10	19 Aries
11	21 Libra	11	13 Taurus
12 *noon*	3 Scorpio	12 *midnight*	3 Gemini

August 5

AM		PM	
1	21 Gemini	1	17 Scorpio
2	6 Cancer	2	28 Scorpio
3	18 Cancer	3	11 Sagittarius
4	1 Leo	4	23 Sagittarius
5	13 Leo	5	7 Capricorn
6	24 Leo	6	22 Capricorn
7	6 Virgo	7	11 Aquarius
8	18 Virgo	8	3 Pisces
9	29 Virgo	9	29 Pisces
10	12 Libra	10	25 Aries
11	23 Libra	11	17 Taurus
12 *noon*	5 Scorpio	12 *midnight*	7 Gemini

August 8

AM		PM	
1	24 Gemini	1	19 Scorpio
2	8 Cancer	2	1 Sagittarius
3	20 Cancer	3	13 Sagittarius
4	3 Leo	4	26 Sagittarius
5	15 Leo	5	10 Capricorn
6	26 Leo	6	26 Capricorn
7	8 Virgo	7	15 Aquarius
8	20 Virgo	8	8 Pisces
9	2 Libra	9	4 Aries
10	14 Libra	10	29 Aries
11	26 Libra	11	22 Taurus
12 *noon*	7 Scorpio	12 *midnight*	10 Gemini

August 11

AM		PM	
1	27 Gemini	1	21 Scorpio
2	10 Cancer	2	3 Sagittarius
3	23 Cancer	3	15 Sagittarius
4	5 Leo	4	28 Sagittarius
5	17 Leo	5	13 Capricorn
6	29 Leo	6	29 Capricorn
7	11 Virgo	7	20 Aquarius
8	22 Virgo	8	14 Pisces
9	4 Libra	9	10 Aries
10	16 Libra	10	4 Taurus
11	28 Libra	11	26 Taurus
12 *noon*	10 Scorpio	12 *midnight*	13 Gemini

August 14

AM		PM	
1	29 Gemini	1	24 Scorpio
2	13 Cancer	2	5 Sagittarius
3	26 Cancer	3	18 Sagittarius
4	7 Leo	4	1 Capricorn
5	19 Leo	5	16 Capricorn
6	1 Virgo	6	3 Aquarius
7	13 Virgo	7	24 Aquarius
8	24 Virgo	8	19 Pisces
9	7 Libra	9	15 Aries
10	18 Libra	10	8 Taurus
11	29 Libra	11	28 Taurus
12 *noon*	12 Scorpio	12 *midnight*	16 Gemini

August 17

AM		PM	
1	2 Cancer	1	26 Scorpio
2	16 Cancer	2	8 Sagittarius
3	28 Cancer	3	21 Sagittarius
4	10 Leo	4	4 Capricorn
5	22 Leo	5	19 Capricorn
6	3 Virgo	6	7 Aquarius
7	15 Virgo	7	28 Aquarius
8	27 Virgo	8	23 Pisces
9	9 Libra	9	19 Aries
10	21 Libra	10	13 Taurus
11	2 Scorpio	11	2 Gemini
12 *noon*	14 Scorpio	12 *midnight*	19 Gemini

August 20

AM		PM	
1	6 Cancer	1	28 Scorpio
2	18 Cancer	2	11 Sagittarius
3	29 Cancer	3	23 Sagittarius
4	12 Leo	4	7 Capricorn
5	24 Leo	5	22 Capricorn
6	6 Virgo	6	11 Aquarius
7	18 Virgo	7	3 Pisces
8	29 Virgo	8	29 Pisces
9	11 Libra	9	25 Aries
10	23 Libra	10	17 Taurus
11	5 Scorpio	11	7 Gemini
12 *noon*	16 Scorpio	12 *midnight*	22 Gemini

August 23

AM		PM	
1	8 Cancer	1	1 Sagittarius
2	20 Cancer	2	13 Sagittarius
3	2 Leo	3	26 Sagittarius
4	15 Leo	4	10 Capricorn
5	26 Leo	5	25 Capricorn
6	8 Virgo	6	15 Aquarius
7	20 Virgo	7	8 Pisces
8	1 Libra	8	4 Aries
9	13 Libra	9	29 Aries
10	25 Libra	10	22 Taurus
11	7 Scorpio	11	9 Gemini
12 *noon*	18 Scorpio	12 *midnight*	25 Gemini

August 26

AM		PM	
1	10 Cancer	1	3 Sagittarius
2	23 Cancer	2	15 Sagittarius
3	5 Leo	3	28 Sagittarius
4	16 Leo	4	13 Capricorn
5	29 Leo	5	29 Capricorn
6	10 Virgo	6	20 Aquarius
7	22 Virgo	7	14 Pisces
8	4 Libra	8	9 Aries
9	16 Libra	9	3 Taurus
10	28 Libra	10	26 Taurus
11	9 Scorpio	11	12 Gemini
12 *noon*	21 Scorpio	12 *midnight*	28 Gemini

August 29

AM		PM	
1	13 Cancer	1	5 Sagittarius
2	26 Cancer	2	18 Sagittarius
3	7 Leo	3	1 Capricorn
4	19 Leo	4	16 Capricorn
5	1 Virgo	5	3 Aquarius
6	13 Virgo	6	23 Aquarius
7	24 Virgo	7	17 Pisces
8	7 Libra	8	14 Aries
9	18 Libra	9	8 Taurus
10	29 Libra	10	29 Taurus
11	12 Scorpio	11	16 Gemini
12 *noon*	24 Scorpio	12 *midnight*	29 Gemini

September 1

AM		PM	
1	16 Cancer	1	8 Sagittarius
2	28 Cancer	2	21 Sagittarius
3	10 Leo	3	4 Capricorn
4	21 Leo	4	19 Capricorn
5	3 Virgo	5	7 Aquarius
6	15 Virgo	6	28 Aquarius
7	27 Virgo	7	23 Pisces
8	8 Libra	8	19 Aries
9	21 Libra	9	13 Taurus
10	2 Scorpio	10	2 Gemini
11	14 Scorpio	11	19 Gemini
12 *noon*	26 Scorpio	12 *midnight*	3 Cancer

September 4

AM		PM	
1	18 Cancer	1	10 Sagittarius
2	29 Cancer	2	23 Sagittarius
3	12 Leo	3	6 Capricorn
4	24 Leo	4	22 Capricorn
5	5 Virgo	5	11 Aquarius
6	17 Virgo	6	3 Pisces
7	29 Virgo	7	29 Pisces
8	11 Libra	8	24 Aries
9	23 Libra	9	17 Taurus
10	5 Scorpio	10	6 Gemini
11	16 Scorpio	11	22 Gemini
12 *noon*	28 Scorpio	12 *midnight*	6 Cancer

September 7

AM		PM	
1	20 Cancer	1	12 Sagittarius
2	3 Leo	2	26 Sagittarius
3	15 Leo	3	10 Capricorn
4	26 Leo	4	25 Capricorn
5	8 Virgo	5	15 Aquarius
6	19 Virgo	6	8 Pisces
7	1 Libra	7	4 Aries
8	13 Libra	8	28 Aries
9	25 Libra	9	20 Taurus
10	7 Scorpio	10	9 Gemini
11	18 Scorpio	11	25 Gemini
12 *noon*	29 Scorpio	12 *midnight*	9 Cancer

September 10

AM		PM	
1	23 Cancer	1	15 Sagittarius
2	5 Leo	2	28 Sagittarius
3	16 Leo	3	13 Capricorn
4	28 Leo	4	29 Capricorn
5	10 Virgo	5	19 Aquarius
6	22 Virgo	6	13 Pisces
7	4 Libra	7	8 Aries
8	16 Libra	8	3 Taurus
9	28 Libra	9	24 Taurus
10	9 Scorpio	10	12 Gemini
11	21 Scorpio	11	28 Gemini
12 *noon*	3 Sagittarius	12 *midnight*	11 Cancer

September 13

AM		PM	
1	26 Cancer	1	18 Sagittarius
2	7 Leo	2	1 Capricorn
3	19 Leo	3	16 Capricorn
4	29 Leo	4	3 Aquarius
5	13 Virgo	5	23 Aquarius
6	24 Virgo	6	17 Pisces
7	6 Libra	7	14 Aries
8	18 Libra	8	8 Taurus
9	29 Libra	9	28 Taurus
10	12 Scorpio	10	15 Gemini
11	23 Scorpio	11	29 Gemini
12 *noon*	5 Sagittarius	12 *midnight*	13 Cancer

September 16

AM		PM	
1	28 Cancer	1	20 Sagittarius
2	10 Leo	2	3 Capricorn
3	21 Leo	3	19 Capricorn
4	3 Virgo	4	7 Aquarius
5	14 Virgo	5	28 Aquarius
6	26 Virgo	6	23 Pisces
7	8 Libra	7	18 Aries
8	20 Libra	8	13 Taurus
9	2 Scorpio	9	2 Gemini
10	14 Scorpio	10	18 Gemini
11	25 Scorpio	11	3 Cancer
12 *noon*	8 Sagittarius	12 *midnight*	16 Cancer

September 19

AM		PM	
1	29 Cancer	1	22 Sagittarius
2	12 Leo	2	6 Capricorn
3	23 Leo	3	22 Capricorn
4	5 Virgo	4	11 Aquarius
5	17 Virgo	5	3 Pisces
6	29 Virgo	6	29 Pisces
7	11 Libra	7	23 Aries
8	23 Libra	8	16 Taurus
9	4 Scorpio	9	6 Gemini
10	16 Scorpio	10	21 Gemini
11	27 Scorpio	11	6 Cancer
12 *noon*	10 Sagittarius	12 *midnight*	18 Cancer

September 22

AM		PM	
1	2 Leo	1	26 Sagittarius
2	14 Leo	2	9 Capricorn
3	26 Leo	3	25 Capricorn
4	8 Virgo	4	14 Aquarius
5	19 Virgo	5	7 Pisces
6	1 Libra	6	2 Aries
7	14 Libra	7	28 Aries
8	25 Libra	8	20 Taurus
9	7 Scorpio	9	9 Gemini
10	18 Scorpio	10	24 Gemini
11	29 Scorpio	11	8 Cancer
12 *noon*	12 Sagittarius	12 *midnight*	21 Cancer

September 25

AM		PM	
1	4 Leo	1	28 Sagittarius
2	16 Leo	2	13 Capricorn
3	28 Leo	3	29 Capricorn
4	10 Virgo	4	18 Aquarius
5	22 Virgo	5	12 Pisces
6	3 Libra	6	8 Aries
7	15 Libra	7	3 Taurus
8	27 Libra	8	24 Taurus
9	9 Scorpio	9	12 Gemini
10	21 Scorpio	10	28 Gemini
11	3 Sagittarius	11	11 Cancer
12 *noon*	15 Sagittarius	12 *midnight*	23 Cancer

September 28

AM		PM	
1	7 Leo	1	1 Capricorn
2	19 Leo	2	16 Capricorn
3	29 Leo	3	3 Aquarius
4	12 Virgo	4	23 Aquarius
5	24 Virgo	5	17 Pisces
6	6 Libra	6	14 Aries
7	18 Libra	7	8 Taurus
8	29 Libra	8	28 Taurus
9	12 Scorpio	9	15 Gemini
10	23 Scorpio	10	29 Gemini
11	5 Sagittarius	11	13 Cancer
12 *noon*	18 Sagittarius	12 *midnight*	26 Cancer

October 1

AM		PM	
1	9 Leo	1	3 Capricorn
2	21 Leo	2	18 Capricorn
3	3 Virgo	3	5 Aquarius
4	14 Virgo	4	27 Aquarius
5	26 Virgo	5	23 Pisces
6	8 Libra	6	17 Aries
7	20 Libra	7	11 Taurus
8	2 Scorpio	8	2 Gemini
9	13 Scorpio	9	18 Gemini
10	25 Scorpio	10	3 Cancer
11	7 Sagittarius	11	16 Cancer
12 *noon*	20 Sagittarius	12 *midnight*	28 Cancer

October 4

AM		PM	
1	11 Leo	1	6 Capricorn
2	23 Leo	2	21 Capricorn
3	5 Virgo	3	9 Aquarius
4	17 Virgo	4	1 Pisces
5	29 Virgo	5	27 Pisces
6	11 Libra	6	23 Aries
7	23 Libra	7	16 Taurus
8	4 Scorpio	8	6 Gemini
9	16 Scorpio	9	21 Gemini
10	27 Scorpio	10	6 Cancer
11	10 Sagittarius	11	18 Cancer
12 *noon*	22 Sagittarius	12 *midnight*	1 Leo

October 7

AM		PM	
1	14 Leo	1	9 Capricorn
2	26 Leo	2	24 Capricorn
3	8 Virgo	3	14 Aquarius
4	19 Virgo	4	6 Pisces
5	1 Libra	5	2 Aries
6	13 Libra	6	28 Aries
7	25 Libra	7	20 Taurus
8	6 Scorpio	8	9 Gemini
9	18 Scorpio	9	24 Gemini
10	29 Scorpio	10	8 Cancer
11	12 Sagittarius	11	20 Cancer
12 *noon*	25 Sagittarius	12 *midnight*	3 Leo

October 10

AM		PM	
1	16 Leo	1	12 Capricorn
2	28 Leo	2	28 Capricorn
3	10 Virgo	3	18 Aquarius
4	21 Virgo	4	12 Pisces
5	3 Libra	5	8 Aries
6	15 Libra	6	3 Taurus
7	27 Libra	7	24 Taurus
8	9 Scorpio	8	12 Gemini
9	21 Scorpio	9	27 Gemini
10	3 Sagittarius	10	10 Cancer
11	14 Sagittarius	11	23 Cancer
12 *noon*	27 Sagittarius	12 *midnight*	5 Leo

October 13

AM		PM	
1	19 Leo	1	15 Capricorn
2	29 Leo	2	2 Aquarius
3	12 Virgo	3	23 Aquarius
4	24 Virgo	4	17 Pisces
5	6 Libra	5	12 Aries
6	18 Libra	6	8 Taurus
7	29 Libra	7	28 Taurus
8	11 Scorpio	8	15 Gemini
9	23 Scorpio	9	29 Gemini
10	5 Sagittarius	10	13 Cancer
11	17 Sagittarius	11	26 Cancer
12 *noon*	1 Capricorn	12 *midnight*	7 Leo

October 16

AM		PM	
1	21 Leo	1	18 Capricorn
2	3 Virgo	2	5 Aquarius
3	14 Virgo	3	26 Aquarius
4	26 Virgo	4	22 Pisces
5	8 Libra	5	17 Aries
6	20 Libra	6	11 Taurus
7	2 Scorpio	7	2 Gemini
8	13 Scorpio	8	18 Gemini
9	25 Scorpio	9	2 Cancer
10	7 Sagittarius	10	16 Cancer
11	19 Sagittarius	11	28 Cancer
12 *noon*	3 Capricorn	12 *midnight*	10 Leo

October 19

AM		PM	
1	23 Leo	1	21 Capricorn
2	5 Virgo	2	9 Aquarius
3	17 Virgo	3	1 Pisces
4	29 Virgo	4	27 Pisces
5	11 Libra	5	23 Aries
6	22 Libra	6	16 Taurus
7	4 Scorpio	7	6 Gemini
8	15 Scorpio	8	21 Gemini
9	27 Scorpio	9	6 Cancer
10	9 Sagittarius	10	18 Cancer
11	22 Sagittarius	11	29 Cancer
12 *noon*	6 Capricorn	12 *midnight*	12 Leo

October 22

AM		PM	
1	26 Leo	1	24 Capricorn
2	7 Virgo	2	14 Aquarius
3	19 Virgo	3	6 Pisces
4	1 Libra	4	2 Aries
5	13 Libra	5	28 Aries
6	24 Libra	6	20 Taurus
7	6 Scorpio	7	8 Gemini
8	18 Scorpio	8	24 Gemini
9	29 Scorpio	9	8 Cancer
10	11 Sagittarius	10	20 Cancer
11	25 Sagittarius	11	2 Leo
12 *noon*	9 Capricorn	12 *midnight*	14 Leo

October 25

AM		PM	
1	28 Leo	1	28 Capricorn
2	9 Virgo	2	18 Aquarius
3	21 Virgo	3	12 Pisces
4	3 Libra	4	7 Aries
5	15 Libra	5	15 Taurus
6	27 Libra	6	24 Taurus
7	9 Scorpio	7	12 Gemini
8	20 Scorpio	8	27 Gemini
9	2 Sagittarius	9	10 Cancer
10	14 Sagittarius	10	23 Cancer
11	27 Sagittarius	11	4 Leo
12 *noon*	12 Capricorn	12 *midnight*	16 Leo

October 28

AM		PM	
1	29 Leo	1	2 Aquarius
2	12 Virgo	2	21 Aquarius
3	24 Virgo	3	16 Pisces
4	6 Libra	4	12 Aries
5	18 Libra	5	7 Taurus
6	29 Libra	6	27 Taurus
7	11 Scorpio	7	14 Gemini
8	22 Scorpio	8	29 Gemini
9	5 Sagittarius	9	13 Cancer
10	17 Sagittarius	10	25 Cancer
11	29 Sagittarius	11	7 Leo
12 *noon*	15 Capricorn	12 *midnight*	19 Leo

October 31

AM		PM	
1	2 Virgo	1	5 Aquarius
2	14 Virgo	2	26 Aquarius
3	25 Virgo	3	21 Pisces
4	7 Libra	4	17 Aries
5	19 Libra	5	11 Taurus
6	2 Scorpio	6	1 Gemini
7	13 Scorpio	7	18 Gemini
8	25 Scorpio	8	2 Cancer
9	7 Sagittarius	9	15 Cancer
10	19 Sagittarius	10	27 Cancer
11	2 Capricorn	11	10 Leo
12 *noon*	18 Capricorn	12 *midnight*	22 Leo

November 3

AM		PM	
1	4 Virgo	1	9 Aquarius
2	17 Virgo	2	1 Pisces
3	29 Virgo	3	27 Pisces
4	10 Libra	4	22 Aries
5	22 Libra	5	16 Taurus
6	4 Scorpio	6	4 Gemini
7	15 Scorpio	7	20 Gemini
8	27 Scorpio	8	5 Cancer
9	9 Sagittarius	9	17 Cancer
10	21 Sagittarius	10	29 Cancer
11	5 Capricorn	11	12 Leo
12 *noon*	21 Capricorn	12 *midnight*	23 Leo

November 6

AM		PM	
1	7 Virgo	1	14 Aquarius
2	19 Virgo	2	6 Pisces
3	1 Libra	3	1 Aries
4	13 Libra	4	27 Aries
5	24 Libra	5	20 Taurus
6	6 Scorpio	6	8 Gemini
7	18 Scorpio	7	24 Gemini
8	29 Scorpio	8	8 Cancer
9	12 Sagittarius	9	20 Cancer
10	25 Sagittarius	10	2 Leo
11	8 Capricorn	11	14 Leo
12 *noon*	24 Capricorn	12 *midnight*	26 Leo

November 9

AM		PM	
1	9 Virgo	1	17 Aquarius
2	21 Virgo	2	10 Pisces
3	3 Libra	3	6 Aries
4	15 Libra	4	2 Taurus
5	27 Libra	5	23 Taurus
6	9 Scorpio	6	1 Gemini
7	20 Scorpio	7	26 Gemini
8	2 Sagittarius	8	10 Cancer
9	14 Sagittarius	9	23 Cancer
10	27 Sagittarius	10	4 Leo
11	11 Capricorn	11	16 Leo
12 *noon*	28 Capricorn	12 *midnight*	28 Leo

November 12

AM		PM	
1	12 Virgo	1	21 Aquarius
2	24 Virgo	2	15 Pisces
3	5 Libra	3	12 Aries
4	17 Libra	4	7 Taurus
5	29 Libra	5	27 Taurus
6	11 Scorpio	6	14 Gemini
7	22 Scorpio	7	29 Gemini
8	5 Sagittarius	8	13 Cancer
9	17 Sagittarius	9	25 Cancer
10	29 Sagittarius	10	7 Leo
11	15 Capricorn	11	19 Leo
12 *noon*	2 Aquarius	12 *midnight*	29 Leo

November 15

AM		PM	
1	14 Virgo	1	26 Aquarius
2	26 Virgo	2	21 Pisces
3	7 Libra	3	17 Aries
4	19 Libra	4	11 Taurus
5	2 Scorpio	5	1 Gemini
6	13 Scorpio	6	17 Gemini
7	24 Scorpio	7	2 Cancer
8	7 Sagittarius	8	15 Cancer
9	19 Sagittarius	9	27 Cancer
10	2 Capricorn	10	9 Leo
11	18 Capricorn	11	21 Leo
12 *noon*	5 Aquarius	12 *midnight*	3 Virgo

November 18

AM		PM	
1	16 Virgo	1	1 Pisces
2	28 Virgo	2	27 Pisces
3	10 Libra	3	22 Aries
4	22 Libra	4	15 Taurus
5	4 Scorpio	5	4 Gemini
6	15 Scorpio	6	20 Gemini
7	27 Scorpio	7	5 Cancer
8	9 Sagittarius	8	17 Cancer
9	21 Sagittarius	9	29 Cancer
10	5 Capricorn	10	12 Leo
11	20 Capricorn	11	23 Leo
12 *noon*	9 Aquarius	12 *midnight*	5 Virgo

November 21

AM		PM	
1	18 Virgo	1	5 Pisces
2	1 Libra	2	1 Aries
3	13 Libra	3	26 Aries
4	24 Libra	4	19 Taurus
5	6 Scorpio	5	8 Gemini
6	18 Scorpio	6	23 Gemini
7	29 Scorpio	7	7 Cancer
8	11 Sagittarius	8	20 Cancer
9	24 Sagittarius	9	2 Leo
10	8 Capricorn	10	14 Leo
11	24 Capricorn	11	26 Leo
12 *noon*	12 Aquarius	12 *midnight*	8 Virgo

November 24

AM		PM	
1	21 Virgo	1	10 Pisces
2	3 Libra	2	6 Aries
3	15 Libra	3	2 Taurus
4	27 Libra	4	23 Taurus
5	9 Scorpio	5	11 Gemini
6	20 Scorpio	6	27 Gemini
7	2 Sagittarius	7	10 Cancer
8	14 Sagittarius	8	23 Cancer
9	27 Sagittarius	9	4 Leo
10	11 Capricorn	10	16 Leo
11	27 Capricorn	11	28 Leo
12 *noon*	17 Aquarius	12 *midnight*	10 Virgo

November 27

AM		PM	
1	23 Virgo	1	15 Pisces
2	5 Libra	2	12 Aries
3	17 Libra	3	7 Taurus
4	29 Libra	4	27 Taurus
5	10 Scorpio	5	14 Gemini
6	22 Scorpio	6	29 Gemini
7	4 Sagittarius	7	13 Cancer
8	16 Sagittarius	8	25 Cancer
9	29 Sagittarius	9	7 Leo
10	14 Capricorn	10	19 Leo
11	29 Capricorn	11	29 Leo
12 *noon*	21 Aquarius	12 *midnight*	12 Virgo

November 30

AM		PM	
1	25 Virgo	1	21 Pisces
2	7 Libra	2	17 Aries
3	19 Libra	3	11 Taurus
4	1 Scorpio	4	1 Gemini
5	12 Scorpio	5	17 Gemini
6	24 Scorpio	6	2 Cancer
7	6 Sagittarius	7	15 Cancer
8	19 Sagittarius	8	27 Cancer
9	2 Capricorn	9	9 Leo
10	17 Capricorn	10	21 Leo
11	4 Aquarius	11	3 Virgo
12 *noon*	26 Aquarius	12 *midnight*	14 Virgo

December 3

AM		PM	
1	28 Virgo	1	25 Pisces
2	10 Libra	2	21 Aries
3	22 Libra	3	14 Taurus
4	3 Scorpio	4	4 Gemini
5	15 Scorpio	5	20 Gemini
6	27 Scorpio	6	5 Cancer
7	9 Sagittarius	7	17 Cancer
8	21 Sagittarius	8	29 Cancer
9	5 Capricorn	9	11 Leo
10	20 Capricorn	10	23 Leo
11	8 Aquarius	11	5 Virgo
12 *noon*	1 Pisces	12 *midnight*	17 Virgo

December 6

AM		PM	
1	1 Libra	1	1 Aries
2	12 Libra	2	26 Aries
3	24 Libra	3	19 Taurus
4	5 Scorpio	4	8 Gemini
5	17 Scorpio	5	23 Gemini
6	29 Scorpio	6	7 Cancer
7	11 Sagittarius	7	20 Cancer
8	24 Sagittarius	8	2 Leo
9	8 Capricorn	9	14 Leo
10	23 Capricorn	10	26 Leo
11	12 Aquarius	11	7 Virgo
12 *noon*	5 Pisces	12 *midnight*	18 Virgo

December 9

AM		PM	
1	2 Libra	1	6 Aries
2	14 Libra	2	2 Taurus
3	26 Libra	3	23 Taurus
4	8 Scorpio	4	11 Gemini
5	20 Scorpio	5	26 Gemini
6	1 Sagittarius	6	10 Cancer
7	14 Sagittarius	7	23 Cancer
8	26 Sagittarius	8	4 Leo
9	11 Capricorn	9	16 Leo
10	27 Capricorn	10	28 Leo
11	16 Aquarius	11	9 Virgo
12 *noon*	10 Pisces	12 *midnight*	21 Virgo

December 12

AM		PM	
1	5 Libra	1	11 Aries
2	17 Libra	2	6 Taurus
3	28 Libra	3	27 Taurus
4	10 Scorpio	4	14 Gemini
5	22 Scorpio	5	29 Gemini
6	4 Sagittarius	6	13 Cancer
7	16 Sagittarius	7	25 Cancer
8	29 Sagittarius	8	7 Leo
9	14 Capricorn	9	19 Leo
10	29 Capricorn	10	29 Leo
11	21 Aquarius	11	12 Virgo
12 *noon*	15 Pisces	12 *midnight*	24 Virgo

December 15

AM		PM	
1	7 Libra	1	16 Aries
2	19 Libra	2	10 Taurus
3	1 Scorpio	3	1 Gemini
4	12 Scorpio	4	17 Gemini
5	24 Scorpio	5	1 Cancer
6	6 Sagittarius	6	15 Cancer
7	18 Sagittarius	7	27 Cancer
8	1 Capricorn	8	9 Leo
9	17 Capricorn	9	21 Leo
10	4 Aquarius	10	3 Virgo
11	24 Aquarius	11	14 Virgo
12 *noon*	19 Pisces	12 *midnight*	26 Virgo

December 18

AM		PM	
1	9 Libra	1	21 Aries
2	21 Libra	2	14 Taurus
3	3 Scorpio	3	4 Gemini
4	15 Scorpio	4	20 Gemini
5	27 Scorpio	5	5 Cancer
6	8 Sagittarius	6	17 Cancer
7	21 Sagittarius	7	29 Cancer
8	5 Capricorn	8	11 Leo
9	20 Capricorn	9	23 Leo
10	8 Aquarius	10	4 Virgo
11	29 Aquarius	11	17 Virgo
12 *noon*	25 Pisces	12 *midnight*	29 Virgo

December 21

AM		PM	
1	12 Libra	1	26 Aries
2	23 Libra	2	19 Taurus
3	5 Scorpio	3	7 Gemini
4	17 Scorpio	4	23 Gemini
5	29 Scorpio	5	7 Cancer
6	11 Sagittarius	6	20 Cancer
7	24 Sagittarius	7	2 Leo
8	8 Capricorn	8	13 Leo
9	23 Capricorn	9	25 Leo
10	12 Aquarius	10	7 Virgo
11	5 Pisces	11	19 Virgo
12 *noon*	1 Aries	12 *midnight*	1 Libra

December 24

AM		PM	
1	14 Libra	1	2 Taurus
2	26 Libra	2	23 Taurus
3	8 Scorpio	3	10 Gemini
4	19 Scorpio	4	26 Gemini
5	1 Sagittarius	5	10 Cancer
6	14 Sagittarius	6	22 Cancer
7	26 Sagittarius	7	4 Leo
8	11 Capricorn	8	16 Leo
9	27 Capricorn	9	28 Leo
10	16 Aquarius	10	9 Virgo
11	9 Pisces	11	21 Virgo
12 *noon*	5 Aries	12 *midnight*	3 Libra

December 27

AM		PM	
1	17 Libra	1	5 Taurus
2	28 Libra	2	26 Taurus
3	10 Scorpio	3	13 Gemini
4	22 Scorpio	4	29 Gemini
5	4 Sagittarius	5	12 Cancer
6	16 Sagittarius	6	25 Cancer
7	29 Sagittarius	7	6 Leo
8	14 Capricorn	8	18 Leo
9	29 Capricorn	9	29 Leo
10	20 Aquarius	10	12 Virgo
11	14 Pisces	11	24 Virgo
12 *noon*	10 Aries	12 *midnight*	6 Libra

December 30

AM		PM	
1	19 Libra	1	10 Taurus
2	1 Scorpio	2	29 Taurus
3	12 Scorpio	3	16 Gemini
4	24 Scorpio	4	1 Cancer
5	6 Sagittarius	5	14 Cancer
6	19 Sagittarius	6	27 Cancer
7	1 Capricorn	7	9 Leo
8	17 Capricorn	8	20 Leo
9	4 Aquarius	9	2 Virgo
10	24 Aquarius	10	13 Virgo
11	19 Pisces	11	26 Virgo
12 *noon*	16 Aries	12 *midnight*	7 Libra

The Elements of Fire and Earth

Vision v. Reality

The Element of Fire

*We can accept the unpleasant more readily
than we can the inconsequential.*

GOETHE

The cycle of the zodiac begins with fire, the gift
which Prometheus stole from the gods to give to
man so that he might have hope and a possibility of
growth and development. And if we are to make any
sense of those peculiar fire signs – Aries, Leo and
Sagittarius – and their often incomprehensible but
always dramatic behaviour in life and in relationships,
we must, as with all zodiacal symbolism, think for a
moment about fire itself. With all the myriad forms that
fire can take, we can make two general comments about
it. Firstly, it brings light into darkness. Secondly, it
cannot be contained in one shape, one size, one form.
It is volatile, unpredictable. So, too, with those people
who belong to the astrological element of fire.

You may see some common descriptions of the fire
signs in any good astrological textbook, or more repu-
table newspaper columns: warm, outgoing, self-centred,
dramatic, lucky. The fire signs seem to have it all over
the others in terms of sheer *chutzpah*. No one can quite
top an Aries for daring: no one can beat a Leo for
personality and impact; no one can come miles within

a Sagittarian for a roving, adventurer's eye. But what really makes fire people tick? All those lovely descriptions are not much use if you happen to be in a relationship with a fiery temperament and are subjected to the more exaggerated idiosyncrasies of fiery behaviour. What does life really look like through fiery eyes, and what do they really need from a lover, a partner, a friend?

One key thought which might help: to the fire signs, life is an endless sea of possibilities. As long as there are opportunities to explore, open doors through which to pass, new twists and turns in a future that is still in formation and in which anything might happen, then the fiery type will be reasonably content – if contentment is a word one can apply to this restless, volatile psyche. But as soon as you take away the possibilities, close the doors, plan the future too rigidly, and remove that little bit of chaos that makes the world go round, then the fiery type panics. You have taken away the very thing which nourishes them: their ability to shape creative things out of random possibilities. And as soon as you've done that you've lost them. Some people need security more than anything in the world. Not so the fire signs. While they like a little, too much of it is like burying them in clay. They suffocate.

Never mind talking to them about reality and responsibility. They see it perfectly clearly, thank you very much. Its just that this isn't *their* reality. The 'real' world to a fire sign is secretly that fantasy world which was supposed to end when the last fairy tale book was tucked away in the cupboard and the brutal truth about Santa Claus was made known. Look into the secret reality of the fire signs and you are in a world of pure romance, pure myth. Fire signs need to mythologize everything: other people, professions, situations, themselves. For fire, all the world's a stage, and no one plays the part with such *panache*.

You may have met that common fire-sign propensity to make vast Himalayan peaks out of perfectly ordinary molehills. It wasn't just a little disagreement, it was a Holocaust. It wasn't a nice film, it was Wonderful, Brilliant, Mind-Shattering. The overwhelming and contagious enthusiasm of the fire signs is hard to resist; so, too, is their anger. Fire signs often exaggerate their behaviour, dramatize it – even when they are alone. They aren't just spoiled brats trying to attract your attention. They need this fantasizing, this injection of brilliant colour and sound into the grey and banal fabric of what the world is constantly insisting is reality. Fire is not interested in the pragmatic approach to life. Take away a fire sign's fantasies and visions of how life might be, and you have crippled them. It is, truly, that serious. If there is one thing sacred to the fire signs, it is their dreams.

You may find the fiery types somewhat egocentric and insensitive. In some respects, they are – as regards the details of earthy reality. But it isn't really insensitivity. It's just that forcing a fire sign to focus his broad and all-encompassing vision on something so temporal and boring as a fact is positively threatening to him. If he stares at a detail for too long he feels that he might miss something. Fiery people like to get the gist of the picture without getting trapped in it for too long, so that they can take their sensitive, colourful impressions and place them in context with all those other impressions they're collecting about life. This is why so many fire signs are ardent and restless travellers. They like to get a taste of the world, of life, of current events, of cultures, of people.

The future is the most fascinating thing on earth to a fire sign. The past is a novel someone else wrote, the present relevant only as a potential doorway into a whole network of possible futures. When confronted with the incessant and monotonous demands of the material world, the fiery type may often drop the situation like the proverbial hot potato and move elsewhere. This has earned them the accusation of irresponsibility or callousness. Not so. It is just that they cannot bear to be imprisoned.

A few more significant comments about the fire signs, before we look at them individually. It is best that you get a clear picture of the type, for they are less likely than their earth, water or air relatives to be able to explain themselves to you. After all, knights on white horses never have to offer explanations in the fairy tales.

There is that wonderful gift that some fiery people have for the magic 'hunch'. Have you ever watched a fire sign assess a situation? They will rarely analyse the components, or if they do, it will be in an afterword, to justify themselves to some pestering earth sign who doesn't believe in hunches. But the fiery type seems to be able to get an instantaneous perception of all the undercurrents going on, and to come to a snap conclusion which just seems to 'happen' in their head. They rarely know how or why. They have an excellent nose, which often flies against the apparent facts of a situation, yet is unerringly accurate. You might even call this mysterious sixth sense a little magical. Actually what has happened is that they have used functions of the psyche other than the senses and the rational intellect to assess the situation. What other function, you may well ask. Why, any fire sign can tell you: intuition.

For this reason fire signs appear to have a lot of luck. They are the ones who win the races and the pools, invest in the one stock which climbs when the market is collapsing, set up a company to see a product which is suddenly needed in two years' time, peer into the smoky lens of the future and write books, make films, design fashions that are a prophecy rather than a reflection of now. And what happens when it goes wrong and the business collapses, the market crashes, the deal doesn't come off? Never mind. Somehow, some way, a solution will appear. There is an infuriatingly unquenchable trust in the future with fiery people. If you meet them when they are down and out, never mind, it will all come right one day, somehow. And what is maddening is that it usually does – if they haven't hooked up with some partner who stomps all over their dreams and convinces them that the way to happiness is the regular small salary cheque, their semi in the suburbs, 2·3 children, 1·5 dogs, and the in-laws over for Sunday dinner each week. If you find any fire signs living like that, get out your handkerchief. There is nothing sadder than a noble knight in rusted armour trying to clip the hedges in Neasden.

Ah, they are romantic, these fire signs. They sound almost too perfect, too magical, too heroic. How can you resist them? Not many people can. Have they no vices, then?

Remember what we said about every element having a secret dark side? Well, here it is, then, the secret vices of the element of fire. A little scenario might help to make this clear.

EARTH: Have you remembered to pay the telephone bill, dear?
FIRE: Telephone bill? Oh, yes, of course. Sorry, I forgot, I was just starting to work out the plot for this novel.
A week later:
EARTH: Have you remembered to pay the telephone bill, dear?
FIRE: Telephone bill? (*Beginning signs of irritation.*) Yes, dear. Look, I'm trying to concentrate on this piece of writing. It's not going well.
EARTH: I've asked you at least a dozen times. We'll have the phone disconnected if you don't pay it.

FIRE: (*Feeling guilty because he hates being accused of being irresponsible*) If you stopped nagging me, I might remember to pay it.

(*Translation: I can't really cope, don't remind me.*)

EARTH: You wouldn't remember. If I didn't remind you nothing would ever get done. We'd have no telephone, we'd be thrown out of the house, there'd be nothing to eat, the children would have no clothes . . .

FIRE: (*Losing temper*) Will you just for once leave me alone? Now you've ruined my concentration, I can't write any more this evening. Why must you bother me with such petty rubbish? It will get paid.

EARTH: (*Taking martyr pose*) I'm the only one who does any giving in this relationship. I cook and clean and pay the bills and you just sit there staring out the window dreaming. Why don't you get a proper job?

FIRE: (*Later, to his mistress*) She just doesn't understand me. She crushes my creativity.

EARTH: (*Later, to her solicitor*) I want the house, five hundred pounds maintenance per month, and the car. I have to take care of myself, after all.

We can summarize the difficulties of the fiery signs by the following general pronouncement: the element of fire has a problem coping with the everyday world. Despite their wonderful vision, intuition, dash and insight, the world is, unfortunately for fire signs, full of the presence of objects and stubborn, conservative people. The world, for many fire sign people, appears to have definite malice aforethought in its tendency to thwart them. They must either conquer it in grand style or withdraw into their strange world of fantasies. These frustrations may take the well-known and beloved form of government structures and red tape, traffic laws, taxes, bills, the necessity of earning an income, and the problem of remembering to feed, clothe and take care

of that old incubus, the body – which, after all, is made
of the substance of the world.

So our fiery friends, though they may be wonderfully
successful in any enterprise which entails speculation
and the inauguration of creative ideas rather than
routine and bondage to detail, often cannot leave the
house without forgetting car keys or wallet or drive
down a street without incurring a traffic violation – if
the car will start at all, brute beast that it is. It is this
kind of experience which forces many fire signs into the
'misunderstood genius' syndrome. But it is not really
society which is creating the problem – albeit it is all
too frequently too conservative, too stolid, and at least
twenty to fifty years behind the leaping intuitive vision
of fire. It is the secret, unknown, unconscious world of
the senses, of matter itself, which poses fire with his
greatest problem. And it is often his body itself.

I have known a great number of fiery people who
hold an active dislike of their bodies. This may range
from dislike of the appearance – and here the peculiar
fantasy life of fire is most evident, for the person's body
may be, by popular standards, very beautiful. But there
is just something about flesh itself – flesh divorced from
the glamorous, hazy images as though seen through a
gauze, denuded of its associative symbols; flesh that
gets sick, grows old, produces hair and warts and
perspiration and cellulite – which is a mystery and a
terror. It may be concluded from this that many fire
sign people are hypochondriacs. You would be right if
you guessed that. It isn't really the poor Virgos; they
merely worry about the possibility of germs and disease,
which is something else altogether. But fire is afraid
of his own body, for it seems, all too often, like an
enemy, an intruder, something into which he feels
stuffed, as it were, like a sausage into a sausage-skin.
Some fiery people will even admit to you, after a couple
of whiskies and if softly asked, that they don't really

want to be in a body at all; it's too confining, too restrictive, too 'formed', somehow. They are blithe spirits, volatile burning marshlights, and dragging around that inert old thing is a damned nuisance – bearable if it goes on running, bloody difficult if it doesn't. A good many health freaks and dietary devas and macrobiotic and massage masters are fire signs trying to deal, albeit, in a rather exaggerated way, with that unknown and fascinating world of the senses.

Which takes us to the thing which will interest you the most, if you are involved in a relationship with the fiery trigon of signs: their sex life. At the risk of incurring an appropriately fiery explosion from my fire sign readers, it must nevertheless be said that the fiery temperament is more prone to feelings of sexual inadequacy than any other group. Feelings, I said. It has nothing to do with performance, about which many fire signs are so obsessive that, were there competitions to determine such things, they would undoubtedly walk off with all the awards. The secret, vague, nagging feelings that one is a sexual failure. It comes from all that lack of understanding about the body. If you don't make friends with your body, your sexuality is going to remain a mystery to you, and you may often feel as though your body is going about its own business while you have nothing whatsoever to say in the matter. And another funny thing about fire is that, being so rooted in the world of fantasy, the body becomes unreliable, and is likely to show the evidence of emotional frustration, resentment, fear, and anger quickly as various forms of what we politely call 'sexual problems'. They are not really sexual. They have to do with the rather tenuous relationship fire has with the earth plane. But they can wreak havoc in relationships nonetheless.

You see, fire lives, if you remember, in a world of fantasy. Objects by themselves are at best boring, at worst frightening. They have to be invested with meaning, charged with glamorous or romantic connotations. In other words, objects become symbols to a fire sign. Simple appreciation of the body and bodily sensations is difficult, without the appropriate fantasy. So the element of fantasy in a fire sign's romantic relations is liable to be very strong. By fantasy we mean anticipation, visualization, expectation, need for erotic stimuli verbally, visually, imaginatively. No one loves the strip club or the porn cinema or the erotic photograph or the black silk underwear quite so much as fire signs. In fact, this element of fantasy is often so strong with a fire sign that it can become more important than the actual sexual act itself. Sounds strange? Not to fire. Sex is, for them, a thing of the mind as much as the body.

Fine, you may say. Erotic fantasies are normal; to be encouraged. We live in an enlightened age. At least, we're supposed to live in an enlightened age. But the problem comes with the choice of partner that fire signs make. We will go into this in much more detail later. Suffice it to say, for the time, that the fire signs as a group are attracted most strongly to earth. And earth is the most literal, the most basic, the most sensual, the least prone to fantasy of any of the astrological elements. So what happens? The poor fire sign often feels as though there is something wrong with him, since his partner is getting off on his hairy chest or muscular arms or cute little paunch while he is desperately trying to conjure the atmosphere of Mata Hari meeting Clint Eastwood in a '30s club in Berlin by candlelight with Marlene Dietrich singing Gestapo songs in the background.

The matter-of-fact approach of earth to sexuality is likely to make our fiery type a little uncomfortable. He may feel as though he (or she) is obliged to 'perform successfully', which is a disastrous expectation. In fact, expecting any kind of earthy performance, sexual or otherwise, from fire is likely to lead to disaster. Unless their fantasy is with them, fire signs often go impotent or frigid. This stems from the complexity of fire's approach to their senses. But the fire sign who 'fails' is liable to blame his partner, since it is very uncomfortable to blame oneself. And the blame may be one of several types.

There is the 'I simply can't perform like a machine every second Thursday,' variety. (Subsidiary subplots run to 'Not tonight, dear, I have a headache' or 'I had a long day at the office' etc.)

There is the 'Our sex life has become boring, there's something missing from it' variety. (Subplot involves either the 'together couple' who explore silk undies/ strip clubs together, or the less together couple who try to replace those elusive fantastic possibilities with 'open' marriage, wife-swapping, lovers, etc.) Fire, like blondes, has more fun? Don't kid yourself. It's no fun having to prove yourself constantly by playing Don Juan or Donna Juana to every available contestant just to make sure you're actually a member of the human race.

Over-compensation, that most common of human traits, often surfaces in the fire signs either in attempts to prove sexual prowess or attempts to prove material prowess. (Even athletic prowess.) The difference between the fiery sports champion and the earthy one though they may seem, to the casual observer, to be the same, is that the earthy gymnast – sexual or otherwise – enjoys the sensations, and does it because it feels good; the fiery gymnast aims to win, because the act is not nearly so interesting as the anticipation and the recollection.

Romantic liaisons, for the fire signs, often begin as a fairy tale and end as a cage. No fun at all, since this propensity for unreliability in relationships leads to tremendous loneliness and a big fat sense of failure.

And to complicate things fire sign people often find it hard to articulate their needs – partly because fantasies are hard to put into words and partly because, even if they could be, more stolid types have a habit of stomping all over them. As Mick Jagger sings, 'What can a poor boy do except join a rock-and-roll band?'

Fire signs are very prone to violent physical passions, which they call love. This unfortunate scenario usually ends with the sad revelation that all cats are grey at night. They can become cynical and brutal, masking their tremendous romanticism and idealism; always seeking restlessly for that spiritual soul-mate who will secretly understand the fears that drive them without demanding that they explain themselves, who can fan their little hearth fire into a mighty creative conflagration; who will contain them without imprisoning them. Are there such people? Not likely. Only in fantasy, since any red-blooded partner, whatever the astrological element, cannot always provide a new scenario every night. Sooner or later the fire signs must learn to balance their vision with a little realism and a little appreciation of the things of the earth. The present can be just as interesting as the past and the future. Facts can be just as exciting as possibilities. But balancing is *not* the same as changing. Anybody who thinks they can tame fire into a meek domestic creature is liable to get badly burned.

Aries

*L*et's begin our description of Aries with a little scenario, which will illustrate some of the qualities of this first of the fiery signs. The scenario might be entitled the Knight in Shining Armour syndrome. It can be found in both male and female Ariens – although in the case of Aries women, it might be subtitled the Joan of Arc syndrome.

ARIES: (*to friend*) I notice you're smoking. I suppose you realize that it will kill you? Give you lung cancer, heart disease, arteriosclerosis, emphysema . . .

FRIEND: Thanks, I've read all the literature. But I still think I prefer to smoke. Now about those books you were asking about . . .

ARIES: Wait a minute. Have you really read the literature? Look, I don't mean to sound pushy, but really, it's for your own good. I mean, I'm really concerned about this smoking issue. Every time I take a train or ride in a tube, and I see all these people smoking . . . I've started a group in my area called the Death to Smoking committee. We're doing a quiet little street demonstration in front of all the local tobacco shops. I figure if we put enough pressure on maybe they'll get some sense in their heads.

FRIEND: (*Lighting up a cigarette in annoyance*) Did it ever occur to you that people may like to choose whether they smoke or not? We're adults, you know.

ARIES: But I know what's best for everybody. You say you're adult, you can choose, but have you *really* read the literature?

The subject might be smoking, or anything small or great which concerns the public weal. Give him a mission, a cause, a battle in which he can trounce the enemy, an evil which he can challenge, and out comes that old suit of armour, kept clean and polished in case of emergency. We don't know whether Joan of Arc was really an Aries or not. The date of her birth is lost. But her absolute conviction, her courage, her bravery, her fanaticism, her vision, her devotion to the cause of the French nation, and her defence of the underdog – an important point, that last one – make her pretty Arien. You may notice the emphasis on championing the underdog. Aries just doesn't feel really right unless there's an underdog to take care of. If we ever really enter a truly utopian society, Aries will be in a sorry state, because he lives and breathes for the great battle. And the great battle must have an ideal. Remember

that Aries is a fire sign, and all fire signs tend to
mythologize life. The ideal justifies the battle, brings
out his courage, draws forth his genius at quick action.
And the ideal, ideally, should be the protection or
defence of the weak, the downtrodden, the abandoned.
Joan of Arc could hardly have become the mythological
figure she did without having a poor neglected wreck of
a disinherited king to defend. That was what gave her
cause pathos and meaning. The restoration of the lost
king to his kingdom, the return of justice. Does it all
sound a little fast and furious for ordinary life? Never
mind. Aries doesn't really believe in ordinary life.
There may not be any more lost kings to restore to their
kingdoms (although one never knows), but Aries can
find a cause in social welfare, in any form of life or
human expression which is overlooked, underesti-
mated, or neglected, or hasn't a chance. Aries is the
natural enemy of collectivization, because collectivization destroys myths and takes away the whole drama
of the oppressor and the oppressed.

There is definitely a chivalric quality about Aries.
Not that he's unsophisticated; some of the most polished, brilliant, intellectually aware statesmen and
thinkers are Ariens. But deep in the Aries soul, the age
of Courtly Love isn't over. He's still looking around for
the knightly order, the Round Table which he can join
to declare himself a True and Devoted Knight, and also
for the damsel in distress that he can rescue. You might
notice that Aries is very concerned for damsels in
distress. Half the fun of a relationship for Aries is the
whole chivalrous display of the rescue. Then the knight
rides away again, of course. Knights never stay home
and fix the fuses in their castles. They need adventure;
otherwise they grow pale and lifeless and distressed.
And Aries needs adventure. It might be making money,
or establishing a school, or developing any new idea
which is bound to change or alter the world around

him. But adventure he must have. Contentment and serenity and sameness give him psychic indigestion.

The ruler of Aries is the planet Mars, the mythological god of war and passion. All his qualities, when you read about them in such sources as the *Iliad*, sound like Aries exaggerated. He's courageous to the point of foolhardiness, and his courage is mixed with a liberal dash of personal glamour. (Behind-the-scenes courage is more a Scorpio trait, the dark face of Mars.) If you read history, you will come across some interesting descriptions of the age of chivalry, and one of the most interesting is the Hundred Years War. The flower of French knighthood lost some disastrous battles at Crécy, Poitiers and Agincourt. They all behaved like Ariens. There was no discipline in the French ranks, largely because each knight was so committed to his own honour and prowess that he couldn't receive orders from a superior. They fought constantly among themselves, because there was no real spirit of cooperation; every knight was a nobleman, and every nobleman an autocrat. They overweighed themselves with flamboyant armour and banners to the point where if a knight fell off his horse there was no way he could get up again without the help of a couple of squires – or a crane, which hadn't been invented yet. Notice the Aries traits? Naturally the English armies, much better disciplined although far less colourful, mowed them down. Not all Ariens get mowed down, of course. But often this quality of foolhardiness takes a few years before it's tempered by the realities of life. Ariens tend to grow up late. It takes a few hard knocks and a few confrontations with other people's stubborn resistance to teach them that it can't all happen right this minute according to their own unique creative vision.

Aries will always behave with honour toward both friend and enemy alike; he will be generous and loyal to his friends, and although scathingly contemptuous, will rarely stoop to revenge or petty behaviour toward his enemies. He does tend to make a few enemies, though, and not just because he's inclined to be rash and impulsive. He also inspires a kind of mean jealousy in other people, because in one way or another he's just a little larger than life. He tends to mythologize himself, and act accordingly. There is also a strong streak of impatience bordering on arrogance in Aries; he doesn't suffer fools gladly. He also doesn't suffer delay gladly, or insubordination, or slowness, or stupidity, or indirectness. In fact, he just doesn't suffer gladly at all, unless it's noble suffering.

Like all the fiery signs, Aries is a child at heart. This sometimes means he can be childish; at other times it means he's childlike in the most spirited, warm hearted way. He can get wildly excited and heated up over things which other, more jaded souls simply miss or overlook; no matter how old he is, from six to eighty, he can still throw himself into his work or his special projects with enthusiasm and energy. Many Ariens are so infuriatingly energetic that you get tired just watching them. They rush about with eighteen irons in the fire, all heating, as though they had some kind of invisible pill which made it unnecessary to eat, sleep, rest, or contemplate. This quality of dynamic energy is one of the most noticeable things about Aries. That, and the fact that he's usually in a hurry, even if there seems no reason to be. He'll walk in a hurry from the living room to the kitchen. He must have movement and colour and life around him, because he gets bored easily. Then you get the notorious Aries querulousness, the irritability and edginess and bad temper which often flare up. Now, the Aries temper can be a little frightening. Have you ever tried confronting Mars on the battlefield? But it helps to remember that for Aries, gestures are stylized and often dramatized. All that fire and smoke and explosion is like a child throwing a tantrum. If he's really, really angry he won't explode so much; he'll just quietly move to destroy what's in his way. But the temper is just that – temper. And once it blows over, Aries hold no grudges. He's too chivalrous for one thing, and too absent-minded for another. It just isn't that important.

I had an Aries client who once told me about his behaviour in childhood. He said that when he wanted his mother to buy him something – a coveted toy, or a sweet – and she had the bad manners to refuse, he had a simple tactic that always worked wonders. He would throw a tantrum right on the street in front of the shop. Not a yelling tantrum, either – all kids do that, and Aries isn't all kids. He would announce in his most heraldic voice, 'I'm going to hold my breath until I turn blue.' And he would do just that – prone on the sidewalk, where everyone would have to stop and crowd around to see what had happened to the poor child. His mother, naturally, never waited to see whether he really turned blue. Also, she obviously didn't know anatomy, or the fact that if he did fall unconscious he would, of course, begin to breathe again. She simply bought the toy or the sweet. Cowed by the god of war, every time.

Naturally one thinks these things end with childhood. But my Aries client made it painfully obvious that although the nature of the tantrum had changed – after all, who would fall for a forty-five-year-old man saying he was going to hold his breath until he turned blue? – the tactics were the same. He had everyone in his household benignly terrorized. But usually Ariens contrive to get everybody else to do what they want. And their approach isn't subtle. No emotional blackmail like Cancer, or long strategic planning with deals and financially viable pressures, like Capricorn. Or gentle, diplomatic statesmanship in the spirit of cooperation, like Libra. No, Aries has a simple approach. 'Do it.' If you don't, you get the tantrum, in one form or another

– maybe a slammed door and an evening of frosty silence, or a harangue, or a few smashed plates.

One way to describe Aries is self-willed. He's unquestionably unaware, a good deal of the time, of the fact that other people might wish to pull in a different direction. It's hard for Aries to understand compromise and cooperation. When he's fired up about something, nothing else seems as right, as true, or as relevant. He's dogmatic. That means that he simply doesn't notice conflicting opinions, unless you shout them at him. And then he's often genuinely hurt that you think he's being selfish or egocentric. In fact he's no more selfish than anybody else, and frequently less so. Because he tends to be generous to a fault, he's an easy prey for a sad story, and can be easily taken advantage of. He's also not a particularly astute judge of character, since he's not a suspicious type and will usually believe the best about people until unpleasantly surprised. Disloyalty, backstabbing, and meanness of any kind can really bewilder and wound him. It's just that he tends to be a little oblivious to the facts of situations, since he lives in his world of ideals. What he sees isn't how things are. It's how they could and should be. And even if everybody else is too tired or too jaded or too apathetic to do anything about it, Aries will go out there alone if necessary (he prefers support, but can do without it) and fight the dragon. And doesn't demand repayment for it either. A little applause, appreciation, perhaps. But no strings are attached to his gifts.

Trying to live with an Aries can often be difficult, if you're the type who likes the *status quo* to remain the same and the partner unchanging. Aries needs action; he needs something to pour his splendid energies into, something that stimulates him and has open possibilities. Ariens do not work well as complacent employees for strong bosses. They need scope and challenge and plenty of personal freedom to follow their visions without interference.

Now, there is a type of Arien who suppresses all this, just as anyone can suppress the natural qualities of his nature. You might see a meek, mild, docile Aries led along by a powerful wife or husband, or kept in his place by a powerful employer. All that fire goes inside, and eats at him from within. Headaches are a common Arien symptom, when the anger goes inside. You can't expect the god of war to be happy tending geraniums in the greenhouse. He'll either tear himself apart, or make life miserable for everybody else instead.

Not all Ariens display the physical prowess of the mythological Mars, although a lot are fond of sports and physical competition. The spirit of competition and winnning is there, but it may be on an intellectual level instead. Many Ariens seem to have this quality of dynamic energy in the mental realm, and whether they are scholars, philosophers, prophets, artists, religious leaders of one kind or another, you are immediately impressed by the vivid life of their minds. They love mental challenge, difficult problems, impenetrable texts which they can battle. Don't think all Ariens wear armour and ride horses physically. Some do it very unobtrusively. But watch out for the glint of the steel cuirass someplace. You'll always find it.

Like all the fire signs, Aries has a problem coping with the facts of the situation he finds himself in. Some Ariens are terribly impractical, about very mundane things – like food, money, taxes. Some are sufficiently protected by an army of secretaries, agents, cleaning ladies *et al.* so they appear to be models of efficiency when in fact, if left alone with their own resources, they would make a hopeless muddle of the material world. Some are a little better with the things of this world, but are oblivious to the limitations of things. For Aries, anything is possible. Of course, anything isn't possible.

But you can't tell an Aries that; he'll simply think you're cowardly, unimaginative, frightened or weak, and walk away to prove that it can be done. And he gets himself into a lot of trouble as often as he wins honours and accomplishes the impossible at the same time.

One of Aries' most dangerous problems is that he can be easily disillusioned and made bitter. Because his reality is so often tinted by the values of the chivalric code, he may be injured over and over again by other people who refuse to recognize the code themselves. Aries doesn't compromise gracefully with either people or life. And if he's unlucky, or pushes too hard, or has visions which are too wild or impossible, he can wind up in a very bitter state. He needs, more than anything else, to learn to see people as they are and to let them remain as they are without crusading. Conquering the infidel didn't work in the thirteenth century; it's certainly not going to work in the twentieth. It's important for Aries to learn balance, a happy medium between his noble visions of how the world might be and the limitations not only of himself but of the times he lives in. If he can find this balance, he sets his aims low enough to be achievable, without abandoning them to the kind of black despair which overwhelmed the knights when the Holy Land was lost.

A strange creature, our fiery Aries. He's capable of profound thought and considerable tenderness; but without warning he'll be leaping on his feet again to stir up another crusade. Life is certainly not boring with an Aries. If he can't find a crisis, he'll make one. There's a certain mischievous streak in him too; he'll poke and goad people and situations which are too staid, too prissy, too stagnant, until the whole thing bursts into a conflagration. He, of course, is out the door first, so that he never gets burned – or almost never. But Aries can be a tease, a gadfly nibbling away at whatever has grown fat and complacent and too sure of itself. He likes to play the role of the Devil's advocate, and doesn't mind having everybody else thoroughly annoyed at him for doing it. At least it generates a little action; and action, for Aries, is synonymous with life.

♈ The Myth

There are two myths which epitomize Aries, one an ancient one from Greece, the other a medieval myth which is still beloved in our own day and continues to give rise to films, television series, and novels. We'll deal with the second one first: the outlaw of Sherwood Forest, Robin Hood.

Now, Robin Hood is a perfect Aries character. Consider first the fact that he's an outlaw. In one way or another, Aries tends to take this stance, for he stands for change and progress. So he often comes to blows with established authority in one way or another – sometimes literally, sometimes simply as the exponent of a new set of ideas or a new method of propagating an idea. The bulwarks of society often don't like our Aries, because he makes trouble and keeps them on their toes. So Robin Hood, self-appointed champion of the oppressed poor and enemy of established, corrupt authority, represents our Knight quite well.

Consider also that Robin Hood has a band of Merry Men. He's not a dark, sinister outlaw skulking about in narrow alleyways; he has a damned good time of it. This too is an Arien quality; for Aries, being a fire sign, is determined to enjoy himself. Life, to him, is exhilarating, particularly when there's danger. The greater the danger, the spicier it is. You'd expect Ariens to be quick drivers, a little reckless. Many are. The idea is to be merry in the face of battle.

The whole background in which the Robin Hood

myth is embedded is also very Arien. There is a Good
King – Richard Coeur de Lion – who is away fighting a
Crusade for the recapture of the Holy City from the
Infidel. There is a nasty, vicious younger brother – King
John – who has usurped Richard's rightful throne.
There are the oppressed poor, and the overweaning and
arrogant rich. There is another nasty, vicious figure in
the shape of the eternal archetype, the Sheriff of
Nottingham, representing authority empty of meaning,
law empty of mercy, class structure empty of rights.

You can see why this whole myth is so Arien. Even
the lovely Maid Marian fits into the Arien dream; she
always has to be rescued. Many Aries play Robin Hood
in one way or another in their lives, shamelessly robbing
from the oppressive enemy to succour the underdog.
And, of course, at the end of the story, Good King
Richard returns. And there's a quirk to this whole tale
that is also pretty Arien. For Good King Richard wasn't
a particularly good King. That, to Aries, doesn't matter;
he often misses the quality of the cause or person he
fights for. Joan of Arc perhaps didn't realize that the
Dauphin, Charles VII of France, might not have been
particularly worth getting burned for either. It's the
vision that matters.

Now let's look at the other Arien myth. It's about
Jason and the Argonauts, and the capture of the golden
fleece. Yes, of course it would be a golden fleece, for
the ram is Aries' symbol. You can take it, if you like, as
a symbol of the ultimate goal of Aries – whether it's the
realization of his own individuality, or the achievement
of his quest, or the rescue of the damsel, or whatever.
Never mind. Jason, like a true Aries, hears about this
fantastic fleece and is delighted to find that it's impossible to find. That only encourages him. So he sets off
with his band of merry men – the Argonauts – through
one terrible danger after another, finally arriving in
Colchis where the fleece is hidden, and capturing it.

The Jason myth doesn't, however, end happily ever
after. It highlights in certain ways the dangers confronting Aries on his quest. Jason is a kind of failed Aries,
where Robin Hood is a successful one. His failure,
wouldn't you know, is due to his treatment of a woman.

In order for Jason to capture the golden fleece, he
must enlist the aid of a sorceress-princess, Medea. Now
Medea, daughter of the King of Colchis, falls wildly in
love with Jason. He's so bold, so heroic, so brave, so
courageous, so noble. She is even willing to sacrifice the
life of her brother to help him, so deeply in love is she.
Everything goes well enough, until they return. All that
golden fleece goes to Jason's woolly head. He begins to
behave more like a very stupid sheep than a golden
ram. He tries to discard Medea in favour of a younger,
more suitable princess. This is a problem with Aries:
once he's reached his goal, he often forgets the help
he's received along the way. Or he becomes bored, and
moves on. It's a common pattern in Aries relationships.
Medea is not the woman to put up with this sort of
treatment. She was probably a Scorpio. Instead of
retiring gracefully to make way for the new favourite,
she slaughters her two children by Jason, poisons the
young bride with a cloak that has been steeped in some
dreadful witch's brew, and escapes in her chariot drawn
by winged dragons. Jason's luck goes downhill from
there. In a sense, you could say that he underrates or
overlooks the power and value of the feminine. And
many Ariens do; to them the world is populated by
heroes and noble deeds, but Aries can often overlook
the power of gentleness, patience, sympathy, compromise, adjustment. Aries women too do this; remember
that Joan of Arc insisted on wearing men's clothes. So
our Jason comes to a bad end – not because he failed to
capture the golden fleece, but because he wouldn't take
into account anything except his own wishes, his own

vision, his own values. And incurred some pretty nasty vengeance as a result.

Both of these myths touch on the deeper needs and motivations in Aries' nature. There is the need to have a goal – without the goal, life for Aries is meaningless. It can be a long-term or a short-term goal, but there must be a goal. There is the need for a quest – either some journey that takes one into danger but ends with a coveted and almost impossible prize, or some battle which runs many risks but defends the ideals and the visions that have given it birth. Aries is a sign of new ideas and a sign of change – and the need to promote change, to look to the future, to conquer the enemy is embedded deep in the sign. We can, if we like, look at the twelve signs of the zodiac as a cycle, beginning with Aries and ending with Pisces, describing the round of life. Aries the first sign, the sign of spring, is the symbol of new life after the cold and barren winter. All of nature heralds the spring with a burst of life and colour, sometimes precipitate, sometimes rash, sometimes premature, but a reminder that everything has a new birth, that no matter how dark or limiting or depressing the winter it always ends with the spring. The whole world responds to the new hope and new life of the spring. For Aries, it's a constant spring, a constant challenge to end the grip of winter, a constant effort to bring new life up through the frozen ground. However impatient and irascible and clumsy he may be, the Knight in Shining Armour makes it possible for life to progress and change and grow. In a way, he must be a little crude or forceful or insensitive to do it; and perhaps in a more sober age, where we have forgotten knights and chivalry and courtly love, where we have learned to compromise too much, the voice of Aries is worth a little closer listening.

♈ The Shadow

Yes, knights on white horses have shadows. And you might expect that with all that shining armour, with the sunlight glinting so brightly on it, the shadow would be pretty dark. All fire signs, because their reality is so coloured by their inner vision of a mythical world, have a shadow that is pretty heavy and earthy. The same is true of Aries. We can apply two words to describe the qualities of Aries' shadow. Sloth and pettiness.

Now, the slothful side isn't something you'd notice, what with the hurry and the impatience and the quickness of the flash of armour whisking by. It isn't usual to think of Aries as lazy. And he isn't lazy, really, in the sense that he lacks physical energy or dynamism. But he can be inclined to be a dreamer, and along with all those lovely images of chivalry and courtly love and the glory of the chase, we should remember another facet of medieval life. This is the attitude of the *noblesse* toward the world: because he's at the top of the hierarchy (even if he's financially impoverished), he should be supported by those beneath.

This connects with a secret dream that many Ariens have: the wealthy patron. Now the dream of the wealthy patron isn't quite the same as Taurus' love of material luxury, or Pisces' gentle passivity which often requires a strong support. Aries can believe so utterly in his own dream, his own talent, his own messianic mission, that he expects that less talented souls should provide the material means for him to achieve it. Even Joan of Arc arrived at the chateau of Vaucouleurs and demanded a horse, armour, a company of fighting men, a groom, a squire, and some nice clothes so that she could be presentable for the king.

This expectation that others should do the messy work and provide the support is a real problem with many Ariens. It's why so many creative, gifted, idealistic Ariens with a real talent come to nothing. They're still waiting for wealthy patrons, still assuming that the world owes them something for their gift. And when it isn't forthcoming, they can become angry and irritable, as though life had injured them. It isn't that Aries is averse to work. He can work harder than any other sign, devotedly, obsessively. It's just that his work must be what he wants to work at. But all those annoying mundane details should be cleared away before he arrives. He doesn't want to be bothered with them.

It's common enough for the Aries man to take this stance in his relationships. Aries tends to be hard on secretaries, manservants, messenger boys, shop keepers. He's impatient, irritable, and annoyed if something isn't done quickly, immediately and perfectly. The fact that he might blunder if he tried to do it himself is irrelevant. He shouldn't have to try doing it. He's Special. He's the Knight. Knights don't polish their own armour or feed their own horses. That's what lesser folk are for. Yes, the Knight can be fairly obnoxious when you catch him at home. His gallantry and bravery and noble deeds compensate well enough; and they also overshadow what a nuisance he can be if there's a speck of rust on the cuirass.

This takes us to the second side of the Aries shadow. I mentioned the word pettiness. Perhaps pernicketiness would be a better word. It's about that spot of rust. Because he isn't terribly well related to the earth plane, Aries can often be a little compulsive about it. He can even display qualities which are usually expected of what is traditionally the Queen of Pernicketiness, Virgo. But the Aries brand is different from Virgo's habitual need for order and pattern and ritual. Aries doesn't want order. Order is a concept he's not interested in, since his universe is primarily filled with the figure of himself.

Order means adjustment of many parts within the whole. For Aries, there's only one part – him – and the whole contains him and his vision. No, Aries is pernickety in another way. What should be done for him should be done perfectly. Spotlessly. Flawlessly. Immediately. The famous Arien temper can be unleashed with great rapidity if something hasn't been done right. Aries has no patience with sloppy service.

He can even make a crusade of it. If a shirt comes home from the laundry with the stain still on the collar, it means a public campaign and many long and emotional confrontations with the cleaning establishment. If the steak isn't well-done, or the chips are soggy, the entire restaurant becomes a place of siege, because the principle takes over, and think of all the other suffering customers, and what is the modern consumer society coming to, and it's the fault of the government, and . . . Well, you get the picture. The tiniest issues can explode with resounding fury in that noble brain, because tiny issues always seem to Aries to be symbolic of big issues. The key to this is the fact that he seems to see everything symbolically. Something isn't just an isolated incident or accident; it's symptomatic always of something greater. So the spot on the collar is symptomatic of the slackness with which people nowadays treat their work, and the soggy chips are symptomatic of the low wages and bad employment practices which emerge from the government he happens to dislike, and so on, until you begin to wish he'd just go off on Crusade to capture the Holy Land and leave you alone.

Don Quixote is a figure who contains much of Aries' shadow. He tilts at windmills. This peculiar trait in the Knight in Shining Armour is most disconcerting, since Aries ordinarily is big in everything – his heart, his wallet, his visions. Yet he can explode over trifles. The trifles are usually mundane things, little trivial details which any earth sign would simply laugh at and get on with life.

A word of advice to the Aries shadow might be: relax and take it easy, because the world is also inhabited by other people who are Important. The Aries who saves up his creative ideas like a virgin saving her maidenhead may be sadly disappointed in life, since the wealthy patron may exist only in his overheated fiery imagination. He may have to get out and provide the means himself, often through work or pursuits which are not initially to his taste. And the Aries who expects that everything must be done for him instantly and impeccably needs perhaps to recognize that other people have other lives, other needs, other dreams, and also other concerns besides him. Moreover, they, like him, aren't perfect. The imperious Aries shadow needs to be tempered a little with the bread and salt of patience and a bit of gentle tolerance. Given some relaxation, all that armour weighs far less heavily; and if you don't beat the horse half to death in your hurry to get to the Crusade, the horse might turn out to help you when you need help the most. Aries can learn a lesson from Henry V's bowmen at Agincourt. They had patience, tolerance, humility, and discipline. And they won.

♈ The Aries Lover

Aries in love is what you would, of course, expect. Love is Courtly Love, and Knights in Shining Armour don't love either meanly or half-heartedly. Often, however, they love the shining ideal, rather than the actual princess who may be a little hot and uncomfortable sitting and watching that bloody joust set up in her honour.

To Aries, half the joy of love is the pursuit. It might be said that for many Ariens, love is the pursuit, rather than the arrival or the catch. Have you ever looked at medieval tapestries of the hunt? It's the hunt in every possible form: the horns, the dogs, the wonderful horses, the ladies in their towering headdresses . . . but never the catch. What would be the point of a tapestry showing the catch? How boring, how banal. Once caught, it's eaten, or hung on the wall as a trophy. The hunter is already, from the moment of success, contemplating the next hunt.

Some Ariens follow this pattern very closely in their relationships. This is why it's often a good idea to be a little reluctant in the face of chivalrous Aries pursuit. You must know how to play the game. Courtly Love is a remarkable, stylized ritual form of human relationship. The handsome young knight falls in love, always, with an Unobtainable Lady. The obtainable ones are in his life, of course – they may even be his wife. But they don't really count. It's what he can't have that he truly loves and adores. He writes her poetry, paints her miniatures, sings her troubadour songs, disguises himself as a poor minstrel so that she can throw him a rose from her balcony. He pines and mourns and watches the moon a lot, and spends lots of time wandering through forests in a kind of sad languorous melancholy. He wears her colours at the joust, and offers his life to perform deeds of terrible danger on her behalf. Eventually, it's hoped, the lady is won. But you never hear about what happens afterward.

It's not that Aries is incapable of either loyalty or fidelity or a constant relationship. It's just that he tends to get a little fidgety if the relationship never changes or provides him with any challenge or conflict. It may seem, knowing the Arien character, that this extremely masculine sign wants a passive, frail, submissive partner – of either sex. Not true. Those happen often enough, but they're practise runs. Aries will stick when he's found a relationship he can't completely dominate. So, submissive souls, take warning.

Aries, like the other two fiery signs, Leo and Sagittarius, is a born romantic. The more prosaic aspects of love don't really interest him, like grilling fish together over the fireplace. Unless the fireplace happens to be a snowbound cottage in the Alps and the rescue team won't arrive for three days, or the fish has just been caught at enormous risk from a capsized yacht where you both had to swim like mad holding the fish between you to reach the shore. As soon as things lapse into routine, Aries – male or female – starts to yawn. Now it may seem an impossible task to always provide excitement and stimulus to an Aries mate. It doesn't actually mean *you* have to provide the stimulus. It does mean you have to be careful not to try to tame the urge for excitement and change and challenge, physical or mental. And it means having your own life and your own interests, so that he – or she – never feels you're totally and utterly a possession. At that moment, the rot sets in.

One way or another, you won't be bored. Unless you have one of those completely repressed Ariens who have turned all their energy and dynamism inside against themselves, Aries is never boring. And even the injured, introverted Arien isn't; even his neurosis is interesting, if taxing. If you want a stolid, placid, contented mate, stay away from Aries. His business is not contentment. It's challenge. Try a Taurus or a Cancer. Otherwise you might get burned.

♈ The Aries Man

The Aries man is the original Knight. He's also the original male chauvinist, because you have to hit him with a veritable brick to remind him that his protection and interference may not be welcome. And you have to virtually turn him inside out to get him to notice that you can protect yourself.

Now, many women don't particularly want to protect themselves, or they are smart enough to know that they can do it quietly without bruising that rather fragile Arien ego. No question about it, Aries has an eggshell ego, to use the phrase coined by Beata Bishop in *Below the Belt*. He's as male as male can be: the original macho man. He often feels obliged to keep this image up even when he doesn't feel very macho: knights get tired too, and cranky, and hurt, and vulnerable, but there too, you never hear about it. Nobody ever describes Sir Lancelot when he has a head cold and needs cosseting. So the Aries man often pushes himself beyond his own limits trying so hard to be the ideal image of male. It helps him a lot to relax and recognize that he's human too. But Aries has a lot of difficulty acknowledging his own humanity, because he's so caught up in the world of myth.

He's capable of alternating between grand gestures of generosity that are downright poetic and hard to beat, and some pretty crude insensitivity and trampling of others' feelings. When he's bad-tempered, he often doesn't realize how he can injure others who are more sensitive; and when he's on his hobby-horse, he expects everybody around to believe so totally in what he's doing that they should drop their own goals and visions. But if you do believe in his dreams, he's an unflinching friend and will defend you and protect you literally to the grave.

What you may have to suffer most with an Aries man is the queer feeling that the goddess he worships, the princess he adores, is some vague glimmering figure just behind your left shoulder. When you try to tell him you're human, individual, he often can't see. Aries is prone to idealization of women. The Eternal Feminine is very much a reality to him, and he perceives and generally loves it as well as desiring it. But the individual personal qualities of a particular woman are not always so noticeable. He generally likes what he considers to be feminine women, and he's inclined to stereotype them, just as he's inclined to stereotype himself into the macho role. It's hard to bring him down to earth enough to let the outlines of two people emerge from all the mythologizing. And sometimes – if he's a more extreme fiery type – the outline of the real person is disturbing, and can send him off on the next quest. It's easier to be in love with an ideal image than a real woman, because the real woman needs to be related to as an individual. That means slowing down and seeing, considering, feeling, adjusting. We've already mentioned that Aries is not particularly gifted at the art of adjustment

With Aries, there's no lack of passion. And no lack of romance either. This isn't generally a once-every-Saturday-at-ten man. Aries can be a Don Juan or a Casanova, but he certainly isn't a quotidian lover. You must appreciate his romance and play to it. Too much realism kills his fire, and too much routine crushes his spirit.

Aries likes to sweep women off their feet. This may be basic and physical, or it may be subtle and intellectual. He also loves to play Pygmalion – change you, create you, fill you with his ideas, stimulate your intellect. Many Aries men love to believe that they begin with unshaped clay and create a goddess. Pygmalion was undoubtedly an Aries. Once again, if you're strongly feminist, this can be annoying. If you're comfortable with yourself and don't need to prove the point, it can be amusing, charming, touching, endearing, and still annoying. The trouble with being the object of Pygmalion's endeavours is that, while you retain the shape he's sculpted, he's fine; but if you develop any ornament or quality which wasn't in his design, he can be hurt and offended and, yes, threatened.

The truth is that Aries is a very vulnerable sign when it comes to relationships with women. There is an amusing film which Clint Eastwood starred in and directed called *Every Which Way But Loose*. The hero, like all Clint Eastwood heroes, is the original macho man – who is tough but sensitive, strong but poetic, able to beat all the bad guys but still capable of tenderness toward old ladies and pets and able to appreciate the scent of summer flowers. He's completely duped and mashed about by a hooker disguised as damsel-in-distress. She looks so frail, so needful, so injured, so abused. She really wants a little money and then a quick farewell. His look of baffled injury at the end of the film is a classic Arien look. Yet it's his own lack of insight, and his blind persistence in taking the feminine at face value as an image rather than seeing and understanding the actual woman, that is responsible for the mess. Because he's so vulnerable to Woman, he often has to be a little heavy-handed to women. This is a paradox peculiar to the fiery signs, and in particular to Aries.

On the other hand, the Aries man has one superb quality which should be emphasized again and again. He loves change, and that includes changing himself. Although capable of arrogance, petulance and downright bloody-mindedness, he's never complacent. This means that, if he can understand that a relationship is a thing which grows and changes and needs insight and attention, he'll happily make that his cause. And then you get all the benefit of the best side of the Knight in Shining Armour. And they are, truly, sadly needed these days.

♈ The Aries Woman

It isn't the easiest thing in the world to be an Aries woman in a world which burns Joan of Arc. The attitude which prevailed in Joan's time is not over yet. When you read the judgments and pronouncements of her contemporaries on her, you find an astonishing thing: what really upset everybody about Joan wasn't her visions, her charisma, her wild myth, her drama, her strange capacity to predict victories. It was her insistence on dressing in masculine garb. Virtually every pronouncement against her mentions this, as the worst, the most unforgivable of her sins.

The Aries woman, however feminine she is, however devoted a wife and mother, also needs a crusade. She needs challenge too, and projects which stimulate and inspire her, and a cause to follow, and a goal to reach. She also needs to feel she is doing something to promote change and progress, on however small a level. Aries women are naturals for executive positions and positions of leadership, because their strength, courage, directness, and conviction give them both personal charisma and authority. They are action people. You can't expect them to sit quietly behind the typewriter, or in the kitchen baking bread twenty-four hours a day. In a way, the world is only just becoming able to accommodate the clear fire of the Aries woman. Traditional astrological interpretations in the past have emphasized her masculine qualities as though these took away from her essential femaleness.

Aries is not, of course, the type of woman who fulfils the fantasies of the lovers of geisha girls in paradise. She is not likely to be pliable, submissive, and an empty vessel into which a man can project all his fantasies.

She is not likely to hero-worship or smile sweetly when her mate is behaving insufferably. She's more likely to argue, shout, throw a temper tantrum, storm out of the house, or place her own career first. And quite rightly for her, for this is a spirited sign which has suffered from the weight of social conditioning placed upon it.

Aries may also not be particularly maternal. Mars-ruled, her energy may need direction through other kinds of creativity. Often Aries women, if they are mothers, are dedicated and devoted, but essentially impatient and much better as companions and friends when the children are older. They lack the quietness and capacity to put up with noise and confusion which needs to be present along with the love in the early years of a child's life. They are also apt to push the child, if it is moving in a direction contrary to the parent's wishes. But Aries women, as mothers, have the unique virtue of not being likely to live their own lives through their children. This is an inestimable gift. It spares the psyche of the child, so that it can develop as itself.

You might say, and of course there are exceptions among individual Ariens, that the Aries woman is a much better mistress than she is a wife. This is because she must have romance and a certain amount of challenge in her relationships. And she is also sometimes ferociously independent, and all too likely to attract an easily dominated mate looking for a Joan of Arc.

The chief difficulty with the Aries woman in relationships is her competitiveness. She is apt to see a man as not only a challenge, but a fellow contestant. One-upmanship can be a real problem for the Aries woman; and her natural egocentricity can also be a terrific bruise. It isn't any worse in the Aries woman than it is in the Aries man. But it seems that the male ego, at this stage of our development, is less equipped to cope with an Aries assault than the female, which has a few thousand years of practice.

The Aries woman is also apt to try to take over and change her loved ones. This kind of interference – known popularly as bossiness – is amusing to some people and infuriating to others. It depends on your taste, and on whether or not you can deal with it productively. Better to fight it, because Aries understands a good fight where she doesn't understand sly inferences and undercurrents and subtle emotional pressures. Often the Aries woman is defenceless against the veiled barb, the indirect hostility; this is why she is often a much better friend of men than of women. It is typical of Aries women to prefer the company of men. In part, it's because she's peculiarly inept at the little undercurrents, subtle jealousies, and inferences which are so much a part of the shadow side of women's friendships. In part, it's because there's always the sparkle of the challenge and the flirtation for her.

This woman is noble, and has a noble spirit. She can be extremely difficult to live with and relate to, for all the reasons we've discussed. Unlike the Leo woman, who prefers the role of the queen, or the Sagittarian woman, who prefers the role of the *hetaera*, Aries is capable of tremendous loyal commitment. She will fight for those she loves, devote herself to them, work for them, believe in them, inspire them. She's capable of being side by side on the battlefield while preserving her innate femaleness. Men with fragile egos which need cosseting, stay away. I have a good friend married to an Aries woman who once, after discussing some trivial complaint about her bossiness, said, 'There isn't anybody like her in the world. I would never want to leave her. It's because she's herself, her own person. She's doing something with her life. She's interesting and exciting. I admire and respect her.' If you are the sort of man who is reluctant to offer admiration and respect to a strong woman, try another sign. But you'd be missing an awful lot.

*L*eo's public relations staff have been very busy in sun-sign columns, portraying the king of Beasts as the top of the heap. After all, his ruler is the sun, the Great Light as it is called in medieval astrology. So we have the traditional portrait of Leo: mane flying, radiating confidence and sunshine, ready to outstare and outshine any foe, loving himself, life, and the applause of the crowd. Most Leos do their best to help cultivate this image. They will be the last to tell you it isn't what the sign is really about. But it isn't.

A reminder might be useful here how to read sun-signs in the horoscope. Being born under a particular sign, or having a lot of planets or the ascendant placed there, doesn't automatically show that you *are* those things, that you have those qualities full-blown and ready to display in the shop window. It means that there is a reservoir of potential innate in you, something to strive toward. You grow into your chart, just as a seed grows into a full plant. The stars correspond to us, reflect us, have a connection with us; but they don't fate us.

If you see someone with lots of Leo in his chart, don't make the mistake of thinking that he's confident, radiant, egocentric, creative, self-assured. It means he's striving to develop confidence in himself, trying to radiate himself outward into his environment, trying to find out who he is, trying to express his creativity. And because these goals are likely to be terribly, intensely important to him, he will spend a lot of time and energy developing them. But Leo, confident? Hardly. His problem is usually just the opposite, which is why he spends so much time thinking about himself. After all, if you look in the mirror and there's nobody home, what meaning can you find in life?

Leo is a fiery sign. The element of fire is concerned above all else with the discovery and fulfilment of future possibilities. In Aries, these possibilities have to do with action, with leadership, with challenge. In Leo, these possibilities have to do with his fulfilling his own peculiar myth. And you don't have to look very far to discover Leo's myth. There is a wonderful book on the meaning of mythology by Joseph Campbell, called *The Hero With a Thousand Faces*. There's Leo: the hero or heroine, in a thousand different guises, playing a thousand different roles, disguised as somebody you know, or maybe even yourself. Beneath the apparent worldliness and bombast of the fire signs there always lies a secret child, who mythologizes life. And Leo, more than the other two fire signs, loves to make a myth out of himself. He is so idealistic it can make you cry. Even the Leo who cloaks himself in the cynicism of the world is really a romantic to the core. And Leo's idealism frequently makes him cry as well, since he's inclined – being rather fixed in temperament – to become fairly solid (put euphemistically) in his attitudes and ways of thinking. In other words, Leo tends to envision life in a certain way – and that way is usually coloured by all the charm and romanticism of King Arthur's court – and once he's got his vision, he really doesn't appreciate having to change it. It takes a lot to convince him that life is not the fairy tale he thought, where villains are always recognizably and totally bad, where heroes are always recognizably and utterly good, where the hero always wins and the villain loses, where the beautiful rescued princess is suitably grateful and adoring. Sometimes villains and heroes, much to Leo's chagrin, have subtle shadings of grey, and are not easily definable. Leo has a kind of black-and-white perception which doesn't readily accommodate the complexities and subtleties of human nature. And those beautiful princesses have a nasty habit, particularly lately, of not wanting to be rescued at all, since they're learning how to do it themselves. What can a poor lion do? Leo courts shock after shock on the plane of real life. Like the other two fire signs, his intuition works overtime and tells him all about the creative possibilities whereby he can live out his myth as hero, creator, sustainer, protector of the weak. It's a tough role to play these days, since people can be so damned unappreciative. Even in King Arthur's time they weren't always willing to play the game. So Leo usually collides mane first with some aspects of life he doesn't like very much. But if he can stick to his inner vision of himself, and relinquish his demands that the rest of the world conform to his ideals, it may one day dawn on him that he is indeed the hero, on a quest for his own Self, and that the rich love of life which blossoms in him is not wasted because he has to occasionally make a few adjustments to reality.

The tendency to cling to the ideal and become bewildered when it doesn't match reality is most visible in Leo's relationships. Both in business and in love, in the family and with friends, he is perpetually baffled by the pettiness, ambiguity, jealousy, and general nastiness that abounds in the human psyche. Not that he doesn't possess these attributes himself. But Leo usually will make an enormous effort to be honourable in his dealings with others, because that's the knightly code. Quite right, he's a living anachronism. There are Leos walking about where you can virtually hear the clank of armour and see the heraldic banners waving in the breeze. Loyalty is terribly important to Leo, and honour – a word whose meaning has become rather tarnished in the marketplace these days. It's perfectly understandable why the lion may so often be found with that hurt, disillusioned look on his noble face.

In the big, broad, colourful world in which Leo lives, the intrusion of the small and the banal are not welcome. Leo needs to paint his canvas with large, unrestricted strokes. Wherever some new, original idea is needed, wherever an impact must be made, wherever some new creative possibility can be envisioned, there you'll find Leo. Freddie Laker is a characteristic Leo. Who would have thought that one man, without the enormous funds and hierarchy of the large airlines behind him, could have succeeded in setting up his Skytrain service with such flair? Notice the ads for his flights. Often you get to see a picture of Sir Freddie himself, smiling and promising his customers the best possible service available. There's the Leo touch: the personal stamp. No cold, impersonal photo of a big, powerful plane as you find with commercial airlines. No, you get to see the man himself. A little exhibitionist? Of course. But that's part of Leo's charm, too – the more distinctive and individual he can be, the happier he is. Some Leos carry this to the most outlandish extremes. Napoleon, for example, wanted to conquer the world. But you'll notice that wherever it's said that something can't be done, there you'll find a Leo determined to do it.

The trouble with all these big, bold, colourful strokes on the canvas of life is that somebody has to clean the paintbrushes and wash up the paint tins afterward. And also during. And you can be pretty sure it won't be Leo, who feels trapped and miserable when he has to deal with the details of everyday life. When you read mythology, you don't often find the hero considering what chemist he should visit for his mouthwash so that he's acceptable to the princess. No, details like that aren't part of the mythological world. Who ever heard of King Arthur shopping at Marks and Spencer to save a quid or two on chain mail? You may have heard that Leo is extravagant. Yes, that's perfectly true. His extravagance stems from two sources: firstly, he loves things to be quality, beautiful, and luxurious, as well as distinctive and stylish. Secondly, he can't be bothered to see whether there's enough in the account to cover it. Leo resents having to adjust, and hates limitations. If he wants something, he believes he ought to have it. Save? Budget? Don't be silly. Somehow it'll get covered. Leo's intuition also gives him an unquenchable optimism. Find him on the dole and he'll have his mind focused years ahead when he'll be on top again. The trouble with all this is that in the meantime it's often somebody else who has to do his worrying for him. It might be reasonable to say that Leo behaves as though he needs a twenty-four-hour secretarial and accounting service at his disposal. Now, your more successful Leo might have this very thing, and life is truly a myth for him, since he can indulge his fancies as he pleases. For the more limited Leo, life can be hell. Or he'll make it hell for his partner, who's the one stuck with reminding him he's got a doctor's appointment, reminding him he owes an electricity bill, reminding him to take his clothes to the cleaners, reminding him . . . You probably have the picture. Leos can give the impression, quite unconsciously, that they expect to be taken care of and cleaned up after, because they're concerned with much more important things.

This can naturally become a classic scenario, and often does. Leo, being a fiery sign, is often attracted into relationships with earthy partners, who seem to offer the stability and realism he needs to complement his big dreams. But you should listen to those earthy partners complain: Why do you always assume you have more important things to do and leave me to clean up the mess afterward? It really isn't deliberate autocracy. Remind a Leo that he's behaving badly and he'll usually be both astonished and hurt. He doesn't mean to treat people like a crowd of courtiers. But his mind is so often on the future, or in his imaginary world of creative vision, or on the big picture, that he fails to notice the difficulties he makes for others. Yet his gifts are often so outstanding that others make allowances for him. For a while.

This connects with another curious facet of Leo's psychology. Because of the slightly dramatized world he lives in, he often can't conceive of the fact that the world outside doesn't orbit around him like his inner one does. So it's often difficult for him to realize that life goes on without him. He needs to feel important to himself, and often tries to find this sense of self-esteem by being important to others. When they don't notice him, he's hurt. Objectivity is not one of Leo's strong points. I once had a friend – a double Leo, both sun and moon being placed there – who, one day finding his tennis shoes too tight, cut off the toes. A couple of days later, a new fashion appeared in the shoe shops (it was Hollywood, the natural habitat of many Leos) – open-toed boots. My Leo friend observed this phenomenon with a certain charming mixture of amazement and complacency, and then said in utter seriousness: 'I wish people weren't always copying me like that.'

There you have it. The thing is, people frequently do copy Leos, because they often have style and charisma; and it's easy to see how a little personality inflation goes a long way. Nothing in the world is quite so important to Leo as his own world. It is genuinely painful and difficult for him to see beyond the lens of his own consciousness, and comprehend that other people are truly different, think and feel differently, and most importantly, that they have a right to be different. At heart Leo is the Divine Child of the zodiac. And to a child, the world is a mysterious and exciting extension of himself. The sun shines for him, the clouds rain on him and for him, and good and bad luck are personally related to the heavens favouring or disliking him rather than being either products of his own efforts or the tracks of random chance.

Leo men and women often find it very difficult to share the stage. Sharing it with somebody else means taking away possibilities for their own creative expression. It also means being limited, because they must adjust to somebody else's needs and feelings. So Leo will often find ways, overt or subtle – and there are many subtle Leos about who don't really look like Leos, but actually are just as true to their sign as the more charismatic ones – to claim back the space which has been usurped. If you are the timid and secretly resentful type, stay away from Leo. Fire signs are not known for their sensitivity to the feeling currents around them, and they don't make good telepaths of other people's needs if those needs aren't voiced. Leo may inadvertantly trample over others' feelings without ever meaning to, or ever realizing it, simply because he's so caught up in his own vision. Therefore you have to make a noise, if you want a piece of the stage. If you have set a precedent of ten years of meek subservience and then discover you've got a stomach ulcer or migraine headaches because you're seething with anger over that Leo's clumsy insensitivity, blame yourself. Remember the child. Although he loves to preen and appear to others as the height of style, Leo is terrified of being unloved, mediocre, unappreciated, unnoticed. And his pride will often not permit him to admit it.

It's sometimes difficult to understand that these flamboyant, always individualistic people are not always the extroverts they seem. Leo is often shy and deeply introverted, but depends so ferociously upon the love and acceptance of others that he will do virtually anything to earn their approval. It is a problem of identity. The first task that challenges Leo in life is the issue of who he is, why he is here, why he is uniquely himself. It's a lifelong challenge. If he can't muster the self-esteem he needs from his own inner resources, he'll crave it like a drug from the audience. But his real journey is within, into the source of his own being. Leo at heart is a religious sign, using the word here as it was originally meant: to reconnect. It is the secret of his intense need to create something which mirrors his own essential substance – be it a company, a book, a painting, a political movement, an airline, a scientific achievement, an empire, a photograph. It is in this process of creating that he finds his real sense of self-value. Leo is a disaster when he tries to follow the advice and instruction of others. A lifetime of following will often kill him with heart disease and frustration.

He needs, in some way, to create something, however small, that is wholly and completely his own.

From others, Leo requires the same nobility that he strives for himself. He can be an intolerable perfectionist both with others and with his own behaviour. Nothing less will do. Shatter his dream and you cause him pain; but pain is the only thing that shakes him out of his pride and complacency. His heart is that of a noble knight. But he needs realism and earthy wisdom, and above all a sense of humour about himself and his own foibles. Heroes, in myths and fairy tales, are not the funny characters. That role is left to the court jester. It seems that when Leo learns how to be the jester himself, and can laugh at himself a little, his true nobility emerges. Flexibility is important, too, for him to learn, for he often lacks this as well. Most of all, he needs faith in himself, in what he stands for, in what he is trying to become. Leo is the most human, the noblest, the most tragic – in the ancient Greek sense – of the signs. This is because the sign is the epitome of Man, that bewildered creature who is half-animal and half-god, and who has not yet understood either his own origins or the fact that the world is populated with other human beings different from himself. The Leo who learns this is indeed the hero.

♌ The Myth

One of the myths which helps to shed some sunlight on the sun-ruled sign of Leo is the medieval legend of Parzival. Although we may recognize this figure as Sir Percival from the Grail stories, Parzival is in fact a much older figure, whose roots lie in pre-Christian Celtic and Germanic mythology. And probably, if we were to assign Parzival a sun-sign, he would be a Leo.

Parzival is the epitome of the hero on the quest. As we have seen, the figure of the hero is close to Leo's heart, since the sign is really concerned with the expression of unique individual potential.

Our mythical hero, like many other heroes, is fatherless at the beginning of the story, and grows up in a wood with his mother. He is ignorant of his origins, since his mother has been at pains to prevent him from discovering them. She is afraid he will leave her and go off into the world. So Parzival is naïve and innocent in his comfortable nest in the forest.

One day a troop of knights rides through the wood, and Parzival sees them and talks with them. He decides to become a knight. His mother, naturally, has hysterics, since this means he will abandon her. She tries to thwart him. But he is determined to seek his future, to find out what he might become. The nobility and chivalry of the knights have fired his vision and his imagination. So he makes himself a very inadequate suit of armour out of sticks and leaves, and rides off.

Strangely, Leo is often fatherless, or has a difficult relationship with the father. It seems as though the deeper significance that underlies the sign requires a kind of search for a true Father, an inner self or spiritual core. And the call to leave what is known and comfortable for the sake of a dangerous but shining future is also characteristic of Leo. Often he must rebel against authority or social mores to begin his quest. No matter where you find him, Leo always has his eye on becoming bigger, better, greater. There is always something beckoning him, more attractive than the place he's in.

So Parzival begins his adventures. After many vicissitudes, Parzival has a vision in a forest when he finds himself in a mysterious glittering castle, surrounded by incense and gold and strange figures. There is a sick old king with a wound in his groin, who performs an elaborate ritual where the poisoned blood is drawn out through the point of a lance. There is an enigmatic and beautiful woman who enters bearing a platter on which rests a sword and an object which comes to be known in later Christianized legends as the Holy Grail – the cup from which Christ drank at the last Supper. In the original story, the Grail – or Sangraal – is not a cup at all, but a stone – the Philosopher's Stone of alchemy, the symbol of the eternal Self. Parzival stares bewildered at this drama, but does not say anything. His mother has taught him never to ask rude questions of strangers, and these people are even stranger than strangers. So he remains silent throughout the ceremony. Finally, a great angry voice speaks and tells him he has made a dreadful mistake and failed everybody because the whole point was that he ask the magic question which will restore the sick old king to health and win Parzival the Grail Maiden as wife and the Grail Castle as inheritance. And the question is: What does this mean?

Parzival awakens from his vision cold and alone in the wood. He realizes that he has been blind and ignorant, and resolves to find the Grail Castle again one day. The second part of the legend concerns the process of his slow maturing. Eventually, a man and a true hero, he rediscovers the castle after much pain and suffering and the passage of twenty years. This time he remembers to ask the question. And he discovers that he is really the son of the Grail King, and becomes the new King and custodian of the Stone of Life.

If we remove the later embellishments which Christianity has placed over this tale, we can see in it the pattern of Leo's life. For the quest of Leo is the quest of the Self: Who am I? What does my life mean? What is it that makes me different from others? It is a deeply introverted and profound quest. Many Leos are not aware in any way that this is their road; but they follow it nonetheless. The showy Leo of traditional readings is usually either a very young Leo who hasn't awakened yet, or an older Leo who has lost the Grail Castle and hasn't the courage to try again. So he seeks his identity in the audience. But Leo is not really the showman of the zodiac. That role must go to Sagittarius, whose profligate ruler Jupiter is a much better representative of amateur dramatics. Leo's path lies within himself, although the fruits of his creative searching are often products which the world sees and acclaims. But the creative process doesn't really have anything to do with the audience. It is between Leo and himself, the thing within him that creates. It is this discovery that an Other, a Something inside is capable of offering creative ideas and images through the medium of one's own mind and hands that is Leo's most important discovery. That's the road to the Grail Castle. The Leo who is courageous enough to pursue this road will come eventually to his own centre. The psychology of Carl Jung is an excellent expression of this quest for the Self. Jung called the process of individuation the process whereby a man becomes himself. It is a lifetime's journey. The central motif of the Self, the inner essence of the personality, is paramount in Jungian psychology. It isn't coincidental that Jung was a Leo.

For this reason too, Leo is self-centred. He has a kind of constant self-consciousness, a sort of watcher that is always watching himself watching himself, that never really allows him to be totally aware of the environment except in relation to himself. It is almost impossible for Leo to detach from himself. Nor should he. His whole journey is about discovering who that watcher is. As the Alan Watts limerick goes:

> There once was a man who said, 'Though
> I think that I know that I know,
> I wish I could see
> The I that knows me
> When I *know* that I know that I know.'

Leo's tendency toward self-centredness can be irritating to other signs. But it needs to be seen for what it is: a powerful drive toward self-recognition. Leo also needs to understand it, because otherwise he can make the mistake of assuming that it's the little 'me' that's the object of all that energy. Then he really becomes insufferable. He can inflate, and think he's the most wonderful thing in the world, God's chosen son to whom all the world owes obeisance. But if Leo ever understands that the Other is not him, but his source, then he has truly come to the vision of the Grail, and becomes a light which illumines the lives of others not by what he does, but by what he is – the true hero who has found his journey's goal.

♌ The Shadow

Leo's shadow is probably one of the better known shadows of the zodiac. This is because nothing Leo does is small or unobtrusive. Everything is big and a little larger than life. That includes his shadow side. We might call it the 'I, the King' syndrome. The phrase 'I, the King' was used by the Holy Roman Emperor Charles V during the sixteenth century, and it meant that he ruled the world and no questions asked. If a document was signed, 'I, the King,' that was it. You didn't discuss, debate, argue, negotiate, or even mention it again. You simply obeyed. The scenario goes something like this:

FRIEND TO LEO: I've decided to look for another job. I'm really sick of working in insurance. I'd like to find something more creative.

LEO: I have just the thing for you. You can work for me. I need someone to edit my film scripts before they go out to the cast. You can do the editing and proof-reading.

FRIEND: But I don't know anything about films.

LEO: I'll teach you (*Tone of voice becomes expansive, magnanimous.*) We'll start you at a fairly small salary, of course, because after all, you've no experience, but as you learn we'll increase it. Say twenty pounds a week.

FRIEND: (*Torn by guilt. Disgusted at the suggestion but grateful to be given the opportunity to enter a new field.*) That's pretty small.

LEO: But you're inexperienced. Don't worry. It'll get bigger.

Six months later:

FRIEND: Thanks for that increase. By the way, I tried my hand at a small piece of scripting myself. I'd appreciate your comments.

LEO: Of course, of course. I'd be glad to read it. I'll bet you've got a lot of potential.

Six weeks later:

FRIEND You used my idea.

LEO: What are you talking about?

FRIEND: That film script. You took my idea and wrote it into your own script.

LEO: Don't be ridiculous. That was my own original idea. Look, I don't like your tone of voice. It was my generosity that got you into this business in the first place. You would still be working in the insurance office if it hadn't been for me. I did you a favour. This is how you repay me. That's really pretty bloody ungrateful. I had that idea a long time ago. You surely don't think I got it from your silly script. Look, you've been working hard. Tell you what, we'll give you another five quid a week and put you on camera direction. That's something you don't know much about . . .

This scenario illustrates several facets of the Leo shadow. The first part sometimes peeps through Leo's magnanimity. Sometimes that generosity is genuine, and nobody in the world can be as generous and open-handed as a Leo. But when the shadow creeps in, it isn't all genuine. There's an ulterior motive at work. For one thing, Leo loves to be needed; he loves to feel people depend on him. Sometimes he forgets that encouraging a person's own individuality is just as important as always giving. Sometimes receiving a gift can be even more important. Leo sometimes gives and gives but won't receive because it puts the other person on an equal basis with him, and takes away the obligation.

Also, Leo sometimes unconsciously surrounds himself with creative people so that he can shine better himself. This happens when Leo isn't doing what he loves, when he hasn't got a chance to create himself. But then he doesn't reward them with the recognition their efforts deserve, and sometimes – unconsciously – takes the idea as his own. He may play on the fact that he was the one who gave them the break, or the favour, and never really allows them to go free to blossom on their own. And when they protest, he has a knack, with all that charm, of making them feel guilty and unappreciative when he has been so generous and so tolerant. It's difficult to know what to do with a Leo in this kind of mood, because it's his own insecurities breaking through that make him behave in this less than honourable fashion. You know you've been had, but there's nothing you can put your finger on. When you've been had by Capricorn, or Virgo, or Libra you know exactly how and in what fashion. In fact, Leo is usually so generous and magnanimous that you can't really think of any situation you can blame him for. So he hangs on to you, and makes you feel good because you've helped him, and the Leo shadow gradually subsumes all your ideas and takes them for its own.

It's a rather dark shadow, this one. But Leo does everything in a big way, and his nobility is equally grand. Leo when he shines stands head and shoulders above everybody else; when he's in shadow, he's that much darker. The real root of this shadow is the I, the King psychology. To Leo, the other people in his life are often extensions of himself. He genuinely believes that their creativity is his, their ideas are his, and that he has a right to help himself, because, after all, it's all his universe anyway, and he's the King. It's a kind of blank insensitivity, a lack of recognition of other people's individualities. It comes from being so preoccupied with his own individuality. He doesn't mean to do it. Some Leos forget to give credit to others for accomplishments when the shadow is at work. Or they fail to offer compliments and genuine encouragement. Leo, the King and Father, often believes that the people he loves are his children. Unfortunately the children have a way of rebelling against this autocracy. Then Leo feels wronged, and tells the world about it.

This is one of the reasons why it's so terribly important for Leo to develop his own creative outlets. He needs recognition for his own abilities, and should be prepared to put plenty of time and energy into making sure he produces something that can earn it. The lion who hasn't created anything too often becomes sour and jealous, and then you see the shadow peeping through. He'll try to steal centre stage from anyone who happens to be on it, forgetting that they might have worked hard to get there.

There are other adjuncts to this shadow. One is the 'I know what's best for you' pattern, which afflicts many otherwise warm-hearted and honourable Leos. They mean well. Really, they do. Their advice is helpful, and they offer it freely, and are incredibly generous with their time and their efforts to assist you. The trouble is, you might not have asked for it. Leo has a reputation for sometimes being pretty interfering. And sometimes it can be maddening, especially if the Leo happens to be your mother or your best friend, when they invite themselves to sort out your life for you and then look so desperately hurt when you reject their advice. Leo needs to be needed. Even more, because his myth is the hero myth, he needs to be looked upon as a redeemer, someone who's really done something for others. If he can't redeem somebody, then how can he be a hero? And if you protest – say, because you don't really need redemption, or would prefer to find your own – then he thinks it's your fault, because you're ungrateful and unappreciative.

A third adjunct of this shadow is the 'I know everything' syndrome. This is the Leo who cannot bear to admit that he can't do something, or doesn't know something. It's got a slight resemblance to the Virgo shadow, another know-it-all. But the motivation is different. Virgo has to know it all because he's terrified of anything unknown. Leo needs to know it all because he's got to be king. Even when his contribution is patently absurd and glowing with florid ignorance, he won't back down. I once knew a Leo like this. He would profess knowledge about all sorts of things, because he needed to have an image of being highly learned. If you questioned him, he would begin to argue. Of course he was always right. How dare you challenge it? What? Not know the answer? Not him. He knew everything. He would even get indignant and angry if you questioned him, to cover up his own inadequacy. I, the King.

What can Leo do with this shadow? Well, a lot of it requires being very, very aware of oneself. Leo has a hard time being aware of the needs of others because he takes a lot for granted. Leo isn't a sign of relationship like Cancer, Libra and Pisces. But Leo needs to make this gallant effort of noticing what his own behaviour does to other people, and allowing them their independence and the credit due them, if he isn't to lose his friends and loved ones through enmity and antagonism. Enmity is agonizing for Leo, who needs so badly to be loved. We've said that the lion doesn't have a mean, petty bone in his body, and that's perfectly true. But his shadow can be a bit of a bully, and trample unnecessarily over the wills and desires of others. Unless he's able to put time into his own creative expression he runs the risk of robbing other people of theirs. It's not an easy task. But it's one worth striving for, and suitable for the genuine nobility of character that is the real basis of Leo.

There is a beautiful image in the Tarot deck which describes Leo very nicely. This is the card for the Sun. It shows a small child crowned with a wreath of flowers, riding bareback on a horse, with his arms and legs thrown out in the air in joy. He isn't even hanging on to the horse, so trusting is he of the bounty of life. Behind him, a huge sun shines. This is the Leo who really trusts his own inner self. He doesn't have to own others then; he's just himself, and it's good to be alive. Shadows have a way of disappearing in the noonday sun.

♌ The Leo Lover

Love makes the world go round for Leo. And love, like every other experience in life, is something mythical to him, something which must be dramatized to the utmost. Love too must be big, bold, spectacular and dramatic. A little fondness isn't Leo's style. He loves to be in love; and he loves to play the lover. And if you're the recipient, whether it's a male or female Leo, it's probably not like anything you've experienced before.

For one thing, there's Leo's magical talent for the right theatrical gesture. He's a romantic, and a generous one; and one of his ways of showing love is to lavish gifts on the loved one. And those gifts aren't just ordinary run-of-the-mill boxes of chocolates. They're more likely to be expensive, exotic, and difficult to obtain; and usually they're things which are meant to be worn so that someone else can admire them. For the love of God, show your appreciation. A Leo who's gone to a great deal of trouble to present his loved one with a gift can be totally crushed and humiliated if the gift isn't acknowledged with suitable enthusiasm. Leo is a better giver than he is a receiver. He genuinely loves to give. But he never does favours offhandedly; there's a self-consciousness about them, and he needs to be thanked.

Leo's ideals in love are different, however, from Libra, the other sign which is concerned above all else with love and relationship. For Libra, love is an exchange, a partnership, a meeting of two different individuals. For Leo, it's a creative act, and he's the sun at the centre. Sometimes you can get the distinct feeling, in the midst of Leo's romance, that he's so in love with being in love, and so in love with the lovely image of his love, that somehow he's missed noticing you. It's a common Leonine problem in love affairs. The partner feels sort of left out of the whole thing, unless he or she is one of those people who also has the knack of stepping in and out of the fairy-tale landscape.

But apart from this problem – and it may be little or big, depending upon the Leo – the lion is really the ideal lover. Male or female, the gift of making a love affair magical, something special, is one of Leo's special qualities. He can always make you feel as if it's the first time anyone in the world has ever been in love. He loves with style, and without inhibition. And it's in his nature to be loyal, too; for although the lion can be vain, and loves to be admired by the opposite sex, he is basically a constant partner, and has an idealistic vision of love as something which endures. If he loves he will move the earth. (If he doesn't love, he will often use.)

Of course, he needs something in exchange for all that loyalty. For one thing, he needs loyalty in return. Leo, male or female, is a jealous cat, and won't tolerate smaller fry pursuing his chosen mate. He can be very obvious and not a little rude about insulting or removing challengers. In a way he enjoys the contest, provided he's on safe ground, since this kind of knightly combat suits his image. What he can't endure is betrayal, which is deeply wounding and rarely forgiven. Leo has a naïve heart, and a wonderfully soaring idealism. Betrayal of trust is a horrific thing to him. Where Capricorn expects it and Scorpio suspects it constantly, Leo simply can't believe it. He'll rarely look beneath the surface at why. To him it's a cardinal sin, the worst sin you can commit. And you'll not be given a chance very often to do it again.

If you want to understand just how deep this sense of honour and loyalty goes in Leo, consider the attitudes in love and war during the Age of Chivalry. France has always epitomized the chivalric code; and a French knight, when taken once in battle during the Hundred Years War, discovered that his captor was a mere peasant, of lower rank than himself. The French knight proceeded to knight his captor, so that they could be of equal rank, so that his own knightly rank wouldn't be insulted. Now, that's Leo. It's said that France is ruled by this sign, and one can well believe it if one reads a little French history. And the French attitude toward love is typically Leonine: it's an art.

Leo not only expects loyalty and fidelity. He or she also expects to be treated like a king or queen. Now, this is a sword which cuts two ways. On the one hand, Leo can be so lovable that you want to treat him like royalty anyway. On the other hand, that I, the King routine can sometimes be a little annoying, because it goes with a double standard. Now, it may be a little unfair to say so, but in spite of this Leo seems to operate on a double standard basis much of the time. (How else could he be, when his primary motivation is his *own* self-realization?) But it's sometimes difficult to remind Leo gently that what's good for him is also good for you. He's apt to forget it.

Leo also offers, in exchange for the loyalty and love he seeks so intensely, a wonderfully protective quality. Male or female, Leo will fight for the person he loves, and defend them loyally. He can be protective and supportive and terribly caring, and is not averse to making some pretty big sacrifices on behalf of his love. (The little sacrifices are sometimes harder for him.) But when it comes to big gestures, Leo won't baulk. He can be completely self-sacrificing, and give up everything, and never begrudge it.

All in all, Leo's love affairs and marriages are interesting but rarely smooth. He's too temperamental a creature, and his visions and ideals are too big to be able to avoid inevitable conflicts in the smaller realms of living. Leo doesn't get along with the mundane reality of relationships and the inconsistency and limitations of human nature. What Leo wants is the total love, the mythological love, the love that was sung in the troubadours' songs six centuries ago. In one sense, that kind of love doesn't exist; and Leo usually suffers disappointment in love somewhere along the line because of it. On the other hand, this symbol of the power of the heart is also a reality on another level, and no sign is as capable as Leo is of bringing the world of myth into the ordinary one, to gently remind other mortals that they're also heroes and princesses. If you're around someone who tries to be a walking myth all the time, you begin to realize that myths are all around you; and a relationship with Leo can convince you that fairy tales aren't so silly after all.

♌ The Leo Man

You might expect the Leo man to be slightly larger than life. He usually is. Sometimes it's in the obvious way – his creative talent, or his success, or his flamboyant personality. Leo often radiates charisma – and whether you like him or not, you're likely to notice him. Sometimes the quieter, more introverted type of Leo appears on the scene, and doesn't make a great roar about his own uniqueness. But if you get to know him, you'll find that inwardly he's just the same, and the same need for mythologizing his own life exists deep within him. Don't be fooled by quiet, shy Leos. They may have more restrained ascending signs, like Cancer or Capricorn or Virgo. But they're lions nonetheless. And that quality of intense self-consciousness, of always feeling as though the stage is under their feet and the audience watching, permeates even the most introverted Leo.

Because he lives so much in his visions, the Leo man is often attracted to an earthier partner. This can be a wonderfully creative combination, and it can also be a disaster. Where it works, the Leo man looks for his stabilizing influence in his partner, and maybe achieves a measure of realism and contact with reality through her – by appreciating her own more earthy outlook. Where it's a disaster, it usually springs from Leo's tendency to undervalue detail and the things of ordinary life. When he takes this stance, he's liable to treat his women as though they were in his life to clean up after him and remind him of his eleven o'clock appointment.

You usually wind up with a very angry and resentful partner.

Leo the romantic can sweep you off your feet. His attitude toward love is neither timorous nor restrained, and those grand gestures – whether they're gifts or magical journeys to magical holiday places or dramatic declarations of emotion – are irresistible. A Leo man can make a woman feel completely feminine and desirable. And it's fairly typical for the Leo man to have a fairly long and insistent crowd of admirers and pursuers. Even if he's not a conventionally handsome or successful man, there's something about him that women find fascinating. Leo is a very male creature. There's nothing ambiguous about him. He can often be the archetypal male, and women's liberation notwithstanding, it's pretty difficult to resist that kind of magnetism.

Where the difficulties arise is later. Once upon a time, in an age when roles were fairly rigid and women had little opportunity and perhaps little desire to live beyond those roles, the Leo male would have, from any point of view, been anybody's ideal image of manhood. For that matter, he still is. The problem is that society has changed and people have changed; and it has become increasingly apparent that men have a feminine component to their psyches and woman a masculine component. The need to express this opposite within oneself is increasingly a demand of our culture. And this is where Leo finds his difficulties, because he doesn't warm much to the idea of having a woman with a life that ranges beyond him at the centre. Many Leo men become intensely resentful when a woman shows too much interest or too much commitment to a career, a creative pursuit, or simply an independent array of interests, hobbies or ideas. Leo needs to feel that he's the sun around which your moon orbits; if you suddenly take off and start shining with a light of your own, he's liable to get a little sullen at best, and at worst to stifle your individuality because his own is threatened. It's a rare Leo – though it's both possible and happens regularly – who can not only acknowledge the need for independent creative expression in his mate, but also his own need for an individual partner. He can only really do this if he's standing firm on a ground of self-confidence and self-esteem. Otherwise, he can be pretty difficult to be around, since anything you do that doesn't place him at the centre is looked upon as a betrayal.

The Leo man probably has more harmonious relationships with the more fluid signs – Gemini, Pisces, Virgo, Sagittarius, perhaps Libra. This is because he's basically a fixed creature; he doesn't change his habits or his viewpoints easily, and certainly not because someone else has told him to. If you try to push or change a Leo man, you're wasting your time. He can be stubborn to a maddening degree, and his pride will rarely allow him to acknowledge the wisdom of your advice. His business is to give advice, not receive it. On the other hand, faith in him, belief in his dreams, confidence in his hopes, and acceptance of his some-times childlike need for constant reassurance and atten-tion, can work wonders. A Leo who knows he's believed in can achieve miracles, outside in the world and inside within himself.

If you're the more independent or self-contained type, Leo can be a big problem for you. He requires lots of time, love, attention, and devotion. He wouldn't be half so interesting and charismatic if he were the self-effacing type, anyway. Besides, who ever heard of a hero who hid in the background while his lady fought the battles? Extreme women's libbers should stay away from this animal, for although Leo usually loves women and loves loving women, he expects his woman to be a woman first of all. If your need is to be recognized as an individual first and a woman second – which is fair enough for many women – you're going to see a little fur fly if you try to make a home with the king of the beasts. On the other hand, if you're the self-effacing, martyr-like type, Leo isn't for you either, because he likes you to be as royal as he is. It reflects back on himself, and he needs to take pride in his partner. A difficult but lively relationship is likely to be yours if you're involved with Leo. It's never an easy sign – far too temperamental. But nothing can match Leo when it comes to sheer life and vitality and colour. And if you want to have a partner you respect and take pride in, then Leo's probably a good choice for you. He's not just anybody, after all. He's himself, at whatever cost.

♌ The Leo Woman

Meek, mild, colourless and self-effacing this lady is not. She's a queen, and expects to be treated like one. Even the more repressed Leo woman will show this side to her nature, although it may be heavily disguised under socially acceptable manifestations of good behaviour. The truth is that the Leo woman is intensely individual and not very good at being everybody's favourite model of conventionality. More often than not she'll be a troublemaker, or a woman who causes people to gossip about her. She has an intense need to live her own life in her own way, and that life has got to have a little colour and a little dynamism to it. Have you ever watched caged lionesses in a zoo, pacing back and forth and back and forth, their eyes furious and glaring, because they haven't got room to stretch out and run? That's what happens to the Leo woman when she's caged either by social expectations or a limiting relationship.

The Leo woman needs some place to express her

creative impulses. Whether these are in the form of artistic talent, organizational ability, public relations ability, or whatever, she needs to be somebody special, and to do something extremely well that will earn her some sort of recognition. Recognition is as necessary to the Leo woman as the Leo man. If a Leo woman doesn't find an outlet, she's liable to try to get her recognition either by getting every available male to fall in love with her, or by trying to play Pygmalion and shaping the lives of her husband and children. And exacting due recognition from them later for all she's done. This dynamic, energetic woman must have a stage on which to perform. Otherwise, she's liable to throw you off yours.

Leo women are often highly competitive. This may be in their field of work, where they need to shine. The Leo woman shouldn't have to be in a position of answering to somebody else all the time; she needs room to work with her own ideas, and come up with her own designs. Often Leo women are also highly competitive with their own sex, and it isn't really a sign that makes for good sisterhood unless the other sisters are willing to play Greek chorus to the main role. The Leo woman must have the role of leading lady. It's very typical to find her with a bevy of friends who all lean on her and need her advice and help. In part, it's because she's strong and also generous, and needs to be needed. In part, it's because she doesn't like competition.

Often Leo women extend this tendency to be the support to a weaker role into their relationships. You often see Leo women with some gentle and pleasant and basically indecisive man, who worships at their feet and gives them the devotion they need so badly, and who is also willing to be moulded. Many Leo women are afraid of stronger men, because they need to dominate; and this can create a great problem, because while it satisfies the Leonine needs it denies the feminine ones. And all too often the pattern in relationship is for the Leo woman to take charge, to make the decisions, to be the strong partner, and then to bitterly blame the man for being weak when she in fact has never given him a chance to be otherwise.

This is why it's so essential for the Leo woman to have some area of life where she can shine independent of her family. If this need is satisfied elsewhere, then she can relate to the people close to her in a less compulsive way.

The Leo woman is also very concerned with the image she gives in society. You won't often find her mousey and self-effacing; she's more likely to dress dramatically, act dramatically, and attract attention because of her sheer style and charisma. Take a Leo like Jacqueline Kennedy Onassis. Self-effacing she's not. She has a Scorpio ascendant, so is perhaps more underplayed than many Leo actresses and performers; but style is terribly important to her, and so is her dignity. Leo women don't like to play the fool or the victim. Their pride is ferocious.

Their gifts lie both in their capacity to be so intensely individual and so intensely alive, and in their loyalty and generosity to those they care about. Even more than the Leo man, the Leo woman is likely to offer devotion and steadfast love in relationships – provided she's treated well. But that's fair enough, because she's somebody special and she knows it. Never, never, never take Leo for granted. The lioness has claws, and isn't averse to making a scene that would make more socially inhibited signs turn white and cold with shock. If you're looking for a woman who is also an individual, an individual to the hilt, then you'll like Leo. In fact, you'll even love Leo, for it's a sign that inspires intense responses. One thing that won't happen: you're not likely to overlook her.

Sagittarius

*7*he centaur is a mysterious composite figure from Greek mythology – half horse and half human – who's always shooting his arrow at some distant target over the horizon and then galloping off in hot pursuit. Sometimes he finds the arrow. Sometimes, however, he gets completely sidetracked by all the interesting scenery on the way, until another target beckons. It is an apt and descriptive image for Sagittarius, the third and most volatile of the fire signs. For this equine archer does indeed aim the flashing arrow of his intuitive visions at some distant goal of the future; and most of his life is spent chasing after one arrow or another. The big question is whether he has aimed true or not. And, after that, whether he can find his arrow at all.

The key theme in all this classical imagery is that what really interests Sagittarius is the excitement of the aim and the fascination of the journey. The goal is really, after all, relatively insignificant. There is a basic attitude innate in Sagittarius that life is an adventure, a journey, a quest – and the real sport of living is to make that journey as interesting, as varied, as expansive, and as informative as possible. Arrival is not the point.

Jupiter, King of the Gods in mythology, is said to be the planetary ruler of Sagittarius. And we can learn a lot about our centaur friends by having a closer look at Jupiter's imposing figure. First of all, he is noble, dignified and majestic. That is, most of the time, when he has his Olympian court around him and plays to the hilt the role of *rex deibus*. He is a consummate actor, our friend Jupiter. He is also the great profligate of the Olympian heights, a god who is always chasing after something or other – mostly women. Some Jupiter-ruled folk take this symbol very literally, and they are the Don Juans of the zodiac. It isn't that they are driven by some insatiable sexual passion, though. It's the ideal that drives them, the possibility of something new and exciting. The adventure, the unexplored mystery, the unobtainable goal, the one that got away. Sagittarius, it seems, has this Jupiterian propensity to be afraid he might be missing something – be it a woman, a project, an idea, a book, a creative work, virtually anything new and untried and unexplored. On a more extroverted level, you'll always find the Sagittarians gathering where a new club has opened up, a hot new restaurant, an artsy film, an exciting workshop or group of some kind. Some people have used the unkind word 'trendy' to describe this behaviour. What it's really about is that

Sagittarius has a remarkable intuitive nose for what's going to be popular before anybody else knows it. It is often the Sagittarius who makes fashion, because he gets there first and gives his often vociferous stamp of approval. And everyone else, knowing that if it weren't good he wouldn't be there, troops after him.

The more introverted Sagittarian may not be found frequenting a new disco or roller skating rink. But he'll usually be miles ahead of everyone else with a new novel, a new philosophy, a new film, a new cultural phenomenon. The same gifted intuition works here, but in a more interior way. And it works, too, with contacts. Nobody has the penchant for making valuable contacts that Sagittarius does. Somehow it's always the centaur who 'bumps into' the director looking for a new lead, the publisher looking for a new work, the record producer looking for a fresh voice. It can make you tear your hair, the way luck seems to pour from heaven onto Sagittarius' haloed head. But it isn't really luck. It's that remarkable eye for the opportunity, that intuitive nose that can spot a potential or a possibility thirty miles away. And also the impulsiveness, rashness, boldness, call it what you will, that gives Sagittarius the flaming nerve to try his luck, where other signs will cower in the wings waiting for something more concrete.

Boredom is the great enemy of this rampant and random sign, and believe me, they get very easily bored. It takes a mere doing something twice in the same way to push the more restless type of centaur out after the next arrow. After all, he's *done* that one. Why do it again? Never mind telling him about the rewards of applied, disciplined effort. Pass that advice onto a Virgo or a Capricorn. Sagittarius isn't interested. For him, it's the exhilaration of the process of getting there, not the kind of reward you can hold in your hand. Besides, if he ever does get to hold it in his hand, he'll no doubt spend it within five minutes anyway.

Let's take another look at Jupiter, for he is full of information about our unpredictable fire sign. For another thing, he's got a very jealous wife. Not that jealousy is the way to keep a Sagittarian in a relationship; fences drive him crazy, and ultimatums are guaranteed to drive him directly into the opposite behaviour. But think again. Without that jealous wife trailing him everywhere and doing terrible things to his mortal mistresses, where would Jupiter be? Where would the spark and excitement of all those pecadilloes go? Right. What makes them fun, in large part, is that Jupiter gets to fool someone, to play the gambling game. If it were all socially acceptable and out in the open, why, he probably wouldn't bother. It would have been too boring. The elements of danger and a little rebellion against social mores are lifeblood to Sagittarius. He may look conventional, but he loves to push his luck.

Another thing about Jupiter. He's always changing shape. When courting, he's apt to be a swan, a bull, a shower of gold, virtually anything else his imagination can create. It's the consummate actor again. Sagittarius loves to play roles – the more theatrical, the better. Being caught in the same costume twice is quite horrific for him. His restless mind is always seeking new ways to approach those goals, new costumes, new poses, new techniques. Change, travel, constant mental stimulus, exploration of unknown landscapes – tell Sagittarius that there really is a hidden treasure under that mountain and he'll be as happy as any Taurus with his bank account bursting. Find a Sagittarian who's forced to circle the same ground over and over again, perform the same routine in endless monotony, and you have found the most miserable of creatures.

Jupiter also has a mighty explosive temper. Think of all those thunderbolts and flashes of lightning. He can be pretty terrifying in mid-eruption. But when it's over,

the anger is gone, and he's jovial again. Not a god to
hold a grudge. And although Sagittarius can sometimes
display a fairly flamboyant sort of anger, complete with
waving of arms and smashed crockery, he really doesn't
brood about it afterward. You won't find Sagittarius
plotting away in the corner ten years later like you will
Scorpio, or nursing his wounds like Cancer. Once he's
yelled at you, he's finished. Often he can't understand
why the recipient of all this blustering and noise is so
hurt by the display. After all, he didn't really mean it,
not really. All those horribly blunt, hair-raisingly honest
remarks he made weren't really true, they were just,
well, for effect. As you pick yourself up off the floor
after his barrage of deadly verbal arrows, you may well
be astonished at how quickly he's recovered his usual
sweet temper. But Sagittarius isn't renowned for his
sensitivity to subtler feelings. His arrows can be really
destructive to the more sensitive signs – like Pisces,
Virgo, Cancer – but he doesn't realize it. Bash him over
the head and he won't crumple with horror. He might
bash back, but it's all part of the game. How can you
remain angry at such naïvete?

Sagittarius can also be downright gullible, if you
flatter him properly. Like all the fiery signs, he loves
mythology – especially if it means he can mythologize
himself. A lovable quality – unless you happen to be his
wife and it's somebody else offering the flattery. Then
what do you do? Absolutely nothing. Offer lots of rope.
With luck, he'll hang himself. The heart of the fiery
signs is always true. But it's true to the ideal, not to the
physical reality with all its imperfections. And it's pretty
hard for this fiery spirit to inhabit a world of boundaries
and limitations. Show him that you understand that,
and you've earned an undying friendship.

Friendship, by the way, is a key word for Sagittarius.
He will often refer to a lover as 'my friend', for this
ultimately means more to him. Heavy displays of

emotion, particularly the soggy kind that don't have any romantic dash to them, are very disturbing to Sagittarius. He can take grand drama – after all, he makes enough of it himself – but he can't stand pathos. Domesticity too can terrify the wits out of him. And this applies to the female Sagittarian as well. Offer her the 3·4 children, the piles of unwashed diapers, the dinner to cook, the beds to make, and no prospect of ever escaping on some exciting journey, and you'll never see anyone run so fast. The world of safe, unchanging domestic security and serenity is not Sagittarius' idea of a happy life. He needs his pack on his back and a mountain to climb. Home is pleasant, so long as the back door isn't kept locked.

What, then, is this quest on which every true Sagittarian spirit must embark? It varies. Much has been written about the sporty side of the sign. But this is more a by-product than the goal of the quest. Lots of Sagittarians hate sport. And travel, although often a favourite Sagittarian pursuit, is really a means of enlarging one's horizon. The Sagittarian traveller isn't the one who books the two-week package holiday in the huge hotel on the Costa del Sol and sits in the sun nursing his tan. He's the one who needs to be mobile, who needs a city to explore, a ruin, a chateau, a library, a mountain, a place no one else has been. And the stranger and more alien the culture, the better off he likes it.

In a sentence, at the heart of Sagittarius there lies a great craving to explore and understand life. Whether orthodox or not, Sagittarius, like Leo, is a deeply religious sign – and the word religious is here used in its original sense: to reconnect. This means reconnection with the source, with the roots of life, with some sense of meaning. Whether you find him travelling as a salesman or an archaeologist, a poet or a scholar, whatever profession or job he lands himself in, Sagittarius is trying to broaden his scope, to enlarge his consciousness. Life is a curious and interesting thing to Sagittarius. It is something to be played with, explored, enjoyed, peered into. And, ultimately, understood.

Watch the typical Sagittarian conversation line. Make an ordinary everyday remark – something like, 'Have you noticed that fashions this summer are getting very ethnic – all that hemp and linen and Indian cotton?' Any other sign would reply with a personal comment. Yes, I really like the look. Or, yes, I really hate the look. Or, it's great because the clothes are so cheap. Or, my mother doesn't approve because you can see through the muslin. But listen to the Sagittarian. Everything, to him, is connected with something larger. Whether in the pool hall or the university, he is an irrepressible philosopher, with or without the vocabulary. Expansion is the keyword. So: 'Yes, I've noticed. I'm sure it's because in our current society there is a deep need for trying to reestablish a connection with nature. Technology has forced man to . . .' And you're off on a deep, broad, often hilariously funny and frequently inspiring philosophical discussion. Sagittarius watches other people a lot, and he has both a strong sense of irony and an acute degree of insight. The leaping intuition of the element of fire is directed toward the world of ideas with Sagittarius – often with great brilliance or, at the very least, with a capacity to grasp broader implications and themes. No Sagittarian, however poorly read or educated, lacks this capacity to make connections between the ridiculous and the sublime.

Jupiter is King of the Gods because he's the biggest. And in an odd sort of way Sagittarius is the biggest sign – in terms of horizons. Better to shoot an arrow high and lose it than to aim low.

① The Myth

We've already talked quite a bit about Jupiter. Now let's look at one of the myths connected with the centaur itself, because this gives us a key to the deeper meaning of Sagittarius.

The most famous centaur in ancient mythology was the centaur Chiron. He was a sort of King of Centaurs, half man and half horse, who lived with his tribe among the wild hills and forests of Thrace. He was renowned because of his wisdom, accumulated over a long and varied life – especially the wisdom he had of life, of nature, of human behaviour. Wild and uncivilized as he was, all the kings of Greece brought him gifts, and sent their young sons to Chiron for instruction, to prepare them for their training as princes. Chiron was the sage, the teacher, the philosopher. He was a mysterious figure, for from his strange union of man and beast came both a deep knowledge of man's bestial origins, and a deep sadness at his own differentness. He was the alien, the outsider. He saw too much. One of the tales about Chiron relates that he received a wound from a poisoned arrow. But because of his wisdom, he had been granted the gift of immortality from the gods. So he couldn't die. But neither could the wound heal, for the poison was from a deadly serpent.

So Chiron is the figure of the wounded healer, the sage who has an incurable injury yet who, because of this injury understands far better the nature of pain. He becomes a healer through learning the secrets of herbs and magic. Yet he cannot heal himself.

In this noble and rather tragic figure of myth we can get a glimpse of the deepest meaning of Sagittarius. Not that this is a tragic sign; far from it, for nobody is as optimistic or ultimately positive in his viewpoint as the Sagittarian. Yet Chiron is also positive and optimistic. His wound is really about the gap between the mortal, animal side of him and the immortal, godlike side. Let's put it another way. Sagittarius, with his intuition and his vision, is often in touch with many mysteries. He may have a deep sense, often unarticulated, that life is meaningful, that man is divine, that all things have a purpose and teach a lesson and offer growth. But the distance between his vision of light and the limitations of being human is a vast one. The reality of tangible, physical life is always imperfect, always in a way poisoned, when compared to the vision he sees. In some strange way, this is Sagittarius' true wound. He may try to avoid his wound, and throw himself into an endless running bout of escape from one excitement to another, striving always to avoid stopping so that he doesn't have to feel any pain. Lots of Sagittarians are those people who walk into their flats and instantly turn on both the TV and the radio and phone a friend, to avoid being alone with their thoughts. The Sagittarius who has the courage to face both his vision and the reality of his life is rare; but should he succeed, he is in truth the wounded healer, for he has learned compassion – a quality which the more naïve or blind Sagittarian utterly lacks. And he is also privy to one of the deepest secrets of life and of human beings – the duality of god and beast that underlies us all.

④ The Shadow

Sagittarius, too, has his dark side. There are a couple of typical manifestations of it. One of them we might call the Groupie. The Scenario goes something like this:

FRIEND TO SAGITTARIAN: I hear you've been away on holiday. Did you go anywhere interesting?
SAGITTARIUS: Oh, Cannes, naturally, I just had to be there while the festival was on. It was really nice to see Stanley and Michael again.
FRIEND: Stanley and Michael?
SAGITTARIUS: Oh, yes, you don't know them, do you? Kubrick and Cimino. The new film is really exceptional. We had a long talk about it over dinner.
FRIEND: I went to Southampton for a couple of weeks.
SAGITTARIUS (*with a profoundly bored look*) Really. That's interesting. I suppose you haven't heard about the terms of Mick's divorce?
FRIEND: Mick who?
SAGITTARIUS: Oh, never mind, you probably wouldn't know. Well, I must be off, Ariana's having a cocktail party tonight, and you know, well, I have the distinct feeling she fancies me, so . . .
(There is a coda to this scenario. It usually involves the friend not seeing the Sagittarian again, because he just doesn't know the right people and isn't up on what's happening.)

The shadowy side of Sagittarius can be a dreadful name-dropper and groupie. There's the literary Sagittarian groupie who knows Lawrence Durrell intimately and stays at his house. There's the esoteric Sagittarian groupie who's intimate friends with Guru Swamikananda and knows all about his private sex life. There's the political Sagittarian groupie who's always having dinner with Jim or Maggie. There's even a scientific Sagittarian groupie, and a legal one, and a medical one. In short, the Sagittarian shadow likes to be where it's all happening, and with the people that it's all happening to; and somehow, with his marvellously intuitive nose, he manages to be in the right restaurant at the right time and meets the right person. One of Sagittarius' gifts is the ability to make contacts and spot opportunities. This gift is put to the service of the Sagittarian shadow when the archer uses other people as his opportunities, and drops them when they're not useful.

Don't think the groupie is limited to the shadow side of Sagittarian women. It's not. There are as many hangers-on among the male sex in these fields as there are women; and the shadowy Sagittarian groupie of the male variety is no more averse to using a sexual relationship with a glamorous or well-known woman to get him into a position of advantage (no pun intended) than the female variety is. Having spent a couple of years working in the Hollywood recording business, I had ample opportunity to observe the groupie phenomenon. It's observable in any profession where fame, glamour, colour and excitement are part of the show. And the really good groupies, the ones who managed to build a veritable career out of basking in somebody else's limelight, were usually the Sagittarians.

The Sagittarian shadow is always the first to hear of a new club, a new restaurant, a new pub where the interesting people hang out. He'll be the first to buy the record, read the book, see the film. And, my, does he talk about it. Part of the fun is that you get to tell all your lesser-connected friends about that wonderful Olympian world they can't enter because they don't have, well, 'it'. And if you're nobody going nowhere, this kind of Sagittarian has no time for you. If you've arrived but are on the decline, his time becomes less and less available. He uses shamelessly, but so charmingly that you're often taken in by it; and somehow he makes you feel shabby and uninteresting if you haven't been to the places he's been and met the people he's met. Oh, well, every shadow looks for power of one kind or another.

There's another facet to the archer's shadow. We

might call it the Promiser. Now, the Promiser is a fairly well-known face of Sagittarius, and has a lot to do with the archer's tendency to overextend himself. The Promiser simply promises. He promises to loan you money when you need it; he promises you that you can stay in his flat while he's away; he promises to help you find a flat, paint your flat, dig your garden; he's going to take you on a trip to India, Egypt, Madagascar, just as soon as summer comes; he's going to ring you Saturday, this afternoon, next week, he's having a party, he's buying a new car; you name it, he'll promise it. And with all these things, material or emotional or spiritual promises, he's never, never able to come through, because he made that promise in a moment of wild enthusiasm both to convince himself and impress you. The reality's different. Usually, you have to be burned at least twice by the Promiser before you spot his game. Then it's like the boy who cried wolf. That's when he drops you and finds more agreeable game.

Yet when you promise him something, you can be sure he'll arrive on the day specified to collect. And my oh my, can he be sour if you haven't got it ready at just that moment. A typical area where the Promiser shows his shadowy colours is with money. He'll usually offer it generously – but not when you need it. When you need it, he's usually broke. To be fair, many Sagittarians are as open-handed and generous themselves as you could possibly hope. But the shadow side isn't. It's downright tight. It sounds generous – that's the talent of the Promiser, to sound good. When you need it, it isn't there. But should you loan money to the Promiser, kiss it goodbye. If you ever try to collect, he forgets, he's broke, he's out of town, tomorrow, next week, next month. And should he loan it to you, he'll never let you forget it – down to the last penny. There's a curious unconscious mean streak that sometimes shows in Sagittarius – and I repeat, unconscious, because the true Sagittarian personality is magnanimous and extravagant and generous and totally unconcerned with material limitations. But it's that damned shadow again. It has other ideas. And it takes away Sagittarius' natural nobility and great heart, and shows you a shrewd commercial nose that would shame any Capricorn into looking naïve.

The root of the Sagittarian shadow lies in his difficulty in adjusting to the limitations of reality. The archer who's unsure of himself in the world, who's afraid of failure, who can't find sufficient maturity or discipline in himself to stick to something and finish it, often falls into the hands of his shadow because it's far easier to ride on somebody else's efforts. At bottom, this isn't a real evil in Sagittarius; it comes from fear. The Sagittarian is often frightened of making any kind of commitment to the tangible world, because then he'd have to face not only the limitations of form but also the fact that his potential genius might not be quite so boundless and cosmic as he thinks it is. Jupiter, king of the gods, is a profligate deity who can't bear limitation. That's all very well for Jupiter, because he's a god and can get away with it. The Sagittarian mortal can't. Granted, he gets away with a lot more than just about any other sign, because he trusts in his luck and he's optimistic; and because he believes in life, life often treats him kindly. But he isn't a god. And it's often hard for him to come to terms with his mortality and his ordinary humanness. Thus he becomes the groupie, hanging on to others' achievements vicariously without daring to venture his own, or the promiser who needs desperately to sound wealthy, successful, important because it helps make him feel that way if others see him that way. It's really like watching a child playing Caesar. Sagittarius can strut about and try desperately hard to live out his fantasies. It's when he allows himself to be the gifted, imaginative, funny, intelligent, restless student of life that he really is that he can allow himself to be loved for his own sake, rather than for the sake of his fantasies.

① The Sagittarius Lover

It's a traditional tale that Sagittarius exhibits a certain reluctance when it comes to things like marital vows. This is pretty understandable in light of all the foregoing; since Sagittarius' great love is of open possibilities, he's naturally going to baulk when he's asked to give up all those future possibilities for one reality for the rest of his life. 'Till death do us part' is a phrase which resonates in his consciousness largely because of the word 'death', which is what such a commitment may seem like to our ever-questing archer. And this is especially true when you find the archer who's already been through a marriage which he made in the days when his idealism was untarnished by the realization that sometimes things don't quite work out that way. Find a once-divorced Sagittarian and he's likely to be very, very shy of getting bitten again. And in many ways a state of non-marriage suits Sagittarius, not because he's necessarily always roving and dissatisfied, but because he at least knows he can exit if he wants to with a minimum of fuss. And just knowing that the back door is open does wonders for his anxieties.

Sagittarius might not sound like too good a prospect for relationship, from all that we've said. This isn't really true, of course; it just depends on the quality of the relationship. His myth is certainly that of the wanderer. But myths portray symbols and psychological realities, not necessarily literal behaviour. The endless seeking after future goals and possibilities, the endless quest for meaning, may in fact be a quest lived within his own soul, and not necessarily through a series of partners revolving around the bedroom. Some Sagittarians, of course, choose the literal enactment. And there isn't a great deal you can do about it, unless you like this sort of open relationship and are prepared to have your own life too. It isn't always a pathology; after all, remember Jupiter. He sets a fine example.

If you've got yourself into an involvement with a Sagittarian like this, it won't do much good to play Juno and become the nagging, jealous, suspicious wife. It really doesn't help at all; and it often drives the Sagittarian, like Jupiter, straight into more sympathetic arms. The same applies to the Sagittarian woman, who may often display the same propensities as her male counterpart. As soon as you remind Sagittarius that he's responsible to somebody for something, he often gets very, very uncomfortable, and has to do something to convince himself that he can't be tied by responsibilities. If you want to do anything at all to help the situation with a profligate Sagittarian, try reverse psychology. But that's for very strong people. Otherwise, find yourself a more constant and homebound sign.

If it's any comfort, try to remember that Sagittarius, being an idealist, is usually driven by his need to pursue his romantic fantasies. The relationships he makes on this basis often mean very little; and he'll usually turn around and come home again, because home is where his stability lies. He both longs for and fears stability, but it's more likely he'll long for it if it isn't placed squarely on the back of his neck like a millstone. Sagittarius is also often driven by a deep feeling of sexual inadequacy. Being fiery, he often has difficulty being in a physical body at all, which involves annoying limitations. Also, his vision of love is likely to be so wishful and so full of fiery drama and perfection and spiritual union that no relationship is going to wholly satisfy his every need. But the pursuit of the eternal feminine is simply part of his pattern, and he must be allowed both to get on with it and get disillusioned by it. Leave him if you must, since this sometimes helps him along with certain realizations – like the fact that other people aren't always going to wait for him to come back. But this is part of his journey, and the young Sagittarian who denies himself exploration in love usually finds in middle-age that he must break out of his conventional bonds. And later in life it's a lot more painful, what with children and mortgages and all that other stuff we tend to accumulate as we grow older.

There are, of course, plenty of Sagittarians of both sexes who are fully willing and capable of making commitments in relationship. But here too you must be careful not to mistake your centaur for another sort of beast. He still doesn't like being caged, even if he's quite happy to remain with one person. This means psychological caging as well as sexual caging. It means that when he needs to go soaring off into his imagination and his fantasy, or into a book which stirs him, or into a philosophical speculation which leaves you gasping and stranded like a fish on dry land, he simply has to go. If he needs to travel – and travel is, for many Sagittarians, an elixir which always serves to rejuvenate their flagging spirits – then let him, or her, travel, and alone if necessary. It doesn't mean the archer is going to go running off. It means he's got to exercise those horse legs a little, feel the ground moving under him, shoot an arrow or two just to keep the arms in practise. You can't really tame Sagittarius' spirit. He's not a domestic creature. Don't even try. If you want a steady, earthy type, try an earth sign. It's tragic to see the archer when he's been gagged and bound by someone who won't let him exercise his spirit. And it can be very subtle – it's not as simple as letting him come in at the hour he pleases. It's a very delicate psychological process, the

way we sometimes control and possess each other; and
much of it involves crushing the other person's dreams.

Sagittarius needs to believe in something, and he
needs to have goals, even if they aren't realistic.
Constant sniping at those goals is tantamount to
destroying him. Reminding him all the time that something dear to him is silly or impossible or unrealistic or
childish is the best way of driving him away for good.
But then, if you didn't believe a little in his dreams, you
wouldn't be with him anyway, would you? Or would
you?

Sagittarius can be the most generous of souls, both
materially and emotionally. But he can't give on
demand, like a hot or cold water tap. If he's left to give
spontaneously, he can surprise you with some exciting
plan or project – usually a trip somewhere – just when
you need it most. His intuition is very good that way.
Demand that he give regularly, in conventional ways,
and he feels crushed and inadequate. He's a rather self-
centred soul – this applies to female Sagittarians as well
– in that there's a certain insensitivity about the fiery
signs. They have to be reminded that they're being
absent-minded or inconsiderate. You have to say,
outright and without ten years of resentment brewing
beneath the surface, 'You're interrupting me, dear.'
Otherwise they really just don't know they're doing it.
And you also need to be a little realistic about the
extent to which they can modify that behaviour; because
even the Sagittarian who's hopelessly in love is still
likely to be insensitive. In a sense, he has to be; if your
eyes are fixed on the distant horizon, you can't pay
attention simultaneously to where you're walking. If
you look closely at every blade of grass under your feet,
you miss the horizon. You can't have both.

Given a feeling that he can be himself, Sagittarius
gives freely of himself. And no one is so entertaining or
stimulating a partner, because life to him is full of

excitement and new possibilities, and his enthusiasm is infectious. It's all a big children's playground. Don't sneer. When was the last time you let yourself go and had a good time? Sagittarius dislikes most those people who keep reminding him he needs to grow up and become more responsible. He knows that voice, he's got one inside him too, and it probably sounds horribly like his mother or father. It's the surest way to get him very angry, and an angry Sagittarian is not like an angry Cancerian who sulks, or an angry Scorpio who broods, or an angry Virgo who nitpicks, or an angry Capricorn who seethes. An angry Sagittarian is likely to smash crockery, overturn chairs, and yell a lot. He'll forget it all later, of course, because his temper doesn't run to morbid brooding. But he can make a hell of a lot of noise in the process.

In relationships, to the male and female Sagittarian, the imprisoning world of dull routine and endless dreary responsibility is a real death. So, too, is having demands made and orders given. Personal freedom is a god to Sagittarius, and he'll give up a lot to keep his god close to him. He also believes in democracy, which applies to the Sagittarian woman as well; so don't try the do-as-I-say routine, because you'll just get laughed at or left. What Sagittarius needs and truly appreciates is a friend who can share his dreams, and be there when he lands with a bump (which he always inevitably does). It isn't really a great deal to ask – what, after all, are friends for?

① The Sagittarius Man

This elusive and fascinating creature can often be spotted either by his tendency to gesticulate wildly or by his tendency to tell very funny stories. Often he'll do both. But one of the things which virtually exudes all over from Sagittarius is his sense of dramatic irony.

You'll often find that the Sagittarius man does his travelling and his wandering on a mental level rather than a physical one. They are often the apparent intellectuals of the zodiac, devouring books, absorbing all forms of knowledge like tasty meals. But Sagittarius isn't an intellectual in the sense that Gemini is; he's not prone to analysing with a fine-toothed comb all the bits of information that come into his head. He's much more intuitive, and more interested in relating fields of knowledge than in dissecting them. And his mind is speculative – whether it's about philosophy, literature, the arts, or the stock-market.

For him, this life of the mind is much more important than what he eats for dinner. In fact, he'll often forget to eat. The Sagittarius man has a peculiar habit of getting involved, particularly in the earlier part of his life, with rather maternal and earthy women who see this absent-minded and endearing quality ('The poor dear, he's so brilliant and he can't even remember to change his shirt') and immediately feel they need to take care of him. Now, what he doesn't need, repeat, doesn't need, is to be taken care of. Yes, of course he'd live in a pigsty without you, and his clothes would be rumpled, and his hair needing cutting, but if you do all these things for him he'll not only grow to resent it in time, he'll also never get to do it himself. Besides, he might not particularly care. Sagittarius, like the other fiery signs, is often attracted to the earthy signs – Taurus, Virgo and Capricorn. And the Sagittarian man with an earthy partner will, for a time, certainly allow her to become the symbol of steadiness, stability, reliability. If you're cast in this role, try to stop playing it right at the beginning, not at the end. It's a tragic mistake that occurs regularly in Sagittarian relationships. You can't mother him until he grows up. For one thing, growing up in his terms means something different from growing up in yours. For earthy people, maturity is synonymous with taking responsibility in the tangible world. For fiery people, maturity is seeing, knowing, understanding. By earthy terms, Sagittarius will never wholly grow up; nor should he. And all that careful mothering and shirt-ironing which is usually aimed (secretly) at binding the dashing, wandering soul to you for all eternity, is likely to backfire in a bad way. Sagittarius, for all his longing for earth and steadiness, needs ultimately to find it in himself. And the less responsibility you take for him, the less resentful you'll be, and the more relaxed he'll feel, and the better the future for you both.

Not that you're to blame. The archer is a stimulating and exciting and dynamic man, and his fleet-of-foot quality, that tantalizing quality of free self-expression and untamed vision, makes him terribly appealing particularly to women who long for a little excitement and adventure in their lives. And there's no doubt that Sagittarius' adventurous soul is guaranteed not to bore you. But try to find adventure and excitement in yourself first, please; then you're likely to enjoy him and his vision much, much more. One of Sagittarius' basic approaches to life is to laugh at it; after all, what's so serious when you really think about it? You have to have a sense of humour yourself; otherwise you won't understand at all what he's laughing at, especially when he laughs at you. Sagittarius can sometimes be a terrible tease, and he's not averse to taking a sly little poke at anyone who carries too much seriousness or pomposity. Fortunately this not very endearing quality is balanced by the fact that he can laugh at himself, too.

The Sagittarian man's biggest problem in relationships is making that dreaded bridge between romantic fantasy and fleshy reality. For many archers it's just too big a gap, and they never succeed in bridging it. Living in the fantasy world, if you've got the money to support it, is the only recourse for this kind of Sagittarian. Some archers despair, and feel they'll never achieve a successful relationship; so they roam through life leaving a trail of broken affairs behind them, unfinished business, unpaid debts, unlived life. The fear of failure here is as big as the fear of material failure to the Sagittarian. After all, what was Jupiter trying to prove? Behind the often contemptuous and ironic attitude which many Sagittarian men have toward love and commitment, you'll often find a frightened child who's afraid his romantic world will be smashed. The child can build a pretty big cynical wall around himself. He can arm himself with a stunning array of quips, jokes, and nasty asides which make you think he has no heart. But inside, he's a child. Don't fall for it. Sagittarius has a heart of gold. It just bruises easily. Eventually, he learns that the idea is to reach the first goal first. And trust and friendship are the guideposts that help him on his way. He can offer these in abundance himself, and he truly deserves them in exchange.

♐ The Sagittarius Woman

There are women adventurers, too. Not all explorers, mountain-climbers, and world travellers are male Sagittarians. And the true female archer is as restless, as hungry for experience, as longing to explore the fascinating carnival that she sees as life as her male counterpart. This woman needs personal freedom to an extraordinary degree, and she's not known either for her readiness to marry or her readiness to take up domestic responsibilities. Frequently she's happier spending a lifetime without both. And she's as likely to have a child out of wedlock and happily raise it as a travelling companion as she is to ensconce herself behind secure walls. Walls, for any Sagittarian, are like waving a red flag at a bull.

Any career which allows space, travel, freedom of movement, and opportunity for new contacts pleases the Sagittarian woman. And the archer who doesn't pursue a career still needs these things. Failing everything else, she'll become a socialite, because at least she gets to throw parties and meet exciting people. There are also more introverted, philosophical Sagittarian women – and some, like Jane Fonda, who may be philosophical but are also more typical of their sign in that they are vociferous about their philosophies. You'll often find the Sagittarius woman involved in a cause of one kind or another, because her astute vision and sense of movements within the group give her an interest and a concern for human welfare.

One thing she isn't, and that is opinionless. Sagittarius is always thinking about something, chewing it over, learning it, reading about it, discussing it. Convictions are terribly important to the Sagittarian woman, although her convictions are likely to change regularly. Sagittarius is a fluid, flexible sign. You'll also sometimes see the more spiritual or religious side in evidence in the Sagittarian woman – often showing as an interest in religion, myth, psychology, and various assorted esoteric or occult subjects. There's a love of the unknown and the challenging, the magical and the unexplained.

There is also a strong sense of fun and humour in the Sagittarian woman. And the famous blunt Sagittarian tongue is also much in evidence here. You can't expect an archer to flatter you diplomatically. More likely she'll deliver a verbal punch between the eyes – not because she's cruel, but because she has a tendency to speak before she thinks, and to not quite realize that you, sensitive soul that you are, have just been irrevocably crushed by the insult. She's usually right, too;

it's pretty difficult to fool Sagittarius' sharp intuition, which has a way of seeing right through postures and hypocrisy.

You may see a touch of the groupie here. The Sagittarian woman often needs to be where the action is, where interesting and exciting people are. Whether it's by her own talents or through somebody else's, she's attracted to anything new and important. And she needs to be moving all the time, working at things, busy with projects. What doesn't work is the nine-to-five routine at the office filing cabinet, or the six-to-eight routine of the kids' breakfasts and the shopping and the ironing. In fact, you might have noticed that many Sagittarian women are terribly inept at dealing with things like tangible organization. If they do it, they often get good earthy help – those Virgos and Capricorns and Taureans who stand quietly in the background and collect the money and wash up the dishes. Never mind. Her gift is at bringing people together, inspiring them, delighting them, teaching them, opening up the world for them. Not, in fact, cleaning up after them.

Sagittarius the romantic can have a problematic time in long-term relationships. Because she loves the new and the exciting, the Sagittarius woman may follow the pattern of her male counterpart, always seeking the knight on the white horse who can take her away from banality and show her a world of fairy-tale romance. This may be a literal escapade or a fantasy one; but those escapades are common and very likely to occur. But she does come back again, if left alone. What you can't do is possess her; she'll fight then, and isn't averse to just walking out. Sagittarian women are very independent. You see it even in the Sagittarian child. You don't tell them to do something. You ask. Nicely.

Sagittarius, like Gemini, needs to be able to communicate. If you're after the quiet, docile type, forget it. Many Sagittarian women are great talkers; and they'll talk about anything they've found exciting and interesting. They have a knack of making it sound exciting for others, too. Sometimes they go on too long, and become bores; and there's no bore like your Sagittarian bore once he gets on his favourite passion or enthusiasm of the moment. But in general, Sagittarius is a conversational animal, and needs a partner who's interested and willing to talk as well. The silent, taciturn type doesn't do terribly well mated to the archer.

All the fiery signs need to be in love. That fine distinction made between loving and the state of in-love-ness is all right for the more rational elements of air and earth. But without the belief in love, fire wilts. And the Sagittarius woman is really, in her heart, in love with life itself. It's to be lived, not caged; and although she'll inevitably take quite a few romantic knocks in the nature of things – not least because her need for personal freedom and independence may drive away a few frightened partners – she never loses her hopes for the future. This woman is an optimist, a believer in the value and vitality of life. Spend any time around her, and you'll begin to believe it too. Sagittarius faith is infectious. But unlike most infectious things, it isn't fatal. Just the opposite. It breeds life.

The Element
of Earth

*The trouble with always keeping both feet
firmly on the ground is that you can
never take your pants off.*

J. D. SMITH

Since earth is what we all stand on, build with,
draw sustenance from and in which we are
inextricably rooted, it might be said that the element of
earth in astrology is a symbol of the three-dimensional
world of matter, the observable conjunction of space
and time. Earth is real, earth is solid, earth is reliable
and factual and present. And the earthy signs – Taurus,
Virgo and Capricorn – possess, as their basic mode of
experiencing life, an attentiveness to and a recognition
of all that occupies the senses. Earth represents the
reality function *par excellence*. Or, if we are to summarize all this, earth people are above all else realistic.

Now realism is a dangerously relative term to anybody but an earth sign. After all, there are lots of
different kinds of realities. But an earth sign will tell
you, That's all very well; but nevertheless, regardless of
all your theories to the contrary, what I perceive is what
I perceive, and therefore I will work with that and
make something of it. Earth is not interested in why,

how, what might be, what was, what could be. It is interested in what works. Pragmatic to the end.

What is really important in studying astrology is not to catalogue behaviour traits, but to understand the real essence, the innermost motivation and way of experiencing life that a sign – or a group of signs belonging to one element – share. Hence, if we catalogue the traits of Virgo, Taurus and Capricorn, they will not do justice to this fascinating, apparently simple, underrated and undervalued element. Probably fewer earth signs study astrology than any other group; I have found fewer Taureans and Capricorns in my classes than any other signs. Virgos tend to like the systematization, and therefore come because they find it useful. But the true earth personality has no time for abstruse cosmological speculations. He is much more interested in what is going on at this moment in this world, how to deal with it, how to master it, how to build security and safety in a chaotic cosmos, how to apply his skills to carve out for himself a life that is productive, useful and full.

Most textbook descriptions of the three earth signs share some common adjectives. For example: practical, efficient, full of common-sense, sensual, realistic, well-organized, fond of money and security and status. To a great extent this is true. In the sphere of reality – or what we consider to be reality via the senses – the earthy type excels. Somehow, to the mystification of more intuitive, volatile people, they manage to make order out of the random array of stimuli which assault the senses by relating to each experience or object individually, studying its laws and its nature, savouring it, and moving on to the next, gradually building up a body of facts and experience which allow them to function in life by dealing with the things of this life. Render unto God what is God's, and unto Caesar what is Caesar's. The fire signs tend to spend a lot of time on God, while the earth signs court the careful acquaintanceship of the needs and expectations of Caesar – or, as the Cathars would have said, of *rex mundi*, the Lord of This World.

Earthy people tend to be at home with their bodies. They like bodies, they feel comfortable clothed in flesh; often they believe themselves to actually be their bodies. If you ask a group of people individually, 'Who are you?' and ask for the first honest spontaneous answer, you will see the elements very quickly coming to the fore. The intuitive will seek to articulate – if possible – that he is his innermost spiritual essence, his creative source. The earth sign will tell you, or experience himself as, his body. After all, what better friend than the body? It is as far as many of us know of reality. So earthy people are usually healthy, because they neither repress nor undervalue the needs of the body.

They are at home with objects, and can usually manage money and responsibilities in an apparently effortless way which is most upsetting to their fiery comrades. Earthy people have a gift for actualizing their desires. They take the time to explore all the practical aspects of a situation, and do not reach for what is impossible. So they are successful in those areas which require discipline, hard work, application, diligence, patience and care. Fire is much too sloppy to be bothered with this kind of patience. Earth knows that every birth must be preceded by a gestation which is awaited with tenderness and caution. If your eyes are kept fairly close to the ground, you won't miss much on the path you are walking.

The problem, of course, is (as the quote at the beginning of this chapter humourously points out) that if you keep your eyes fairly close to the ground, you never get to see the sky; and you are likely to form a picture of the universe which, rather than spanning the broad, interconnected canvas of fire, will be bitty, and reduced to a constant monotonous round of daily details and facts. The failing, the one great danger with the earth signs lies in that secret dark side which we have been talking about. Because there is a tendency to ignore or undervalue or repress the wilder, grander, more fantastic visions and leanings of their natures, earthy people are prone to dogmatism, narrowmindedness, over–possessiveness, over–simplification, and a compulsive ordermaking. Just as the details of mundane life threaten the fire sign's vision, too much vision threatens the security of earth. Fire fears order; earth fears disorder. As the French poet Paul Valéry wrote,

> The world is constantly threatened by two things: order and disorder.

Because the innate chaos of life, its randomness, its movement, its incessant propensity to shift and change, are so terrifying to earthy people, they have a tendency to build bastions in which they can retreat and feel safe from the ever-present threat of the unknown. As fire loves what it does not know and has not yet seen, earth cherishes what is known, familiar and trustworthy. Life is, perhaps, a paradox containing both. While earthy people can manage with ease the complexity of the world of objects, they are dangerously liable to miss the inner significance of their own lives. Because of their fear of chaos and that which is unknown or changeable earthy people are often beleaguered with irrational fears and vague apprehensions.

Sometimes you will see earthy people who have stamped so ruthlessly on their imagination, their intuition, that they live in an endless grey twilight of labours and routines that, while gradually increasing the pile of objects around them, never ease the real hollow space. And deep inside you can hear the plaintive cry, the longing for some sense of purpose, some feeling of being a part of a larger life, some hope for the future. All those labours make it hard to live creatively. Another way of putting all this is that the earthy person's problem is: he doesn't know how to play. He has forgotten the state of childhood, which does not leave us just because our bodies are 'adult'. There is a secret child in all of us, full of wonder and naïveté and the hope that life will bring surprises, joys, bounties unexpected – like Santa Claus on Christmas morning. If fire is the eternal child, earth is the eternal old man or old woman. He is often old when he is young, being more sensitive to and more willing to undertake responsibility; and this very gift which allows him to look realistically at what he must accomplish in life is also his greatest enemy. Unless he can break loose from the treadmill of his bondage to what he calls reality, he is especially liable to fear death as the final reckoning: a definitive summation of his own life, whose underlying significance has somehow eluded him.

Fire signs often have a terribly intense secret longing for the very security, stability, and 'ordinariness' which in public they may be heard to condemn as drab and suffocating. Earth signs by contrast, have an equally intense, equally secret, equally unspoken longing for the spiritual. This is frequently in the guise of superstition, which is even more embarrassing, since they are so quick to demand the facts, and so apparently anything but gullible. But there is no more spiritually gullible element than earth, although you may have to get your earth sign friend drunk to get him to admit that he knocks on wood all the time, won't pass under ladders, and has a horror of spilling the salt. Earth signs are often fascinated by ghosts, psychism, and other parapsychological phenomena which are an everyday part of the life of fire. But the earth person will often not consider these things as part of the universe, a natural part which is perhaps not yet understood. He 'believes' in the 'supernatural' in a covert way without recognizing the implications of such a world. So – predictably – he will look for these qualities in a partner. Earth is attracted to fire, just as fire is attracted to earth. The earthy type will often be seen in careful, systematic pursuit of a love-object which symbolizes the medium, the inspiration, the creative spirit – the guide who can share with him the secrets of the cosmos, the bringer of drama and fire and life. Unfortunately these fiery partners, who may perhaps be in touch with some inner mystery be it spiritual or unconscious, cannot parcel out this kind of insight like bread and cheese. Such experiences are wholly individual, intensely personal, and inexplicable in concrete terms. As Lawrence Durrell wrote,

Intuitives find language an obstacle, a clumsy hurdle. The eyes understand wordlessly – for words conceal more than they reveal.

You can imagine what sort of a problem it is for the earthy person to understand the abstruse and volatile symbolic language of fire.

For earth can accept nothing unless it is backed up by the testimony of his senses. He is often like a dog bound by a long lead to a post. He runs round and round, yet can never get beyond the circumscribed length of the chain – a chain forged by his insistence that the senses are the only means of apprehending reality. What a problem! The following is a typical dialogue one may overhear at parties:

EARTH: But don't tell me you believe in all that sort of rubbish.
FIRE: I don't 'believe' in it, and it isn't rubbish. I just know certain things. I've had experiences.
EARTH: Maybe you were on drugs at the time. What kind of experiences?
FIRE: Oh well, you know. I can't explain it. But I believe things happen which we can't explain rationally.

EARTH: Nonsense. Everything has a rational explanation.

At this point the earth sign is thinking that fire is a loony, and the fire sign is thinking that earth is a narrow-minded bore. Reality *v* vision. What can a poor boy do?

Earth signs may be wonderful builders, providers, homemakers, conscientious servants of the needs of those they love. Their really big sin is never lack of care or effort. It is their lack of vision, which often stifles those who are close and crush their own as well as other's nascent creativity through over-insistence on the practical.

EARTH PARENT to FIRE CHILD who is learning how to paint/play piano/study philosophy/master the architecture of smoke-rings:
Why are you wasting your time on that rubbish? You should be out learning how to make money.

We know well enough what this attitude has done to younger generations. You might say that the earth-sign viewpoint – understandable enough in an earth sign – became the common collective standard of our society for a time, after the horrors of two world wars and severe economic depression. We have by now two entire generations of dropouts and runaways who have rebelled violently against these excessively earthy values forced upon them by well-meaning parents who have lived through the economic and political nightmares and insecurity of this century and have forgotten that the future always contains new possibilities. Earthy people value only what they know and what they perceive through their senses; and they miss a lot that way. Who would want to spend his last shilling on hyacinths for the soul when a good bowl of soup would do as well?

The trouble is that earth will spend a lifetime providing others with the things he believes they want because he wants them himself. And when that fiery partner shows a predilection for hyacinths, it is like a slap in the face. The problem here is the same as for us all: recognizing that different people see different realities and need different things.

Now let's talk a bit more about the earth signs in relationships. It should be pretty obvious by now that if an earthy person is reasonably satisfied sexually, and has a situation which gratifies his need for material stability, he will generally remain solid, loyal and immovable (or at least mostly) in relationships which would drive the other elements, particularly fire, wild. As earth gets increasingly secure, fire gets increasingly imprisoned. And although earth's sensuality will often lead him into extraneous affairs which are pleasurable in the same way as a really fine meal, he will rarely do anything to threaten the structure of a long-standing relationship or marriage if it satisfies his need for security and social acceptability. Ah yes, we didn't mention social acceptability. It is terribly important to earth, because society is a place where one can seek safety. Pillar of the community, and all that. Society is an earth-sign creation. It protects and sustains. It upholds tradition and offers laws by which life and behaviour may be systematized. Earth people love all that stuff. Fire hates it. Fire is fiercely individualistic and will generally feel he is outside, beyond, or ill-fitted with society. Too conservative, traditional, and safe. Ugh. There you have another typical problem.

EARTH: Darling, how could you have behaved like that in front of my friends? You shocked them. I won't be able to face them again.
FIRE: But all I did was talk about my belief that there are really flying saucers.
EARTH: But that stuff is nonsense, everybody knows

it's marsh gas or the lights from Japanese squid boats.
You made me feel ridiculous.
FIRE: You're so damned afraid of what everybody
thinks. I have a right to express my own opinion.
EARTH: No you don't, not when it upsets people like
that. It isn't NORMAL.

Now normal and abnormal are two words you'll hear
a lot in dialogues between earth and fire. Normality –
whatever that is – is safe, stable, a measure by which
earth can organize its reality. Abnormality is sickness.
To fire, normality is a bore – who wants to be mediocre?
Abnormality is simply another word for individuality to
fire. Each secretly fears and desires the opposite. Earthy
people would like, once in a while, to be perfect
lunatics. And fiery people would like, once in a while,
to be drearily ordinary.

Because he bases his reality on what is in front of
him, the fact that a partner is physically present, that a
marriage actually exists, means that a relationship
exists. All that stuff about 'something missing' is pretty
incomprehensible to the earth signs. Duty, loyalty,
responsibility, commitment and security are much more
important than wild romantic idealism. The subtler
nuances of relating often escape him. Tragically, his
partner often escapes him as well, seeking more of the
chaotic burning stuff of spiritual passion and soul. It is
fire who will usually abandon a relationship with an
earth sign, unless the fire sign has one affair too many
and the earth sign leaves out of wounded vindictiveness.

Sexual problems *per se* do not often afflict the earth
signs. Inhibitions about fantasy do, though; they tend
to be a prudish lot when it comes to the more exotic
aspects of erotica. They appreciate the senses, not the
imagination. You can imagine where this leads.

Taurus

Ferdinand the Bull, in the famous children's story, is a lovable creature. He amuses himself by smelling the flowers, listening to the birdsong, enjoying the summer breezes. He doesn't do very much, our Ferdinand; but he's easily contented, and at home in his pasture. Then one day he sits on a flower, and on the flower is a bee ... Well, you can work out the rest. Ferdinand the Bull is a perfect Taurean. And the story of many Taureans' lives runs along those lines – the contentment of the field and the flowers; but there is always that damned bee.

Taurus, the Bull, is ruled by the planet Venus. In mythology, Venus is the goddess of love and beauty. She's also the most indolent of all the Olympian deities, preferring her considerable pleasures to the nuisance of hard work. All this describes very nicely one side of the Taurean nature. A few words encapsulate it. Peace, serenity, pleasure, calm, stability, placidity. The famous patience of the Bull isn't so much patience built upon discipline and cynicism, as is Capricorn's. It's the patience of nature, of the earth itself, serene and living each day for the pleasures it holds, while tomorrow – so long as it can be guaranteed that tomorrow will be the same as today – is forgotten.

There are other sides to Taurus, of course. In a sense, you can place Taureans at one of two phases in their lives: before and after that most dreaded aspect of life to Taurus, the thing that goes innately against the grain: Change.

Among the traditional associations to Taurus is the realm of material stability and security. And there's no doubt about it, Taurus likes his security in tangible, unchangeable forms – like gold bullion, or valuable antique furniture, or a really superb Ferrari. Abstract wealth, tied up in investments, or wealth of a noncorporeal kind (like knowledge, self-understanding, friends, and other less graspable commodities) is not really wealth to a Taurus. Security is what you can trust. What you can trust is what doesn't change, corrode, leave you, disappear, or depend upon others for its value. Once he has it, he can relax. Often he relaxes so much that he barely moves again.

There's another aspect to this security-building impulse in Taurus. This has to do with Taurus' way of looking at life. When we discussed the element of earth in general, we mentioned that it had to do with dealing with reality – concrete, tangible reality. Taurus, the first of the earthy signs, excels at this 'realistic' viewpoint.

Taurus is never foolishly idealistic. Never naïve about the requirements and demands of ordinary life. A true Taurus always has one eye cocked toward how he can sustain and preserve himself in life. He's always realistic in his goals, always setting them where he can fulfil them. Taken by itself, Taurus isn't an ambitious sign. He can quite happily remain the unseen power behind the scenes: the investor, the accountant, the one who keeps the business running without getting the public laurels. Taurus is realistic enough to know that you can't eat laurels, and they won't fix a leaky roof.

The other side of the coin with this great realism is .hat Taurus often misses what's not visible to his earthy eye. He values simplicity and basic facts; but many aspects of life are neither simple nor reducible to formulae. We might call this the Boring Pragmatist syndrome. He's boring largely because, if he can't hold it in the palm of his hand, he has nothing to say about the matter, let alone any appreciation for its nuances. Never mind all those hyacinths for the soul. A scenario might run like this:

FRIEND TO TAURUS: I have the most wonderful idea. You know that novel I was working on? Well, I thought it might go really well as a film script. All the battle scenes staged at night, with torchlight and bonfires and stuff . . . really dramatic! And the fifteenth-century costumes . . .

TAURUS: I can't understand why you're bothering with that stuff. It isn't making you any money.

FRIEND: Well, not yet. But if I'm lucky, I can get some help from this friend who . . .

TAURUS: You'll never get into the film business. It's too competitive. Besides, what good is a historical drama? Who cares about history? It's dead. I don't see why you're wasting so much energy on it.

FRIEND: It's not dead. It has all kinds of symbolic significance today . . .
TAURUS: Symbolic? What are you talking about? Something's dead or it's not. I don't understand what you're talking about. Why don't you train at something that can make you a little money?

This scenario has several different versions. It can apply, as here, to the complete lack of understanding of the symbolic, the romantic, the dramatic. Taurus likes his meat and potatoes plain, without sauce. They must, of course, be of the absolutely best quality; but he doesn't appreciate frills. He also doesn't appreciate possibilities. For something to be real to Taurus, it must be more than possible: it must be definite.

Other versions to this scenario occur in all areas where the physical reality of something isn't immediately apparent. Many Taureans are notorious sceptics of anything they consider 'mystical' – like astrology, for example. I've noticed over a decade of teaching that fewer Taureans enroll in my courses than any other sign. There are also very few Leos. For the latter, of course, it's probably that they would rather be teaching themselves; and also, Leo doesn't like to learn from anybody else. But Taurus will be terribly cautious about something like astrology unless he can be shown, definitively and scientifically that it works. And not once but several times, in case the first time was a fluke. I once had a Taurus client who, although he was quite ruffled and impressed by his horoscope reading, doubted that I could repeat such a performance. He wasn't prepared to accept that the chart worked; he thought (which seemed an even wilder interpretation) that I had somehow acquired my information psychically or telepathically. He asked if he might sit in on several other chart readings for some of his friends. Because he was a Taurus, and I knew there was no other way, I conceded. After about fifteen such sessions he begrudgingly admitted that there must be something to it. And like a good Taurus, once a change of attitude had taken hold of him, he swung into action. Not content with merely accepting it, he decided to learn it. He learned in the way Taureans do when they have finally got moving: obsessively. Now he's a practising astrologer.

This pragmatism about things which might be foggy, woolly, charlatan, or false, works to Taurus' advantage as well. It keeps him out of mischief, and helps him to establish the absolute reliability of anything he allows into his life. This applies to relationships as well. Taurus is the kind of person who prefers to know a lot about you, to 'check your references' in a bizarre sort of way, before he makes any commitment. After all, that's the sensible, realistic thing to do. Although he has a sentimental, gentle, romantic streak, it's backed up by healthy cynicism. In the midst of the bouquets of roses, he might quietly have a peep at your bank balance and inquire about your family. It's not that he expects you to provide the riches for him. He just likes to know that everything is stable, secure and reliable. Including you.

Let's consider the famous sensuality of Taurus. The true Taurean is an undeniably sensuous creature. This means not only in the sexual realm, but in anything that pleases the senses. Colour: Taurus often has a real flair for design, for colour, perhaps for painting or photography. Sound: Taurus is well-known for its love of music, and many Taureans have become famous singers (like Barbra Streisand) or composers (like Tchaikovsky). Touch: this means not only responsiveness to physical touch, but a love of texture. Silk, velvet, satin, fur. Yes, of course it costs money, but Taurus isn't interested in anything cheap. Taste: well, that can be a problem. Love of good food leads many a Taurean into weight problems. Lots of Taureans have a sleek well-fed look – not floppy fat, but solid flesh, the sign of the person who eats not only what tastes good but is also good quality. Perhaps a little too much good quality. Your Taurus friend is bound to know all the best restaurants – not the fashionable ones, necessarily (that's where the Geminis and Sagittarians go) but the really reliable ones with excellent food. Smell: Taureans are terribly sensitive to smell, and usually have a great affinity for luxurious scents of various kinds. From flowers to priceless perfume, Taurus likes to surround himself with good smells. Often the senses of the Taurus are so acute and intense that he finds it unbearable to be around anything that looks, smells, or feels sordid or cheap or ugly. Taurus has a strong instinct for harmony.

Taste is another quality often to be found in Taurus. Taurus' tastes tend toward the conventional, rather than the startling; if you want shocking taste, try the fire signs, or perhaps the air signs. Earth, being more realistic and conscious of the demands of society, tends toward things of good quality which are not likely to suddenly go out of style in six months. Taurus is not a 'fad' person. But within the confines of his more solid, almost bourgeois palate, his taste is usually impeccable. Never obtrusive. Maybe a really good car, like a Bentley or a Rolls Royce (never something as flashy and unreliable as a Lamborghini, which always has to be in the shop to be tuned). Something solid and reliable that speaks not fashion, but solid wealth. Taurus has strong roots in tradition. And often there's a love of the old and the antique – antique furniture, antique lace, antique shawls and jewellery, old masters' paintings. Solid, ageless, valuable.

With Taurus' love of beauty, he's bound to create an environment that has as much beauty and pleasing atmosphere as possible. On the other hand, he's often so occupied with physical beauty that he may miss what lies underneath. Taurus is the original sucker for a pretty face; he can value beauty so much, in objects and people, that he overlooks and underestimates qualities such as perceptiveness, wit, intelligence, and character. It isn't that difficult to fool a Taurean if you are beautiful. Sad to say, many Taureans are hopelessly ensnared by appearances. It's one of their great failings.

Taurus is also a collector. Of objects, money, and people. What he collects must have value to him. He will treasure it, take care of it, shower attention on it, and hang on with both tough fists tightly encircling it. This is why Taurus is often the partner people seek when they seek the real security of a stable, unchanging relationship. No matter what happens or what you do, Taurus will stand by you. He may not always understand your motives; but he'll remain loyal regardless.

The collecting instinct in Taurus can get out of hand. He may collect for the sake of collecting, which is fine for objects – they don't seem to mind – but very disturbing if you are a person. Sometimes it takes some rude shocks and a few quarrels to convince a Taurus that you have your own individuality and your own private inner life. You have to tell him. He can't telepath, and often misses subtle signals. And he has a hell of a time trying to disentangle motives.

Because the gods seem to resent complacency, there is usually a bee in the flowers. It seems to be a necessary part of the life pattern. Often the Taurus himself courts this bee without realizing it, unconsciously setting up a situation where he is shocked aware while thinking it happened by chance or was someone else's fault. But without the sting, he remains charming and childlike. Many adult Taureans are so childlike that it's astonishing. Life is terribly simple to them, black and white, with no shades of grey in between. They have it all worked out, logically, systematically, and simply. Good people are good and go to heaven; bad people are bad and go to hell. Childlike and trusting. What the bee offers is a capacity to take this precious childlike simplicity and combine it with a little earthy realism. It's a lovely combination, once achieved. For you have a person who not only knows the realities of life and can deal with them, but who can also live happily and contentedly in the moment, capable of abandoning himself to his pleasures in the wholehearted way that children have before it's pounded out of them. Remember the goddess Venus. She is, in many ways, the eternal child.

♉ The Myth

Mythology abounds with motifs about bulls of one sort or another. For about two thousand years the bull, the symbol of Taurus, was one of the main religious symbols for the Taurean Age – which occurred roughly between 4000 and 2000 B.C. In pagan religion of this time, the bull and the cow were symbols of the fertility of the earth, for this epoch coincided with the emergence of the great agricultural civilizations of the Tigris and Euphrates and the Nile.

Of all these motifs, one of the best known and the most apt for Taurus is the myth of Theseus and the Minotaur. It is a complicated myth with many facets; but it helps to illustrate both the main difficulties and the main challenges of the deeper journey of the sign.

Minos was the king of Crete, and had a herd of exceptional bulls which were dedicated to the god Poseidon. He made a deal with the god, and promised him a particularly beautiful white bull in offering if Poseidon could give him mastery over the seas. The god agreed to the deal, and Crete flourished.

Minos, however, was covetous and greedy (a characteristic Taurean problem) and when the time came to sacrifice the bull, he decided to cheat the god and keep it for himself, offering a lesser specimen in its place. The god, in revenge, asked Aphrodite (Venus), goddess of love, for aid in a plan for retaliation. Aphrodite afflicted Minos' wife, Queen Pasiphaë, with an uncontrollable lust for the white bull. (Uncontrollable lust is another virtue ranking high on Taurus' list.) Pasiphaë, unable to suppress her desires, enlisted the aid of Daidalos, the palace master craftsman, to make her a wooden bull in which she disguised herself so she could mate with the white bull. The offspring of this union was the Minotaur, a dreadful beast with the body of a man and the head of a bull, which fed on human flesh.

Now, the Minotaur in our story is a symbol of Taurus run amuck. With human body and bull's head, his humanity is completely overshadowed by his rampant desires. The Minotaur, being a mark of Minos' shame, was enclosed in a labyrinth which was so complex and so impenetrable that the beast could not escape. Into the labyrinth regularly were thrown a quota of youths and maidens from Crete's conquered vassals, to feed the endless appetite of the Minotaur for human flesh.

Theseus, the son of the King of Athens, volunteered to join this sacrificial quota to slay the Minotaur. With the help of Minos' daughter Ariadne and her famous ball of thread, he found his way into the labyrinth and killed the Minotaur with a club, and found his way out again through the skein of thread. Having completed his quest, he was made King of Crete – marrying the King's daughter and adopting the hereditary title of Minos.

Both Theseus and the Minotaur are aspects of Taurus. Like every myth, this one portrays many things, and can be peeled for meanings like an onion. But one way you can take it is that within each Taurean is this basic conflict between the human, heroic side and the bestial side with its rampant appetites, product of more compulsive desire on the part of both its parents. Desire is a dominant force in Taurus, whether it is desire for sexual satisfaction, food, drink, money, status, or anything else you can think of. When Taurus becomes obsessed with the object of his desire, there is no withholding him from it. He's like a fully wound up steam roller; it may take him a while to find out what he wants, and a while to get warmed up, but once he gets moving, nothing on God's green earth will stop him. The trick is to harness the desires to work for the man, rather than the desires dragging the man behind them. And to make sure that the desires, whatever they are, don't – as the picturesque mythological image suggests – devour human flesh.

Notice that Theseus succeeds because of the ball of thread. The ball of thread has to do with plan and purpose. Ordinarily, Taurus would blunder into the labyrinth blind, because he didn't look forward far enough to the time he might want to leave again. The Bull doesn't always possess foresight. But armed with it, the task is made easy. Also, the labyrinth is the tangle of human motives and emotions that so often defeats Taurus. Because of his love of simplicity, and his intense dislike of inferences, convolutions, half-shaded and ambiguous suggestions, undercurrents and nuances, he often loses his way in the labyrinth of human relationships and of his own inner life. He badly needs a ball of thread – that is, a clear path and an idea of the map of the place. Given that, he's on his way.

There's another myth which is pertinent to Taurus as well, and describes more the strengths and abilities of the sign. Theseus and the Minotaur portrays one of the basic life problems of Taurus. Vulcan (Hephaistos, in Greek) is the god who represents a different side of Taurus' nature. In mythology, Vulcan is the husband of Venus. He is the divine artisan, the builder, the worker. He works at his forge, which is at the heart of a volcano, and creates on his anvil all the tools and objects of beauty that provide the other Olympian deities with their powers. Vulcan is responsible for making Zeus' thunderbolts, Mercury's winged helmet and sandals, Pluto's invisible helmet, Minerva's magic shield. Every deity owes Vulcan something, for it is Vulcan who forges from the earth itself the attributes of power. He is an alchemist: from the raw substance of the earth itself he produces gold and precious things. He is an indefatigable worker, with immense strength in his shoulders and arms. He represents the qualities of creative power that Taurus possesses, unleashed and directed toward a useful and purposeful end. If Taurus can only find his purpose, his meaning, some field of work which can occupy his tremendous drive and energy, he is a true artist – whether it is of a piece of sculpture, a symphony, a building, a government. First, of course, he must get that bee sting which reminds him that he can't spend the whole of his life chewing grass contentedly, while chasing other bulls out of the pasture. Deep in every Taurus is a need to be useful, to produce, to build something solid and permanent and tangible that stands as a testimony to his abilities and to his existence. Taurus is seeking a symbol of his own value, his own worth. To accomplish this, he must make something that lasts. Until he settles into his life work, Taurus is often aimless, or lethargic, or passive, or dependent on the support of others. But his real nature is as much Vulcan, the earth-fire god, as it is Venus the beautiful, indolent one. Put the two together – as the Greeks did in their myth – and you have some marvellous offspring.

♉ The Shadow

Let's consider the undertow that exists in all earthy signs: that of fire. And let's remember that this undertow often shows itself in a strange kind of religious fervour or fanaticism. Here you have the Taurean shadow, completely hidden in many Taureans and unleashed in full force in others. Nobody, but nobody, is as good at founding ersatz religions as a Taurus.

Notice the quality of the religions. Let's take Karl Marx, a Taurus. Now, dialectic materialism is supposed to be a political philosophy. It's meant to explain the forces operating in history – all explained in true Taurean fashion, with regard for the economic motivations but with complete unawareness of other currents and motives. The importance of spiritual needs, for example, is grossly ignored. The impact of powerful personalities is missed. And the substrata of myth, the basic patterns and structure of the human psyche, is sadly missing. Dialectic materialism is an anti-religious religion. Witness the religiosity with which its partisans attempt to convert the world. Instead of the old Inquisition hunting heretics, it hunts capitalists. And the impetus is Taurean: fixed, persistent, determined, obsessive, and fanatical.

Let's take another Taurean: Sigmund Freud. Now, modern psychology owes an immeasurable debt to Dr Freud, for he was the first to postulate the existence of what we call the unconscious, the hidden side of man. However anachronistic Freud's theories seem to us now, it is worth remembering that he was the real founder, the builder, of a new outlook of man. Since Freud's time, man has become much more aware that he is a complex creature with many facets not apparent to the ordinary eye. Freud was a true Taurean in that he was an empiricist, non-mystical, pragmatic, thorough, scientific, and a builder. He was also Taurean on the shadow side, for Freudian psychology is like a religion. When you read Freud, you realize that he is offering us a new Bible, a new face of God, a new expulsion from the Garden. The sexual drive, to Freud, is a god; it has the power and absoluteness of God. Freud's own religious propensities found their way into his psychology. It's dogmatic, fixed and orthodox. Its adherents, when strict, are so closely akin to those of the Church that it is amusing to see them such arch antagonists. Freud's work is banned in Ireland, stronghold of the Church. Yet they bear strange similarities.

This religious fanaticism often permeates Taurus' endeavours. The list is very long, and ranges from the very light – Buddha was said to have been a Taurus – to the very dark – Hitler was also a Taurus. What do they have in common? Well, it's an unfair comparison. But the story of Siddhartha is a Taurean story – all or nothing. So is Hitler's. And in Hitler's you can see the Taurean shadow run so rampant that we have not yet recovered from it: a religious fanaticism so intense that the western world is still reeling under the impact of Wotan unleashed in the twentieth century.

In ordinary life, this fanaticism can peep out in lots of different places. The most typical form is intolerance. Taurus is not known for his easy acceptance of others' viewpoints. He simply negates the existence of anything that doesn't fit in with his scheme of reality. For a realistic sign, Taurus is prone to the strangest sorts of gullible fervours. Often his pragmatism has the undercurrent of gross, blind fanaticism – a very unpragmatic quality. He usually doesn't recognize it. In his own eyes, no one is more realistic. But the bull can be so one-pointed that it can only see red.

Intolerance has a close relationship with prejudice.

And prejudice is one of Taurus' chief difficulties on the shadow side. Once he makes up his mind that a particular ideology, religion, race or type of person is a loss, there his mind stays. There's no moving it, no budging it. And he can be incredibly offensive in his criticism of others' values. For Taurus, his values are the only values. He's not averse to being either rude or insulting if you contradict them.

There are other facets to the Taurus shadow, connected with these just mentioned. One of them is Taurus' tendency to use people. It ties up with his longing to find meaning, his search for the glamorous, the mystical, the dramatic. Sometimes, failing to find these qualities in his own life, he becomes a kind of spiritual groupie. Or a real groupie. You'll find a lot of Taurus women riding arm in arm with famous pop stars, film actors, peerage. Taurus is sometimes capable of selling himself for a piece of somebody else's action. It's a fair exchange for him, barter of his own value for something he values more. There is a side to Taurus, both male and female, that likes to be kept by somebody else, bought by somebody else, because it states a price, a value. The higher the price, the greater the value.

Fanaticism and opportunism: two distorted faces of the repressed fire in Taurus. The fire signs themselves have both but in a different way, diluted and more honest. With Taurus, these are shadowy qualities, and he is usually unaware that he is displaying them. How to deal with them? Well, like all shadow qualities, it helps to know about them. In the case of the fanaticism, the religious fervours, it helps if Taurus is willing to recognize that life is full of things which are not recognizable through the five senses alone. There are mysteries and layers of meaning to life which elude the pragmatic, statistical approach. This means not trampling, bull-like, over others' values, and it also means not stealing others' values, as in the case of the

opportunism of the Taurean shadow. It involves building one's own values, and learning to value one's own
self. And it means learning flexibility and tolerance.
Then, like Theseus, the Taurean can deal with his own
Minotaur effectively and become what he is truly suited
to be: the preserver, the sustainer, the builder, the
artist, the giver of gifts. Taurus is not a lukewarm,
milksop sign. You'd expect him to pack a pretty
powerful wallop on the shadow side. Likewise, you'd
expect him to have enormous strength and endurance,
patience and courage, on the positive side. Never mind
those mild, pretty descriptions of Ferdinand among the
flowers. Remember that he's a bull. The power of the
earth itself flows through him.

♉ The Taurus Lover

Let's deal first with the obvious. Taurus is a very
physical sign. It's a rare Taurean that doesn't possess a
strong, intense desiring nature. Taurus is sensual, loves
beauty, and can be entirely sybaritic. This is not the
sign for the ascetic, unless you want one hell of a
religious fanatic instead.

For many Taureans, the sexual side of a relationship
is the thing which takes top priority. Where there's
good sex, there the Taurus remains. It would be a
mistake to assign any particular morality to Taurus; it
depends on his personal viewpoint, his generation, and
his private values. If he chooses to be faithful, he's very
faithful. If he doesn't, he'll happily pursue his sensual
pleasures on the side, getting enormous satisfaction
from them, yet never allowing them to interfere with
the stability of a marriage. Remember that stability is
really important to Taurus. So, of course, is satisfaction.
The way to keep a Taurus in a relationship is not to

play sexual games of now-you-can-have-me, now-you-can't. He'll just find something more available.

Taurus, being Venus-ruled, has a sense of the romantic. It isn't stylishly romantic like Libra, or slightly dissipated like Pisces, or intense and shady like Scorpio. It's good old storybook romanticism, because Taurus has a conventional streak. The old time-honoured rituals and ways work best. A true Taurean keeps promises, doesn't promise unless he's sure, and isn't sure until he's checked all the facts on the situation. No, that isn't very romantic. But his romanticism, heavy-handed though it sometimes is, is genuine. He really believes in engagement rings and white wedding dresses. They're concrete representations of his feelings. Taurus is apt to give gifts, to demonstrate emotion. This can be both flattering and difficult, because often emotion doesn't come easily to his fixed, cautious nature.

Because he's very conscious of stability, it's a rare Taurean that flies in and out of relationships. He may fly in and out of sexual encounters, but 'relationship' to him has a heavy sound. Often his sense of responsibility, coupled with his need for security, will keep him in a relationship which has long since lost its charm. In this case he'll very likely find the charm elsewhere, so long as it doesn't rock the foundations of the secure home. And Taurus can be maddening in his simplicity. Relationship means you're physically present. It's difficult to talk about deeper nuances with a Taurus. You must be literal, because Taurus often has trouble with inferences. He's likely to believe what you say, and be equally blunt himself. When you talk about things like unconscious hostility and emotional blackmail and other undercurrent stuff that a Scorpio would take to like a duck to water, Taurus will often turn his head away in disgust. What are you talking about? Show him. Put it in the palm of his hand. Often he won't look at the forces building up underneath that so often wreck the best relationships, simply because his vision is tied to what is in the shop window.

Taurus can be poignantly gentle, tender and affectionate. Because it's a very physical sign, most Taureans need tactile expression of love. Once again, this can either be flattering and nourishing, or it can be suffocating. You may have heard about the famous Taurus possessiveness. Taurus is indeed a possessive sign; though for different reasons from Scorpio, also notorious for his jealousy. Taurus possesses, which means that like the treasured paintings, the valuable antiques, the rare old books, you're *his* (or hers) and that's that. Taurus will often demonstrate this in public by physical gestures of the property-ownership variety. It depends upon your taste. Taurus is not the sign to get involved with if you like detachment and open relationships, not if he's in love.

It takes a lot to goad a Taurus into anger. The endless patience and easygoing calm in this sign are a blessing and a relief to anybody who seeks tranquillity and peace in a relationship. On the other hand, push him too far, and you have the proverbial angry bull. And once he's angry, Taurus can be physically violent. He's rarely subtle enough to deliver verbal bites like Virgo and Gemini, or manipulate poisonous atmosphere like Scorpio. His language is simple: smash the china, or punch you in the face.

One way to observe this violence is to flaunt your freedom from him. Once an agreement has been made, it's a sure way to anger Taurus. Another is to threaten his material security. Taurus women, in divorce or separation, are apt to hang on to the house, the car, the furniture and the bank account with teeth bared and fingernails poised for the attack. Take away his possessions, his stability, and you have a very angry – and a very insecure – bull.

For loyalty and steadfastness, no one beats a Taurus. For calmness verging on complacency, too, no one beats a Taurus. Like all sign combinations, matches for Taurus depend upon your personal taste. Taurus is often attracted to fiery temperaments, who possess the daring, childlike abandon, gambling instincts, love of danger, imagination and rashness that he himself doesn't dare express. Taurus needs fire to warm him, loosen him, show him that other dimensions of reality exist. He needs fire for faith in life, since his own faith is largely built on what's in the bank. He also needs fire for creative inspiration, as a muse. And the more volatile temperaments, the gypsies and the wanderers, the visionaries and the prophets, need Taurus, because like the earth he supports and sustains, protects and cherishes, and because his strength in coping with the ordinary problems of life is endless. And because, unlike more complicated signs, he simply wants to be happy; and happiness for him is not so difficult to find. And his simplicity and love of the natural make it a little easier for others to find too.

♉ The Taurus Man

The bull is an extremely masculine animal. Although Taurus is considered to be a feminine sign, the male version doesn't display much femininity – unless you consider as feminine the qualities of gentleness, sensuousness, and love of beauty. But Taurus tends to run a little macho in many men – largely because it's so physical, and also because Taurus is a sign that's very sensitive to the collective roles which society offers. So the Taurus man is apt to collect the accoutrements of what society considers masculine, from clothes to stance to his possessiveness of his woman.

Many of the characters in romantic historical fiction appear to be Taureans. The strong, silent hero – a sort of cross between Clint Eastwood and Hercules – is a Taurean figure. He's usually terribly handsome (and Taurus usually is – if not in the conventional, regular-featured way, then in a pleasing, earthy, sensual quality) and also beautifully dressed. That last is one of Taurus men's frequent traits: sometimes known as vanity, other times known as good taste. Taurus likes elegance, and many Taurus men – although not necessarily 'foppish' – spend an awfully long time with hair, shoes, finger-nails, aftershave. These are all physical pleasures, signs of physical beauty and physical style. It's a rare Taurus man who hasn't got that streak of vanity tucked away somewhere. After all, Venus rules them – and Venus was perpetually before her mirror.

The powerful passions are another fictional hero's trait apparent in many Taurus men. If you like strong sensuality, Taurus possesses it in abundance. Many Taurus men also pride themselves on their sexual prowess; physical love, like physical beauty, is important to them, and not something to be either hurried or done badly.

On the other hand, you may not like strong, silent heroes. You may like a lot of chatter now and again, or a little ambiguity. In that case stay away from Taurus. He's not good at games. And even when you find him in the worst possible situation, somehow he seems wholesome. You just can't remove that sheen of the good earth itself from him. D. H. Lawrence's 'natural man' (you can find him in *Lady Chatterley's Lover* and other novels) must have been a Taurus. The explicit sexuality, the complete absence of embarrassment over any aspect of the human body, are typically Taurus.

You may, however, like a little more flair, or some-thing a little shadier. Try a Libran, a Scorpio or a Pisces. Taurus men can be infuriatingly simple. When they don't wish to understand something, they block it out. They tell you you're being unreasonable, irrational, or silly. And they patronize. This is one of the more irritating qualities about the Taurean man: he can be smug. Because he's not easily ruffled himself, he often has contempt or a blank response to someone else's anxiety, fear, or nervousness. Then you get the pat on the head and the suggestion to take an aspirin and get a good night's sleep. Or a good night in alternative ways, a great cure-all in Taurus' health handbook.

When you're a mess, he can be a rock of strength and calmness. On the other hand, he probably won't understand your mess, so don't bother attempting to explain it unless you can explain it simply. He has no patience for 'female hysterics'. Everything should have a simple solution. Some things unfortunately have no solution. In these cases Taurus refuses to see the dilemma.

And be careful not to betray him. Expecting understanding for convoluted games gets you nowhere. Taurus is terribly vulnerable where his more romantic feelings are concerned; if he's invested you with his romantic ideal, he will simply be wounded and bewildered if you give double messages. It's possible to string a Taurus along for a long time, because he tends to love with fixity; but once you've pushed too far, he's equally capable of throwing you and all your belongings out of the house and never speaking to you again. Fixed is fixed, in love or hate. And Taurus isn't terribly good at forgiving. Forgetting, perhaps; or simply not discussing. But forgiving, no. He'll remember, for a long, long time.

You also may have heard of the famous laziness of the Taurus male. Yes, it's true. Taurus can be incredibly, overwhelmingly indolent. His idea of relaxation may be a can of beer in front of the TV watching *Match of the Day*, while you have more glamorous things in mind. He also has a tendency to sit with feet up on the table

waiting for dinner to be served: not an attitude calculated to win the heart of the feminist. He loves being
spoiled, and often takes it as his due. It depends once
again, on your taste. Remember that, no matter how
lurid his past or iconoclastic his views, deep down he's
conventional, and probably will always have a touch of
the male chauvinist about him. But that isn't really so
bad, if you remember that it's nice to have an identifi-
ably male male around. Taurus men have a way of
making women feel very female. Who can complain?

♉ The Taurus Woman

As the bull is a supremely masculine creature, the cow
is supremely female. Sometimes, in modern usage,
cowlike is considered to mean dull, slow, boring. But
the Greeks saw the cow differently; they named the
goddess of love and desire, Venus, the Cow-Eyed. And
the Egyptians also had a cow-goddess, Hathor, a symbol
of the fertility of the earth and of woman. The female
Taurus is often the epitome of the instinctual feminine
– the dream-image of many men, and with all the
softness, strength, wisdom, patience, and passion of her
goddess-antecedents.

There seem to be two distinct types of Taurus woman.
The first is the real Venusian Taurus. These are the
lovely ones, with perfect complexions, surrounded by
beautiful scent, dressed in sensuous, expensive clothes.
Janet Reger probably does a thriving business in glamorous, pure silk, underclothes for the Taurus women of
this world. Pampered, indolent, sensuous, and very
concerned both with their own attractiveness and their
capacity to please a man, they owe a lot to the old
temple priestesses in the days when the power of the
earth goddess represented the power of life itself. This

228 Star Signs for Lovers

kind of Taurus woman is the ideal feminine for many men. Her problem is that she often doesn't do much, or think much, of anything else.

The Venus Taurean woman is devoted, and usually loyal – provided you give her security, and take care of her, and pamper her. She will offer everything of herself, and her tenacity and faithfulness is admirable. Sometimes it's too admirable; try to release yourself from a relationship with a Taurean woman like this, and you have to be either very callous or give up, since she'll hang on with that incredible Taurean tenacity until you give up and come back out of sheer exhaustion. Taurus women can wait; and they often do wait, and wait, and wait, for the commitment or the promise. As we mentioned earlier, Taurus is attracted to fire. Many Taurus women are fascinated by the fiery types – unfortunately the least reliable of all the men of the zodiac. They love glamour and success and a little dash, a little fleet-of-foot unpredictability. They themselves are willing and ready to play earth mother. Be sure you want an earth mother. Flirtatious at the beginning, Taurus settles into stability very easily and quickly. The benefits of the care and love of a Taurus woman are inestimable. If you prize your freedom, however, try another sign, like Gemini or Aquarius.

The other type of Taurus woman is the 'natural' type. She is still an earth-mother and her qualities of devotion, gentleness, steadfastness and strength are as much present here, perhaps more so. But these are the women who eschew makeup, eat healthily, live in the country, despise cigarette smoke, and want to go back to the old ways of life. If you have that secret fantasy of the cottage in the country covered with climbing roses, with your own horse stabled in the field behind, and the lovely smell of fresh-baked bread wafting out from the kitchen, this kind of Taurus woman is for you. Be careful, though, if you get fidgety easily. If you like to travel, give her at least three months' notice. And don't, for God's sake, change plans at the last minute.

Taurus women are often very literal. That is, they believe what you say, and hold you to it the next day. If you're one of those people who changes his mind a lot, be careful. Taurus is capable of hurling at you, 'But you said you loved me' 'But that was a year ago,' you reply. 'So what?' retorts Taurus. 'You promised.' And so it goes. If you promise, mean it. She simply doesn't understand, otherwise. And you get cast in the role of the bastard.

No matter what the Taurus woman goes through – from expensive call-girl to business manager – there is an innate naïveté and wholesomeness, a naturalness, that experience doesn't seem to be able to quench. Even the Taurus woman, whose practical abilities and business acumen and persistence have led her to build a career for herself in the world, possesses this naïveté. Simplicity is perhaps a kinder word. It can be both – charming ingenuousness or unfuriating literalness. But the great gift of the Taurus woman is her ability to keep things within the realm of common sense, whether it's in a domestic environment or at a job. Her eye for the realistic, the stable, the reliable, is inerringly accurate. She's a poor judge of people, because people are more complex and have layers. Her eye for facts of a tangible kind is fantastically accurate. And her common sense is a wonderful elixir for the jaded visionary who has seen so many possibilities, and dissipated so many talents, that he can't see the point any longer. Taurus brings things down to earth. And because it's a gentle sign, it's likely to be a soft landing.

Virgo

7o begin with, we can throw away everybody's favourite image of that eternal ashtray-emptier and furniture-duster. The neat, orderly, tidy soul with the perfectly balanced bank account and the immaculate kitchen is a picture which sends most Virgos into fits of cynical laughter. And even the virtuous, virginal lady with the unbound hair (discreetly clothed) which adorns jewellery and zodiacal knick-knacks doesn't have much to do with our theme either. For some rather elusive reasons – reasons which might just lie, as so much astrological misunderstanding does, in the attempt during medieval times to Christianize or make 'moral' a symbolic system that is far older and more inclusive than Christianity – Virgo is sadly misinterpreted. Some signs come out rather badly when you try to moralize symbols into social concepts, and Virgo and Scorpio have been hit the hardest – you're caught between the eternal secretary and the eternal sex maniac. Well, like many Scorpios, Virgos are getting pretty resentful about all this misrepresentation. Especially the untidy ones, who are quite shamelessly slovenly and not in the least concerned with whether they arrive at one minute before eight or one minute after. It has been suggested that Virgos have not yet come into their own because the real ruler of Virgo – Vulcan – has not yet been discovered. There has been, however, a discovery made of a strange little 'planet' between Saturn and Uranus, which astronomers were quick to call Chiron for reasons best known to themselves but which might just fill the bill. We don't know yet. Never mind. What is Virgo really about, if not the eternal janitor of the zodiac?

Let's bear in mind first of all that each sign has a deep, fundamental drive in it, a basic motivation which always spurs the individual, whether he is aware of it or not. This basic drive shows in different ways for different people. We've already touched on these – how, for example, the drive toward understanding that motivates Sagittarius makes some Centaurs travellers and others scholars. Physical or emotional or mental, the expression still comes from the same source. And suffice it to say that Virgo's basic drive isn't toward cleanliness. It has been suggested that perfectionism is a Virgo characteristic. I haven't found this to be the case. Discrimination, yes. Absolutely. No one is more discriminating than the Virgo. A simple yes or a simple no doesn't work; it's yes to this part and possibly to that part and probably no to that middle one unless A or B can be changed, and certainly no to the last. Never black and white. Black and white choices imply a simple universe, and to Virgo the universe is rarely simple. It's more like a huge, boundless jigsaw puzzle, and it drives Virgo crazy if he hasn't got a picture of the puzzle on the top of the box before he begins to assemble the puzzle. Discrimination is a finely developed faculty with Virgo. You can see it in his choice of friends, lovers, food, ideas, lifestyle, clothes, reading, artistic taste, or any other area where choices are to be made. But to be a perfectionist means you have to be idealistic, since you have to have an ideal of what constitutes the perfect. And Virgo is no idealist. It's one of the most realistic, possibly the most realistic sign of the zodiac. Virgo harbours no impossible rosy visions of a perfect utopian world, or even a perfect utopian kitchen. Virgo uses what comes to hand, what appears on the plate. The element of earth, remember, is the element that pertains to acceptance of earth plane reality. And no perfectionist ever accepted reality.

It has been suggested, too, that there are two types of Virgos, the neat ones and the sloppy ones. This is probably true as far as it goes. There are two types of any sign – the introverted and the extroverted. The extroverted version of any zodiacal sign tends to express himself out in the world. So the extroverted Aries finds challenges in the world, the extroverted Sagittarian explores the world, the extroverted Pisces projects his visions into the world, and so on. The extroverted Virgo no doubt tries to apply his need to classify and order and synthesize at a worldly level. The introverted versions of the signs express their natures through an inner reality. So the introverted Capricorn is spiritually or psychologically ambitious, the introverted Sagittarian travels the boundless leagues of the mind and spirit, the introvert Pisces communes with the depths of his own inner ocean with its mysterious denizens, and the introverted Virgo attempts to synthesize and order himself. Which means that the sink may well accumulate a truly ripe treasure-trove of week-old dishes, the house may accumulate a formidable array of objects in general disarray, and the world may well go to pieces so far as Virgo is concerned – so long as he's performing that long, alchemical labour within his own depths, on himself.

Notice that word synthesis. It offers much more of a key to Virgo's basic motivation than perfectionism. Synthesis means bringing together different things, like a good cook performing miracles of culinary genius with a random array of leftover bits from yesterday's meals. Synthesis also means finding compatible things or ideas or aspects of life which most people find mutually exclusive. Virgo's compulsion and gift both lie in this area of synthesis. Everything must be fitted together and made to blend. That means finding out where everything fits by naming it, learning about it, categorizing it, classifying it. A friend of mine once referred to Virgo as the Great Classifier. With Mercury, god of intelligence and communication, as the present ruler of the sign, you'd expect a love of acquiring knowledge. The difference between Virgo and Gemini, however, both of which are ruled by Mercury, is that Gemini loves bits and snippets of knowledge for their own sake. For Virgo, knowledge is relevant only if it's useful.

So in a way, you can say that this little internal voice is always echoing in poor Virgo's mind with every new experience he meets. How can I synthesize it? he says, and then, How can I use it? If he can't synthesize it, he'll pretend it doesn't exist, or begin a dogged pursuit of names and definitions which will allow him to pigeonhole that experience to make it manageable. If it can't be used, he'll discard it with a certain flippant arrogance. Yes, that's fine for more impractical souls.

The drive to discriminate sometimes makes Virgo harsh. He will throw aside people or ideas or careers or things of beauty because they may not be effectual or applicable to what he considers practical reality. Sometimes he throws romance out as well, which is a tragic thing since you then find that type of Virgo for whom life is work and drudgery. Often he's a cynic, looking at reality with jaundiced eyes; he knows perfectly well that you have to be clever to survive, and he's prepared to hustle a little and make the effort of polishing the goods because that makes them more saleable. If he's going to do something, he'll do it well, both from pride in craftsmanship and from a good marketing sense. Idealistic perfection? Hardly.

Sometimes the only tidy thing you see around Virgo is his bookshelf, for many Virgos respect to an inordinate degree the entire field of knowledge. His books are to him the personifications of his mind, and his mind is often like one of those intricate workings of a delicate Swiss watch, ceaselessly moving and cataloguing and reflecting and considering and labelling. He may live with a heap on the living room carpet, but you can bet he's cleaning up his psyche. A lot of Virgos take to astrology like ducks to water – that is, if they can ever get over the resistance to the aura of vague spiritualism which popular columns have mistakenly cast upon the study – because astrology and other cosmological maps offer them confirmation that the universe is basically orderly, and that God Himself is innately tidy.

The impulse to be of service also runs strong in Virgo. Virgos need to be needed, and they need to feel useful. The typical Virgo is not particularly ambitious; he lacks the onesidedness necessary to go after one goal wholeheartedly. In many ways his tendency to look for wider and wider pieces to complete the great jigsaw puzzle takes away any propensity for him to focus everything on one piece. It's a rare Virgo who aims for the position of obvious power. Most of the time you find them as advisors or counsellors to someone else who's silly enough to have taken the throne and subjected himself to all that trouble. Virgo, clever as always, prefers to lurk behind the throne and keep himself out of the line of fire. Realistic, remember? Foolhardy Leos and Ariens and Capricorns aim for the top. Virgo knows that what goes up must come down; he'd rather keep his feet on the ground, thank you very much. Unless a Virgo has a lot of Leo in his chart, or the sun strongly placed in the horoscope, you'll usually meet him only through his work, rather than through his outgoing personality. Most characteristic Virgos are quite shy, or if not actually retiring, then subtle and quieter than their friends born under other signs. Being earthy, Virgo does like his security, and the need for security is often a problem because it keeps Virgo from trying out creative possibilities that require daring and a little bit of a gamble. Ask a typical Virgo to gamble and he'll get a white, shocked look. Gamble? How horrible! You never know when life might deal you a blow; better to plan and prepare for the future. You often meet Virgos who have been rooted in rather limiting jobs for many years, where their natural intelligence and imagination are stifled, because of the wonderful security of that regular salary cheque. Besides, Virgo is more curious about what makes the wheels on the car run than he is being the driver and entering the race. He's a student and observer of life rather than a gambler or an entrepreneur. It's said that Virgos make better servants than rulers. This is undoubtedly true. Remember the historical characters like Cardinal Richelieu. Being a power behind the throne suits Virgo very well. Craftsmanship and craftiness often run together in this subtle sign. Mercury, in mythology, was also the god of thieves and liars, and presided over the business deal.

There's another trait, sometimes endearing and sometimes infuriating, that's worth noting here about Virgo. This is his obsessiveness. He may be obsessive about order or tidiness in the obvious way, but equally often he's obsessive about emotional orderliness and tidiness. That is, never show your own emotional weaknesses. Virgo is a great controller of emotion. In fact, if you watch a more obsessional Virgo for a while, you begin to get the queer feeling that he's organizing rituals to keep the forces of darkness at bay. Whether it's the object-obsessive Virgo who puts all the yellow shirts on the left side of the cupboard and falls into a hysterical fit if you introduce a blue one, or the tight-lipped emotionally constricted Virgo who analyses everything in a kind of frenzied desire to keep any ripped psychological seam from showing, the root is the same. You guessed it. All that chaos and emotional sensitivity and sloppiness and romanticism and vision lurk secretly in the recesses of Virgo's soul. He has to fight against his own chaos far too often to be tolerant of vagueness and woolliness in others or in the world around him. There's too much of it in him. Virgo's apparent hardness and ruthlessness – no sign is quite so adept at saying 'no' – is often his way of protecting himself against an intolerable sensitivity. His famous meanness – and no doubt about it, many Virgos are really mean with money – is often a coverup for a streak of innate extravagance. And his insistent compulsion to stick to practical realities helps him to escape the mystic in his own soul.

A queer bird, Virgo. Not far beneath the cool and analytic veneer you find a sentimental romantic. Virgo may be brusque in manner, and don't try to borrow money unless you've proven you can repay it. You'll rarely find Virgo as you find Pisces, who will offer his last pound to the drunk in Picadilly Circus. Virgo's more likely to deliver a stern and frequently insufferably irritating lecture about self-help. But often this is because he's too acutely aware of the drunks, derelicts, rejects and flotsam of life, and has a real horror that he might become one himself. Planning for and guaranteeing the safety of the future is an obsession with Virgo, because his acute sense of the world as it is often makes it hard for him to have faith or trust in life. He can't cope with that reality he's so plugged into. It threatens his sense of stability. So he shuts it out – discriminating like mad against any elements of it he can't deal with – and looks out for number one. You'll often find Virgo being generous and apparently altruistic, giving freely of his time and skills, especially when it comes to teaching somebody how to do something. He loves to show his competence and is genuinely generous in sharing his knowledge. But you'll rarely find Virgo giving beyond that ring-pass-not. He usually learns his lesson early. It's almost as though he has a secret Piscean in him somewhere, and he's learned Pisces' lesson – with no boundaries comes self-disintegration. After all, it's only realistic.

♍ The Myth

Modern language sometimes does some very funny things with words and concepts that come from the pre-Christian era. For example, take the latin word *virgo*. This is usually interpreted as virgin, with all its sexual implications. So the typical Virgo portrayed in popular astrology is virginal, i.e., prudish or inhibited or sexually cool. One need only look at some well-known film personalities born under Virgo, like Sophia Loren and Jacqueline Bisset and Sean Connery, to feel a little silly about equating Virgo with lack of sexual interest or appeal. Remember that the key word is discrimination, and you'll have a better idea of the nature of Virgo's sexuality. But more of that later. Let's go back to what the word *virgo* once meant. It had, in fact, nothing to do with sexual virginity, but simply meant intact, self-contained. The great mythical figure that stands behind Virgo is the Great Goddess, the Magna Mater, and she was no virgin. In fact she is often portrayed in myth as the Great Harlot, the fecund one. There is a magnificent statue of the virgin goddess Artemis, one of many names for the Great Goddess, portrayed with fifty breasts to show that she represents the nurturer and giver of life to all of life. But she is *virgo* in the sense that she is self-possessed, her own person. In early mythology, from which we inherit the figure of the Virgin Goddess, before the Hellene invasion from the north into the agricultural civilizations of the Aegean in around 2000 B.C., the Goddess did not owe her powers or her status to a divine husband as we see her in later mythology. She ruled alone, self-contained, husbandless, yet offering her femininity freely as she chose. She was the consort of all life. This is a clue to the deepest meaning of Virgo: the ultimate goal of this apparently humble sign is nothing less than the self-possessed psyche, the person who is integrated within himself and can therefore give freely because he need not fear losing himself in another. He can choose life's experiences from his own place of completeness, rather than because his need for finding himself in another drives him into relationships or situations which destroy him or rule him. Sometimes you see this pattern of becoming one's own person lived out in the lives of Virgos through the necessity to live alone for a period of time. In fact this seems to be almost a requirement for Virgo to develop himself or herself. Difficult as it is for any person to face loneliness, many Virgos impose it on themselves, not because they don't need others, but because something in them says that you must first learn to be yourself and love your own company before you can allow another person to be himself.

The zodiacal circle of twelve signs is divided into halves. The first half – Aries through Virgo – is often taken to symbolize the stages of individual development. The second half – Libra through Pisces – is often taken to symbolize the individual's relationship to the larger whole, society, other people, the world.

Virgo is the last of the first half of the zodiac, the cycle of individual development which we mentioned earlier. This means that Virgo in its deepest sense is about the real synthesis and integration of the individual, the refinement and ordering of all the experiences which have come from the first five signs. In an odd way you can see this in Virgo, just as you see it in Pisces, the last sign of the second half of the zodiac. In Pisces you can see the world, for the sign stands at the end of the great round. Pisceans contain the whole of human experience. It's why they can identify with anybody, sometimes much to their cost. Virgo contains all the stages of individual development. He's been through the rash impulsive courage of Aries challenging life. He's been through the building and acquiring stability of Taurus. He's been through the curiosity and fascination with ideas of Gemini. He's been through the need for warmth and family and roots of Cancer. He's been through the need to be creative and individual in Leo. You can see a sort of matter-of-fact Yes, I've done that quality in many Virgos when they watch those other signs. It's as though it's stored somewhere in their memory banks. And their job, their business, is about taking all those different stages and kinds of experience and not specializing in one but rather making a refined and well-functioning whole out of it. It's one of the reasons you find so many Virgos obsessed with health and diet, and equally many obsessed with psycholgy and self-help. They're trying hard to knit the whole thing together, to become the efficiently functioning person who can deal with any experience. But because Virgo is the final summation of the first cycle, any experience means any personal encounter, not an encounter with the group. Virgo isn't ready to go out into the bigger life of society. He keeps himself to himself. That's Libra's job. The compulsive self-perfecting that you find in so many Virgos, the endless stream of books and workshops and talks and lessons about how to be healthy, how to learn this, how to master that, all these things have a deep symbolic root. It's the need to prepare the vessel, to craft it, shape it, refine it, for some vaguely sensed next phase for which Virgo waits without really knowing what it is he's waiting and preparing for.

All myths are profound, and unless we make a little effort to think on a level of life other than what's for dinner, and on a level of astrology other than that Virgos make good typists, there's no way out of the snakepit of meaninglessness we have built with our own smallness. As we watch our Virgo friends and lovers and children busily rushing about with their dietary fads, their psychological self-development techniques, their new methods of do-it-yourself house building or auto repair, their obsessions and compulsions, we can see here – as with every other sign – a deep drive and a profound myth trying to express itself. Ashtray-emptying aside, the Goddess as self-contained nurturer of life is a fitting and noble image for this underplayed sign.

Virgo is also connected with the strange picture-language and concepts of medieval alchemy. Every Virgo, in some way, little or big, is an alchemist. Now, medieval alchemy doesn't really have anything to do with the practice of making gold, any more than Virgo has to do with virginity. If you read old alchemical texts, you'll hear them constantly saying that alchemical gold isn't ordinary gold. It's transmuted substance, inner gold, spiritual gold, creative gold. It's about purification, of taking something clumsy and crude and base and transforming it so that the real potential shines out of it. Whether it's his car or his body or his psyche, this laborious process of transmutation goes on throughout Virgo's life. One way or another, whether it's himself or other people or the disorderly world, his business, his environment or the products of his skilful hands, Virgo is attempting the alchemical transformation. It isn't really the outside world he's trying to order and synthesize. It's life. And life, ultimately, is himself.

♍ The Shadow

With a sign as obsessive as Virgo, you might expect a fairly twitchy shadow. How right you are. Virgo's shadow side is complex, like his ordinary consciousness. One main face of it we might call the 'I know it all' syndrome. It goes something like this.

WIFE: (*to Virgo husband*) I've just discovered something really interesting. It was in my oil painting class. If you dilute oil paints with turps and float them on water and then dip paper . . .

VIRGO: Yes, yes, I know all about that. I learned to do it years ago. But you have to make sure you don't use too much turps, or it gets too runny. Next time let me help you with it.

WIFE: But my paintings came out really well. (*Feeling slightly deflated because it would be really nice, once in a while, to surprise him with something he didn't already know.*)

VIRGO: I'm sure they did. It's just that I might be able to help you mix the colours better. It's not easy.
WIFE: Oh, and I read in the paper today . . .
VIRGO: I know. About the new budget cuts.
WIFE: Yes. I really think that if the government expects to help the economy, they ought to . . .
VIRGO: Before you criticise the bill, you should really learn more about it. I studied political and economic philosophy for years. I'm convinced it's the best thing they could possibly do.
WIFE: But . . .
VIRGO: Never mind, I know I'm right.

Sounds fairly innocent on the surface. Just an ordinary know-it-all. But the destructive side of Virgo's shadow takes a long time to bear its fruits. Try this on somebody over a period of a few years and you never allow them ever to learn anything, find out anything, think anything, that they can give you. You've taken it all already. You know it beforehand. It's one of the most insidious and deadly ways of crushing another person's creativity that could happen. And it's one of the darker edges of Virgo. The Virgo shadow slowly and in tiny, unnoticeable steps, completely erodes another individual's trust in their own self, mistakes or not. The Virgo shadow, as one of its compulsions, has a positively horrific fear of being mistaken or wrong. There is something about having something not quite known, labelled, classified, that is intolerable. But life is full of mistakes, and so are people, and so, probably, is God. The Virgo shadow, in its own way, kills life, because it tries to remove life's unpredictability and unevenness.

Another similar face of this shadow is the I-told-you-so syndrome. No great detail is needed to describe it, since we've all met it, in somebody else or in ourselves. It makes you feel like killing. That smug, faintly satisfied look that Virgo can sometimes get – when he warned you about something and you blundered and he knew all along that you would – makes you want to fill the bathtub with piranhas. It's another way of never permitting anything to happen which is unexpected, messy, incomplete. It's Virgo's way of saying, 'But I never would have blundered like that, I know better.'

You get the picture. What is this shadow about? Well, for one thing, it stems from Virgo's fear of the unknown. When a Virgo is really being true to himself, he's ordinarily maybe a little cautious, but not ridiculous about it. He's sensitive, he knows it, the world is difficult and full of changes and problems, and he usually works to find skills and tools which can help him cope. But a Virgo who is really insecure just goes off limits with his caution. Tell him anything new and he'll either pretend he's learned it already, or tell you it's untrue. Show him a side of yourself he hasn't met yet and he'll criticize it or tell you how to fix it, because it threatens his pattern. Show a little spontaneity and he'll try to crush it, because it terrifies him. Show some unexpected emotion and he'll go blank and numb because he doesn't know how to classify it or deal with it. All this is part of the Virgo shadow. It has to do with control, as do all shadows. And with Virgo, it's a kind of crazy, naïve, ludicrous attempt to control life so that it won't contain any unknown and threatening elements.

There's another type of Virgo shadow you sometimes see, and this happens when Virgo's sensitivity has been bruised too badly. We might call it the Hustler. The Hustler is a face of Virgo which appears when reality and its difficulties weigh too heavily on the scale, while hope and faith and trust weigh too light. Then the Hustler appears. He uses Virgo's naturally canny commercial nose and twists it so that everything must be bargained for. The Hustler makes everything into a deal. He's also prepared to sell anything, at a price. In some ways the ancient mythical image of the Great

Harlot has here become the mean hooker. Translated, it means, sure, I'll sell that, what's it worth to you? Anything to get a little salted away. Any individual is a potential customer, a potential soak. And this is perhaps the most tragic side of Virgo's shadow, because this happens only when Virgo has become so disillusioned or so frightened that he must put up barriers against everything. Even love is for sale then, and the 'suitable' marriage must include the right amount of money in the bank account. It isn't beyond this side of Virgo's shadow to check your credentials before that first date is accepted. It's also sometimes known as psychological usury.

Sadly, this side of the Virgo shadow appears most frequently in male Virgos. I have come to the conclusion that it's because society makes it a little difficult for the Virgo man. This is a sensitive and receptive sign, not naturally ambitious, and often very aware of subtle undercurrents and intuitive interchanges which elude the thicker-skinned signs. It's also a sign naturally inclined to flow rather than lead. These aren't part of the conventional macho image men are supposed to carry in our culture. The Virgo man often has a hard time being himself in a world which requires him to be more insensitive than compassionate, more successful than skilful, more leader than craftsman, more money-maker than lover of nature. So the Hustler side of the Virgo shadow appears, and it isn't a very loveable one.

All shadows dissolve when light is brought to bear on them. This one is no exception. For a Virgo seeing himself in the light – complete with what he's really afraid of – is a great healer. For him to try, just once, to trust himself and others and life rather than demanding that everything be named and guaranteed is also a great healer. And for him to recognize that life has mysteries he'll never understand or explain, and chaos that maybe shouldn't ever be ordered, and pockets of mistakes and slips and messiness that perhaps don't really need tidying, is the greatest healer of all. In other words, Virgo the realist isn't really very realistic. The reality he sees is only the tangible one. It's the other one he needs to find, and to trust. Then he can become what the myth portrays: the one who can heal and nurture and bring life, whether to people or ideas or his art, because he's made peace with the unknown.

♍ The Virgo Lover

I once came across a kind of joke horoscope which gave a particularly insulting paragraph to each sign. For Virgo, it said, 'Virgos are apt to fall asleep while making love. They make good bus drivers.' Well, amusing enough. But it reflects the general attitude most popular astrology holds about the Virgo lover. And sadly, many Virgos do nothing to dispel this image.

I once knew a Virgo man who kept by his bedside one of those ubiquitous sex primers which told you which erogenous zone the left hand should be placed on after the first five minutes of foreplay. He actually attempted to follow the instructions, as though he were following a recipe. Virgos tend to like instructions, on boxes, packages, books, or whatever. Take the instructions away and they often panic. This Virgo wondered why it was that he didn't seem to be able to keep his lover's interest. It goes back again to the problem Virgo has with the unknown. And sexuality and love are both mysteries about which we know virtually nothing. As the novelist Robert Musil wrote,

> There is still a great deal unknown about this phenomenon capable of transporting an ordinarily 'civilized' man and woman into a state which under other

circumstances we would associate only with a frothing lunatic.

This isn't, however, what Virgo's nature is really about. It's just that he often sees himself as the potential frothing lunatic, and tries to make sure it doesn't happen. Then you get the apparently cool and unromantic Virgo, perhaps sexually skilled but emotionally invisible, who tells you that having it three times a week is good for you because of whatever book he's just finished. Ah, whatever happened to the Great Harlot?

Virgo unleashing his sensuality, however, is a different creature altogether. In common with Taurus and Capricorn, Virgo is earthy, and that means metaphorically as well as astrologically. His sexual needs are often deep and sensuous, and his sensitivity and delicacy allow him – or her – to be aware of another person's needs in a very acute way which hastier signs don't notice. The problem, as always, is in releasing that sensual side. It's said that Virgo takes a long time to warm up. This is probably true. In part, it's because of that old fear of the unknown, the chaotic. Passion isn't exactly something that can be defined and rendered safe.

Another reason for Virgo's apparent slowness in love is that he's not really easily fooled or a sucker for a pretty face, male or female. Virgo thinks too much. That means that he needs to communicate, to have some basis for relationship other than a sexual one. Often his work life is terribly important to him – Virgos frequently identify with their work and validate themselves according to how well they fulfil their jobs – and if you don't want to share his interest in his work, or talk to him about it, then he'll get pretty tired of even the most voluptuous or exciting partner. Emotion and sexuality aren't enough to hold Virgo. Remember that the sign is ruled by Mercury, and like Gemini, there's got to be some – however slight – meeting of minds.

Virgo's realism also enters the stage here, and makes it rather difficult for this sign to try a wild moonlit love-at-first-sight passion. He observes the world too much, and knows too much, to take that very seriously. Also, he doesn't like gambling, and gambling with instantaneous passions is liable to be hurtful and disillusioning at best. So he may sometimes go very cold and shut out someone to whom he's attracted, because he mistrusts anything sudden, uncontrollable, or unexplainable.

Sometimes you find Virgos apparently kicking over the traces. But look closely. You'll usually find that their hearts haven't really been touched. Male or female, it takes a long time for Virgo to truly thaw on a feeling level. He may even allow himself to fall in love, but to love is for him something that takes time and careful nurturing. He's realistic, you see. In the end, he'll choose the reliable over the flamboyant. You can see that in his taste, his furnishings, his habits. Always pick the useful, the safe, the knowable, the quality, over the bright, the spontaneous, the unreliable, the unpredictable. It can be a terrible bore, or, tempered with a little humour and a sense of fun, it can give a quality of understanding and warmth and wisdom which is both magnetic and highly attractive. The operative word is fun. In love, Virgo often needs to learn the word.

Like everybody else, the things Virgo represses in himself are often the things he seeks in a partner. Virgo, the 'earthbound builder of planes, landlocked craftsman of ships', often orders himself into a meaningless maze. Not seeing the forest for the trees is one way of putting it. He's so busy trying to perfect the vessel that he forgets it's meant to contain something. So Virgo's greatest terror in life is usually his greatest fascination in love: the fiery chaos and spontaneous self-expression of the intuition and imagination, personified by those dashing and unreliable fire signs who seem to have secret pacts with the gods and actually gamble, yes, horrors, gamble, rather than display due caution. When Virgo meets a fiery type, all the repressed child in him longs to escape and be free. Earthbound, Virgo often starves himself of sheer joy in life. He'd rather work, thanks, there's too much to do. Virgo men and women can often be seen with long lists of what must be done each day, and they will inevitably put play as the least relevant of priorities. And Virgo's pattern is often to choose a partner who represents all the irresponsibility and drama he won't allow himself, all the instability and 'selfishness' (Virgo likes to use this word to apply to people who don't follow his priorities). Naturally, these relationships can go two ways. Either Virgo warms up and loosens up and balances himself out, or he tries to play Pygmalion with this lovely raw stone by chipping it into shape. Then comes the scenario of the fiery partner spitting fire like a dragon because he or she is always being 'nagged' or 'criticized'. Relationships are rarely smooth and easy for Virgo, unless he plays terribly safe and finds himself another earthy type who fits into his safe universe. And then, sadly, he's always a little bored, and life's a little dreary, and he feels he's missed the boat, somehow. The recipe for happiness is the same here as for the Virgo shadow. A good liberal dose of the child: to gamble, to play; a dash of recognition that what is useful is not always necessarily what is living and meaningful. And occasionally to be mistaken. To occasionally be a fool, because in our most ancient mythologies the fool is holy.

♍ The Virgo Man

Some of the best Virgoan qualities make their appearance in the Virgo man in love. One of these is his desire to be needed, and his generosity and helpfulness if you need support, talking, understanding, or material assistance. Always reasonable, the Virgo man will often draw you out about your problems, and he loves to offer advice. Give him a problem which is solvable and he'll attack it like a chess game, and often his detached insights are useful and constructive. There's also a safe feeling about him, and a love of truth and accuracy. And Virgo rarely pretends to be anything other than himself. You won't get pushed into the corner to play adoring audience as you might with a Leo or Aries man.

On the other hand, the Virgo man's self-control and coolness can be infuriating. He's sometimes the sort of person who insists on hanging his coat up carefully before he kisses you, because first things must come first. Sometimes he's horribly socially sensitive, and will avoid touch in public because 'somebody' might notice that he's not completely in control, or discover that he has passions. And taken to extremes, you also might have to cope with the scheduling of everything including courtship – which always comes second to work – and even sex – which also often comes second to work.

Remember that it isn't easy to be a Virgo man. The sign, like Pisces, is sensitive and vulnerable, and doesn't easily match the cultural male image. Virgo men often have a chip on their shoulders, because they're trying so hard to be cool and in control. Any emotional need which isn't expressed in neat, structured verbal terms can then seem like an overwhelming demand. There is a strangely self-contained quality in Virgo, which goes back to our myth about the Goddess. For a lover or partner to be able to tolerate this shutting-off tendency in Virgo, he or she needs to keep a sense of humour, because otherwise the criticisms can be taken hurtfully and the entire relationship can blow up with resentment.

The thing that saves this complex and sometimes insufferable temperament from being really intolerable is that Virgo, if you can tell him the truth quietly and clearly, will always listen. It's one of the most endearing qualities in the Virgo man. If he's hurt you, or been cold, or been too structured, try articulating it. Quietly. He'll usually listen. If you express it emotionally, he won't. If you're the combustible type, with a lot of Scorpio or Leo, try a more resilient and less highly-strung temperament. Virgo simply can't take angry explosions and tempestuous scenes, or long weeping sessions with lots of soggy handkerchiefs. You'll often see Virgo men fidgeting, smoking heavily, biting fingernails, and doing other little acts which betray the tightly-strung nervous system of the sign. Given the fact that the Virgo man will usually overwork himself anyway, it doesn't help his naturally fidgety temperament. He needs lots of play, rest, and nature to heal him. Usually he can't be bothered to make time, since that list has 'work' at the top of it. So the onus falls on you to cajole him, reason him, or drag him to someplace where after his initial whingeing he might even discover that it's quite pleasant to sit in the sun and do nothing.

For all these reasons the Virgo man in love is not always every woman's *Brides' Magazine* dream of the perfect husband. It's a sensitive, high-strung, and complex temperament, rarely aggressive, more likely to let trifles and difficulties nag and nag inside before direct action is taken. Virgo isn't Don Juan, although there are some fairly good imitation Don Juans floating about in the form of terribly insecure Virgos trying to pretend

to be Sagittarians and Leos. Trust, quiet, warmth, and
safety are necessary for him to show any of that more
mystical, sensitive side of himself, the one you osten-
sibly chose him for. Hopefully you didn't choose him to
provide you with security, for you're making a sad error
if you think he'll be able to play Supportive Father for
very long. He's too fluid and changeable, and too
terrified of his own propensity to change, to tolerate
being somebody else's rock. Appreciate his intelligence,
his wit, his cynical wisdom, his craftsmanship, his
shrewdness, his kindness and his sensitivity, and you'll
have a very rare creature as a lover. For those who
appreciate subtlety, and wit, and respect inner solitude,
Virgo makes those more flamboyant signs seem pretty
boorish in comparison.

⑪ The Virgo Woman

If you're looking for the perfect housekeeper and have
just read somewhere that Virgo women are masters (or
mistresses) of the art, you should probably bestow your
insult on some other sign. The main gift of the Virgo
woman is her intelligence, not her orderliness; and
when you find the compulsive housebound type who
dusts three times a day then you're courting trouble
because you've got yourself a Virgo who's fallen into
the shadow side of the sign. And all that good house-
keeping will pale into insignificance beside the shrew-
ishness which goes with it. This isn't, we repeat, what
Virgo is about. And it certainly isn't what the Virgo
woman is about. As a by-product it can be a nice bonus,
and there are plenty of Virgo women who take an
interest in their homes and like an orderly environment.
But Virgo as it expresses itself through the feminine
psyche seems to be about things like good taste, and

subtlety, and understanding, and a keen wit about people and life.

There are catches, of course. The self-contained figure of myth is very much in evidence in the Virgo woman, and it's often difficult for Virgo to really be 'married' in any deep sense of the word. There's a quality about the Virgo woman which is psychologically untouchable, and if you try to invade it you get the same reaction as if you tried physical rape. Virgo women aren't usually the clinging, helpless type. More often they're amazons who show a frightening degree of capability and efficiency, either on a physical level or a mental one – or even sometimes both. Good points for Women's Lib, but bad points if you want to be the sun around which a happily reflecting moon orbits.

For one thing, Virgo women have opinions. Mercury's connection with the sign seems to come out in a need to communicate, to talk, sometimes to simply gossip or chat. Many Virgo women talk endlessly. Sometimes it can make you cover your ears and begin screaming, just to make the sound stop. It may not be the traditional Virgo criticism, either. It may be all about the latest book she read, or the film she saw, or the person she's lately been taking apart and analysing psychologically. Virgos love to talk about other people, in great detail. So if you're after the beautiful, silent type, forget it. Virgo women also have a sometimes admirable, some-times infuriating propensity to question your word and your knowledge, too. Tell her something and she'll ask the source, complete with footnotes. Virgo tends not to believe anybody else until the definitive reference work becomes available. It's hard to be more knowledgeable than a Virgo, because they won't allow it. It's got a good and a bad side. It does wonders for your intellec-tual scope, and horrors for your ego.

Many Virgo women come close to the figure of the Earth Mother, because the peculiar sensitivity of the sign expresses itself through a love of nature and a healing and skilful touch with all crafts. It seems to be a typical Virgo skill to have a 'knack' with handicrafts of all kinds. The arts for their own sake rarely attract Virgo, because things must be useful to be relevant. But the Virgo woman often displays immense skill at gardening, and craftsmanship in many areas. And the quality of needing to be needed which attracts so many Virgos into the helping professions, from nursing to dieticians to psychologists and counsellors, is very much an aspect of the Great Mother archetype which is connected with the sign.

The thing is, you often have to find it behind the high-strung nervous system, the edginess, the need for solitude, the apparent coolness and detachment. It's hard for a Virgo woman to be spontaneous. Often she can only show love or affection by doing physical things for you. The same situation applies here as to the Virgo male: emotion and passion are disturbing and frightening, and can only express in an atmosphere of complete trust. Break that trust and you'll get the sarcastic, cutting edge of the Virgo tongue, which can be really vicious because she's been observing with minute care all the weaknesses and foibles which you didn't think anybody noticed. Virgo women have a disconcerting habit of noticing the carefully hidden frayed cuff, the razor nick, the scuffed shoe, the word-slip, the nervous twitch you thought you were controlling. They observe minute things because for Virgo the vast spectrum of life is best reflected in the small. For the Virgo woman, the great art is the art of the small.

It may be appropriate to remind you again of those Virgos who are anything but tight-lipped spinsterish shrews: the Greta Garbos and Sophia Lorens and Jacqueline Bissets of the world. But you can see a thread which runs through these women as well as every other Virgo woman, from Lauren Bacall (another

Virgo) to Twiggy. Notice the attention given to skill. Whatever Virgo does, it does well, and Virgo women are no exception. These are skilled actresses, with polish and impeccable performance. Whether cooking or sculpting or teaching or whatever, Virgo women take pride in their skill. Appreciate it and you'll earn her warmth. Ignore it or undervalue it, and you've made a ghastly mistake. And if you're one of those men who doesn't think it's appropriate for a woman to be skilled in anything except pleasing a man, you're courting real trouble with a Virgo woman. Curiously, Virgo needs lots of respect – a need which isn't always evident in the other signs, which are less likely to identify with their skills. Also notice the quality of cool self-containment about these women. Married or not, they all radiate some mysterious aloofness which is not so much a 'keep out' sign as a 'welcome, but respect my separateness'. It's evident even in the heat of sexual passion or intense emotion with Virgo. Self-contained. If you can learn to deal with the shadowy side, the know-it-all quality, the occasional fits of ordering and tidying either the environment or you, then you can reach the other side of Virgo. Isn't it nice to be able to appreciate someone who is capable of being her own person? While all women, and all people, ultimately strive for this, Virgo makes a career and sometimes an art of it. Virgo won't adore you blindly. She'll more likely love you for your flaws and imperfections, because she's a realist and also it makes her feel needed. And it can either terrify a man into running eighty miles an hour in the opposite direction, or it can be a wonderful cooling bath to actually be able to be yourself. But then, it depends on the sort of man you are, doesn't it?

Capricorn

The Capricornian goat is no ordinary billy-goat munching grass in the pasture. Look closely at the symbol for this most mysterious of the earthy signs, and you will see that he has a tail, a kind of cross between a fish and a serpent. The goat who climbs the awesome mountain of worldly success and material achievement also has another entirely different and usually hidden side to his nature. People who think that Capricorn can be summed up by mundane ambition are sadly mistaken. If we take a look at ancient symbolism, we find that the serpent is one of the oldest representations for instinctual wisdom and the secrets of the earth itself. And the fish is also a creature that swims in the depths of the unknown waters of the psyche. Our mountain goat – hard-working, plodding, cautious, materialistic, shrewd, ambitious – is also, in his secret heart, a kind of magician, a seeker after mysteries. To manipulate and organize the stuff of the world is no mean feat, and takes more than just patience. Whichever realm Capricorn achieves in – the inner or the outer – he applies the same principles to it, and those principles can be summed up in one word: mastery.

It isn't easy to get to know a Capricorn. For one thing, he's usually learned by the tender age of about three that you let the other guy show his cards first, and that sometimes it's necessary to keep an ace or two up your sleeve. There is a curious thing about Capricorn children: sometimes you can look into their eyes and be startled by the little old man peeping out from that childish face. Many Capricorns follow the classical goat's pattern of having to carry responsibility or hardship very early in life. The goat doesn't take kindly to having his secrets probed too quickly. He must first know exactly where he stands, and exactly who you are, and exactly what you want, before he is willing to show his hand. Suspicious? Yes, you might say that. Suspicion is a natural propensity with Capricorn; sometimes it goes the wrong way and becomes profound mistrust of life and people, but the better face of it is caution and realism. Capricorns learn from childhood on – and childhood for them is often no childhood at all, but a too-early initiation into the hard facts of life – that one should always check one's capital and assess one's possible losses before entering any deal. And everything to Capricorn is a kind of deal, even when his motives are the noblest and most altruistic ones. Remember that the keynote of all the earth signs is realism.

This is, in a way, the sign of the ulterior motive. It's also a sign of immense subtlety: never imagine you've worked out all his motives, because there's always one you haven't thought of. Nothing is ever done by a Capricorn without a purpose. All that canny waiting and assessing, hard work and labour, are always directed toward an end. And you don't always see the goat showing his goal on his sleeve like any Sagittarian, or talking about it like any Gemini. Often he'll play the humble servant, the one who has no ambitions, who only seeks to help, while he waits and assesses and plans. But there's no time for wasted time with Capricorn, no space for useless leisure and play. Serious? Yes, you might say that about Capricorn too. His wit is often of the ironic kind, full of a sense of life's incongruities, rather than the broad slapstick of some of the other signs. That ironic wit is part of Capricorn's underplayed charm. But to most goats, life is a serious business, because it has to be mastered if you want to survive.

Survival is another key theme for Capricorn. To the goat, the world isn't always a friendly, bountiful place. It's as if his antennae are always plugged in to what might go wrong, rather than what might go right. As J. D. Smith says,

> The world is nothing but a vast, concerted attempt to catch you with your pants down.

Nothing is ever taken for granted by the goat, least of all luck, which to Capricorn is a highly untrustworthy and often nonexistent commodity. He'd rather replace luck with good, solid hard work, unlike his fire sign cousins. And goals, of course, are another keynote to our perplexing goat. Without goals, Capricorn slides back-end first down that steep mountain path and lands with a rude bump in a big, black depression. Since the world isn't basically a friendly place to him, his goals give him his sense of meaning, and achievement to him is what romance is to the fiery signs. Besides, Capricorn will be the first to tell you, romance is all very well, but it isn't very permanent, and it doesn't put a roof over your head. Achievement can outlast your lifetime, and often comes in the form of good, hard cash.

Let's consider Saturn for a moment, Capricorn's planetary ruler. He's got a peculiar reputation in astrology, since he's always been considered the symbol of limitation and discipline. Also of isolation and loneliness. In mythology Saturn is one of the Titans, the earth gods, children of the great Earth Goddess Gaia. Earthy indeed: there isn't any greater pragmatist than Capricorn. Saturn is also often portrayed as a ruthless figure in mythology, who will stop at nothing – even his own father's destruction – to seize power. Ruthlessness may often be seen in the goat, and the field of politics swarms with Capricorns. But it's always a necessary ruthlessness, and rarely stems from wanton malice or cruelty. Power, too, is attractive to many Capricorns, both in the world and in their personal lives. This in fact is one of the goat's biggest problems in human relationships: he finds it immensely difficult to relinquish control. Male or female, Capricorn must always hold the reins. He's downright terrified of what might happen if he loses control – not only of the situation outside him, but of himself as well. You might guess from this that Capricorn isn't likely to be the great gambler in the sphere of the passions. You'd be quite right. He's more known for having the wit to choose the conductor over the second violin.

Yet in Roman mythology, Saturn's rulership over the world coincides with the Golden Age of man. Vines bear abundant fruit, rivers flow sweet, the sky is blue and cloudless, the earth yields its riches, and the children of men no longer have to labour by the sweat of their brows. In some ways the earth signs have made peace with the world, and the world, pleased to be recognized as something other than a grubby, sleazy and unspiritual cesspit (we're taught, after all, that it's pretty hard for rich men to enter heaven), will often show a kind face in reward for the long labour which the earth signs are willing to expend. And you often find that Capricorn, once he's paid his worldly dues to the ferryman and accomplished something in the way of success or skill, will settle back and begin to develop the deeper, more profound side of his nature. Capricorn, far from being a ruthless materialist, is a reflective and often deeply introverted soul who knows that he'll never have the freedom to pursue his love of the mysteries without first learning to live in the world. Visionary and mystical he isn't; the qualities of faith in the intangible are hard for Capricorn to muster. But he's often drawn to the occult, which involves learning the laws of the energies that govern life. That's a very different path.

Peculiar people, these Capricorns. With a powerful and fateful ruler like Saturn, it's no wonder they're difficult to know. There's another strange paradox, too, in Capricorn: the conflict between society and individual will. Many Capricorns are unusually sensitive to the opinions and values of the world, and pay a lot of attention to things like good credentials and acceptable training. The right clothes are important – never too flashy, but always good quality, the sort of thing that's understated and always in impeccable taste. The right neighbourhood is important, the right schools for the children, the right social image. Capricorns often have a remarkable skill at appearing to be the pillars of society, and although in youth they are as rebellious and iconoclastic as any young person can be (remember that Capricorn is interested in the world, and often in changing it) they usually become increasingly conservative as they grow older. It was most probably a Capricorn who said, 'If you're not a socialist by the age of twenty then you have no heart; but if you're not a conservative by the age of forty, then you have no brain.' You'll also often hear the famous, 'What will people think . . .' out of Capricornian mouths, for the goat is often unduly concerned with not being noticed within society's protective embrace. Sometimes Capricorn can be downright crushing with his insistence on obeying the silent dictates of what is right and appropriate. Yet deep within, he's a fierce individualist, and his game with society is usually yet another of his immensely subtle methods of making sure that the world around him doesn't disturb him while he works out his own particular destiny. It's based on the principle of rendering unto Caesar what's Caesar's, and rendering unto oneself what's yours.

The pattern of Capricorn's journey usually divides his life into two distinct halves. Often in the first half – which includes that frequently restrictive or burdensome childhood – the goat is frustrated or thwarted by some responsibility, and is in a sense at the mercy of society or of his tasks and responsibilities. Hardship – inner or outer – seems to be part of Capricorn's training in the school of life, and if life doesn't offer it to him then he'll make it himself. You often see Capricorns entering a kind of voluntary bondage in the early part of life, as though they actually wanted to experience this term of frustration. It might be taking care of ill or ageing parents, or working at a job they dislike intensely, or embroiling themselves in a restrictive marriage. Whatever the nature is of the restriction, there is a curious kind of psychological hair shirt which Capricorn dons for a time. In medieval mysticism, the hair shirt symbolized the individual's way of purifying himself of his carnal sins in order to prepare him for the experience of God. Capricorn's symbolic hair shirt is a kind of perpetual self-punishment or self-imposed labour. Try to get him to enjoy himself and he'll give you a thousand excuses why his responsibilities won't permit it. And like the British officer of the old school, he's convinced that what tastes bad must be good for you. No allowances made for luxury or sybaritic indulgence. He can show an ascetic streak even when there's lots of money around to be enjoyed. He's more likely to horde it and live as though he didn't have it, than spend freely like the Leo or the Libra on beauty and pleasure.

But those first thirty years of training serve a purpose. Even when it's happening at a deep, unconscious level, Capricorn is planning his ultimate destiny. He may be a nobody, someone who has to take orders from others, or work at things he detests which offer no challenge to his real capabilities. But watch him when that term has passed and he's released from his self-imposed prison. All the while a powerful determination and ambition have been breeding in him, and an immense strength of will. It might be a worldly goal he envisions – to run his own business, to make enough money to buy a piece of land, or whatever. It might be ambition in a creative sense – to develop a formidable skill as a painter, a writer, a musician. It might be an inner ambition – self-understanding, or something more occult. You can see this side of Capricorn in such people as Gurdjieff and Krishnamurti. But whatever the goal is, those first years of life have developed a steely determination in our goat, and although he may be a little late in getting on the road, once he gets moving nothing is going to get in his way, no matter how many setbacks and obstacles confront him. Capricorn is very tenacious. After all that work, he's not going to just dump the project because the road's a little rocky. If you want to bet money on someone succeeding in life, bet it on a

Capricorn. It's not that there aren't any Capricorns who fail. Lots do. But the Capricorn who's really expressing his basic nature is a sure winner. It may take him seventy years, so don't expect it in a hurry. But he'll get there.

Work and success aren't the whole picture to Capricorn. Because he's very concerned with tradition and structure, his family life is also often highly important. Structure is yet another keynote for the sign, and marriage and family commitments are often taken with great seriousness and responsibility. Capricorns don't like to break promises; they like to be thought responsible, and it's important to their self-image to have the world see them that way. The idea of leaving a marriage, or offending the family, is extremely painful to Capricorn; he'll often endure a marriage that has gone loveless for many years because his sense of commitment to the structure and security is so strong. This trait is usually more typical of the older Capricorn, since most sun-signs don't really show their colours until around thirty and Capricorn sometimes even later. But Capricorn can carry the duty bit so far that he makes his own life a living hell and sometimes the lives of the people around him. Duty is a two-edged sword. And guilt often plagues our goat: vague guilt which he can't always pin down, but which makes him take up responsibilities that others should be handling. Many Capricorns willingly pick up the threads other signs have blithely dropped, because they somehow feel vaguely responsible for keeping the world turning on its axis, and feel horribly guilty if they don't step in. It might just stop spinning if they do. It's hard to pry a Capricorn away from his guilt, because it makes him feel he's contributing something. The trouble is, it often leads other people to lean on him and take advantage of him, which only increases his sense of suspicion and his mistrust of others' motives. And he rarely realizes that it's his own doing.

Capricorn's real place is out on the world's stage, moving things in the environment – little or small – so that he leaves the place a little better organized than it was when he found it. His gifts lie in the realm of organization and control, discipline and initiation of changes within already existing structures. He's often more of an idealist than you'd expect, in that he may have a vision of how to improve the world, or the small corner of the world he inhabits. Mystical he isn't, and his ideals are always attainable ones. He makes sure of that, and usually also makes sure he has the resources and the skills to achieve them in his lifetime. He won't sit idly by and let others bring to birth his vision; he hates to delegate responsibility, and usually believes he must do it himself. It's usually only in maturity that he discovers it's okay to relax occasionally and enjoy the fruits of his labours. Sometimes he has to be prodded by an infuriated wife or lover, or a weeping child, to take a little holiday and let himself be sloppy and human. But in his heart he's a builder, and often a selfless one, building for others with his immense skills and power of will. It may take you a while to get to know him. But beneath the often overly conventional garb he's seen a lot of life, and hopefully a lot of the funnier side of it too. In kabbalistic thought the symbol of Saturn was equated with understanding – profound, rich wisdom based on real experience rather than theories and philosophies. It's worth a little time and effort to be able to tap that vein of gold.

♑ The Myth

There are many figures in mythology who can teach us about Capricorn's life journey. The old Titan Saturn is only one of them. But we can summarize all of them by saying that this sign of the winter solstice, which begins on the shortest day of the year in the northern hemisphere, is linked with the myth and mystery of the Father.

Now Father is a pretty complex thing. It means more than just Dad. Dad enters into it, certainly. You often find that the early life of the goat is heavily marked – sometimes downright scarred – by a difficult or intense or highly complicated relationship with the father. Sometimes this means the loss of the father, and the incurring of responsibilities of a fatherly kind early in life. Sometimes Capricorn has a stern father, or an aloof one, or a weak or unstable one. Sometimes he's an overidealized figure, a pattern which you see with many Capricorn women; they go on looking for this adored and overidealized father for a long time, often making marriages early in life to men who can play the fatherly role. Sometimes the father is a glamourized figure against whom the Capricorn child feels he can never compete, or whose love seems hard to obtain. Whatever the circumstances, Father is a mystery and a challenge and often a problem to be solved. This is why the first thirty years of Capricorn's life are often difficult. Many Capricorns are busy rebelling against the father during that time, or trying to live up to his expectations. But no matter what kind of father Capricorn has, the relationship is almost always complicated. It seems that only in adulthood does Capricorn – man or woman – realize that he or she must in some deep sense become Father himself or herself. The qualities of strength, control, will, protectiveness, stability are all things which can't be found in somebody else, or in a job, or in the all-embracing arms of some big hierarchical business or company to which so many Capricorns are initially attracted. These qualities, which are qualities associated with the symbol of Father, have to be built inside, the long, hard, slow way.

There's another mythical image which we should add to Capricorn. This is the Eastern teaching of the Bodhisattva. In some Eastern teachings, there are two types of enlightened souls: the Buddhas and the Bodhisattvas. The first reaches self-realization or enlightenment and remains in the mystical state of oneness with God. The second, having reached the portals of the divine, turns back and sees the rest of humanity suffering and labouring in darkness. He could, like the Buddha, remain in his wonderful realm of oneness with the Light. But he chooses voluntarily to return and travel back down into the dense, dark world of ordinary life, in order to help those who are still imprisoned. Only when they are free does he feel free to leave his self-imposed prison. This is a profound symbol, and one which portrays Capricorn's real destiny. Whatever the mountain peak he seeks – material or spiritual or both – he cannot remain at the top. He must descend again into the world, although he may no longer need to remain with that particular job or commitment, because his skills are needed.

This Eastern teaching about the Bodhisattva is also reflected in many aspects of Christian teaching. And it's not coincidental that we celebrate the birthday of Christ on the 25th of December, while the sun is in Capricorn. In many pagan religious teachings, the sun-god is always born under Capricorn, because he is a Redeemer who voluntarily offers to incarnate into the hard, painful world among mortals to help lift them up to the Light. Maybe it's a little glamorous for many hard-working Capricorns who have no greater ambition than to own their own small business and get on with the business of survival and the support of a family. But somewhere in each Capricorn there's a seed of this ancient figure who is really much older even than Christianity, who chooses of his own volition to remain in the restrictions and heaviness of ordinary life and responsibility in order to change things just a little bit and leave them just a little better or brighter.

♑ The Shadow

The shadow side of any zodiacal sign is connected with the parts of the personality which the individual can't recognize and can't express. And you might expect that with all Capricorn's realism and earthy wisdom and emphasis on the mundane and the practical, all those repressed emotions and dreams and fantasies have to go somewhere. After all, Capricorn is complex and sensitive, and is much deeper than he often appears. So we might call his shadow side the Fanatic syndrome. This particular figure is connected with another one, which we might call End Justifies Means. The scenario goes something like this:

> FRIEND: I hear you're standing for Parliament. That's really good news. I always thought you ought to pursue a career in politics. What do you see yourself doing?
> CAPRICORN: Well, I have some long-range plans. If I can get this seat, then I can begin to get my ideas about cleaning up Soho accepted.
> FRIEND: Oh, come now. Why do you want to clean up Soho? I thought you were such a realist.

CAPRICORN: (*looking stern and patriarchal*) It's about time this country returned to the good old values of our fathers. All those disgusting pornographic films and prostitutes on every corner and the police can't even control it . . .

FRIEND: Oh, surely they don't harm anyone, and besides, it probably fulfils a useful function. Lots of people need to let out the seedier side of themselves.

CAPRICORN: It's total self-indulgence, greed, in fact it's sinful. Why, it's destroying the family as the basic unit of society. Young children can go and see those disgusting shops where you can buy all those terrible things, and they're corrupted before they even go to college. I'd shut every shop and close every cinema. I'd arrest anyone who . . .

FRIEND: I thought we had freedom of speech and press in this country.

CAPRICORN: But it's for the good of the whole. Oh, I suppose it would ruin a few people who make their money peddling those revolting things, but in the long run . . .

The Capricornian shadow gone fanatical may have an axe to grind about just about anything. When you first hear him going on, you might laugh. Ah, well, silly man or woman, moralizing that way, doesn't he or she know that you can't change human nature? But the Capricorn shadow thinks you can. And whether the issue is about sex, or money, or religion, or politics, or just giving you lots of unwelcome advice about how you should run your life, the Capricorn shadow got out of hand can freeze your blood, because it's like Yahweh in the Old Testament: do as I say and don't question it. The shadow side of Capricorn isn't necessarily politically conservative, either: remember that Stalin was a Capricorn too. What it's really about is that Capricorn, gone over to the shadowy side of his nature, always has a plan to change society, which of course necessitates changing it his way, which of course means there's no room for dissenters, which of course means you either forcibly remove them or pay them off. Richard Nixon, too, is a Capricorn. End justifies means.

The thing that needs changing in Capricorn's eyes also needn't be a big section of society. It might be you: the husband or wife, lover or child. And you see the same fanatical gleam in Capricorn's normally wise and knowing eyes. Get him on his favourite hobby horse and he'll tolerate no opposition. Refuse his advice and you've permanently offended him. And he'll often manipulate in the most outrageous way to get you to go along with his plans, because he's convinced that he's right and that in the end whatever means he's used – however unscrupulous – will be rendered tolerable by the results.

The thing is, Capricorn rarely allows his vision or his imagination any scope, because he's so busy being realistic. He'll never permit himself any fantasies about what the world might be like, because he forces himself to keep his eyes on what's practically obtainable. Yet he has a powerful imagination and a lot of vision. And it's got to go someplace. And you often discover that Capricorns have a secret vision tucked away somewhere about what they'd do if they ever got into the big driver's seat. The trouble is, keeping a fantasy like that locked in the basement for twenty or thirty years has a tendency to make it turn a little funny. It inflates. When it comes out, Capricorn loses his wonderful realism and gets carried away by his own messianic visions. Of course the world, or you, can be changed. And he's the man to do it. And if you oppose it, well, it's only your own delusions or foolhardiness or stupidity or whatever that causes you to be so unintelligent as to not recognize the Absolute Truth of his conviction.

If you're not the recipient of his Great Mission, you

may be in the position of being the person closest to him who has to listen to what he plans and who is expected to offer every last ounce of your own energy to see that he achieves it. This is where Capricorn's shadow can often make others suffer, for in a relationship or family situation he is prepared to sacrifice everybody else's will to his own. Whether it's his morality or his views on money or whatever his conviction might be, everyone else is expected to go along. This is the Capricorn father who believes – fanatically – that hardship is good for you, and keeps his children on allowances of tuppence a week when there are thousands of pounds in the bank; it's the Capricorn mother whose stern moral views or social codes are ruthlessly imposed on husband and family; it's the Capricorn friend who takes it upon himself to interfere in your personal life because he believes it's really good for you to tell you your boyfriend's been cheating on you. In short, the Capricorn shadow attempts to bend everybody else's will to its own, and everybody else's needs, desires, ideas, and lifestyles to its own concept of how life should be run. And for realistic Capricorn, that's hardly realistic. Only a deluded fool believes that he can change other people's natures simply by issuing a command. And only a deluded fool believes that he even has the right to do so.

Capricorn, because it's a powerful sign which usually accomplishes much in the world, has a dangerous shadow. It's that much more important for the goat to come to terms with this fanatical streak in himself, because he's always likely to end up in a position of responsibility in some way and usually has other people needing his strong, guiding hand. If he misuses that hand, it's far more deadly than the little shadow plays of people who have little influence over others' lives. Tolerance is hard sometimes for Capricorn to learn, because he's often had to discipline himself and his own needs in a ruthless way to get to the goal he's after. He can't understand why others aren't either interested in or capable of applying the same discipline, because he doesn't realize that their goals may be different, or that they don't have any goals at all in the sense that he does.

Capricorn, as we said, is connected with the myth of the Father; and the shadow side of the Father is the tyrant. You can't be a tyrant unless you've blinkered yourself pretty tightly to any point of view other than your own. The recipe for the Capricorn shadow is often a little effort in understanding that different people have different lives to live, different myths to express, and different needs and desires. Capricorn can often benefit from astrology because it can teach him that there are twelve basic life paths, not just one. Beneath the suit of armour which Capricorn must don on his journey through an unfriendly or challenging world, he is as capable of love and devotion as any person. He needs to be able to remember his capacity to love, and also to remember that loving another person means recognizing them, not just guiding them. The Father – whether the figure appears in a man's or a woman's psyche – is in his positive form the one who offers support, guidance, wisdom, training in the ways of the world. The Father in his negative form offers support only if you're prepared to take his advice; he offers guidance only if you accept his views *in toto*; he offers wisdom only if you recognize no other source for it; and he trains in the ways of the world according to his own image of the world. This kind of Father withholds love if there is no obedience. The root of it is the intense emotional drive which Capricorn so often represses, and which eventually begins to eat away at his usually reasonable thinking processes, making him blind just when he believes he's got sight. The more the goat can express his powerful emotional needs in human relationships, the less likely they are to muddle up his vision. And the more he allows himself to relax sometimes, the more he can see that less disciplined souls are no less worthy, but often hold a key to joy in life that he himself may have missed. Then you have a really mellow goat, who can dance as well as climb.

⑥ The Capricorn Lover

Relationships aren't easy for Capricorn. You might expect this, since control is always important to him, and letting down the solid protection of that suit of armour takes a lot of effort. He's been wearing the armour for so long that very likely it's rusted at the hinges, and you hear some pretty loud groans and protests as it comes off. You usually find that no matter how much the goat loves, there's always a last special place inside which he isn't prepared to share, a last area of self-control which he isn't about to relinquish. Capricorn is often a loner, a self-isolated figure climbing his own private mountain. And sometimes he won't allow himself to accept either help or sympathy when the going is rough. Thanks very much, he'll manage himself. It's difficult to do Capricorn a favour. He can often be seen doing favours for his friends and loved ones; he knows how to give, especially when it comes to the things of the world. But sometimes he can't receive very well. He has a ferocious pride, and a real terror of being dependent or weak. No goat can bear a situation over which he has no control.

If you ever have a chance to scratch the surface of Capricorn, you'll find that he's a secret romantic. He shares this in common with the other earthy signs. But his romanticism is almost never allowed to dictate his decisions. He'd much rather sacrifice the great romantic love for the safe, suitable partner who is a social asset as well. When they marry early, many Capricorns run the risk of choosing for security and suitability, and living to bitterly regret this choice. You'll rarely find Capricorn throwing all away for love. He might throw all away for the sake of a conviction, or for the preservation of his family. But love? Well, marriage isn't always motivated by love for Capricorn, and certainly not solely. Back in the days when marriages were arranged and you learned over many years of sticking together (divorce just wasn't done) to develop a deep fondness and respect for your partner, Capricorn would have found that arrangement just right. You can imagine what the Pisceans and the Leos and the Sagittarians would have done. But Capricorn takes his vows seriously, and he wants to be very sure before he makes them that the investment is likely to turn out successfully. Most Capricorns either marry early – in which case they're either looking for fathers, or trying to play fathers – or they marry late, having scanned the market carefully. But on impulse? Rarely.

Not that it's a bad way to be. Capricorn places more value on deep respect, duty, loyalty, and the power of the family bond than he does on a few months of wild passion. Not that he's not capable of passion. This is an earthy sign, remember, and the sexual drive is often strong and the physical nature very basic. But many Capricorns keep this side of themselves out of their serious relationships, because they don't often trust their passions.

If you are involved with a Capricorn, you must accept the fact that he or she will try to take charge. Capricorn doesn't take kindly to either positions of submission or humiliation or one-upmanship – unless he's the winner and you the one who submits. If you hurt his pride, or take away his self-respect, he'll take a long time forgiving, and an even longer time forgetting.

Because of his earthy, controlled nature, Capricorn sometimes finds it difficult to express his love and affection in a relaxed way. He may feel it deeply, but you may never know it. And he's usually attracted to those who can loosen him up a little bit – the extroverted emotional type, the irresponsible and playful temperament, the child. The same thing that makes many Capricorns secret religious seekers also makes them seekers after people who are able to open up the romantic side of life for them. Underneath the realistic and pragmatic surface of Capricorn, you'll find all sorts of fantasies. But it's not likely he'll tell you about them. Capricorn is very frightened of chaos. This is why so many Capricorns shy away from the supernatural or mystical side of life – or, put another way, from the unconscious, the unknown depths in themselves. An emotional eruption or a nonrational experience can leave Capricorn feeling embarrassed and vulnerable. Yet he longs for these qualities in a partner, someone through whom he can learn to trust all those things he doesn't dare trust in himself or in life.

So this old-young man or woman will seek someone who can help him free the child in himself. And this kind of relationship can often heal him and release his real creativity. The trouble is that, having found someone who personifies the fiery side of life, Capricorn will often take role of a stern parent with a child, repressing rather than encouraging spontaneity. If it's you who has been cast in the role of the child, that well-meaning parental tone can get a little suffocating, not to say restrictive. It's really the child in himself that Capricorn keeps trying to keep in line, the restless, volatile wanderer who might upset all his plans and suddenly call the world's attention to his own difficulty in commitment. Capricorn's parent-child marriages (and he'll usually taste both sides of this arrangement, since he'll very likely play the child in youth and the parent later in life) can be either creative or destructive. Gone sour, they can develop into a never-ending prison for the more spontaneous partner, and a growing sense of suspicion and mistrust for the Capricorn. Or the stern, stiff streak in Capricorn can let himself be thawed by the gift of love, and learn through it that life can be trusted. And if the suspicious goat can learn that, well, then, he has the world truly at his feet, since he can begin to enjoy the rewards of all his labour. It's truer for Capricorn than for any other sign that life begins at forty – and often love as well.

♑ The Capricorn Man

Meet this man while he's still in his twenties and you'll probably not really see the goat. You'll meet a goat in formation, and often he'll seem like a worldly failure, or a wanderer who is unsettled and unsure of his direction. Or he'll seem to have given up and saddled himself with an unpromising future in some job he dislikes. But stick with him, or meet him later, and you'll see the goat in true form. And he'll almost always have a goal he's working his way towards. And his way of showing his love is generally to share that goal with you, and his expectations in love are that you do everything in your power to help him achieve it.

Capricorn men tend, on the whole, to belong to a more traditional school. Once again, this may not be in evidence in the early part of life, since the goat must learn by hard experience and hard experience means he must try a lot of things in youth that he'll moralize fiercely against later. But because of his emotional complexity and inhibitions, and because security means a lot to him, sooner or later he'll usually look for a stable, solid relationship which can constitute a family for him. You'll also notice that it's important to many Capricorns to have sons, since the strong patriarchal streak in the sign may love and adore women yet still secretly feels the world should be run by men. Capricorn men aren't really very good members of the feminist movement like many Aquarian and Libran and Piscean men are. They have a strong sense of what masculine pride and dignity and achievement are about. If you want to get a Capricorn to consider your opinions or wishes, you must learn to be a diplomat. After all, he respects diplomacy. What he doesn't like is rebellion.

Often you'll see a real fatherly quality in the Capricorn man. He can be wonderfully protective and supportive, and he's usually the kind of man who when he says, 'Don't worry, I'll take care of it,' really does. He can be a pillar of strength and a great source of wisdom and help. The difficulty with this paternal side of him is that you sometimes only get the best face of it when you're prepared to be the helpless one who needs support. Many Capricorn men dislike capable women; it takes away their need to be the strong figure in the relationship.

Sometimes you see this reversed. The Capricorn man who hasn't come to terms with his father relationship may behave like an adolescent still rebelling against the father. Then, in a queer way, he looks for those paternal qualities in his women. There is a whole breed of Capricorn male who let their ladies support them and make the financial decisions. They sit back and play the child to a woman-father-lover. It's a curious phenomenon, and you find it when Capricorn has been badly scarred or hurt by his childhood. But more often the Capricorn man is only too happy to play the strong, supportive, capable role. It's just hard for him sometimes to share it.

You also have to accept, in relationships with Capricorn, that the career comes first. That means that if he's moved by his firm from London to Stoke-on-Trent, you learn to like Stoke-on-Trent. If it's his ambitions that might be fulfilled by a move of house, a pruning of the social circle, a change in any of the things which give comfort and pleasure in personal life, then it's his ambitions which come first. If you have any of your own, you're expected to adjust. This means that you have two solutions. Either you accept with grace and joy the ancient male-female role relationship, which has much to commend it, or, if you're the more independent sort, you learn to maintain a relationship with Capricorn that isn't very close. That usually means a sexual relationship without any commitment. He's not going to commit himself to you unless he knows that you're prepared to commit yourself to him and his goals. And he may simply run a few casual affairs for a time until he finds the woman who can be the kind of emotional support his enclosed nature needs to blossom.

It's obvious that this kind of man is the perfect mate for some women, and a disaster for others. It depends on your taste. But you can't dominate a Capricorn man, except by the most devious methods of emotional blackmail – and he'll usually spot those and learn to despise you in time for it – and you can't make yourself more important in his life than his own inner convictions and commitments. And what this sums up is a man who is a pretty good embodiment of the masculine principle in one of its most ancient and traditional forms. Many women prefer more ambivalent men, who are able to lean a little more toward the middle, and have more tolerance for the feminine side of life. Not Capricorn. He's not in the least ambivalent. He usually knows what he wants – and if it's you, then he'll generally be fairly tenacious about getting you to surrender – and he rarely deviates once he's decided. You can either love and respect it, or leave it alone. It's almost impossible to change a Capricorn, since his business in life is to change both himself and the world. And nobody can do it for him.

♍ The Capricorn Woman

It may be hard to imagine a woman who embodies the principle of the Father. But in fact it doesn't make Capricorn women masculine. If anything, they often have a quality of femininity which epitomizes the fantasies of many men. Take, for example, Marlene Dietrich. Masculine? Well, not in any sense we understand the word. But look again. The typical Capricornian woman is usually subtle, and sensitive, and perceptive. She'd rather use diplomacy than argue aggressively; her voice is usually cool and calm and low-pitched. She's often beautifully and tastefully dressed, never gaudily, and never in clothes that follow a fad, but in classically tailored feminine things. She's smart enough to know that silk underwear and expensive perfume are far more effective than blue and green-dyed hair. She's also smart enough to know that you don't confront power directly; therefore, if she wants something from you, you usually end up thinking that you came up with the idea yourself, and she's managed to twist you around with such finesse that you're convinced she's fragile and helpless and you begin to feel such a hero that your biceps begin to visibly swell. Ah, poor soul. No Capricorn is fragile or helpless. All Capricorn women are born with stainless steel spines.

This doesn't mean that all Capricorn women use people. Many do; their strong cynical streak makes them choose partners who can provide support and security, or can help with a creative career. But many are also devoted lovers and wives and mothers, offering their powerful wills and business astuteness and wordly wisdom and shrewd judgment to help you in your own career. Playing the unseen power behind the throne suits the Capricorn woman very well. She's realistic enough about herself to know that being the obvious power in the relationship is much more dangerous – you earn the enmity of society that way – than appearing to be the follower. But the love and devotion may be truly selfless, and the manipulation and subtlety offered to help the person she loves achieve something in his own life.

The thing is, Capricorn needs to manage something, and this is as true of the female Capricorn as the male. If no career appears in a Capricorn woman's life, her need to fulfil a useful role and organize and direct generally falls on the members of her family. Then she'll organize your life and direct your energy, often to your gain, sometimes to your detriment because the goals you think you've got are frequently hers. The Capricorn mother whose managing instinct is thwarted will usually stage-manage the lives of her children. It's important for the Capricorn woman to have some place in her own life where she can apply her gifts of organization, administration, care of others, outside her personal relationships. Whether it's a creative skill or a desire to offer physical service such as nursing or medicine or osteopathy or some other typical Capricornian profession, or a shop or trade which pleases her, the Capricorn woman needs to have a place to unleash her ambition to achieve something either in her own eyes or in the eyes of the world. Capricorn needs to feel accomplished in something. Beware of the Capricorn woman who has accomplished nothing, or doesn't recognize that she even has the drive. Unconsciously, she'll gradually begin to make you her accomplishment.

We've already mentioned the propensity with many Capricorn women to seek men who can play the role of father during the early part of life. The Capricorn woman, like the Capricorn man, often has a complex and problematic relationship with the father. Sometimes you find a type of Capricorn woman who is Daddy's little girl, who needs to be adored and given gifts and taken care of while she expresses her charming, frivolous, irresponsible self. Then she's trying to live out that strong, earthy Capricorn nature through her man. At some point she'll usually go through a crisis; sometimes the marriage breaks down because the man goes off, or her problem with commitment in relationships takes her through so many failed love episodes that she begins to question herself deeply. You can also find a type of Capricornian woman who is busy rejecting the father because he's too stern, or possessive, or controlling, and chooses men who can lean on her. Then she plays father, and often suffers as far as her feelings about her own womanhood are concerned. Either way, the Capricorn woman seems to mature into the warmest, richest side of the sign later in life.

The Capricorn woman who has learned to become her own Father and stand on her own feet in life is free to release the gentler, more sensitive and caring side of her nature in relationships. The feminine side of the earthy signs shows its face here, in the form of real sensitivity and generosity with time and energy; also in the form of loyalty and dedication. As we mentioned already, life is a serious business for Capricorn. And the Capricorn woman who has passed the test of her own survival, and learns that she can function in the world through her own efforts, has also learned wisdom and compassion along the way. In kaballistic teaching Saturn represents the feminine principle of wisdom and understanding, as we have said; and it is also called the Great Mother. The profound depths of wisdom and insight which lie in the still pool of Capricorn's heart can flow into relationships once the Capricorn woman has learned to rely on her own strengths and resources, and has also learned that life can be a pleasure as well. If you're looking for a showgirl, this isn't the sign to choose; even the Marlene Dietrichs of the world, offstage, are wise and self-disciplined women, with a realistic eye and a hard-earned knowledge of human foibles.

Some Last Words...

*T*here is a classic scenario which illustrates with glorious clarity one of the patterns which fire-earth relationships may follow. The scenario as it is given here portrays the fiery man and the earthy woman; but it can as easily be reversed, and contain essentially the same pattern. We may see it when one of these two elements is entirely missing from one partner's horoscope and is present in abundance in the horoscope of the other. It is (granted) a caricature. But threads of it, nuances, aspects, may be found in every typical relationship between fire and earth. It is, in essence, a collision between vision and reality. Like all other collisions of opposites – a phenomenon which appears to compose most of our human relationships – it has two forks, a left and a right. To the left lies the ugly manifestation, with which all divorce courts are familiar. To the right lies the less frequently trod but more creative path, which is an attempt to fuse the opposites so that both people can learn from and grow with each other. Our stars may fate us in temperament. But which of these two forks is taken is our own choice.

The reader of mythology may recognize, in his imaginative journeying, the ubiquitous mother-goddess who in the pagan world symbolized the womb of life, maternal caring and solicitude, the power of creation and procreation in nature, the embodiment of the feminine. Along with her solicitous and loving aspects she inevitably, in myth and in folklore (and in the secret fantasies of men) possesses a dark side, represented in innumerable sculptures, frescoes, mosaics and bas-reliefs as snarling dogs, savage boars or bears, predatory birds that flank her and warn the profane away. And with her, well-known to any student of Frazer's *The Golden Bough*, is her golden-haired son/lover, the beautiful winged youth whom she bears, loves for a season, and who is tragically dead or vanished as summer turns into autumn and autumn into the grim austerity of winter. And he is born anew with the spring, and re-appears once more winged and golden-haired with the budding shoots.

What, you may well ask, has the mythology of antiquity to do with our relationship problems? Or, for that matter, with astrology? Second question first. Mythology and astrology are both picture languages which portray, in the oldest system of cosmology known to man, the forces of life and how they work outside and inside us. The planets in astrology bear the names of the gods of antiquity, and are characterized by the same qualities which these gods also are given. To understand real astrology, you have to know a little about mythology, for in the end they stem from the same source: the deepest creative depths of the human psyche.

Because myths and fairy tales portray the workings of the secret inner psyche of man, they pose typical human problems and typical human solutions. Some of the great myths are portrayals of the major events in the cosmos: the creation of the world, the fashioning of man himself. Some are smaller, and tell about the bizarre, often grotesque, often hilarious vicissitudes of one or another hero or demigod. All are relevant, for we walk with myths and live them without ever knowing the deeper and more profound meaning behind our ordinary everyday behaviour. Many people, for thousands of years, have found comfort and relevance in reading the great myths. You will see, when you have met the Mother and the Eternal Youth, what we mean.

So myths have a good deal to say about the patterns and general messes we make in our relationships with each other. Some of us are Theseus, or Odysseus, or Persephone, or Atalanta. Others are the ghastly gorgons, dragons, demons and sorcerers. Or all of the above. Anyway, the myth of the great earth goddess and her eternally dying and eternally renewable youthful son-consort lives on in that lovely couple next door, whom we may see act out a pattern so typical, so farcical, so tragic and so noble, so banal and so ridiculous, that only the realization that it is an innate human pattern gives it any dignity or meaning.

So on with our scenario. Enter the Eternal Youth. He may be truly youthful; but all youths are eternal, and the Eternal Youth of our scenario is a character we meet more often when he is past thirty. He has been described in other works as someone with a mature body and adolescent emotions. Astrologically we find him most often as someone with a preponderance of fire in the horoscope, and little or no earth. Remember that the element of fire has to do with intuitive possibilities, with creative vision and with the future. The element of earth has to do with actualization, with coping with the facts and situations that present reality offers. Beginning to get the picture?

The Eternal Youth is usually good-looking, (every mother's darling is), since if he weren't, he would have had to learn to cope with reality long ago. He is sometimes highly successful at some creative or speculative enterprise; or sometimes he is full of ideas but is 'someday' going to get them all down and make a million. Whatever he does – successful or not – he is generally dissatisfied with it, because he is bored, or restless, or 'not getting his creativity out'. In other words, reality, no matter how bountiful, is imperfect because it sometimes makes demands on him, or requires him to limit himself. This really annoys him. On Olympus, you aren't subjected to this sort of annoyance. Gods aren't supposed to adjust to reality.

And oh my, does our Eternal Youth love the ladies. Or at least this is the impression he gives, and most people are fooled by it. He loves them so much that he must have more than one at once. More extreme Youths will rarely be seen with one lady for more than a week or two; less extreme ones almost always have mistresses along with the wife or regular girlfriend. You can often see a distinct propensity for slightly shadier ladies as well; this is the boy who is fascinated by the dark; by the hooker, the stripper, the porn cinema, the expensive call-girl. Whether he lives these fantasies out depends on his generation, his culture, his morality. But you can bet your sweet bibby these fantasies populate his nighttime (and often daytime) imagination.

The Eternal Youth radiates a magnetic and very distinctive aura. That is, it's distinctive until you realize that these charming boys are hard to tell apart when you get to know something about them. They are types, not yet individuals. They don't become individuals until they are men. Sometimes they never get there. But the Eternal Youth projects a quality of dash, charisma, magic. He is untameable, undomesticated, uncommitted, sparkling, exuding the mysterious atmosphere of a thousand journeys, a thousand women. He has just stepped off the plane from Shanghai on the way to Madagascar, always in a slight hurry so that his distraction is explicable on these grounds instead of the real ones – which are that he is simply distracted from life in general, never willing to be wholly here now. He is *en route* somewhere, to something. It is what Marie-Louise von Franz, a well-known Jungian analyst, called 'the provisional life'. He is cool and romantic, with a hungry lady in every port dreaming that maybe she will be the one to snag him. Somehow he never quite gets snagged. And if he does – wife, children, mortgage, etc. – he manages somehow to get out of it, albeit on the sly. He is the sort that doesn't 'look' married, whatever that means. And he radiates a loud unconscious message: 'no woman understands me, no woman has ever been truly able to satisfy me, I am a misunderstood creative spirit looking for the understanding woman whom I can at last settle down with, commit myself to . . . perhaps you are the one . . .'

Silly girl. This fellow is still emotionally married to his mother, for better or worse. Why? That takes a complicated answer, and it's a different answer for each Eternal Youth. But astrologically considered, apart from whatever Mummy has done to bind her son in this way, when you find a man who lacks earth and is loaded with fire, you have a gifted spirit who simply doesn't find it easy to cope with the responsibilities, limitations and requirements of ordinary life. As Goethe said, the unpleasant is easier for him to bear than the inconsequential – and anything that isn't part of his vision of the future is inconsequential. Result? He is always looking for Mummy to come and clean up after him, pay the bills, decorate his arm, understand, comfort, forgive, tie his shoelaces, listen. The trouble is that if you are foolish enough to think you can be his Mummy, you are in for a nasty shock. For the deep dark truth about this Eternal Youth who seems to love the ladies so is that, fundamentally, he doesn't like Mummy. Mummy, after all, suffocated him, and almost crippled him. So if you play Mummy, why, lady, you get kicked.

Does this sound cynical? It is. But there is hope. It stems from each person's capacity to heal himself, become conscious of himself, make the effort to reflect a little on those things within himself that he is wont to blame others for. A little healthy contact with the

unconscious, you might say. How many of us are willing
to try?

Back to our Youth. Irresistible? Yes, to some. Those
earthy ladies who are prone to identify with their
sexuality and express affection through sensuality,
through maternal caring and ordering of another's life,
fall victim like so many drugged fruit flies. At first it's
wonderful, a mating made in heaven. The Eternal
Youth loves sexy women. He loves the compliment they
pay to his masculinity, having a beautiful and obviously
warm lady on his arm, since he is habitually in doubt
about his masculinity anyway. Ssh, we say that in quiet.
Tell him that to his face and you might get punched.
But it's his darkest secret. No earth, remember? No
earth, no relationship with the body.

Remember what we said about fire signs? They are
not really comfortable in matter. The body is alien,
something into which one has been stuffed like a sausage
into a sausage-skin. Idealistic dreamers about what life
might, and could, and should, and will be like – but
never what it actually is from moment to moment. And
present the Eternal Youth with a more basic earthy
demand – emotionally or sexually – and that fleet-of-
foot creature will show you his heels in a hurry. Gone
with the wind, a lot faster than Rhett Butler.

And the lady? Ah, the earth goddess. When young,
she is every man's (or at least, every fiery man's)
fantasy. Because she is identified with and takes care of
her body, and is secure in her femaleness – at least on
a sexual level – she makes the best of her looks. She is
often capable, either domestically or financially or both.
She usually wants children, although often 'later'. And
she gives the impression of being a lot looser, lighter,
less attached than in fact she is. If she isn't bit by the
charm of our Eternal Youth, she can lead him a merry
rejection dance. If she is bit, then the tables reverse.
Later. She is warm, accepting, patient, ultimately

female. What she lacks is that innate sense of humour about life, the ability to gamble. That's why she falls for those Eternal Youths. You see, she's earthbound, and often can't find any meaning to her life beyond the relationship she's in. The spark is missing. People who lack fire often can't see the wood for the trees.

So: enter the couple. Dashing Eternal Youth with Earth Goddess on his arm. They are madly in love; and this is the one, he tells himself, the real one, and the sex is great, and she is in charge at first (earth takes a while to warm up), and he is so romantic he begins to make you think he owns stock in Interflora.

We come now to the fork. For this early stage of earth-fire relating is fascinating and compulsive. But when the initial fantasies begin to wear away, and the parties concerned begin to get older and more mature, something happens. It can go to left or to right. That all depends on how aware each partner is of himself or herself, and how aware they both are of the kind of temperament belonging to the other one. And most importantly: how aware they both are of what they are trying to live through the other person because they will not dare live it themselves.

The Eternal Youth is, after all, an Eternal Youth. Untrammelled and unaware, the real process of relating scares him half to death. It involves nasty stuff like commitment, honesty of feeling, acceptance of imperfection, menstrual cramps, sickness, children, responsibility, *et al.* Reality, in short. Relationships on a mythical archetypal or fantasy level are real as symbols, but they are paradoxical, for they are banal and boring and take work as well. If you only see half the paradox, you are in trouble. The Eternal Youth sees the vision, the symbol, the ideal romance in fantasy. The Mother sees the responsibility, the commitment, the day-to-day caring and nurturing of another human being. He lacks realism, she lacks vision. Anything short of the dream, the fantasy of the first weeks, begins to feel to the Eternal Youth like a cage. Oh no, it's his mother again. He thought he had got away from her. So he takes a step back. The dream has begun to tarnish. He isn't quite so romantic. Maybe a night goes by when he isn't particularly turned on. A few less flowers. An hour or two later at the office.

The problem with this behaviour is twofold. Firstly, if you are secretly, quietly, unconsciously drawing away from somebody, they know it. We don't really fool each other all that much. She might not know it overtly – but on some level, deep down, it is obvious. Something has gone wrong. And earth, being so oriented toward the senses, gets very upset and insecure when the tangible declarations of love begin to wane. Instead of taking it in stride and waiting for the cycle to reestablish itself – which requires a certain amount of having your own life as well – the earth-goddess becomes a little more clinging, a little more demanding of affection. He takes another step back. She takes another step forward. Funny tango, this. She will look for things to quarrel about, in the hopes that it will bring the heat back. Quarrelling, to him, equals demand, which equals imprisonment. Commitment is a four-letter word. The left-hand fork has arrived. He takes another step back, a large one, straight into the arms of his secretary/ cleaning lady/hooker/stripper/best friend's wife, who understands him a lot better, of course.

She, naturally, gets the house, the car, and large maintenance payments. The world sees him as the bastard, and he sees himself as the bastard as well. She is equally partner in the dance, though; think of all that emotional blackmail, all that nagging, all that demanding, all that asking an adolescent (albeit disguised as an adult) to carry the burden of the responsibility of her happiness and her meaning in life, when he is still busily seeking his own. By this time there are inevitably children, since mother-goddesses are, after all, mothers. Children also seem to them a means of cementing a relationship. Nine out of ten 'accidental' pregnancies (have you ever heard such a silly thing, in this day of easy contraceptives?) happen to earth-goddesses who are afraid of losing the Eternal Youth. And he being such a child himself, the arrival of a real child complete with howling and dirty diapers is enough to pitch him into a very nasty mood indeed. Mummy has truly become mummy; and it is a courageous Eternal Youth who can face the fact that he is about to heap upon his woman a very false and very unjustified identification with the old woman still waiting at the airport.

I quote here a passage from Marie-Louise von Franz.

> If a man is too much impressed by the figure of his mother, whether by her fault or by his own disposition, so that she interferes with his contact with reality . . . he may, like some sensitive men, not have strong enough masculine brutality to escape the mother and fight his way to freedom. (Masculine brutality here partakes of a good many qualities of earth.) So, he escapes into the intellect where generally she cannot follow. One leaves the earth, takes an airplane and goes 2000 metres above the earth, where the old lady cannot reach, and one feels a man and free, but this naturally has a disadvantage. This is a very widespread type of young man . . . as soon as he wants to touch the earth, either to live sex, or to get married, or anything of the kind which means descent to the earth again, there the old lady stands, awaiting him at the airport.

Not, you must admit, a happy picture. What can a poor boy (or girl) do? Let's assume we have a couple who are willing to take the relationship itself as something serious, something that requires honesty and consciousness. Let's say they are willing to recognize that different astrological signs and elements speak different languages and see different realities. The Eternal Youth can, after all, grow up if he wants to. But he needs to come to terms with that ancient enemy of the element of fire, the world of concrete and banal reality. Reality meaning what is now, not what might be, once was, could, should, ought to be. What exists, complete with warts. And earth can, after all – mother earth being very old and very wise at heart, and infusing us all, since we live in physical bodies – turn out to be something quite different from the dreary and dismal trap which the fiery signs often envision in their nightmares. It isn't that this marvellously dynamic, creative group of signs need become old men burdened with material responsibilities. Fire is still fire, and the Eternal Youth still remains Eternal even if he learns to deal with the world. He keeps his sparkle and his creative spirit. There's nothing wrong with being an Eternal Youth, ultimately; it keeps us in touch with the things which are eternal, the things of the spirit and the imagination. But the more difficult side, and the sad ending, of so many earth-fire relationships can be helped a lot, and turned into a much more creative form, by remembering that old oracle at Delphi:

Nothing in excess.

The Elements of Air and Water

Harmony v. Truth

The Element of Air

The intellect in every man is God.

MENANDER

I think,' wrote Descartes, 'therefore I am.' This famous quotation ushered in the Age of Reason, from which we have not yet recovered. The society in which we live continues to uphold Descartes' maxim not only as the underpinning for its educational methods and philosophy, but also as the underpinning for what is considered ability or quality in an individual. We live in an age of tests of the intellect. It is the smart child who passes the IQ test with glowing ease who is considered the one to watch, the one to help, the one who will some day in adulthood contribute most to the world he lives in.

But Descartes' proposition is a little tricky. For one thing, it is awfully lopsided. How about, 'I feel, therefore I am'? Or, 'I sense, therefore, I am'? Or even, 'I am conscious, therefore, I am'? The interesting thing about twentieth-century Cartesians – and this includes virtually the entire spectrum of the sciences, education, economic and business studies, and even, sadly, psychology – is that they still cling stubbornly to the belief that the intellect, the reasoning faculty in man, is the only thing in him that is really worthwhile, and the only mode of judgment and evaluation that is accurate and truthful. Reasonable, we call these people. Rational. Logical. Lovers of truth. Astrology takes this perspective of life and links it up with the element of air.

Now air, apart from being necessary for life and breath, is, of all the four astrological spheres, the least tangible. Fire can burn or warm you, water can refresh or drown you, earth can bury or grow crops for you. But you can't see air. Like the mind – on which endless philosophical speculations have rested for many centuries – air is volatile, breezy, shifting, clear, transparent, and, you might say definitely abstract.

Astrology uses picture language to describe certain truths about life and people. When you look at the traditional symbols which are associated with each sign, and with each element, certain things are communicated which fifty pages of conceptual dissertation fail to do in such a succinct fashion. Take the three images for the three airy signs. Gemini: the Twins. Libra: the Balance. Aquarius: the Waterbearer. Now look at the symbols for the other three elements. Fire contains the Ram, the Lion, the Centaur. Water contains the Crab, the Scorpion, the Fishes. Earth contains the Bull, the Maiden, the Goat. Notice anything? Right. Air is the only element without any animal symbolism. The air signs are, to sum it up in a word, civilized. No bestial behaviour for them. They think. Therefore they have a chance to think about morals, values, principles, concepts, systems, right and wrong behaviour, social rules, and anything else that can be processed into means for evaluating experience. In fact, the air signs are so civilized that the only inanimate object in zodiacal symbolism – the Balance – belongs to Libra, an air sign. I think, therefore I am human, and no longer animal. Air is the most human element, the quality which has enabled man to create societies, rules for living together, codes of ethics, writing, learning, and the vast and awesome array of gifts and curses which fall under the umbrella of modern technology. Air has made man master of his planet; or so he thinks.

Now what do you notice about a person who is predominantly airy in temperament? The old medieval word for an airy temperament was sanguine, and a sanguine person was always optimistic, never ruffled, never upset, always positive. First and foremost, the airy temperament is reasonable. He is less likely to go hysterical when things do not fall his way, because he has developed the knack of seeing viewpoints other than his own. He is objective enough to recognize that the world is larger than just him; so he is prepared to cope with disappointments and vicissitudes in a rather philosophical way. Even when angry, he will try to reason with his opponent, and he is a great adherent to the ethical code of integrity and honesty in all human dealings. He is usually prepared to consider society as an organism which is built for the benefit of those who belong to it, so that he will deliberately fight what he considers selfish or irrational behaviour. It just isn't fair, from his point of view. And because he is often well-educated, and at least self-educated, he has a wide variety of sources from which to draw for his attitudes and his beliefs. Air is rarely narrow-minded. He may be horribly narrow in other ways; but his mind is always open to ideas.

The airy person will, because of this constant propensity for reflection, rarely react spontaneously. He will assess a social situation carefully, rather than feel his way into it. He is logical, and must have explanations and names for the things which come into his field of awareness. They need not be tangible, but they must be explainable. He is sometimes so logical that he can make you scream, when he asks you to explain feeling states or moods or nonrational intuitions which in a million years do not lend themselves to the careful scrutiny of his analytical brain. He can make you feel as though you have teamed up with a cross between a computer and a refrigerator. Naturally those sterling virtues would have to be balanced with some pretty sterling problems. And air's greatest problem is what appears as coldness in ordinary human relationships.

Yes, air people can give the impression of being exceedingly cold. Not, mind you, in the ordinary social sense. There is no element so adept at the graces of group interchange: ordinary chit-chat about a wide variety of interesting topics, objective and intelligent discussion, stimulating conversation, genuine tolerance of others' viewpoints. But that arctic breeze brushes you sometimes when you are alone with him and you want to talk about how you feel, and he does a lot of thinking about how he feels, and some more thinking about how you feel, and then a lot about how he thinks he thinks he feels, and by the time he has got round to working it out to his satisfaction – structured, named, analyzed, evaluated, and slotted into the grid which to him offers the final differentiation of his values in life, the moment – as they say – has passed.

Having already said that there is no such thing as total objectivity, it should be said that the air signs as a group try harder than anybody else to achieve it. And they do come close; they have the priceless gift of being willing to consider people, events and ideas outside their own personal range of experience as equally valuable and deserving of attention and energy as those things that touch their personal lives. In fact, it's sometimes weighted so heavily on the larger picture that the smaller picture – particularly that of personal relationships – often recedes into the misty distance and you are left feeling peculiarly unimportant and ashamed of your own demandingness. Well, nobody's perfect. Without the element of air, we would still be hitting woolly mammoths on the head with rocks, and there never would have been a wheel; it is the element of air which gives us the ability for abstract thought.

Another way of getting some understanding of the airy temperament is to watch the way an air type strives to understand things. He will perpetually ask why, in contrast to his fellows who will either react with a simple 'I like it' or 'It's horrible,' and leave lofty speculations about the nature of man and the cosmos to the philosophers. But air, even uneducated, is a natural philosopher. Questioning the structures behind the manifest world comes as naturally to him as breathing. Even on a prosaic level, the scientific minds of air will be at work ferreting out the secrets of the economic structure of a business, the composition of fertilizer, the organization and systematization of farmland, the tensions and pressures and laws at work within social groups. One keyword for air is reason. Another is logic. And a third, equally important, is system. Air is the element of systems. Everything must make a coherent pattern. If it doesn't fit into the pattern, either the airy type will make up a new pattern – often called philosophy, psychology or religion – or he will refuse to recognize that thing as a reality. Things that don't fit into patterns are extremely annoying to airy people. That includes irrational inexplicable patterns of behaviour, unwonted emotions and moods that do not fit into the *schema*, unusually charismatic or strangely magnetic personalities, and actions that do not stem from any obvious cause. Watch the air sign when something like this, some denizen of the oceanic depths of the nonrational side of life, smacks him in the face like a mermaid's tail flicked out of the water. You can virtually see his brow furrow as he begins the long chain back to what might possibly explain this phenomenon, so that he can understand it. Expecting him to accept something without understanding it is hopeless. He must understand everything. His whole picture of the universe rests on his capacity for comprehension. Take it away and you will see a very frightened individual.

A long time ago I noticed that the field of psychology was full of air signs. At first this struck me as odd; after all, apart from the odd pastimes of chasing rats in the laboratory which go under the misnomer of academic psychology, the field itself deals with the 'soul' of man (the word means the study of the soul), and thus concerns itself with inner states, mainly emotional. I expected lots of Scorpio and Cancer and Pisces. Instead I found an overwhelming number of Aquarians, large groups of Geminis, hordes of Librans. Eventually it began to come clear. The air signs, because they must understand everything, must make systems to describe the phenomena they encounter in life. The one phenomena they perpetually encounter and find perpetually difficult to comprehend is the human being. Hence psychology, for to air it is a way of understanding that which intrinsically cannot be explained, let alone defined. But as we said, air tries harder.

I suspect air signs gravitate toward astrology too, for the same reason. You find most of them working on the research side, attempting to systematize the cosmos itself. God, to the air signs, is alive and well and hiding in systems. Very well. It doesn't do to knock it, when for the element of air this is where reality lies.

We must, of course, talk a little about the dark side of air. It is, after all, such a light element by nature – sanguine. You might have guessed the dark side is pretty dark. And you can guess as well that the side of life which defies systematization most consistently, which refuses analysis and structure, which cannot be explained verbally or conceptually, is both the most annoying thing in the world to air and also the most fascinating. Emotion.

Air, as we said, can give the appearance of being rather cold. In fact, airy people are often afraid of this quality in themselves, and try particularly hard to show sentiment at the appropriate moment, lest they get the reputation of being heartless. The sense of being cut off is a common experience for those living with airy people. It is as though the person is there one minute and then gone, leaving his body sitting in the chair talking. But there is the distinct impression that the room is empty, that you are alone in it. It is a highly amusing experience if you aren't involved, since you can see the flick of the light switch as the air sign abruptly pushes his emotional responses into the unconscious and the machine registers nil. It is exceedingly hurtful if you are in love, since it's like somebody cut the cord and left you utterly alone. But there it is. Air represses emotions he cannot deal with. By repress we don't mean control, either. That too. But it's much more serious than that. He just blanks them out. He's no more aware of them than you are. They vanish into the vault, and the surface reveals a smooth, glassy consistency. Angry? Of course he's not angry. Hurt? Don't be ridiculous. Jealous? Why, he never feels jealousy. You begin to feel distinctly crude and irrational and bloody-minded in the face of all that nonreactiveness. Don't let it fool you. You should recognize what he doesn't know about himself. The element of air masks an intensely emotional nature, which positively terrifies the pants off him. If he's lucky, it will remain unconscious for a long time. Or maybe I should say if he's unlucky; for the longer he blocks off his feeling responses, the worse the inevitable explosion will be. Yes, inevitable. Nothing dies that isn't lived out. Psychic energy doesn't vanish because you don't like it. It just goes underground and then surfaces when your back is turned some dark night.

Beneath that sanguinity is a lot of sensitivity, an acute sensitivity that allows the airy person to be much more easily hurt than others and much more deeply wounded.

It also causes him to be more inclined toward emotional dependence, and a profound need for tenderness and sympathy which he cannot for the life of him ask for in any straightforward way. The other elements, when they feel weak, frightened, needful, jealous, hurt, angry or rejected, or wildly in love, will tell you so. Earth will buy you flowers, maybe, and fire will write you a flamboyant poem. Water will positively inundate you with emotion. But air? Why, air will discuss the weather. What did you expect? Or the political situation in Iran. Or the state of the labour unions. And if you're a telepath or know something about astrology, you can learn to pick up the body language, the dilation of the pupils of the eyes, the movements of the hands, the feeling tone, the intangible communication of an emotional fact that – if he faced it – would embarrass him immensely. Be patient. Nobody blushes like an air sign.

Emotionally, in short, the air signs – most sophisticated of all in the realm of thought and understanding – are children. They have the entire spectrum of a child's nature too, both the dark and the light. On the one hand their naïveté is touching and beautiful, and every emotional experience has a depth and meaning which the more jaded types quite miss. Air can really be enchanted, because on this level he is childlike, and children still respond to wonder. He can also be touchingly trusting, in a way which makes you always want to show your best face and treat him with integrity. The idealism inherent in his feelings is a powerful pull toward living up to the ideal. There is a purity of emotion, a lack of worldliness, which he may find embarrassing, but which is a rare and precious gift if you happen to be the recipient.

He also has the egocentricity, dependency, crankiness, clinginess, and oversensitivity of the child. Remember the tantrums that children throw when you neglect them? Well, you may never see a real tantrum.

More likely you'll see a sulk, or a very subtle coolness
which makes its point loud and clear. You rejected me.
Now I'm going to reject you. So there. This kind of
sulkiness and unconscious moodiness is very difficult to
endure if you don't understand it. Especially when you
try to tell him about it. The dialogue runs something
like this:

'What's the matter, dear? You seem to be in a bad
mood.'
(*Translation: you've gone cold. What have I done?*)
'Nothing's the matter. I'm not in a bad mood. I'm
perfectly all right.'
(*Smirk of secret satisfaction that you've been rebuffed
and noticed.*)
(*Translation: I never have moods. It's you that's
emotional and moody.*)
'But I know something's wrong.'
'Look, just leave me alone, will you? I keep telling
you nothing's wrong. Don't be so damned demanding.'

This is a classic scenario. And the annoying part of it
is that the air person isn't lying. He's telling you the
truth as he understands it. He always tells the truth,
which is one of his great failings. (Like when you look
terrible, or he announces to you that he isn't sure if he
loves you today.) He really doesn't know. And for him
to ferret out what has happened means he must become
aware of his own emotions. Which means the hurt he
imagines you dealt him, the neglect, the jealousy, the
whatever that is the last thing in the world he wishes to
admit he is experiencing. It just isn't civilized.

No question about it. Of all the elements, this strange
animal is the most difficult of all in love affairs. That is,
if you aren't an emotional telepath. If you are, then
you're all right, for the glory and the tragedy both of
the airy people is that when they really give their hearts,

like children, they give them forever. The trouble is that they can give it and not know it, and leave the relationship (or be left) and discover it thirty years later, when it's much too late. One of the paradoxes of human nature displays itself in glowing colours here. Each element of the zodiac is related to a sphere of life, and each has a special gift for expressing in that sphere of life. But each element also has a secret underside which is just the opposite, like the undertow of the tide as it's coming in. In behavioural terms, air is a somewhat chilly element. But if you really pierce the layer on the surface, and get past that constant analysing and rational structuring that goes on habitually in the airy mind, you will find that the airy person's feelings run deep and strong – so deep and so strong, in fact, that they terrify him. Emotionally, air is a child. A child's feeling nature is naïve, intense, and not very flexible. In feeling matters, air simply isn't very sophisticated, although you'd think from all that polished social charm and the ease with which he flirts and chats and makes clever innuendoes that relationships are an easy matter for him. Not so. What you have, really, is all the vulnerability, sensitivity, and needfulness of a child's feelings in an adult's body. And a good piece of advice to anyone involved in a relationship with a strongly airy temperament is: handle with care, for the person usually isn't aware himself or herself of the depth to which the emotions can reach. Airy people can often be infuriating because of their lack of warmth in close relationships. You get the feeling they are treating you the same as everybody else: fairly, with polite interest, but nothing special. But if you can understand this side of air's nature, and coax it into expression gently (airy people often come near to paralysis when confronted with violently expressed emotional demands), then you're rewarded with all the delicacy and depth of this naïve but powerful love. Beneath the cool wit, air is an incurable romantic in emotional realms, and is truly incapable of using feeling for diplomacy or manipulation. Children, after all, are the only truly honest souls among us.

Gemini

*I*t's said that Gemini is one of the easiest signs to recognize. In the first place, Geminis usually talk a lot, so you have a chance to observe quickly that urbane, witty, cosmopolitan charm in any social situation. (Remember people like David Niven and Marilyn Monroe, two famous Geminians.) Gemini is also recognizable because he's often not where you last left him; and it's common astrological knowledge that you can't tie the Twins down with a heavy cord and expect this sylph of the air to remain with docility and patience until you give the cord a tug. More likely he'll perform a Houdini-like trick and vanish before your very eyes, leaving you with the cord. Unpredictable is another word which generally applies to the typical Geminian; changeable as quicksilver, loving disguise and mimicry, fascinated for a little while with just about everything, quick to become bored and move on. Interested in many subjects, proficient in few, for the world is too large and there is too much to know and too much to talk about to waste time plunging into depths and missing all those other opportunities. To a greater or lesser extent, Gemini is the butterfly of the zodiac (some butterflies are smaller and nimbler than others, but they all fly), gracing your vision for a brief moment while settling on some choice flower, and then moving on. Of course there are Geminis who have become skilled at some particular study or art or profession – but even these Geminis must somehow find variety and versatility within it. You'll never find a Geminian actor, for example, always playing the same type of role.

Gemini has been accused, on the negative side, of being superficial and shallow. But this is neither true nor fair. The Geminian mind is perfectly capable of depth and concentration, when necessary. The sphere of ideas is his natural hunting ground. It's just that Gemini's mind works in a curiously non-linear way. He knows that if you spend too long with one thing, you're liable to miss all its associations and connections. And Gemini's aim is not to acquire specialized in-depth knowledge of any one thing. He's after a broad and comprehensive spectrum of knowledge, which can only be culled by stopping at every port. He appreciates satire, and the sentence which in short-hand somehow communicates the whole picture without the necessity of delving into great detail. And he also appreciates what's interesting in the moment. His concentration isn't foggy, like that of many Pisceans; nor is he absent-minded. It's just that he's liable to be distracted easily. Too many things catch his attention. And why not? Life, to Gemini, is full of moving things; and where they move, he moves with them.

Sometimes Gemini's sly mimicry can be cutting and embarrassing, just because he's a master at picking out the gesture, the expression, which offers the whole situation at a single glance. He usually doesn't mean to be cruel; but dwelling in the heights as he does, he isn't often aware of the emotional reactions going on around him. He isn't terribly vulnerable himself, and has the precious gift of self-laughter as well. You can mimic him if you like. What he can't understand is the poor soul who bursts into noisy tears because of his little joke. What did he do? Never mind, it's obviously time to move on.

Gemini excels in the media, particularly at journalism, the kind of writing or reporting which communicates the entire picture in a few clever images. And the urge to communicate is powerful in this sign as is the urge to learn. There is something eternally childlike about Gemini's mind. If you take the cycle of the zodiac as a symbol of different stages of man's development, Gemini, being the third sign, represents the stage where the thinking processes begin. Watch a child when he's interested in something. His interest may be short-lived; but as soon as he discovers something, he must tell everybody about it. It's as natural to him as breathing. Geminis often monopolize conversations for hours, not because they want to draw special attention to themselves as many Leos do, but because if they know something interesting then it's the most natural thing in the world to tell it to everyone else too.

And Gemini is also the great democrat of the zodiac. You couldn't really expect him to be otherwise; he treasures his own capacity to think and certainly isn't prepared to give over the right of decision-making and concept-forming to anybody else. Tell him what to think about something and you'll see his back receding into the distance very quickly. The immense pleasure that Gemini takes in discovering something for himself, finding something out, learning something, is so obvious and so bright that you could scarcely imagine him following someone else's opinions with any docility. And because he likes to be well-informed, it's hard to fool him or swing him emotionally. He's interested in people, from a distance, and loves to find out how they tick; and he will talk to just about anybody to find out a little something about something because to him everything is interesting. You'll rarely find conservatism or prejudice in Gemini's lively, stimulating mind.

He pays a price for these shining gifts, of course. No one can be everything, and we're all pretty lopsided to start with. In order to preserve that smooth, polished world-view that comes from skimming over the surface of an amazing variety of life's experiences, Gemini must often sacrifice his capacity for deeper relating. The more he spreads himself among the flowers, sampling here and there, the less likely he is to be able to sustain a close relationship. Gemini isn't really the person to choose if you like long intense discussions about emotions. It makes him feel trapped, crushed and possessed. He'll usually make a joke or a witty quip about the things he feels most intensely about. And he'd prefer that you quip too, rather than pour out your deepest soul in grand, theatrical gestures. It makes him turn pale with embarrassment. Then he's liable to do his vanishing act, and you're left to clean up the mess.

With all that knowledge clattering about inside his skull, you'd expect Gemini to also have knowledge of himself. Not so. He is the least introspective sign of the zodiac, and it takes some pretty cricitcal or difficult experience to get him to actually sit down and sort out his own motives. It's not his style. Like a child, he's capable of having several different and distinct personalities, and being quite unaware of it himself. He's also capable of plunging into some pretty sour emotional states or moods, which don't last very long (no mood does with Gemini) and which he rarely analyzes or understands. His demand for personal freedom is so strong that he'll often recoil with resentment if you try to get him to change or alter his natural changeability. And he's fully capable of practising big and little deceptions, both on others and on himself, when he feels too pinned down.

You'll notice that references to childlike qualities have been mentioned several times. In a nutshell, Gemini is the eternal child of the zodiac. This doesn't mean he's childish, in the sense that we use the word to describe people whose behaviour has embarrassed us in some way. It means childlike, which is not the same thing. His lively interest in learning, his tendency to go off in several different directions at once (I know several Geminis who watch television and read books simultaneously, or carry on phone conversations and write letters, or any other sleight of hand you can think of), and his dislike of having to carry responsibilities which he can't understand are all qualities which give him a lot in common with children. In fact, many Geminis get on brilliantly with children – not from the emotional, motherly point of view like Cancer does, but because they love things that amuse them and are downright brilliant at keeping the wandering interest of a child's mind because their own minds wander in the same way.

No, Gemini doesn't care for responsibility very much. He's usually got a strong ethical code – all airy signs do – and he'll deal with people fairly. In that sense he's one of the most responsible of the signs, because he's an idealist as far as how he sees people and their interrelationships. But duty for duty's sake doesn't interest him, and he likes to travel light. He's generally happier with a few back doors open, in case he decides he needs a little journey to refresh him. Tie him down to one place and one job doing one thing for any length of time and he'll either go to pieces in a mass of nervous fidgeting, smoking, nail-biting and paper-shredding, or he'll leave. Gemini needs mental and physical mobility. Put him where he can talk to people, travel a little, and he's fine, and perfectly capable of discharging responsibility. Put him with a partner who talks a lot about duty, and you're guaranteeing a failed relationship.

Words are fascinating things for Gemini. Whether he's the more verbal type of Gemini who talks a blue streak or the quieter type (yes, there are some) whose minds may be spinning with all kinds of things but who are too introverted to tell you about them, language is usually a wonderful and eternally stimulating game for him. I have met many Geminis who are incurable punmakers – a form of humour which seems to be peculiar to only a couple of signs, Pisces being the other – because they love to play with language. Self-expression through language is extremely important, and Gemini also often loves to hear himself talk – not because he thinks he's so wonderful, but because he's fascinated with what words can do. Often he'll learn other languages quickly, and word-plays amuse him where clumsier forms of humour leave him cold. And language means a lot to him, too. Language is the expression of a whole people, and tells you a lot about the psychological traits of the country where it's spoken. Marlene Dietrich is said to have once made an amusing observation on language. In French, she said, the male genital organs are feminine gender; in German, the female are masculine gender; and in English, both are neuter. That's the sort of thing that Geminis notice. Why? Well, because it's interesting. And it makes you think.

Life isn't a terribly serious business for Gemini. For this reason many Geminis drift, uncertain as to where their skills or vocations lie, because so much is interesting and they often show a little talent at a lot of things. Even if Gemini has one definite talent, he'll generally be pretty restless and dissatisfied dedicating himself to it, because, well, only one thing to do is pretty boring. In some ways it's good general advice to Gemini to always have either two jobs, or a job and an important hobby, because that way when one gets boring the other seems fresh and interesting. We aren't taught to look at careers like this; we're supposed, in this world, to do one thing and do it well. Often the Gemini is sadly shortchanged by this policy, because his real gift isn't at doing one thing well, but at finding the links between two completely disparate things. He's really a bridge-builder in ideas. And he's happiest when he can translate one sphere of life into the language of another.

You can generally spot Gemini by his eyes. Not that they're peculiar or anything. It's just that they're generally moving, even when he's talking to you and deeply interested in what you're saying. But he simply can't help noticing someone new who has walked into the room, or some new object which has appeared on the table or the wall. This is pretty disconcerting to many people who like to feel that all his attention is focused on them. If you're the sort of person who needs this kind of concentrated attention, avoid Gemini. He's simply not capable of shutting out the stimuli around him. It doesn't mean he's not interested. It does mean he's not that involved. Deep involvement or commitment is difficult for him. It's not that he needs a lot of rope. It means he needs no rope at all. Then, if you're not paying too close attention, you might discover to your surprise and pleasure that he's still there.

Ⓘ The Myth

The most famous twins in our mythological heritage are Castor and Pollux, the sons of Zeus who were hatched from an egg laid by Leda after she mated with Zeus disguised as a Swan. That tells you something right away: Gemini is half-bird anyway. From the soaring seabird to the mimicking parrot, Gemini has a lot in common with our feathered friends.

Now, Castor and Pollux are a most peculiar pair of twins in myth. This is largely because, although both are brave and clever warriors, one of them is human and one is divine. When one of them dies, the pair are so close that their pleas finally reach the ears of Zeus, and he makes a deal with them. (Geminis, by the way, have a real talent for making deals.) They're allowed to alternate their immortality. While one is spending a little holiday on Olympus with the gods, the other gets to have a turn being a mortal man on earth. Then they change places. It's sort of like foreign exchange students at university. And each time they change they get to spend a little time together, to exchange notes.

This myth, playful as it sounds, gives us a lot of insight into the deeper meaning of Gemini. There is often an awareness of a highly spiritual and ethereal kind in Gemini. I mean spiritual here not in the ordinary religious sense – which is often anything but spiritual – but a kind of delicate tuning to a transpersonal or different realm of consciousness. Many Geminis show this in a very finely developed intuition, which registers all sorts of things at a nonrational level which can be deeply distressing to the more intellectual and rational side of the person. Also, I don't mean spiritual in the sense of seance parlours and spiritualism. It's a feeling of an other, higher world. Gemini has a sense of the eternal, of the secret currents at work in the fabric of life. It's part of the reason why he often doesn't take life or life's responsibilities that seriously. Something deep within him knows that isn't all there is to it.

The trouble is, those perceptions aren't consistent, and they also often aren't welcome. As the myth tells us, one twin dwells in the heavenly realms while one stays on earth. They aren't both in one place at the same time. Often Gemini's intuitions clash violently with his more carefully structured, analytical mind. Often he's a stranger to himself, not knowing whether he's a scientist or a mystic, an artist or an intellectual. Sometimes he tries to forcibly block one of these twin sides of himself from expressing – and it may be either one – and causes himself a lot of anguish in the process. Gemini's alternations, his periods of light and dark moods, of extroversion and introversion, of vision and analysis, are curious to him as well as to others. Which one is he? Both, of course. And somehow, during the course of his life, he needs to learn to translate what goes on in one realm to the language of the other. They're both reality for him. It's like an alternating battery current. Sometimes he's really in touch with his own secret inner Self, and then he shines and it's like the sun coming out on a spring morning. He's the beautiful butterfly, the eternal child, the sparkling one who brushes gold dust on each thing he passes. Then, suddenly, he's alienated. He's no longer on Olympus, but stuck on earth, in a mortal body. Life is a little bitter and sometimes dark and mocking, and he's liable to get cynical and unpleasant, and thinks a lot about death. He goes away to brood, because the connection has been cut and he's only mortal after all. And his mortality, the fact that he must grow old like everybody else, weighs heavily on him.

You can't interfere with Gemini's cycle, or expect

him to change it. He needs his period of collision with mortality just as he needs to breathe the scent of the Olympian heights. This cycle is his alone, and you're very foolish if you think he's doing it against you or because of you. More sensitive souls, like Pisceans and Scorpios and Cancers, can be hurt and feel horribly rejected when Gemini is going through one of his dark turns. He can be pretty nasty and chilly while it lasts. But it isn't personal.

This alternation in Gemini can be described in another way. You might say that it has to do with a polarity in him: intellectual and emotional, or male and female, or conscious and unconscious. One is human, the other is divine. Often Gemini becomes confused about whether to make a rational judgment or an emotional one. Sometimes he gets into a lot of sexual confusion as well, because there's quite a bit of both sexes in him – whether it's a Gemini man or a Gemini woman – which isn't a reflection on his sexuality, but really means that he's both intuitive and rational, sensitive and decisive, reflective and outgoing. Masculine and feminine in Gemini are meant here in their broadest sense, and a lot of Geminis are pretty confused about which role or image to play because they discover both in them, and relate to both men and women equally well.

All this makes for pretty inconsistent behaviour. Sometimes it helps if Gemini can at least differentiate when he's being Castor and when he's being Pollux, and try getting them to talk to each other. You'll often hear Gemini talking to himself anyway. Well, of course. There are two of him, aren't there? One moment the world is shining and full of light, the next it's dark and imprisoning. It's one of the reasons why Geminis are so good are reporting and writing and dealing with the public. They're acutely sensitive to both faces of life, and are usually well-stocked with both idealism and cynicism. They see both and are both.

There is another mythical image which is important to consider if you want to understand Gemini. The planet which rules this sign is Mercury. Now, Mercury is the smallest and fastest planet in the solar system – in itself a good symbol for the speed and mobility of Geminian perceptions. In mythology, Mercury is the messenger of the gods. He carries messages and information from one god to another, and from the gods on Olympus to men on earth. He is also known as the god of thieves and liars, the protector of the roads, and the lord of commerce. Get the picture? He is an amoral god, fluid and flexible, and concerned always with bridges; between gods and men, between man and man, in the form of ideas, money, channels of communication both tangible and intangible.

Mercury is also knows as Mercurius in the medieval symbolism of alchemy. And this tells an important thing about Gemini. Mercurius, as the alchemists try to describe him, is a symbol of the process of understanding, of connecting, of integrating. When you suddenly realize something or understand it, and the light dawns, and two things suddenly click that didn't have any relationship before, the alchemists would have said that was the trickster spirit Mercurius at work. Remember those cartoon strips where somebody gets a bright idea and it's pictured as a lightbulb suddenly flashing on over his head? That's Mercurius. In alchemy Mercurius connects male and female, and allows the Great Work to complete its transformation of substance. He's called the Great Transformer, and is pictured as being androgynous, male and female both. He's the one who bridges the opposites. Bear with us. It may be esoteric, but it's important. For here is the key to Gemini's real path in life, the thing toward which those with the sun in Gemini are really striving. It's the interpreter, the translator, the messenger. But to perform this work of intermediary, Gemini must first find ways of bridging the opposites inside himself. He needs to be able to accept both the male and the female in himself, the mind and the emotions, the spiritual and thé material, the light and the dark. For much of his life, Gemini often wanders in a split and dissociated state, trying first one opposite and then the other, before he learns that he can be both. If you stand in the middle between two struggling opposites, you notice that what you thought was conflict really isn't. It's complementariness, one thing helping and supporting the other, rather than them being mutually exclusive. Opposite things aren't really enemies at all. They're part of one holistic view of life. And that's what Gemini is really after.

Ⅱ The Shadow

What kind of shadow does the god with winged sandals cast? Well, as you would expect, there seem to be two distinct Geminian shadows. Some Geminis display both, and some only one. The first we'll call the Irresponsible Child syndrome. The second we'll call the Plotter. The first one we can illustrate with an actual dialogue which took place between a friend of mine and a Gemini at a party.

GEMINI: Anyway, let me tell you my views on how this country should be run. First of all, I'm really opposed to the materialistic society. I think people have got their values all mixed up. All they're after is bigger houses and bigger cars and more furniture, and nobody cares at all what happens to his fellow man. I think we should return to individual self-sufficiency.

FRIEND: By the way, what do you do? (Noticing the expensively tailored shirt and the large solid gold ring.)

GEMINI: Who, me? Look, I don't want to talk about me. When people ask you that at a party, they're really saying, 'How much money do you make?' We were talking about what's wrong with society. If you really want to know, I do a bit of songwriting, and that sort of thing.

FRIEND: But how do you support yourself, since you're opposed to the conventional lifestyle of working an ordinary job?

GEMINI: Oh, I manage. I just hate the sort of mentality that goes to work from nine to five, and takes out a mortgage, and gets all hung up with the bureaucracy of society's rules and values. By the way, can you give me a cigarette?

The punch line is that last question. Our friend, shadow-Gemini, having waxed eloquent about what was wrong with the materialistic world, then genuinely expected my friend to generously give something which she herself had worked at one of those dreary nine-to-five jobs to pay for. She refused. Our shadow-Gemini was outraged, and immediately classified her as a selfish, materialistic philistine. That's the Irresponsible Child: like the god of thieves and liars, our Mercury-ruled shadow here wants to only have the divine twin, and dispense with the human one.

The Plotter, in a sense, does the reverse. He can't find his divine twin; so he feels terribly isolated and rather neurotic most of the time. He can't connect with himself, so he feels disconnected. You get this kind of typical scenario:

NEW GIRLFRIEND TO GEMINI: I don't know much about you. Tell me about that place you come from – Penzance, was it?

GEMINI: Oh, you wouldn't know it, it's just a village, look, I must just run out and get a morning newspaper. (*Later*)

GIRLFRIEND: You mentioned something about a contract. Look, what is it that you actually do? I'm really interested.

GEMINI: Oh, that, it was just a contract, do you think we can go see *Nosferatu* tonight, I hear it's supposed to be really spectacular and I love Herzog's films.

GIRLFRIEND: (beginning to feel slightly uneasy) But you didn't answer my question.

GEMINI: No. Quite right. I didn't. I'm just watching your reactions. When I don't tell you something, you get kind of pale and nervous. I wonder why you want to know so much.

GIRLFRIEND: Know so much? I'd just like to know something about you. Look, we've been going out for six weeks. I have a right to know.

GEMINI: Don't use that word right. No one has the right to know anything about anybody. If I choose to tell you, then that's my privilege. I suppose you're used to extracting information out of your guys, so you can control them. Well, you won't get any from me. I know that game. Why don't we just go to the film, all right?

The Plotter is Gemini's paranoid shadow. He's a plotter not because he plans things against others, but because he's convinced everyone wants something from him, and he works out long convoluted ways of not giving it, whatever it might be. His characteristics are chronic evasiveness and often chronic lying; and he's also been known to deliberately try to trap you while you're attempting to pry into his secrets, so that he can justify the fact that he's busy hiding. This is a really difficult face of Gemini to deal with, and it stems from his sense of emotional alienation. Because he has a problem relating through feelings, he often can't trust; and he'll deny even the simplest confidences to another person because he's conviced that, if you know too much, you've got control of him. Gemini at his best is playfully evasive, and doesn't like a lot of prying and probing. Gemini fallen into his shadowy side is extremely difficult, because he's capable of being extremely hurtful and using the pointed darts of his nimble tongue to shame you into silence when all you were doing was showing interest. And when this shadow side of Gemini surfaces, you can't take anything he says literally, because more likely than not it's meant to be a red herring so he can go on concealing something which he doesn't understand.

With both sides of the Gemini shadow, the same difficulty lies at the root. It's the problem of the opposites, and of finding a way to live them both. Gemini when he's lost in his divine child side can be charming but a hopeless sponge on others' money and time. He takes for granted the fact that he's entitled; remember that Father Zeus gave him immortality! He's entitled to Special Exemptions. As he gradually comes to realize that he must also live in the world and submit himself to boundaries and responsibilities, he grows and changes, and can bring some of his lighthearted trust in life into everything he does, brightening the lives of those around him. When Gemini is lost in the earthbound side, he fears life. He often tries to analyze it to pieces in the hope that he'll be spared from hurt, and develops a profound mistrust of other people's motives. He loses his sparkle, and simply becomes cunning. As he gradually discovers something worth loving inside himself, something that makes him unique and different, he can open up a little, because he doesn't feel so horribly vulnerable. And whether he's your local newsagent or John F. Kennedy, another Gemini, he will have managed to hold the bridge between two realms so that others can pass across and taste a little of both worlds.

Ⓤ The Gemini Lover

In traditional astrology, Gemini is said to get on best with the other two airy signs, Libra and Aquarius. This sounds great on paper. But no person is just one sign, and also like doesn't always attract like. Sometimes they bore each other. And while Gemini has a lot in common with the other air signs, and may communicate well with them in the realm of ideas, he has an irresistible attraction to the water signs – Pisces, Scorpio and Cancer. This is because Gemini usually has a pretty hard time both knowing what he feels subjectively about things and expressing those feelings to anyone else. When he gets around those watery types, he loosens up. He's often fascinated by their disinterest in rational explanations, and charmed (or alternatively, terrified) by their lack of embarrassment about their own emotions. Now, we've mentioned a little about air-water relationships. They often produce steam. Fog. Mist. Sleet. And other manifestations of two queerly incompatible yet magnetically attracted elements.

A Geminian friend of mine once referred to discussions about emotional affairs as 'swamp trips'. This pinpoints very nicely Gemini's characteristic attitude toward relationships when they begin to get a little heavy. Like a swamp: damp, suffocating, dangerous, dark, full of things that bite and pull you down into the mire. The typical Gemini is often positively terrified of emotional demands. Yet he has a propensity, over and over again, of landing himself in relationships with people who are basically feeling-oriented people. And these watery folk are often full of admiration and fascination for

Gemini's versatile mind, yet need a more instinctual
kind of rapport for their own fulfilment.

It's almost as though Gemini, the eternal butterfly,
trying to solve the mystery of the multiple people he
feels himself to be, longs for a safe and emotionally
secure relationship to help him feel a little less frag-
mented. If he can find someone who loves all those
different faces in him, then maybe, he hopes, he'll learn
to love them himself. Gemini's relationships, when
they're of this kind, can go one of two ways. The left-
hand fork ends with the partner feeling emotionally
frustrated, starved for affection and closeness, rejected
and shut out. Gemini, in his turn, feels oppressed,
suffocated, bored, and caged. It's a sad scenario, this
one, and fraught with heavy blame on both sides –
although you won't often hear Gemini complaining
loudly about his emotional vicissitudes. He'll more
often make a joke of the whole thing, or an ironic and
witty remark, and keep the entire thing quietly buried
along with other disturbing encounters which he doesn't
dare probe to understand. And he'll probably come
away from it with a little less confidence in his own
reliability – which is never very great anyway – and will
then move on into the next relationship, without quite
realizing what went wrong.

The right-hand fork of this road is a lot happier.
Given time and communication (any relationship for
Gemini must have communication) and understanding,
Gemini can often ground himself a little better through
a relationship, and learn to look inward a little more.
He can begin to discover his own needs and sensitivities,
which he often overlooks, and this discovery – that he
has feelings too – helps his habitual condemnation of
other people's needs as devouring and possessive. All
too often, he attracts highly maternal types who smother
him with solicitous care and gently condescending

motherly love. No wonder Gemini all too often remains a little boy – or a little girl – with a dark secret face.

In common with the other two airy signs, Gemini usually has a high code of ethics in his relationships. Although he's often evasive, and dislikes being probed for secrets, he'll usually not deliberately lie or lose his integrity in dealing with others. The element of air has its code of principles, and its principles are high. Many Geminians try with almost superhuman effort to live up to their ethical codes, and fail because the ethical code doesn't allow anybody to react in an inconsistent way, and then crumple beneath the anger of an emotionally hurt partner. Gemini takes the path of deviousness when there isn't any other way to go. But usually there isn't any other way because he simply can't understand emotional language. How can you explain yourself in the face of an accusation you simply don't understand? If you make a demand of Gemini – like, 'You've been ignoring me all evening,' he is likely to offer an evasive answer on principle, because he's aware of so many possible answers and so unaware of his real feelings. Usually he won't even know what you're talking about. It seems perfectly all right to him.

One of the most difficult combinations of signs is Gemini and Scorpio, whether you find this within one person's chart – one the sun, the other the ascendant – or between two charts. They personify the opposite poles of air and water beautifully. Scorpio is a water sign, and therefore highly subjective, with feeling-based responses. And the typical Scorpio will rarely put up with evasiveness, since his nature compels him to dig to the bottom of any issue to discover its hidden roots and motives. Gemini can't bear to be psychoanalyzed, largely because he's terrified of what he'll find underneath. Many Geminians are scornful of the whole realm of psychological exploration, because they have a gift of analyzing things and figure that once you've named a problem it'll go away quietly. Of course it doesn't since intellectual analysis isn't any help with the feelings. Gemini will often be flippant when accused of some dark and convoluted motive. Or he'll make something up. Or he'll go cold, and simply not answer, or walk out. The truth is that he doesn't know, and what he doesn't know frightens him. Have compassion. Gemini often seeks help from intellectual maps and systems and structures in his attempts to find out what he really feels about things.

There are Geminis, both male and female, who always remain children, in both the best and worst sense of the word. They are the eternal butterflies, gilded and charming, delightful and about as substantial as *zabaglione*. If you get involved with this more extreme type of Gemini who's never come to terms with the other twin, enjoy yourself, but keep your eyes open. Gemini needs lots and lots of rope. He may or may not hang himself with it. But commitment is terrifying to this type of Gemini, and he's usually not prepared to look beneath the sparkling and effervescent surface of his own mind, full of cross-currents and ripples and mirages, to see what either his needs or yours really are. It's just too much trouble. If you're a strongly maternal type, like Taurus or Cancer, or the gentle sensitive type like Pisces, or the intense and jealous type like Scorpio, make very sure that you've got a life of your own, so that you don't expect Gemini to carry all your emotional needs for you. He simply can't. And maybe you'll learn something from him or her: like how to let go and allow Gemini the air he needs so badly. Geminis become positively psychologically asthmatic when they can't escape.

And if you're lucky enough to find one of those Geminis who has a little self-understanding, then you're lucky indeed. For although Gemini will always be elusive and challenging, and will never take kindly to having to explain motives and reasons, and will rarely learn to enjoy dramatic emotional scenes, he'll meet you halfway. Then he's truly the Mercurius of alchemy, the translator and transformer, for he can show with the magic wand of his wit the distant mountain heights where the air is clear.

Ⅱ The Gemini Man

Several qualities are noticeable about the Gemini man. For one thing, he's usually in constant motion. Sometimes physically: he's liable to fidget, and even if he isn't fidgeting his eyes are generally moving around pretty restlessly, checking out each thing in the room and inspecting each person with immense curiosity. The hour-long gaze of intense passionate silence that says everything just isn't the Gemini man's style. Many Geminis simply can't hold their attention for that long, and besides, they don't like to be 'sprung' by somebody staring into their eyes either.

Another thing that's readily noticeable is Gemini's conversational gift. It's a rare Gemini who doesn't possess a quick wit and a cursory knowledge of just about anything, which enables him to talk to just about anybody for a little while and appear to be interested. Gemini is also a bit of a gossip – yes, the trait appears in the Gemini man as well as in the Gemini woman – and a less pleasant adjective would be 'nosy' to describe the intense curiosity with which Gemini approaches other people. He loves to find out interesting things, not because he's looking for power over you like a Scorpio would, but because it just happens to be interesting. He's gifted at drawing out several pertinent and interesting facts about you very quickly, and then, when you ask a few questions of him, dodging them with skill while he deftly shifts the subject onto the strange mating habits of greenfly.

Gemini's contact with people is always a light one. He's neither heavy-handed nor intense. It's rare to get an outpouring of intense emotion; and if you do, it will most likely come in the form of a letter, and be full of amusing anecdotes and gossip. Some people find this lightness of touch disturbing; it seems shallow and superficial. But it isn't, really. In fact it's a gift that Gemini offers – the ability to communicate and share feelings while keeping a sense of humour and a perspective. Gemini might be romantic, but it's not the romance of heavy operatic tragedy. It's the sort of light, frothy stuff that makes for lovely summer evenings drinking champagne in the rose garden; but it's not Romeo and Juliet. On the other hand, Romeo and Juliet had tragic ends, which isn't really a vision of romance that appeals to Gemini.

Absolute devotion of the kind that precludes ever speaking to or looking at another woman also isn't Gemini's style. He's interested in people and people are interested in him; besides, he can be a charming flirt, which is just one more part of the way in which he approaches life. The butterfly flirts with life itself; you can't expect him to play Othello to your Desdemona. He'll rarely show jealousy (that's all in the unconscious, along with all the other more terrifying emotions) and doesn't expect you to either. And it's impossible to keep him by your side at a party, because the whole point of a party is to talk to people. People means others besides yourself. It's also embarrassing to Gemini to seem to be too attached to one person; it spoils the image of the cloak-and-dagger mysterious secret agent which he sometimes gets a kick out of projecting. Many Geminis do their best to seem single even when they've come in the door with you, just because it's amusing to try the role on. It's a rare Gemini who obviously displays himself as half of a tight couple. Once again, it's not his style.

Words fascinate Gemini. Emotions don't, unless they can be expressed in words. The more articulate you are, the better he likes it. And he does have a thing about writing – love notes, stories, letters, jokes, whatever. Gemini-type heroes in film and literature (like Errol Flynn and David Niven) don't get their charm from heavy-handed emotional intensity or physical prowess. They get it from some cosmopolitan *panache*, a touch of culture, a taste for good wine, a love of ballet or theatre, an eye for a good book, a polished and versatile mind. If you want to be physically swept off your feet and strong-armed to the altar, avoid Gemini.

Most of all, the Gemini man is interesting, and likes to be with other people who are interesting. That means his partner must be interested and interesting; otherwise he has a very low boredom level, and has been known to seek his interests elsewhere with frequency. This doesn't mean one must be a brilliant intellectual to make a good match with Gemini. But it means that the mind has to be alive. Talk to him all day about what the baby ate and you're asking for trouble. Obviously no one can become what they aren't. But if your idea of partnership is to sit silently in front of the fire holding hands and sipping eggnogs, try a Taurus or a Cancer. You notice the signs immediately when Gemini's hit his boredom level. He fidgets. His eyes wander around a lot. He looks longingly at the telephone – an instrument of communication which many Geminis love, because it allows them to chatter without the discomfort of emotional confrontation – and waits with positively frightening eagerness for the post to be delivered. When you see those signs, either sharpen up your own wit, or take him out to the theatre. The butterfly is preparing to take off.

The most glorious thing about the Gemini man, the

thing which makes his peculiar moods and delicate evasiveness bearable, is the fact that he's really interesting. Now, to some people that might not sound like much. But to those who have had a fairly satiating dose of boring and dull people living boring and dull lives, where imagination never takes wing and humour never sparkles and everything is horribly serious and responsible and one never, never, never behaves in a zany or unpredictable or childish fashion, Gemini is like a draught of the elixir. He reminds you that life is new, and fun, and something fascinating to be explored. And having spent some time around the butterfly, you might even discover you've got wings.

Ⓘ The Gemini Woman

If you think all women should be sweet, emotional creatures without a great deal of intelligence, whose true role in life is to bear children and devote themselves to their mates, you shouldn't be reading this book in the first place. And you particularly shouldn't be reading about the airy signs, since women born under this element are even less likely than anybody else to want to fulfill that lovely traditional image. Air sign women think; and the Gemini woman, in common with her Aquarian and Libran cousins, can generally out-think most anybody you know, male or female. Her thinking might not always be either scientific or consistent; but she's a person of ideas, who needs mental stimulation and interesting people in her life. It's not that the Gemini woman is incapable of being loving, or maternal, or domestic. It's just that these things aren't usually at the top of the list of priorities. Gemini, whether male or female, must have air to breathe and space to explore.

There's often a quality of sophistication about the Gemini woman. Whether you see her in a small country village tending her home and children, or at an art gallery opening in New York City, she'll usually be the one who's read everything she can get her hands on about just about every subject you can think of. She may know something about Iranian politics, and Persian mythology, and knitting patterns, and rare butterflies, and the breeding of horses. One thing she's not: provincial. She needs company and stimulation, and you can't expect her to be happy with a life of strict routine. And she needs to be appreciated not only as a woman, but also as an interesting person. Many Gemini women become neurotic and terribly unhappy because they try to adapt themselves to somebody else's – society, family, husband – image of how they should behave, and underrate their own versatility and restlessness.

Yes, restlessness. The Gemini woman, like the Gemini man, often needs two jobs, or a series of hobbies, or a regular class or group discussion, to keep her happy. Her desire to learn is one of her strongest motivations, and needs to be developed and encouraged – whether this means attending university, or attending evening courses in one or two subjects which interest her, or just going down to the local library a lot. In career terms, the Gemini woman often makes an excellent solicitor, advertising or marketing executive, translator, teacher, journalist or photographer – and the whole world of the media, films, radio, television suit her admirably. She also needs contact with more than one person. The Gemini woman, limited to just a husband and children to talk to, will often vent her frustrations by becoming an intolerable gossip, because she simply must communicate.

Problems with emotional expression are characteristic with the Gemini woman as they are with the

Gemini man. This is true of all the airy signs. The natural Geminian tendency to hold in emotion, to negate it, to analyze it away, often means that the Gemini woman lives a kind of near-hysterical extroverted life running and running away from feelings of loneliness or unhappiness. A good case in point is Marilyn Monroe, who perhaps might have been spared the tragic conclusion to her life if she had been more emotionally honest with herself. Her attraction lay as much in her wit and her sparkle as it did in her looks, for Gemini radiates a kind of fascination whether he or she is conventionally attractive or not.

You often see Gemini women who are terribly highly-strung and nervous. It's a characteristic Geminian response to repressed emotion. It's got to do with that other twin, the one we talked about earlier. For the Gemini woman, the polarity in her nature often consists of her feminine self and her intellect, which are frequently at odds with each other. She'll have in equal proportions the same needs and drives which motivate any woman, and the Geminian intellectual drive as well. And they don't always get on too well together, these two faces, because if you pursue the mind with all its butterfly weavings and turnings, you can't afford to commit yourself either to love or to maternity. It's a hard tangle for the Gemini woman to sort out. She's often more at home in conversations with men than with her own sex; and unless her children are interesting themselves, and able to keep her mind fascinated, she often finds the nonverbal side of communication with children difficult. Many Gemini women have great academic expectations from their children, especially if they have not developed themselves along this line; and it's probably a more sensible exercise for the Geminian woman to satisfy her own love of learning and travel and excitement first before she attempts to raise a family. Otherwise that low boredom level, and the dislike of routine, can become pretty difficult.

No astrological sign is deficient in any basic human need or expression. It's just that each sign suggests a bias, a propensity to lean one way more than another. With Gemini, ruled by Mercury, the need for knowledge and experience and stimulation is often greater than the need for security. It's a question of trying to allow room in one's life for all one's needs to be fulfilled. This is why Gemini, as a sign for a woman, requires plenty of room for personal freedom, development of ideas, and contact socially beyond the family circle. Air signs, as we've said several times already, need air.

The quality of delicate romanticism exists in the Gemini woman as well as in the Gemini man. It isn't a heavy or strongly emotional romanticism; it's light, cultured, and airy. Gemini needs to be frivolous, and love for Gemini must contain some humour and some frivolity as well as more intense emotion. Also, it needs to be talked about. The Gemini woman loves words as much as the Gemini man, which means that the tacit assumption that your presence bespeaks your love doesn't accomplish any miracles. The Gemini woman appreciates a man who can be articulate, especially about his feelings. And Gemini also likes a few games; things shouldn't be brutally honest or stark or without style.

Sometimes you see a strong aesthetic sensitivity in the Gemini woman. Taste is important to her. She's often fashion-conscious and trend-conscious. She's rarely the old-fashioned type for whom the sentimental memories of Victoriana suffice. More often she'll be intensely modern in her tastes, from clothes to cars to the films she enjoys and the books she reads. Nostalgia is a Cancerian trait, not a Geminian one.

The Gemini woman can be a fascinating creature. She can also be an elusive one, and a thoroughly confusing one if you attempt to type her. She's particularly confusing if you expect her moods to be consistent and her interests focused. But once again, remember the butterfly. Butterflies aren't provided by nature for utilitarian reasons such as our food supply or the wood from which we build houses. Whatever nature had in mind, we enjoy butterflies for their beauty, for their grace, for their freedom, for their brightness. To stretch the analogy to unbearable lengths, we do derive one useful commodity from the efforts of this kingdom of nature: silk, the most delicate and luxurious and exotic of fabrics. Gemini is often like silk: you can't expect to repair your car in silk, or subject it to the brutalities of a washing machine, but treated delicately and appreciated for its beauty, it's the most cherished material in the world.

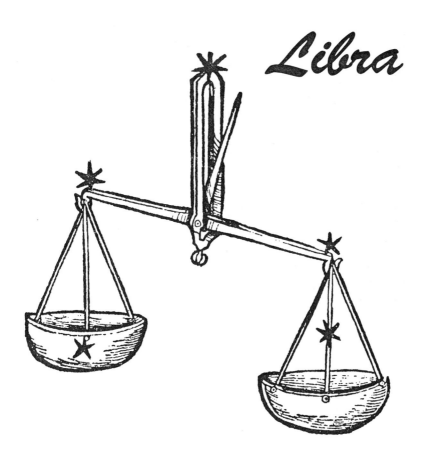

$\mathcal{Libra}$

One of the more notorious Librans of recent fame is Brigitte Bardot. She serves as a reminder that the ruling planet of Libra is Venus, goddess of love and beauty in ancient mythology. You'd think Libra would be the most obvious, easiest sign to understand. All they need is love, right? Wrong.

Remember that Libra is an airy sign. And air is concerned with ideas and principles above all else. Love, yes, of course. Every Libra thinks a lot about love, just as he thinks a lot about anything that pertains to relationship. But the operative word here is *think*.

Libra's idea of love isn't necessarily your idea of a warm, cozy, delightful tête-à-tête. More likely, it'll be one of his many theories on the nature of love and marriage, his ideals about the perfect relationship, his concepts about how people ought to behave toward each other, his urgent vision of a world where everything is absolutely balanced, polished, perfect, symmetrical, harmonious. It can drive you mad. This sign, whose symbol is the scales of balance, has less to do with ordinary sweaty human coupling than any other. What? Libra soil his hands? Never. Love, for Libra, must always be in the appropriate style: a ritual of courtly love, complete with the right gestures, the right words, the right perfume, the right satin sheets, the right scented candles, the right flowers. Be careful. Libra is the great perfectionist of the zodiac. Not Virgo, as you may have heard. Love, ah, yes. Love, for Libra, makes the world go round. But his love is a theoretical one. He knows less about love than any other sign, although he thinks about it more. That's why he's always searching for it in the most idealized possible forms. Like Aquarius and Gemini, Libra's emotional nature is often childlike and naïve.

The planet Venus symbolizes, in astrology, the urge for relationship. Let's look closely at that word. Relating one thing to another doesn't necessarily involve emotion. It's the art of comparison, of differentiation, of making balanced and symmetrical patterns. Relationship is an integral part of dance, of geometry, of mathematics, or warfare. Relationship can mean a delicate and masterly sense of which colour blends with which. Or whether the lines of a Porsche 928 are superior in style to those of a Ferrari. This is what Libra is really concerned with. Marriage, yes. Most Librans think a lot about marriage, too. It's rare to find a Libra who remains unmarried for long. There's something about the ritual, the ceremony, the sense of togetherness, the rings, that appeals to the delicate quality of stylization in Libra's nature. It's the marriage of opposites, the balancing of things which are incompatible and mutually exclusive, the cleaning up of rough edges, the ordering of the pattern. Marriage to Libra is often like a sixteenth-century dance. Every step, every gesture, has a ritualized meaning. Libra is the great sign of ritual. And remember that Libra's symbol, the balance, is an inanimate object. Libra tries to lift ordinary human living onto the level of Platonic ideals. Not that he's incapable of being erotic or deeply sensual. But often sex itself must be ritualized; otherwise it turns him off.

You'll hear the words 'fair' and 'equal' mentioned a lot in conversations with Libra. The Libran's sense of what is fair is so acute that he can spot an imbalance miles away. He believes passionately in fairness, and this often causes him a great deal of unhappiness, because life and people aren't always fair. Again and again his idealism collides with an imbalanced world full of imperfections and rough edges. Libra believes passionately in equality, too, particularly in relationships. If you do him a favour, he does you a favour. If you pay for dinner, he'll pay for the theatre tickets. In many ways he's a truly enlightened soul when it comes to male-female relationships, for he understands in a very real way what equality and fair play mean, and won't use sex to tip the balance. Here, too, he often meets with sad disillusionment, because finding a relationship where each partner gives exactly the same amount and takes exactly the same amount, where there isn't one slightly stronger or one who loves slightly more, is like finding a unicorn. But Libra believes in unicorns too, and may often be seen moving from one relationship to another, one job to another, one country to another, believing and believing and believing that one day, some day, he'll find that perfect companion, that perfect career, that perfect environment where no ugliness or coarseness or human tragedy intrudes.

Like Socrates, Libra seeks the Good, the True and the Beautiful. Even the Libra who's learned to use his notorious charm to manipulate people and situations still seeks these things. He seeks them in whatever field of life you find him, in whatever relationships he enters. He usually knows by the time he reaches the mid-thirties that the Good, the True and the Beautiful are concepts and symbols rather than facts which he's likely to meet on the street. But he'll go on trying. And one of the nicest qualities about this curious sign is that in his eternal efforts to change the world and make it a place where the Good, the True and the Beautiful can make their abode, he often succeeds in making life just a little better, a little more beautiful, a little more harmonious than it might otherwise have been. Like his planetary ruler Venus, he has the gift of creating style and grace and harmony wherever he goes. More earthy souls often don't appreciate Libra's special gift. But those who know that hyacinths for the soul are as necessary as that extra five pounds a week on the salary cheque appreciate Libra.

Libra has a quality of initiation, a need to have goals, which the sign shares in common with Aries, Cancer and Capricorn. All these signs have as a basic characteristic the need to be working toward something. Libra is usually working for order, for perfection, for an ideal of relationship. Because he's always aware of other people's viewpoints, he won't often show aggressiveness or pushiness in his encounters with others. But don't forget that he possesses just as much initiative as his more overt cousins born under Aries and Capricorn. He's always after something. The difference is that, in order to really feel confident about achieving it, Libra needs a partner. If you spend some time with a Libran, you'll learn to recognize the royal Libran 'we'. Aries simply says, 'I want that. Do it.' Libra is far more diplomatic, far cagier. He's born with a downright frightening awareness that the world is full of people who have opinions which differ from his. He'll always listen to other opinions, frequently agreeing with them in order to encourage his partner or opponent to talk more. In the end, he does exactly as he pleases. But somehow he always succeeds in giving the impression that he's done it because of your cooperation. In fact, you might even walk away thinking it was really your idea, and that you pushed him. Instead of 'Do it,' Libra would much rather approach gently, with the famous charming smile, and say, 'You know, I was thinking that it would be really nice for everyone here if we . . .' And you're hooked. How thoughtful he is. How genuinely concerned with others' needs and ideas. How unassertive. How diffident. Why, you'd be glad to do it. In fact, you'd even thought of it yourself. You're so glad to have his support . . .

It's no wonder Libra has a reputation for being a skilled diplomat and a masterful statesman. He has a rare gift of being able to achieve what he wants with the minimum of offence. How can you be offended by somebody who's always consulting you about your opinions? Here's the art of Venusian relationships at its most fluent.

The problem with this, of course, is that more direct souls don't believe a word of it. They see Libra as a chronic hypocrite and flatterer. From one point of view, it's sometimes true; Librans have been known to smile sweetly and pay you an endearing compliment when they actually hate the ground you walk on. They're also prone to agreeing with your side of the argument when they take their place as mediators – 'Yes, I agree with you completely, he's perfectly dreadful' – and then turning around and doing the same thing to your opponent – 'Yes, I agree with you, she's behaving horridly.' It's hard, if you're the sort of person who likes friends who'll bleed and die for you rather than show the faintest sign of disloyalty, to learn to trust Libra, who'd rather be friends with everybody than bleed and die for anything. And more suspicious types like Scorpio and Capricorn don't appreciate Libra's gift for flattery either. They don't trust compliments in general, these signs, and they certainly don't trust somebody who always approaches with a 'You're looking marvellous today' when you know you look horrible. Viewed from the other side of the fence, Libra doesn't come across as particularly trustworthy. Diplomats never do.

But on the other hand (an expression you'll hear frequently on the lips of Librans) this isn't hypocrisy, nor is it dishonesty. From Libra's point of view it's all true. He'd much rather compliment you than insult you, not just because he likes to be liked, but because he tends to look for the beautiful and the positive in people and in life. Yes, the diplomat is at work. But sometimes it's nicer to be courted by a diplomat than bludgeoned by one of those types whose excessive love of 'truth' causes him to destroy brutally your most delicate dreams and needs. The Libran photographer, for example, will usually use a soft-focus lens and flattering lighting to enhance a woman's appearance, because he knows that most women like to appear beautiful; you'll rarely find him in the harsh realist school which insists on portraying every last spot, wrinkle, and superfluous hair because it's true to life. True life to Libra is tinted with his visions of the beauty it might contain. Even if he lives in a dark, dreary one-room basement flat, he'll do his best to disguise its limitations with a few flowers, some bright colours, some clever use of design. And when you're there, you have the illusion that it's bigger, brighter, more luxurious than the physically big, bright, luxurious homes of less tasteful people. Which is the reality?

Libra's royal 'we' isn't sheer hypocrisy either. Of course the diplomat is at work here too, because Libra is smart enough to know that you can get a lot more done when people are on your side than when they're fighting you. And he also has a positive hatred of quarrels and emotional storms, and a real terror of being disliked. It shatters him to know someone despises him. He'll often do everything in his power – which is considerable – to win the opponent over. But apart from the diplomat, Libra also has a genuine interest in other people's ideas and feelings. He really does care, although the degree of it varies with the individual Libran. The interested listener isn't just listening because he knows it makes you like him better. He's also truly interested. And if he doesn't show his disagreement, well, that's not wholly hypocrisy either; he's also smart enough to know that even if he disagreed, it wouldn't change your mind anyway, so why bother? Much more pleasant to have pleasantness.

An interesting case in point is Alexander the Great, one of the more influential Librans of history. He's generally known for conquering most of the known world. But Alexander wasn't your usual run-of-the-mill dictator carving territory out for himself for love of power. He was a Libran, after all. He was an intense idealist, and held a belief for the whole of his life that the disparate peoples of the ancient world – Greek, Persian, Indian – could mix and intermarry and create a united world under one king, with different customs and religions co-existing happily side by side. He himself married the defeated King of Persia's daughter to set an example, and arranged marriages between his Macedonian troops and Persian women. A true Libran dream, this one. Alexander's tragedy, like that of any other idealist, was that after all this painstaking work Greeks still hated Persians and Persians still hated

Indians and fire-worshippers hated earth-worshippers and people still wanted to rape, loot and pillage.

Alexander's military tactics are also pure Libra. He never just blundered into battle, attempting to win by brute force. His genius was his strategy. Time after time he worked out what his enemy was going to do by psychologizing him, and then playing with this knowledge. He also led his men with true Libran finesse; he ate with them, drank with them, starved with them, knew all their names, never set himself above them. No ordinary conqueror, this one, but a wonderful example of many Libran qualities at work.

Frequently, with all these gifts, the one to suffer is the Libran himself. This is because, if you're going to spend your life with the kind of acute awareness of everybody else that Libra's got, you don't have a chance very often to express your own emotions honestly. And this is Libra's biggest problem. He often finds his own emotions very painful to deal with, because they so frequently contradict his ideal of the Good, the True and the Beautiful. Libra likes to think that emotion should always be pleasant, agreeable, loving and harmonious. When he feels things like anger, hatred, jealousy, intense desire, it frightens him. One shouldn't feel such things. He often carries a pretty sizeable guilt complex around with him, over all those nasty things that churn around in his secret soul. Like the fact that he doesn't really like everybody after all. In a nutshell, Libra often represses his own emotions mercilessly, both because they conflict with his image of how people should be, and because they get him into trouble (meaning that other people sometimes get angry at him) when he shows his real feelings. His unreal world of perfect harmony and companionship often becomes so unreal that it's impossible for him to deal with ordinary human conflict. And repressed emotion like that, sooner or later, surfaces in a variety of unpleasant and indirect ways – like depression and physical illness. Or like secret and unintentional snipes at the people he's trying hardest to be pleasant to. Then he says the worst possible thing at the worst possible moment, and doesn't even realize what he's done. His pent-up anger and hostility have come out in an indirect way, and he's usually the last one to know he's doing it, until he's lost all his friends in the process.

Libra, the great lover of Truth, is often emotionally dishonest, both with himself and with others. It isn't intentional. It's just that this sensitive idealist, with a perfect image of the world rattling around in his very capable brain, takes a long time adjusting to the rougher currents in the sea of life. And all too often he'll just avoid the challenge of adjusting his idealistic nature with a bumpier world by trying to hide behind a relationship which can protect him and offer a warm, secure cocoon so that he doesn't have to deal with such difficult issues. Put briefly, Libra is often terribly dependent on his friends and loved ones, because he wants protection from life. The thing is, he has so much charm that you can't resist protecting him, and perpetuating the vicious circle.

Libra also often has a great problem with what he calls his selfishness. It's hard for him to assert his own wishes without consulting everybody first. Now, Libra is pretty notorious for the famous indecisiveness he's said to possess. But it isn't real indecision – it isn't as though he had no ideas about his own wishes or his own tastes. Left alone, Libra can be pretty quick to make choices. It's just that when he gets around somebody else, he keeps trying to adjust his choice to get the maximum cooperation. In part, it's because often he doesn't really care that passionately about having what he wants; it's more important to him to have company. He's made his choice, and it's to choose harmony. In part, he often feels vaguely guilty for wanting some-

thing, because it might be selfish. So he makes an effort
to consider the other person, and winds up caught in
between. And in part he thinks aloud. Libras often
work out their thoughts by talking to others; in the end,
they make their own decisions, but their thinking
processes often crystallize in conversation. It's a good
idea not to take a Libran's statements too literally when
you're in mid-discussion. He's usually trying things on.
Later, when he's alone, he'll work out what he really
thinks.

But when you're subjected to the classic Libran
routine of 'What would you like to do tonight, dear?'
answered by, 'I don't mind, whatever you want,' don't
fall into the trap of trying to force him to give you a
definitive answer. His definitive answer is that he'd
rather you decided – not because he's incapable of it,
but because he'll have a much more pleasant evening
with you if he knows you're happy than if he imposes
his own wishes on you. If you're the sort who likes to
have your decisions made for you, try an Aries or a
Leo. It's just not fair to poor Libra to expect him to
play that role, when his real gift is in finding a happy
medium.

Sometimes you'll see Libra getting argumentative.
He often shows this side to his nature in discussions.
You take one point of view, he'll take the opposite. But
watch carefully. If you shift around and begin agreeing
with him, he'll slide over and take the point of view you
started with. And you discover that he's not really
arguing; he's trying to find the mid-point between both
of you. Some Librans show their need for balance by
disagreeing with everything you say. It's their way both
of working out what they think, and of trying to cope
with their innate tendency to always agree. Sometimes
they over-compensate, like everybody else. But the real
Libran nature isn't argumentative. Nor is it passive and

compliant. It's just that Libra doesn't like extremes. And cooperation is a real god to him.

It's a funny thing about Librans, with all this polarizing going on inside them: people either really love them, or really dislike them. It's rarely anything in the middle. Either their charm wins you over, or you're sure Libra is playing a deceptive, hypocritical game. And this pattern fits Libra too, because everything for him always comes in twos. He's always caught in the middle between extremes, trying first one side and then the other, always searching for the perfect balance. Maybe he recognizes some secret in life that others don't see: that it's possible to be more than we are, better, more Good, more True, more Beautiful.

 The Myth

There are lots of myths and fairy tales about marriage and its problems, and all these have some bearing on Libra. But there is a Greek myth which can help us get some insight into what Libra's real life journey is about.

The Greek myth of Tiresias, the blind prophet, also has some relation to Libra. It's a curious myth, and we'll deal here with only part of it, the part that really pertains to our curious subject.

Tiresias, because he has the favour of the goddess Hera, is given the chance to observe a miracle: two serpents coupling in the goddess' sacred grove. He asks the goddess which of them experiences the greater pleasure; and because she cannot answer, she grants him the boon of spending part of his life as a woman, so that he can experience both. At the end of his period of transexual initiation, he returns to his male form, and is called before Zeus and Hera and asked which experiences the greater pleasure – male or female. At first he tries diplomacy, because whichever answer he gives he knows he's bound to offend somebody. But eventually he tells the truth – that the female experiences the greater pleasure – whereupon Zeus, furious at this insult to masculine vanity, strikes him blind.

Now, blindness in Greek myth is often a symbol for inner sight. All the great prophets and bards are generally represented as blind, either in one eye or both. Oedipus, when he makes his great discovery about his origins, strikes himself blind – that is, he sees inwardly at last. So for Tiresias, the result of his experiences is that he now has inner sight, and becomes a prophet.

What has this got to do with Libra? Well, it's the polarity. Male and female are as enigmatic a pair for Libra as good and evil, or perfect and imperfect. It's a curious thing, but many Libran men have a great appreciation of the feminine side of life – beauty and culture, the arts, harmony, relationship. Not that they're effeminate. In fact, this touch of the artist often makes them devilishly attractive to women. But it's as though the need for balance means, among other things, that they're trying to balance the sexes as well, within themselves. That's where Tiresias comes in – he tries out both. Some Librans, of course, do this literally. More often it's in a psychological way – an interest in women and in the feminine things in life. And many Libran women possess an unusual share of masculine gifts – a fine intellect, the gift of strategy, of statesmanship, of organization. Margaret Thatcher, with the sun in Libra, is an excellent example. Her manner is completely feminine; she's always diplomatic and soft-spoken and subtle. But her mind can function with as much strength and clarity as society has traditionally thought only men's minds could. Whether she's hated or loved, whatever one's political persuasions, this aspect of Libra is evident in her character. Many Libran women have this gift of clear sight and logic and intellect, and need some sphere of life where they can put their gifts to use beyond the sphere of home and family. And there's Tiresias again – playing both sides of the fence.

We should remember that this isn't a sexual issue in the physical sense. It has to do with qualities of mind – for with Libra we're always dealing with the mind. But the fact is, Libra often displays strong qualities and gifts which are usually associated with the opposite sex, often in the most graceful way and without any cost to his or her own sexuality. It's part of the Libran charm; and part, too, of the reason why so many Libran men and women get on better with the opposite sex as friends as well as lovers.

The further Libra goes into his ivory tower of perfection and isolation from ordinary human life, the harder he falls, and the more painful the growth which eventually allows him to make a relationship between the world of his ideals and the reality around him. Sometimes this journey happens to Libra through marriage. It's common enough for idealistic Libra to find fault with an imperfect partner, and dream of the ideal and often find the ideal in the form of a lover, only to discover that both are human and both imperfect. Libra's real lesson in life, his real task, is about love – and about the bringing of love down from the level of an intellectual exercise to the level of the heart. Or maybe I should say bringing it up to that level. For Libra often values the head above more ordinary human manifestations of affection. And it isn't that Libra doesn't need affection, or that he's incapable of offering it. It's just that he often places unnecessary qualifications on it, based on his ideals about how love should be expressed.

And what about the god's anger in the myth? Well, it may be a little specious, but it seems true enough; this quality of blending and balancing opposites in Libra often causes immense jealousy. Many Librans have a very hard time of it with their own sex, because they so often have deep sympathy for the opposite. It's something I've heard over and over from Libran friends and clients: rather than the typical 'stay in your own camp' attitude which so many men and women take with their own sex, they cross camps and overtly sympathize with the other point of view. Many Libran men are unusually sympathetic to women's problems in society, to women's drive for equality and acceptance as individuals. To the horror of their more chauvinistic comrades, they can be heard stating their treacherous viewpoints openly. And many Libran women, happier in the company of men than with their own sex, often show great sympathy and understanding for the problems and challenges which men must meet in the world. And they're not usually thanked for it by their own sex, who feel it's a betrayal.

The Tiresias myth is a profound one, and shows a profound side of Libra's journey. For Libra isn't just about finding the perfect love, the perfect marriage, and perfect society. It's about blending the opposites, bringing together people and things which would otherwise fight each other without understanding. With his great gift of diplomacy, Libra can straddle the fence and comprehend both sides, and act as intermediary because he recognizes both within himself. He may not be very balanced, but balance is what he's ultimately striving for. The sooner he climbs down from the ivory tower which is his protection against emotional pain and disillusionment, the sooner he can begin his real work, which is first to marry the conflicting opposites within himself. Whether it's his intellect and his emotions, his maleness and his femaleness, his spirituality and his materialism, Libra will always find deep conflicts in himself which represent the deep conflicts in life. And as he gradually carves for himself the thin road in the middle, he can truly become the bringer of the Good, the True and the Beautiful – because they no longer exist only in his mind.

⊜ The Shadow

With all that Good, True and Beautiful stuff going on, you might expect Libra's shadowy side to be Bad, False and Ugly. Actually, the Libran shadow is a little subtler than that. We might call it the Coy Maiden syndrome. Shades of it can be found in the figure of Scarlett O'Hara in *Gone With the Wind*. What it's about is a person in whom all that craving for love and approval has got so inflated that all human relationships become competitions where the object is to get the victim to fall in love with you. Then they're rejected, with another notch carved on the bedpost.

It's a little difficult to portray this in scenario form, because it should probably be portrayed in a novel. In fact a number of novels reflect it, not only in Scarlett O'Hara, but also in figures like Madame Bovary, and in men like Casanova (who actually existed, but made his life read like a novel anyway). What this shadow really hinges around is a series of manoeuvres, apparent in both Libran men and women, the object of which isn't sexual conquest so much as adoration. It's sort of like the line in Snow White:

> Mirror, mirror on the wall,
> Who's the fairest of them all?

And to the Libran shadow, everybody else is a mirror.

To accomplish these ends, the Libran shadow draws on all of Libra's best qualities. The charm, the flirtatiousness, the gift of flattery, the instinctive knowledge of what the other person thinks and wants – all are put to the service of the shadow. When you're being charmed by one of these

Librans, be terribly careful. They have a unique talent for seeming to believe you're the only one. They make little wistful sounds like, 'It would be wonderful if we could go away together . . . But I know it'll never be possible.' They display a real genius for taking one step forward and two backward – for if you show too much enthusiasm, you're suddenly confronted with the evasiveness and chilliness which are also air characteristics and which Libra can wield very effectively. It's known in the trade as playing hard to get, and nobody can play it as well as the Coy Maiden which is Libra's shadow. They also display an impressive ability to convince you that you're the only man/woman who can really fire up their nascent sexuality hiding beneath all that cool, aesthetic distance.

Lovely stuff. The trouble is that not a word of it means anything, because there's no real feeling in it. The Libran who's fallen into his shadow like this won't usually recognize consciously what he's doing, because it would be too painful – he'd have to face the fact that he has a shadow, which everyone has in one way or another, but which isn't a welcome fact of life for idealistic Libra. Usually, while he's playing Coy Maiden (and Libran men do this brilliantly as well as Libran women) he'll convince himself that he's really interested in you. But it's curious how quickly all that attentiveness disintegrates into pale cool wisps the moment you're actually available. That's not really what the game's about. And the Libran shadow, in true Scarlett O'Hara fashion, is quite capable of starting quarrels among the competitors, just to get a little excitement generated. Playing one person off against another is common fare for the Libran shadow. It takes the form of either a casual mention – 'Oh, John was all over me at the party, he kept trying to convince me to leave you and go away with him. It was hard to say no, he's very handsome, after all.' Or a deliberate although unconscious arrangement where one competitor bumps into the other leaving/entering the flat, or dates are confused where two people arrive at once, or . . . Well, you know the game. When you're embroiled in it, it's extremely painful. When you're the Libran who's got so insecure that you have to use your gifts of relationship to manipulate people in this way, it's very flattering. And when you're the observer, well, perhaps you feel a mixture of compassion and disgust, depending on your viewpoint.

What is it really about? Well, it stems, in part, from Libra's craving for approval. The need for affection and acceptance from others is a basic Libran need, and is most obvious in the fact that Librans usually hate being alone. They want and need companionship, not only of the romantic kind, but of the friendship kind as well. This game of flirtation and competition isn't only limited to sexual encounters. Librans do it to their friends, their business partners, even their parents. It's universal and isn't only limited to sexual insecurity. The only way Libra can really confront his shadow is to first see it in operation, reflect on how it feels to be put in the situation oneself, consider the fairness (since nothing ever penetrates a Libra's mind without having relevance to his principles) of it, and try to like himself a little more, so that he doesn't depend on an entire army of admirers to do his liking for him. Which gets us down to the nub of it: Libra's tendency to esteem himself too little and others too much. The Coy Maiden is the inevitable result of somebody who's just too insecure to believe one lover, one friend, is enough to convince him he's lovable.

The other reason for this curious game is Libra's tendency to identify with and sympathize so much with the opposite sex. Many Librans, as a result, question their own sexuality. Like Gemini, another sign which is concerned with opposites, Libra often feels dissociated from its own sex. This can be especially so because Libra is a refined sign, and the cruder aspects of both masculinity and femininity can be offensive. But to dissociate from one's own sex means paying a price; and the price is a vague feeling of sexual insecurity. Besides, being as mind-oriented as they are, Librans aren't always comfortable with their bodies, and often feel unattractive or ugly because some little thing isn't just exactly right. So everyone else becomes a mirror, to convince Libra that he's the fairest one of all.

Even Alexander had that problem. So, too, did Napoleon, a Leo with Libra on the ascendant. So have many other famous Libras both in the arts and in the world of politics – the two spheres where you most often find them.

The Libran shadow isn't after all, Bad, False and Ugly. But it can be a little too Good, True and Beautiful for its own good. Anybody playing this role finds pretty quickly, too, that you have to keep moving from admirer to admirer, because if you stay too long with one, the mirror might suddenly wake up one morning really sick of saying, 'You're the fairest of them all,' and say something distressing like, 'What are you really like?' Then the game's up, and Libra has to confront a real relationship. Which is, after all, what his journey's truly about.

≏ The Libra Lover

Most of what we've been saying applies to the Libran lover, because Libra is always in some sense a lover – even if it's a country he's wooing. But a few further remarks might be in order. One important thing to mention is that Libra – man or woman – shows his best qualities in a relationship which contains plenty of harmony and communication. Because his needs and his gifts all lie in the realm of peace and harmony and interchange, you're barking in the wrong kennel if you're one of those people who likes tempestuous, violent scenes with slamming doors and smashed crockery and lots of tears and torn clothes. Although it's certainly possible to drive a Libran to this point, it takes a lot of work, and having accomplished it, you usually find that the Libran, far from enjoying it, loathes every minute of it, loathes you, loathes himself for reaching that disgracefully bestial level of behaviour, and never forgets it. And the next time he's even more diplomatic, and more evasive, and less truthful than before.

If you want to discuss love problems with Libra, you must discuss them. You can't emote them. And make sure you puncture your virulent accusations with a good helping of 'Yes, I know that part is my fault,' because otherwise his sense of fairness will insist that he doesn't deserve all the blame. He'll gladly take fifty per cent, but don't try to heap it all on him, or he'll take the opposite stance and say it's all your fault. Fair is fair, and Libra believes in equal-sized helpings.

It can all get too intellectual for some. Libra is capable of spending hours discussing a relationship – what's wrong with it, what's right with it, how it can be adjusted, how 'we' can make it better. In the end he shows a surprisingly small capacity to actually act on these realisations; he may know them and understand them, but it's hard for him to show them emotionally. Remember that Libra's feeling nature is quite childlike, often very powerful, and usually repressed. And when he's being horribly reasonable and discussing it like a political debate with pros and cons and suggestions for bills and amendments, you feel like doing something simple and basic, like clubbing him, or tearing his clothes off. This sort of behaviour usually has the effect of producing a bland, tolerant look and a statement

like, 'When you're feeling more reasonable, we'll discuss it, dear.'

Having a reasonable lover can be a great boon. It
means you can reason with him or her. On the other
hand, there are times when reason has no place in love,
and this is often Libra's most difficult and painful lesson
in the realm of human relationships. One can sometimes
wait a long time for Libra to offer a genuine and
spontaneous emotional response which hasn't been
reflected over, pro and con, for hours preceding it. But
a little understanding of Libra's need for harmony and
peace and a place where things can be happy and
romantic and free of rejection and darkness often
makes a lot of difference. Sometimes Libra can be
coaxed gently into trusting his own emotions in an
atmosphere of trust. What he can't do is become
somebody else, which means that if you can't accept his
innately agreeable and harmony-loving nature, you
should try something a little more explosive like an
Aries or a Scorpio. Libra is capable of putting an
enormous amount of time and energy into relationships,
which is a rare thing to find; and he or she is usually
willing to try adjustment and compromise because it's
innate in Libra's nature to see the need for adjustment.
The need for companionship also makes Libra terribly
companionable, and if you're the violently independent
type who likes to do everything alone, you're liable to
have a difficult time with Libra, who likes to do
everything together. Some Librans take this togetherness to such extremes that you begin to wonder if they'll
fall apart if expected to eat or sleep alone occasionally.
Some Librans in fact fall apart that way. But in general,
it's a mistake to think this is a weak sign; it's a people-
loving sign, and even the quieter, more introverted
Libran needs a mate and companion to share his dreams
and ideals with.

Librans know a lot about relationships, and the

partner is the beneficiary of all of it. It's quite a big bonus, especially if you've had experiences of the opposite kind. But at the beginning and the end, Libra is an airy sign, not a watery one; and you may have to teach your Libran partner that discussing love is not the same thing as showing it, or feeling it. Never mind. For the romantics of the world, that's a pleasure too.

⚖ The Libra Man

One of the most noticeable things about the Libran man is that he possesses a good deal of taste and also a good deal of vanity. The typical Libran isn't one of your rough-and-ready macho types who changes his shirt every three weeks and occasionally checks the mirror to see if he's cut himself shaving. Libran men are usually concerned about how they look, which can produce either a really well-dressed and attractive man who looks and smells good and likes quality and luxury in everything, or a preening peacock. Probably you'll see shades of both. But it's understandable, since beauty is always important to Libra – beauty of ideas if not beauty in form.

He's also terribly responsive to beauty around him, and as with everything else this carries a plus and a minus. The place he lives in will generally be tasteful and pleasant and often luxurious; and this isn't the man who lives in a pig's heap and then expects you to clean it when you arrive. If you live with a Libran, he'll often wish to be involved in decorating a flat or house; if you don't, he won't usually abide in traditional bachelor digs, but will often have a downright imposing array of comforts around him. He's also someone who appreci-ates other people's care over their appearance; and Libran men aren't embarrassed or stiff about offering compliments. The nicest side of all this is that you can feel really appreciated, and not just in the first two weeks of the relationship.

The darker side of all this love of beauty is that the Libra man is often incapable of getting past his hangup about physical perfection. He's often the 'sucker for the pretty face' who can only court beautiful women, and who is frequently fooled and badly hurt because he thought that what looked Good, True and Beautiful actually was. It takes a long time, sometimes a lifetime, for Libra to recognize that the surface is not necessarily a good index to character. Also, his ideas of beauty are frequently culled from popular collective attitudes, since he pays a good deal of attention to other people's opinions. If all the guys at the office think she's beautiful, so will he. He frequently suffers a lot from having to define his own individual taste.

This problem of loving beauty and being unable to recognize it in other than collective and conventional forms sometimes shows in odd ways. Like a great difficulty in accepting, or finding attractive, the ordinary manifestations of the human body – lumps and bumps and moles and hair and body smells and period pains and other things that make us human and humanly loveable. The Libran man's image of women is often something that stepped straight out of the pages of *Vogue* magazine, polished, plucked, and perfect. Nobody, of course, looks like that except in photographs. The most beautiful women in the world still perspire and get dark circles under their eyes. The Libran man loves women who take pride in their femininity and do everything they can to enhance it. He doesn't usually appreciate the 'natural' look. As a cynic once said of nudist camps, People actually look better with their clothes on. This is often the Libran man's viewpoint. If you're the kind of woman who enjoys clothes and cosmetics, this man won't laugh at them, or demand that you look like a fresh-scrubbed and whole-some country milkmaid. He likes style.

Ah, yes, the famous extravagance. He likes style so much that he's sometimes prepared to bankrupt himself for it. Libra has a reputation for extravagance, and he earns it. It's not for the same motives as Leo, the other big spender of the zodiac, or as Sagittarius. Leo likes to impress; his idea is to have the most different, the most unique, the most impressive thing. Sagittarius just enjoys spending, because he can't be bothered with ordinary mundane things like budgeting. Libra spends for beauty. He'll spend money on beauty faster than he will on necessities; it isn't uncommon to find the Libran man who's blown the entire savings on a beautiful car and can't afford meals for the rest of the week. On the other hand, he'll spend on his friends too, and on his lovers. And Libra is usually generous. A sucker he's not; but if you don't take advantage of him (remember, fair is fair) he's usually open-handed with money, and never begrudges money spent on pleasure or luxury or beauty or entertainment.

You might find one of those Libran men where the shadow has taken over. They're a disaster for anyone, because the constant playing hard to get can corrode even the most confident woman. This kind of Libran is an incurable Don Juan, so if it's fidelity you're looking for, forget it. You're more likely to be regaled with stories of how many women pursued him that afternoon, than you are of how desirable you are to him. But the more balanced Libran is usually quite prepared to have a relationship, as opposed to a fling, because he likes companionship and wants more than a good roll in the hay. He has a mind, after all, and often a brilliant one, and he needs friendship and intellectual companionship too. Librans are often marriage-minded, and many Libran men marry very young. They also frequently marry more than once, since the first one isn't perfect.

And if your life path is about learning to relate, then often more than one relationship is needed to learn. The frequency of broken marriages among Librans shouldn't be looked upon as failure. If you're seeking the depths of a particular experience in life, you need to try a lot of things to find out about it.

The Libran man is also a real romantic. He understands things like flowers, soft music, quiet evenings in intimate restaurants, elegant parties. He needs them too much himself not to recognize a woman's need for them as well. And what he can't bear is an unromantic partner, a partner who has no time for his longings for the fantasy life. However long you're with a Libra, he still adheres to the tenets of courtly love. Never take him for granted. He usually won't take you for granted either, unless you've crushed his love of romance by being too flat-footed and prosaic and trampling on his dreams. Then he'll seek his romance elsewhere, and show the chillier side of him, the one that keeps the marriage together because it's convenient.

Definitely not an easy man to get along with if you're very basic by nature. And he has a tendency, too, to retreat into his head to such a degree that you don't know what he's talking about. He can get pretty abstract, or just wander off into some inner theoretical landscape that leaves you feeling very cut off and alone. But all the airy signs do this, and they do it in excess when they've been threatened emotionally. It's hard for them to remain in the world in the midst of other people's physical and emotional problems and desires for very long. Libra needs to escape sometimes to his ivory tower, in whatever form it takes. And anyone involved with a Libra must allow it, because it's part of his nature. Provided, of course, that it's in balance. And if it isn't you can't drag him down from it. You can only coax him, be reasonable, and trust that eventually his need of relationship will always bring him from whatever airy heights he's climbed back into the world of human interchange.

⎍ The Libra Woman

With the curious magic of polarities that occurs in this sign, the Libra woman, although she shares in common with the Libran man the love of beauty and style and elegance, often has a mind like a steel trap. This lady is not the vague, fluffy bundle of fur and giggles that will stare open-mouthed at your mental acrobatics. She's very probably either got a string of academic degrees or might as well have, and has worked through whatever it is you've just taken two hours at in about ten minutes.

Libran women can be quite unnerving. They often show the enormous paradox of the sign in the contradiction between their appearance and their real nature. Sometimes you meet a Libra woman who has gone off to the opposite pole, and is the opposite of physically attentive; these are often the women you meet in the masculine (so-called) professions who prefer to find their beauty and elegance in the world of ideas. But even here you can see the style and the diplomacy at work. And the Libran woman is usually very aware of her appearance. But her appearance often belies the capacities and capabilities of her intellect. She is, however, generally too tactful and diplomatic to allow this to be immediately known. In fact you may not find it out for years.

There's often a strong intellectual drive in the Libran woman, whether this shows itself as love of knowledge in a theoretical way or as love of organizing. Libran women often need strong careers to allow them expression of their gifts. And there is often a real ability to work with groups, to get people together in cooperative action. Sometimes there is real political ability, and a concern for human welfare. The masculine pole of life expresses itself through the Libran woman as an ability to work with structures, forms, organizations, concepts. It can be very disconcerting to many men, since this is usually the woman who will happily spend a day being pampered at the beauty salon, and will very agreeably spend a fortune on clothes. But no Libran, male or female, is simple.

The tendency to repress emotion exists in the Libran woman as well as in the Libran man. It's more difficult, in many ways, since society expects women to be emotional. The detached and often intellectual approach which many Libran women show toward others is acceptable when evidenced by their masculine counterparts, yet often reproached in the Libran woman. A true Libran is not a creature of feeling; and whatever the biological or sociological differences between the sexes, it's generally easier for the Libran woman to reason things out than to react out of instinct. This is both a great boon and a great problem. A boon in the sense of potential for achievement; a problem because in the domestic sphere, dealing with children and dealing with relationships, the Libran woman may be uncomfortable and find it difficult either to spontaneously show emotion or to respond to emotional outbursts or demonstrations of need from others.

The key here, once again, is romance. Libra's tightly corseted emotions can usually be reached through the ritual courtship of romance; if feeling is passed through this tinted lens which raises it up onto a different level, then Libra feels safe and can allow some feeling to be expressed. And the Libran woman is definitely a romantic, even if you find her displaying those frighteningly rational tendencies and claiming to be a logical, reasonable person. One rose goes a long way; one compliment goes an even longer way.

There seem to be two kinds of Libran women, in fact: those who are unashamedly the bundle of contradictions that the sign contains, and those who overcompensate for the intense need of relationship by retreating into the intellect. The latter is usually a frightened Libran, who finds it too painful to deal with her emotional needs. Love and acceptance do wonders for Libra, and even the painfully tight Libran with emotions tucked firmly away in a safety-deposit box will eventually display the gentle and affectionate side of the Libran nature. The trouble is that a good intellect, which is common with Libran men and women both, can be frightening when it appears in someone who looks as though she should be swathed in furs over scented candlelight; and it seems that if you want to relate to a Libran woman, you've got to accept both the man and the woman in her. For she possesses both, and the Libran woman who's found her own balance is comfortable in both worlds – that of the mind, and that of her own femininity.

Aquarius

When the moon is in the seventh house
And Jupiter aligned with Mars,
Then peace will rule the planets
And love will rule the stars.
This is the dawning of the Age of Aquarius . . .

*T*hese are lines from a song in the rock musical *Hair* which became a hit while Flower Power reigned in America during the late 1960's, and which has just – perhaps a little anachronistically – been released as a film in the late 1970's. For a while everyone was talking about the Age of Aquarius as a kind of New Dispensation, a time when wars would cease and everybody would love everybody else and the New Utopia would arrive, seen through a haze of marijuana smoke and acid rainbows.

Now, a decade later, people are still talking about the Age of Aquarius, but with a certain unease. It appears to consist now of things like terrorism, revolution in Iran, Arab-Israeli conflict, a diminishing supply of fuel for the world, and general malaise. Did the Age of Aquarius fall flat on its face? Did it ever arrive? And is Aquarius really about love, brotherhood, and Flower Power?

Well, yes, in part Aquarius is about love and brotherhood. Or perhaps we should say, with more accuracy, that it is about ideals – and the ideals of love and brotherhood are among many which are formulated in the forward-looking Aquarian mind. Particularly ideals about the group, the welfare of humanity, the future of society.

Aquarius is also, broadly, about science, and knowledge, and invention, and discoveries which will improve the lot of man in the generations to come. *Fraternité, égalité, liberté* – the cry of the French Revolution – is in many ways an Aquarian *cri de coeur*. The noblest of human visions are spun from this last of the airy signs, which in its most profound meaning symbolizes the genius of human invention extended to its furthest limits, applied to the control of nature by the will of man and the structuring of humanity into a civilized society.

So what happened to the age of love and brotherhood? The same thing that happens to many Aquarians.

The ideal was ahead of its time, as the ideals of many Aquarians all too frequently are. The ideal hit a head-on collision with the reality of human nature, which can't really be explained and governed by ideals alone. Without the ideal, no progress of any kind could take place. Yet the anchoring of an ideal takes time, and flexibility, and a sensitivity to the limitations of human nature. Aquarius is not overly gifted in any of these three things. He is usually impatient, and wants to see the ideal made flesh right this minute. He is not very flexible, although a great lover of truth. And he has very little understanding of, or patience with, the seamier side of human nature.

You can see here the dilemma, the gift and the curse of the Aquarian. His symbol is the Waterbearer. Notice carefully that the Waterbearer carries his jug to offer the water of life to humanity – but doesn't get his own hands wet. As an air sign, Aquarius finds his reality in his ideals. Because he is concerned with issues that pertain to the group rather than the individual, you can see the traditional Aquarian link with welfare and human rights. Fields like social work and education and politics are natural for the forward-looking Aquarian who wants to set the world to rights. It's truly the sign of liberty, democracy, and human equality. And Aquarius, as far as his ideals are concerned, is usually truly democratic. One of his nicest qualities is his sense of fairness and integrity. He has a pretty finely honed conscience, which is often so sensitive that it makes his life unbearable. He often has a horror of being what he calls 'selfish', which is very noble but not very psychologically healthy. Regardless of his personal likes and dislikes, his dedication to his beliefs is unshakeable. And this dedication is often to the objective perspective, the broad canvas, a code of ethics or principles by which he believes he should live. And, of course, he is often dedicated to Truth. Yes, it's capitalized, that word Truth. For Aquarius, there is generally only one Truth.

Never mind whether he hates you bitterly. Fair is fair. Aquarius will still deal with you with integrity, because, vile thing that you are, you're still a human being, and all human beings have certain innate basic rights. Sometimes you wish he'd show a little honest unfairness. But no. Fair is fair.

Look at some of the famous Aquarian figures of the past. Abraham Lincoln is one of the best-known. Of course it would be an Aquarian who declared equality between black and white in an age of slavery, and abolished slavery with the result of the American Civil War. He was shot for his pains. Many Aquarians suffer the retaliation of the more conservative elements of society for their contributions, which are frequently suspected. You will also see among the distinguished Aquarian names figures like Thomas Edison – great thinkers and inventors whose discoveries are not intended for personal satisfaction or gain, but for the benefit of the human race. Their dedication is absolute; try to find out anything about their personal lives and you're astonished to discover that they seem to have no personal lives. All their energy and ability is taken up with the dedication to the goal, the ideal.

The list of noble, couragous, dedicated idealists is very long when it comes to Aquarius. So is the list of scientists and philosophers. Can we say anything at all bad about this sign?

Of course we can. For as we near the end of the zodiac, the signs become increasingly complex. Their extremes become more and more extreme. By the time we get to Aquarius and Pisces, you are dealing with an enormous spectrum of human abilities and foibles. There is an element to Aquarius which can only be described as intellectual bigotry. That courageous fixity of ideals can become stubborn fanaticism – the rigidly rational scientist with no heart, who is a caricature in this modern age. This is the fellow who invents a new weapon because it's scientifically interesting and immensely effective, without the wit to realize that people don't possess the psychological maturity to handle such a thing with any responsibility. A little closer to home, this is the fellow who doesn't worry about the few people who might be harmed by a faulty nuclear reactor – or who disguises the actual percentage of radioactivity in the atmosphere – because, well, those are only a few little people, and they don't really have anything to do with grand things like Our Country's Defence and Power.

Also in the shadier reaches of Aquarius are to be found the rampant communist who believes in a utopian state where all wealth is levelled and all people equal – without regard to the fact that people are fundamentally different and are emotionally incapable of coping with this. George Orwell's *1984* is a horror story of an Aquarian Age run rampant. Lest we think that the ideals of love and brotherhood as expounded by the more fanatical adherents of the sign are the answer, enforced by a totalitarian state, read and re-read this little book which was once considered science fiction and now looks horribly like prophecy.

And what about the individual Aquarian? Well, typically, he encompasses these two extremes – genuine love of and concern for the welfare of the group, and personal intellectual bigotry. His ideals and his true sense of democracy are immediately noticeable. Even the non-political Aquarian who lives an ordinary life and doesn't concern himself with movements, will often be found defending the underdog in his business. His ideals often make Aquarius stand out by a head above the crowd. He thinks about other people, about their needs and potential. Or maybe we should say he truly *thinks* – a rare commodity in an age of slogans and opinions.

On the other hand, he doesn't much like individuals. Aquarius is the fellow who loves humanity and doesn't like people. He can be brusque, cool, unfeeling, insensitive, rigid, dogmatic, and downright stupid when it comes to the subtleties of human relationships. He can stand by principles when principles are the least relevant thing in the situation. His fairness can be blindly infuriating when what is most needed is a little bias. In those typical situations where you're hurt by someone else's offhand remark, and turn to your Aquarian for sympathy, and get a pronouncement fit for a trial where point by point the reasonableness of the remark is discussed, it's a wonder there aren't more Aquarians murdered every day.

Aquarius is often embarrassed by emotion, and finds it distasteful both in himself and in others. I've known quite a few Aquarian women who consider it shameful to cry; this sign is proud and self-controlled, and displays of emotion are seen as a weakness. Those tears that according to romantic novels melt the hearts of the hardest men don't work terribly well on Aquarians. After you've sniffed delicately into your lace handkerchief and looked up at him with moist dewy eyes, you may find either that he's quietly left the room during your fit, or that he's got his newspaper out and is reading about the political situation in Uganda. Or he may sit quietly and watch you, and then, when you're certain he's about to tell you he really loves you after all, or that he understands, or that he's sorry he hurt you, he opens his mouth and says, 'Good, now that you've finished, we can discuss this reasonably. I do so hate it when you get irrational like that.' And when you're about to throw the teapot at him in a screaming rage because he hasn't understood at all, he'll look at you coolly and say, 'Now, don't throw another scene, it's really selfish, you know. Can't we talk about something else? People are suffering and dying all over the world. Did you know that the Tanzanian troops waited three days outside Kampala so that the inhabitants could escape? I think that's really a humanitarian thing to do.' Having made you feel utterly and abjectly guilty for having been so emotional in the first place, he can indulge in a little smug self-satisfaction because he succeeded in keeping his mind on the Really Important Things.

Obviously, not all Aquarians are this unfeeling. Aquarian women in particular have an immense capacity for devotion and loyalty. But here too it's so bound up with their ideals and their ethics that they often don't adjust very well to the changes and nuances of relationships. And most important, with all this obsession about the rights of others and what they ought and ought not to do and be, they forget about themselves – to such an extent that they mince their own emotions to pieces through simple lack of expression.

Here's a little scenario to illustrate the point. We might call this the Noble Soul syndrome.

AQUARIAN TO FRIEND: I'm fine, thanks. A little tired, that's all. It was an awful lot of work moving into the new house, and getting the kids ready for their new school.

FRIEND: But last time I saw you, I thought you said you didn't like that house. You weren't going to take it.

AQUARIAN: Well, it's much more convenient for John's work. It only takes him twenty minutes. With the other place, it would have been an hour and a half commuting.

FRIEND: But what about you? You said you hated the neighbourhood, and the shops aren't very nice, and . . .

AQUARIAN: Oh, I was just being silly. Selfish, you know. I'm terribly selfish like that. I should never have gone on like that. John always Comes First. After all, where would we be if I always thought of myself? My mother always told me never to be Selfish, it's the worst thing you can do. A Good Mother always thinks of her husband and children first. No, the house is just right for John.

This is very noble. Truly good. But our Aquarian, if you see her a few years later, is liable to be a little messed up. She might be on Librium, to keep her nerves from acting up. She might have high blood pressure, or have developed a few nervous habits like a tic, or compulsive cleaning. All that natural aggression has been submerged. And when you track her into old age, she's had to become incredibly rigid to keep all that stuff repressed for so many years. She's gone cold by then. That's when the Aquarian goes fanatic. When years and years of being Unselfish and adhering to Right Behaviour have made a dog's breakfast of their spontaneity and love of life.

Aquarius often has a wonderful gift for logic. He can discuss things reasonably, rationally, and often brilliantly. So when you challenge him – or present an emotional grievance – he has it all sorted out to begin with. He can work it out rationally, analytically. He's got all the answers. He has a gift for analysis of human temperament – many Aquarians reach prominence in the psychological field – so he can tell you exactly what your motives are, what his are, why you said this, why he said that, and what the solution is to the problem. It's so neat and pat it makes you swoon with admiration. The trouble is, there's no room for any emotion in it. I've had discussions with psychologically 'aware' Aquarians who have taken an interest in the whole realm of the human psyche. They can list their complexes, use all the latest jargon, draw the latest psychological maps. The human being, like an airplane or an automobile or a well-constructed society, operates on certain basic principles. There isn't any room for chance, or fuzzy edges. Emotion has fuzzy edges. People to Aquarius are mechanisms – wonderful, divine mechanisms, but nonetheless mechanisms. And that well-read Aquarian who knows all the latest about the psyche, while he can discuss it with brilliance, often doesn't know anything about himself at all. It's because he doesn't know what he feels – it's all an idea. His idea of what he thinks he feels, what he thinks he ought to feel, what he thinks he should and shouldn't feel, and what he thinks you can think about what he thinks he feels. Confused? You should see the Aquarian in the midst of all that. Simple phrases, like 'I love you' or 'I hate you' or 'I'm bloody angry with you' are very difficult for him.

The fact is, Aquarians have very deep and complex emotional natures. It isn't that they have no feelings. It's that they are often frightened of their feelings. Aquarius is a true air sign. What can be understood by the mind is safe, because you can reason it out. What can't be understood is often relegated to the realm of the 'imaginary' or the 'emotional', dreaded or simply reasoned out of existence. Is there room for any romance in this formidable temperament? Yes, but it's usually unconscious. Aquarius is often very embarrassed and awkward – you might even see him blush – when the subject turns to romantic matters. This is the fellow who, out of sheer embarrassment, will neglect to give his woman flowers during twenty years of marriage. He often can't understand the need for flattery, compliments, sentimental displays of affection. Everything has to have a reason. He may love deeply – but he won't show it very often, and especially not in the ordinary little ways that make a love relationship so enjoyable.

He is capable of sacrificing his life for a loved one. But sometimes the loved one feels like saying, 'That's very nice, but flowers would have said it better.'

I once knew an Aquarian man whose wife left him after six years of marriage. They had two children, a large house, an opulent lifestyle, and he was extremely successful in his profession. His profession involved quite a lot of travel, which meant long periods when his wife was left alone. It never occurred to him that she would mind this, because it never occurred to him to ask. He could handle it; he simply clicked off on those trips, something Aquarians seem to be able to do with ease. They simply shut down shop and shift to another department. He also found it extremely difficult to show his wife any affection in ordinary situations. To him, this was superfluous. He had proved his love because he had married her, fathered two children on her, took care of her, and was reasonably faithful to her. During one of his trips she ran off with a friend, who had won her starving heart by writing her love poetry. My Aquarian client was beside himself with shock, grief and bewilderment. 'She kept telling me it was the love poems,' he said, baffled. 'Why? What difference does it make if somebody writes her love poems?'

His wife never came back. To this day he still finds it impossible to comprehend that the poems were to her a symbol of something – a recognition that she had feelings, that she was romantic, that she had a heart. To him, it was all terribly unreasonable.

I have seen a number of Aquarian marriages go this way. When it's the reverse way round, with the woman an Aquarian, there's a different base. There the complaint on the part of the man is often, 'She's so good, so fair, so self-disciplined. She makes me feel irresponsible and selfish.' And sadly, the unspoken part of this is that she can be pretty boring. Anybody who's unselfish and highly principled all the time will drive a lesser mortal into some fairly nasty actions, just to get an ordinary human reaction.

What, then, can Aquarius do? Perhaps recognize that his abstract love of humanity should extend to include himself and his loved ones. Often this simple point eludes him. Generosity of feeling toward oneself and those close is part of the ideal of love; often, Aquarians miss it. Some of the zodiacal signs have a knack with personal relating; others don't. Aquarius has perhaps more difficulty than any other sign, because he often has so little sense of the 'personal' – including his own 'person'. Aquarius' ideals often mean too much to him because he hasn't got a sense of himself. We can, historically, make excuses for the Lincolns and Edisons of the world. In retrospect, we're glad they were such personal failures, because their humanitarian achievements were proportionately great. Perhaps that's Aquarius' role in the human family. But with a little balance, if you're not a Lincoln or an Edison, you can be human too.

The Myth

There is one figure in ancient mythology who epitomises the destiny and the meaning of Aquarius. That figure is Prometheus, who stole fire from the gods. His inspiration and his suffering are part of the Aquarian myth.

Zeus, King of the Gods, was jealous of the aptitudes and abilities of mortal men. So he withheld from them the use of fire, for fire – the symbol of creative spirit – would have made them too much like the gods.

But Prometheus, a god himself, or more accurately, a Titan, took pity on man, for he could see man's potential and knew that Zeus' attitude was intrinsically wrong and unfair. So he stole fire from heaven, and offered it to man. Zeus was enraged, for once the gift had been made, it could not be undone. But he took vengeance on Prometheus, by chaining him to a rock. Each day an eagle came and gnawed out Prometheus' liver. Each night it grew back again, so that his agony continued until Hercules came into the underworld and set him free.

This myth contains many themes which are profoundly important to the deepest meaning of Aquarius. The noble impulse is the brightest face of the sign – a selfless impulse, from which Prometheus can expect no personal gain. His gift was given because he saw the potential of the as yet undeveloped human race, and because he felt it unfair that their own potential divinity should be withheld from them. His payment is also important to the psychology of the sign, for it implies that the gift of fire – whether we interpret it as knowledge, creative power, recognition of godhood – costs dear. Nature resents her secrets plundered, or, putting it another way, the gods do not like to share their divinity. An echo of the Prometheus myth may be found in the myth of the Garden of Eden, where God jealously guards his godhood by forbidding Adam and Eve to eat of the tree of the knowledge of good and evil – and the tree of life – lest they become like gods. Prometheus is also the serpent, the goad which insists that knowledge is better than blind faith. To Aquarius, knowledge is always superior to blind faith. Aquarius has no room for superstitious devotion; and he also has no patience for unexplained authority. To him, all individuals in the end should be their own ultimate judges. And he will, if necessary, defy the gods to obtain their secrets.

The dedicated scientist who plumbs the secrets of matter and the universe is truly Aquarian. In earlier days, this probing mind, dedicated to truth, would have been burned at the stake as a heretic, because of the defiance of the authority of religion. To the modern world defiance of religious belief is still a heresy, although the times are changing as we enter the Aquarian Age. But man's demand to know more about the universe around him, to penetrate to the secrets of the meaning of life, is part of the better face of our Age of Science. And Prometheus willingly makes the sacrifice, and endures his agony, which after all is not eternal.

There is an even deeper message to this figure of Prometheus. At the risk of reading things into the myth, we might simply suggest that the punishment which Prometheus calls down on himself is from within himself. In other words, the price the Aquarian pays for his search for truth is a deep and ingrained sense of guilt. For there is a side to Aquarius which is conventional and attached to law and order. Aquarius has two planetary rulers: Saturn and Uranus. Saturn, the symbol of structure and order, gives these qualities to the Aquarian mind. So Aquarius loves principles, and needs a strict code of ethics by which to run his life. This is why so many Aquarians can be intellectually rigid in their ideas, as well as self-disciplined. Saturn structures their thinking, and Saturn also offers devotion to the past, to tradition, to order.

The other ruler, Uranus, is the inventor, the magician, the liberator. It is this planet which symbolizes the strong drive in Aquarius to find freedom, to pierce the veil of the mysteries, to shatter hidebound structures. The Uranian side of many Aquarians is predominant, and they are iconoclasts in one way or another. They foment rebellion – figuratively or literally – because Uranus drives them to seek freedom. It is no wonder that Aquarius is such a complex sign! These two planetary rulers often collide with each other. Aquarius is often torn between his love of truth and his respect for tradition.

We should mention one more myth which has relevance to Aquarius. This is the myth of Pandora, who opens the forbidden box and releases the entire array of human ills and sufferings, along with Hope. Here too one can read the deeper meaning of Aquarius. With his probing intellect and his curiosity about life, he often causes more destruction than good, for his inventions and his insights give us powers we are ill-equipped to handle. But with Aquarius there is also always hope, for he has a deep and ingrained faith in human potential and human nature. This is partly why so many Aquarians favour a democratic or socialist system of government – they believe that ultimately the individual is capable of his own choices and of a noble concern for his fellow man. Whether Aquarius is right or wrong in his conjecture is an issue that continues to rage in every country of the world. But from the viewpoint of this idealistic sign, there is always hope.

The Shadow

As you might expect, the dark face of Aquarius, the secret side which he often can't face, springs from his complete dedication in ordinary life to his ethical codes. Where Aquarius consciously strives for selflessness, his shadow side is completely self-centred; where his dedication to others is often faultless in ordinary life, his shadow is dedicated to the upholding of his position of control.

You can see this shadow side peeping through especially in those situations where Aquarius is on his ideological hobby-horse. Watch him corner the centre of the stage, and push anybody else off who happens to disagree with him. Usually reasonable to a fault, all that repressed longing to be somebody special in his own right sometimes drives him to rather odd behaviour. The result is that he frequently can't practise what he preaches, especially in personal relations. Equality is fine for humanity, but not for you.

There is also another side to the Aquarian shadow, connected with the first. This is his secret longing to be liked and admired by everyone – to the degree where he can often be pushed uphill against his principles for fear of what others think of him. It's sometimes termed weakness of character, or wishy-washiness. And it's rather surprising when you see it next to the kind of courage of conviction which is more usually his behaviour.

What all this boils down to can be put into one rather unpleasant word: hypocrisy. This is the greatest danger, the greatest foible in the Aquarian temperament. He says one thing and often does another unwittingly. And it's frequently those closest that suffer for it. Take his ideals of equality, for example. You'll hear many Aquarians wax eloquent on this theme. Whether it's equality between races, or freedom to worship as one pleases, or equality of rights between the sexes, Aquarius can go on for hours on his theme, once he gets warmed up. But you'll often see a pronounced inequality displayed in his personal life – especially toward those who display the emotionalism or irrationality which he so fears and despises. His wife, often, is given no real 'equality' – he simply can't be bothered to listen to anything which isn't presented in a logical form. His children are often given no real 'equality' – their demands are too selfish, or too emotional, for his taste. His real equality is reserved for verbal debate, when he will always offer his opponent the right to speak. But equality of heart is often difficult for him, because his concept of equality is limited to the realm of ideas and intellect.

Another adjunct to this peculiar shadow side of Aquarius is his propensity to reform everybody. This, too, is contradictory to his belief that all people are entitled to their own beliefs. It translates out to mean that all people should be granted freedom of choice, so long as they agree with him. Watch a zealous Aquarian pursuing his pet subject – whether it is women's liberation, socialism, distribution of weath, ecology, or whatever. Usually his hobby-horses always concern the benefit of some group or other. But if you don't happen to agree with him, you're given short shrift. No equality for you. You've disagreed; and of course there's only one truth, isn't there? Often Aquarius can't see the paradox in his behaviour. The epitome of it is in what Marx called Dialectic Materialism. Or perhaps in Democracy, an ideal which sprang into being on a wide scale coincident with the discovery of Aquarius' ruler Uranus, falling between the American and French Revolutions. Democracy: government by the people, of the people, for the people. And if you don't agree with it, then, by God, you'll be made to. The innate contradiction in all this is very elusive to the Aquarian mind. The worker for whom the revolution is fought is coerced into a behaviour pattern and a life in which he has not a jot of freedom – to pursue either his own religious inclinations, his own creative enterprise, or his own freedom of speech. Yet the battle was fought for his freedom. It is pretty difficult to refrain from commenting on the hypocrisy of this attitude.

Now, the hypocrisy of the Aquarian shadow isn't deliberate. He genuinely doesn't see it, doesn't know about it. If he did, he would be abjectly shocked – because he doesn't mean to be unfair. You might say that this strange shadow side appears because he's so rigid in his expectations of himself and of others. His attempts to reform human nature are, in many ways, a projection onto others of his belief that he should reform his own. But he often doesn't realize that all such attempts, like charity, must begin at home.

Another facet to this is the practise-what-you-preach exercise. Aquarians usually don't. This type of Aquarian is most in evidence in the learned professions. He knows a great deal about the maps, models, techniques, mechanisms and behaviour patterns of his favourite subject of study: man. But he often can't learn these in application to his own behaviour patterns. Because he's so often out of touch with his own emotions, they sneak up on him, and make him do things he doesn't see or understand. Anger, resentment, jealousy, longing, need, helplessness, fear – the ordinary gamut of human foibles – are often things he will simply not. acknowledge, because they make him nervous. He has them, the same as anybody else. He just doesn't see them. But then, it's typical of the shadow of every sign. You don't always see the shadow you cast behind you, because the light is in front of you, and you're busy looking at the light.

Nobody has any testimony about what Mrs Lincoln thought of her husband. Or what Mrs Edison thought. We can only conjecture. But you can see the Aquarian shadow in a lot of places: the Aquarian politician campaigning for equality while he can't be bothered to give the time of day (or any freedom) to his family, the Aquarian psychologist who knows all the theories but hasn't spotted his own emotional needs, the Aquarian doctor who devotes his time and energy to his patients while his loved ones must find a clinic for treatment . . . The list is long. The solution? Like the shadow problems of all the signs, this one needs awareness. It also means that ideals, in order to be worth anything at all, have to be tempered with not only compassion, but with realism. Human nature just isn't perfect yet – certainly not perfect enough to behave in the fashion in which many

Aquarians demand. Total selflessness is simply an impossibility. Like the other airy signs, Aquarius often doesn't remember that though we have our heads in heaven, our feet are on the earth and our bodies have evolved up through the animal kingdom. To Aquarius, man is not a dual creature; he is a son of the gods. As Menander said, the intellect in every man is god. When Aquarius understands that the feelings and the visions and the body of every man are god as well, then he can become what he truly is at heart: the visionary and the prophet, the server of the race, the contributor to the welfare of humanity in great ways or small.

⊛ The Aquarius Lover

We've already said quite a bit about the emotional propensities of Aquarius. Perhaps a little recapping is in order. Remember what we said about the air signs in general: they live in the world of ideas, and tend to be frightened of emotion. This is truer of Aquarius than the other two airy signs because Aquarius is what is called a 'fixed' sign. This means exactly as it sounds. Fixity can also be translated as strength, stubbornness, or rigidity, depending on how extreme it is and whether or not that fixity is in agreement with you or not.

So Aquarius tends to repress his emotions. He often sees his emotions as a weakness, something embarrassing. You might deduce from that that he's not the world's most romantic or effusive lover. He's often charmingly naïve in matters of the heart, and displays a winsome clumsiness which falls in weird counterpoint to his usually sophisticated ideas. In some ways, it's delightful, because he's usually incapable of playing the Don Juan unless he really means it. And then he's likely to make a somewhat less than suave one. Aquarius' gifts are not known to lie in the realms of courtship and romance.

So we can count sincerity of feeling and loyalty among his virtues. Because he's generally clumsy with emotion, he usually means what he says if he ever does tell you he loves you. Also, Aquarius is a truth-addict. This means, on the one hand, that he doesn't like lying, so you can believe him most of the time. On the other hand, it means you should be careful not to ask for those little declarations of emotional reassurance that lovers need. Instead of the compliment or the reassurance, you might get a pronouncement like, 'Well, to be strictly truthful, I don't actually love you at this moment.' I once knew an Aquarian man who felt obliged to announce, at various times of the day, whether he did or didn't love me – not for any particular reason except that he felt I ought to always know the truth at all times. It can be pretty wearing on the ego, to say the least.

Aquarius' loyalty springs from double-edged sources as well. On the one hand, he's probably more capable than any other sign of adhering to a promise kept. So if he promises fidelity, and means it, he very likely will be – because he's loyal to the ideal. And he does have a lot of self-discipline. On the other hand, his loyalty also springs from the fact that the realm of romantic escapades isn't really his style. He's awkward and unsure of himself in it, and often finds it more relaxing and less troublesome to remain loyal because he can get on with what he enjoys the most – things of the mind. It's not that Aquarius lacks passion. Not at all. But he's not particularly sensuous, and often doesn't spend long hours with his erotic fantasies in the way that you would expect of Taurus and Scorpio and even Pisces. He's busy thinking about the World and what can be done with it.

To balance the scales more in his favour, Aquarius is

a truly interesting companion, and he also knows, more than other signs, how to be a friend. This should not be underrated. Friendship often means more to Aquarius than love, partially because he doesn't understand love – it's too complicated and problematic, and he has trouble defining it – and partially because friendship's ideals are easier to uphold. So Aquarius, man or woman, can be a wonderful friend in all the senses of the word. He is loyal and honourable, and is capable of much self-sacrifice; he cares about other people, and so long as you don't expect him to participate in your emotional scenes, he's a wonderful listener and a careful, objective advisor. No friend could be more friendly or tolerant, or understanding. In a marriage or a love relationship, this quality of detached and undemanding friendship is often a true blessing. It means you can have your own ideas, think your own thoughts, discuss things, have companionship and camaraderie without the clutter of an expectation of roles, or a lot of emotional possessiveness. Aquarius, although he has as much jealousy in him as anybody else, will very rarely show it. He will rarely even admit it. He appears to be the least possessive of lovers. Don't let it fool you. But on the other hand, it doesn't intrude. If he believes in letting his partner have freedom, then by God he'll make sure he grants it, even if it minces his gut to pieces unconsciously.

If you're looking for a great deal of sentiment and romance, stay away from Aquarius. You're more likely to have lengthy political and ideological discussions, and very few whispered sweet nothings. On the other hand, if you seek a friend as a lover, Aquarius puts the other signs to shame. He's genuinely interested in people, and genuinely interested in you. Just don't try the heavily emotional approach. And buy yourself flowers.

♒ The Aquarius Man

It seems that the psychology of the masculine combines very well with Aquarius to bring out the intellectual bias of the sign. So the epitome of the Aquarian male is the thinker, the dreamer, the philosopher, the scientist. Also, the problem men in our society have confronting emotional situations generally is aggravated in Aquarius. Aquarian women, while they don't handle their own emotions very well, are usually at least aware of them. But no one is more out of touch with his own feeling nature than the typical Aquarian male.

So the Aquarian male is often one of the most infuriating people you will ever meet when it comes to relationships. First of all, the coolness of his attitude is infuriating – and deceptive. Remember that this sign has a lot of pride. Control of emotion is a big thing for Aquarius. No matter how much he's hurting, unless he's about to have a breakdown, he will often not grant you the satisfaction of knowing about it.

Another problem he's got is that he often sees emotion as a demand. Remember that Aquarius is very big on the idea of freedom. This is often carried to outlandish extremes in personal relationships. Typical of it is the Aquarian man who refuses to tell you what day and time you'll see him again – because he doesn't 'believe' in time. Or the Aquarian man who 'believes' in open relationships, and tells you truthfully (because he believes in truth, and feels everything should be open between you) about the three other lovers you have to compete with. Not that you asked. It's just that he believes in truth, and doesn't understand why you should be hurt and make a scene. It's unreasonable and possessive, and you shouldn't be so self-centred. Everybody, he will tell you, benefits from it. Shouldn't we all love each other? If you love him, you should love his other girlfriends, because they love him too, and he . . . Well, you know the story. It can make even the most tolerant lover develop homicidal instincts.

You may have the sort of Aquarian who simply refuses to discuss personal feelings. Or he may tell you you're being very 'heavy' and too emotional. The problem is, he's often grossly hypocritical about all this. When the tables are turned on him, he's capable of behaving as much like Othello as any Scorpio is. But he won't be as honest about it, because he'll drag in things like honesty and loyalty and other concepts which damn your behaviour without conceding that the real root of his upset is his feelings, not his principles.

The only way to deal with this kind of Aquarian is to out-Aquarian him. That means challenging his beliefs, so that he can find out whether he really believes in them or not. It means being a little unpredictable yourself, or requesting your own freedom of behaviour. Remember that this is a fixed sign. Fixed signs aren't adaptable; they don't adjust easily to other people. They have their own world, their own values. They don't like being pushed. That reforming instinct in Aquarius simply doesn't apply when you try to reform him. You've got to have a good deal of your own detachment, and some source of creative life of your own, if you want to make a relationship work with an Aquarian. He's not prepared to put that much into relationships on an emotional level. You simply have to get used to it, and learn to read his signals, not his words. A good deal of the time, what Aquarius says about his feelings should not be taken literally. You can take his word for it on his ideological views, or his special subject of study. He's pretty reliable there, and usually knows what he's doing. About his own emotions he usually knows very little. Learn to use your instincts, and learn a little telepathy. But don't expect an honest expression; you'll get what he calls honesty, which usually has nothing to do with it, because in this realm he isn't very honest with himself.

On the other hand, expect a good deal of unconscious emotional dependency. That independent spirit, with his mind in the clouds and his eyes on the future, is more sensitive than he can ever know. He's terribly vulnerable emotionally, rather childlike, which is why he takes such great pains to mask his emotions from everybody including himself. He would consider it weakness. If you need overt displays of it, avoid Aquarius. If you're confident enough in yourself to know you're worth loving, and can appreciate the friendship this man offers, you're fine. And who knows? You may even reform him, within reason.

♒ The Aquarius Woman

There are two types of Aquarian woman. Both share all the basic Aquarian qualities of strength, independence, original thought. One type turns the immense self-discipline and dedication of the sign into a purely personal sphere. The other goes out into the world, to try her muscle on society. Either way, this is no helpless, malleable creature. Her self-sacrifice is wholly self-motivated, and due to her own ideals, not your wishes.

Many Aquarian women find that the sphere of home and family is insufficient to exercise their intellectual abilities and interest in the larger group. So you find numerous Aquarian women in the political and helping fields, combining their wide-ranging ideas and spirit of concern for others with their innate femaleness. The typical profession here is the social worker or psychologist. Also the teacher and educator. Remember that it may be Aquarius on the ascendant that we are talking about here. But wherever you find this woman in professional life, she will be motivated by her ideals.

As you might expect, Aquarius is not a sign that is exactly conducive to sexual role-playing in relationships. In fact, many Aquarian women are intensely dedicated to the Women's Movement, for it is a natural to this sign. The logic and necessity of it is obvious to Aquarius, where it might not be to the more personal-oriented signs like Cancer, Taurus or Virgo. A great many Aquarian women must, at some point in their lives, become involved with a cause of some kind, even if it concerns only the three families on the street they live in. And this kind of dedication to a cause brings the best out of the sign.

It's a little more difficult on the emotional level. Aquarian women sometimes have as much difficulty as Aquarian men in expressing feeling. Sometimes it's recognized but held in – and you get a kind of stiffness, a rigidity, a stiff-necked pride. Sometimes the emotions are completely unconscious, and then you see an appearance of coldness, remoteness, aloofness in personal relationships. The 'don't tie me down' syndrome is as typical of the Aquarian woman as it is of the Aquarian man. Because of the resentment toward role-playing, there is also a great liberality in sexual behaviour often in evidence with Aquarian women. These are the women who are much more likely to recognize frankly their own bisexuality, their need for more than one relationship, their need for purely sexual affairs and escapades outside marriage. Aquarius is a masculine sign; it combines with more or less grace with feminine psychology, either in a true marriage which produces the gifted thinker who also has a heart, or in an uneasy conjoining where you have the woman who is basically embarrassed by her own femaleness. This can often be a problem with the Aquarian woman, since 'female' sometimes seems to her to mean weakness, emotionalism, or the victim of masculine domination and suppression. Not an easy sign for a woman to carry, and get it right. But with effort, you have the woman who can be both man and woman, true to her own female self yet with a strong masculine quality that allows her to concern herself with issues beyond her own personal satisfaction.

From all this, it will be obvious that Aquarius is not the woman to choose if you want, *a* the devoted and silent helpmeet who will adore you and listen uncritically to everything you say, or *b* the domestic creature who is only interested in you, your meals, your work, your children, and your cleaning and ironing. On the other hand, for those who are genuinely able to accept women as people, Aquarius can be an inspiring companion and helpmeet and friend, as well as a person in her own right. From this angle, the Age of Aquarius has a lot to do with the Women's Movement – and no sign is closer to the vanguard of the movement than Aquarius, in both its more violent and its more reasonable manifestations. And whatever you have to complain about in the Aquarian woman – whether it is her rigidity, her dedication to her own principles, her stubbornness, her detachment, or her refusal to regard her loved one as the penultimate hero, you must admit that this woman is interested and interesting. Men who are afraid of intelligent women should stay away.

The Element
of Water

A sentimental person thinks things will last. A romantic person hopes against hope that they won't.

F. SCOTT FITZGERALD

*W*ater, we are told by science, is the simplest of the elements: two atoms of hydrogen and one of oxygen, and presto! we have water. Water is also the most unshaped of the elements: temperature can alter its constitution to ice or steam, objects impose their shape on it. The greater percentage of the human body – something like 85% – is composed of water. Water is all around us, the source of life. Water covers two thirds of the earth's surface. And from water, the Koran tells us, all life begins.

The element of water, astrologically, is the most enigmatic of all the elements. It is the most 'primitive' in that it is furthest from the rational realm which we are pleased to call human thought. Look at the symbolism of the three watery signs, Cancer, Scorpio and Pisces. All three are cold-blooded creatures in nature, very far on the evolutionary ladder from the warm-blooded mammalian kingdom which has produced its dubious fruit of man. All three inhabit areas of the earth where man cannot live: the depths of the ocean, the barren seashores, the desert. When we examined the symbolism of the element of air, we saw that there were no bestial figures among them. The Twins, the Scales, the Waterbearer. An absence of 'animal'. Now, when we look at water, we see an absence of 'human'. What this means is not that the water signs are 'cold-blooded' in the sense we colloquially mean it. Far from it. But it may mean – among other things – that the structures, theories, and principles of differentiated human thought are not the mode of operation of these ambiguous signs. The water signs move like the realm of nature: with instinct, at home with that which is nonrational, unexplainable, sometimes magical. They are all motivated by feeling – and feeling, as everyone except a few obsessively fanatical material scientists will admit, is not something you can measure by statistics, define by hypothesis, contain within rationally understandable laws.

> Where does reality lie? In the greatest
> enchantment you have ever experienced.

These are the words of the poet Hugo von Hofmannsthal. They describe one of the water signs' basic attitudes toward life: what is felt is real. And because what is felt is something terribly intimate and subjective, its reality is apparent only to the person experiencing it. Water signs are never very good at explaining themselves to people. Generally, they don't try, but rely on their sure instincts to take them through complex situations. They can rarely tell you 'why' they have done something, from a rational point of view. When pressed, the water temperament will either go sullen and silent, or begin to offer some very half-baked and patently absurd rationalizations. The language of the heart is not translatable.

It's amusing to speculate about things like the development of language and rational thought. We in the West place great emphasis on the processes of the intellect. Our inheritance is largely that of ancient Greece, with its concentration on philosophy and meaning and balance and rationality. The classical Greece which underpins our modern systems of law and education is an air-sign phenomenon. We have forgotten that there are other languages, other modes of communication. Touch, for instance. Feeling. Images and symbols. Colour and music. All these belong to the realm of the water signs. Many water people do not think conceptually, but imagine things in pictures. You can see them as children, excelling at languages, the arts, history, finding a lot of difficulty in mastering algebra, logic, chemistry and physics. It isn't that they lack intelligence. It's that their intelligence is most gifted in other areas. Today we consider the 'smart' child as the one who does well in IQ tests. But as a water-sign friend of mine once said, IQ tests are excellent determinants of how well a person does at IQ tests. Nothing more.

For the water signs, the most important thing in the world is feeling, and in particular the objects of feeling – which are usually human beings. Relationships with people are the breath of life to the water signs. More than any other element, they fear aloneness and isolation. They need the constant contact of other people, the constant flow of feeling, the security of love and relationship. A water sign who has pulled in on himself and withdrawn from others is a sad creature. For many water signs, others are the most important thing in life – hence their sometimes rather suffocating tendency to live through others at their own expense.

Let's take a typical example of this tendency to live through others. Carl Jung uses an interesting analogy, in his work, of a relationship being a combination of two factors: a container and a contained. Picture it like this. One person is usually something like a large house with many rooms, most of them unexplored. The other person is like a small, comfortable, self-contained flat within that house. Both people, for a while, are content to remain in the warmth of the flat. It's safe, it's cosy, the alien world outside can't intrude. It's secure and unchangeable. You know its boundaries.

But the person who is the container becomes aware that the house is really much bigger than anybody thought. He – or she – begins to become restless. What's in all those unexplored rooms? What's the world like outside? Granted, it's unknown, and probably unsafe. But it's fascinating just because of that. So the container begins to fidget, and finally he gets up with a torch and a length of rope and decides to explore the basement. The contained panics. Will he come back? Will he shatter the peace and security of their world? What will happen?

The contained in relationships are usually the water signs. Within their own world, they can create anything, for imagination is usually one of the strongest gifts of this element. Water people have wonderful imaginations. They are also sensitive, perceptive, and profound. It is rare to find someone with a strong water emphasis in his horoscope who is shallow and superficial. But they are frightened of anything that might disrupt the peace of the nest.

Not that water people never change. They change all the time – with a rapidity that is upsetting to the air signs in particular. But it's their feelings that shift and change. One day up, the next day down. Most water-sign people are moody. Now moodiness is something we tend to see as neurotic. This is our air-sign education again, establishing standards of consistent behaviour. In fact the feeling nature in any person is not consistent. Feeling is like water. It flows and shifts and takes a new shape depending on what it meets. And water people, at least those who are brave enough to express their real selves to others, are not consistent in their moods.

It never bothers them. They're used to it; and ups and downs are not frightening. Neither are anger or fear, love or hate. But these things are distressing to the more rational types, who can't cope with their own changing emotions.

Water is also an incredibly subtle element. Nothing is simply black or white to the water signs. If you watch a typical television western of a decade ago, you can see the kind of values which air signs make: there are good guys and bad guys. To water, things aren't that simple. Good guys often have a secret bad streak, and bad guys are capable of acts of nobility. To water, people are complex and must be taken as they are, not as one would ideally like to think they ought to be. In this way, the water signs are the most realistic of all – that is, about human nature. They may not make a great noise about it. But they know. No person is wholly one thing.

There is a kind of relative quality about the values of the water signs because of this. They may have strong likes and dislikes – and this is one of their typical characteristics. Water people tend to react instantly to others. Yes, I like him. No, I don't. Often they can't explain why. Here's a typical air-water dialogue:

AIR: Well, what did you think of my brother?
WATER: I don't like him.
AIR: Don't like him? But he's my brother. Why not?
WATER: I don't know. I just don't like him. I'd prefer not to see much of him. There's just something about him.
AIR: What do you mean, 'Something about him'? What kind of remark is that? You must have a reason. Look, he's a really decent guy. He's always helped me when I've been in trouble. He gives a lot of money to charity, and votes Labour. He's good to his kids, and faithful to his wife. How can you not like him?

WATER: I just don't like him, okay? I don't care what he does or doesn't do. I'm sorry he's your brother. I don't think he's very honest. Maybe it's his shoes. I don't know.

AIR: What a silly, irrational thing to say.

Silly and irrational. This is generally the attitude more rational people give when the water signs produce their instant feeling judgments. But water is democratic enough to know that his own response is not a universal one. Most water signs won't say 'He's an evil person.' They'll own up to the fact that it's their own feelings. It's just, 'I don't like him.' And that's that.

Feelings have their own logic, however. And the values of the water signs are just as complex, just as subtle, just as carefully built of associations and nuances as the theories and ideals of the air signs. It's just that the process doesn't take place in their heads. It occurs, in popular jargon, in the gut. Usually the water person isn't aware of the process. The whole intricate mechanism of establishing a set of values and measuring something against those values takes place somewhere in the depths of the psyche. They don't know why. They just feel, one thing or another. Pleasant or unpleasant, beautiful or ugly, comfortable or uncomfortable: it's like the result coming up in the little window in the computer. The figuring is done inside, through processes which defy the intellect. The infuriating thing is that they're usually right in their assessments.

Another facet of this peculiar ability to 'sniff out' the feeling quality of a person or a situation is a thing which we call taste. Now, taste is a very difficult thing to define. It connects up with all kinds of things like aesthetics and art and beauty. These are so hopelessly relative that you can get into a good flaming row about it any time. Taste is a deeply personal matter. But good taste seems to be something that the water signs possess in abundance. Knowledge of the theories of aesthetics may elude them. But knowledge of the theories of aesthetics often produce monstrous taste.

I once attended a lecture with slides about the work produced by a particular school of art. It displayed the 'modern' products of a particular class, along with the reasons for each work. These works of art – by the artists' definition – were primarily comments on social and political states. They made powerful and important statements about the depersonalization of urban society, the oppression of the working-class, and other ideological attitudes. They were incredibly ugly. Worse, they were tasteless. There was a violent debate among the audience following the show of slides. Several people protested that these might be valid and important socio-political statements, but to define them as art was a dangerous thing. They might or might not be, depending upon who looked at them. Four people in the audience were particularly vocal in their disgust. I inquired later about their birth signs. They were all water signs. The *objets d'art* had offended their taste. They could accept them on the level of political or social statements. But they were ugly, they were offensive to the eye. Here is the subjective judgment: I don't like it, it doesn't please me. It's a simplistic but good illustration of the difference.

Water and air see very different realities, and value very different things. To the air signs, the idea is everything. Feelings must be subjected to the dominance of the idea. To the water signs, feeling is everything, and the idea must be bent to the feeling. Air, for this reason, tends to be more liberal in its politics – sometimes excessively so. 'Humanity' is always a big issue for the air signs. Water tends to be more conservative in its politics – sometimes excessively so. 'Humanity' is not a relevant concept for the water signs. It means nothing. Mrs Thomas across the street who at eighty cannot pay her fuel bills because her pension is too small – well, that's a reality, provided you know Mrs Thomas. One Mrs Thomas is enough to influence the political viewpoint of a water sign.

You can argue unto eternity with these two. They are both right; they see two sides of a coin. Water sees what is here and now, the reality of the pain, suffering, loneliness, dreams and needs of other human beings. Air sees what ought to be, what should be, what from an idealistic point of view might be. Because the water signs cannot grasp broad principles very easily, they can often become bigoted in a small way. Rarely in a large way, because they aren't concerned about large wholes. But if one black or one Jew or one Arab offends him, a water sign will often form a value judgment against the entire race or nationality. Why? Because he, personally, had a bad experience.

The water signs are usually pretty well acquainted with the darker side of human nature. Because they are naturally sympathetic, people unburden themselves, and they learn a lot of secrets. They are also acutely sensitive to all the undercurrents of feeling within a person, whether they are spoken or not. They have a strange ability to feel what somebody else feels, and enter into his emotional state with ease. For this reason many water signs make wonderful priests, doctors, counsellors and teachers. The gentle, delicate touch of the water signs never prods or pushes. It just shows empathy and understanding. And it opens hearts. The trouble is, there has to be a direct, personal contact. Discuss human suffering in the abstract and it means nothing to water. Show him an individual who is in trouble, and he will respond.

With all these virtues, you might expect some pretty strong vices. They can be phrased in one simple word: reason. Water signs have a problem with reasoning. I'll say again that this has nothing to do with intelligence.

Intelligence is something which has many different ways of working. You can have a person who is a brilliant mathematician and who is perfectly stupid about other people. You can have someone who has wonderful insight about people yet can't add to save his life. There are all kinds of intelligence. One is probably no better than another. With the water signs, the intelligence is of the heart. It's intelligence about people, what they need, how they feel. But water isn't a very objective element. It's hard to see beyond the garden wall.

Consequently, watery people are often unreasonable. They are also often unfair, which is infuriating to the air signs. They will quite blatantly set one standard for themselves and another for others. And you can't argue with it, because they can't argue. If they try, you will get the most amazing flow of opinions second-hand, make-shift ideas, 'they say' and 'everybody knows', third-hand quotes from unread newspapers, and a lot of completely irresponsible declarations that may or may not exist in reality. In other words, water is capable of bending the truth, for 'truth' as an abstract is something known only to the element of air. To the water signs, there are a lot of truths, depending on which side of the apple you bite.

Some water signs are charmingly infantile about the world of abstract ideas. This is the 'helpless female' type of both sexes who knows 'nothing about all that political stuff' because it's just so terribly complicated and boring. These people – and it should be emphasized that they are not only women, since I have heard it from a number of water-sign men as well under the guise of 'I'm only a simple labourer working to make a living' – refuse to recognize that 'society' is not some abstract thing that knocks on the door when it's time to pay taxes, but is a conglomerate of individuals. In a word, water can be pretty irresponsible on a broad social level. There is a story told to me about a water-sign woman who formed a friendship with an IRA terrorist wanted by the police. She didn't know his extracurricular activities at first. When she found out, she didn't do anything at all about it, despite the vague and uneasy feeling that he was the one responsible for the deaths of twelve people. Asked why, she said, 'But he's such a nice man. He's always been nice to me. If that other is true, it isn't any of my business, is it?' Charming. But it gives you pause for thought ...

Instead of rational thought, you get opinions. Instead of objective conversation, you get gossip. Instead of disinterested observation, you get bigotry. This is the uglier face of the water signs. It runs along side by side with the compassion, the gentleness, the empathy, the wisdom, the understanding. But as any water sign can tell you, nobody is only one thing.

Water's biggest problem in relationships is that he can often see nothing except relationships. This translates either as suffocating solicitude or clinginess or possessiveness. Now obviously it depends on your taste. The constant attention of the water signs to their loved ones is a gift not to be undervalued. Many air signs, frozen in their own feeling natures, misinterpret this tenderness and concern as a cloying possessiveness – not because it really is, but because they can't respond or receive the gift graciously. But the truth of it is that sometimes water is a little cloying. When the loved one is the most important thing in your life, it can be a little difficult for the loved one – firstly because he can never get away from you, and secondly because you've made him responsible for your own happiness. That's a pretty large burden. The water-sign parent who hates to see his or her children grow up is typical. When they're babies they need that love and attention. And water signs need to be needed. It's a basic trait in their nature. The best of them is brought out by someone else's need.

They are literally capable of sacrificing their lives for a loved one. Air will sacrifice for an ideal; water for a loved person. But when that child grows up, he wants to breathe fresh air, to move away into his own world. That's often when the water signs become frightened and begin to cling. What, leave me alone? After all I've done for you? The heavy obligations they place on their loved ones can be deadly. If you sacrifice your life for somebody, he's going to feel pretty guilty about it. Nine times out of ten, he'll repay you with resentment, because nobody likes to feel that guilty. It's important for the water signs to learn to let go once in a while. And, even more important, to take for themselves, to balance the scales. If you are always the giver, it's a pretty lopsided arrangement. The other person never has a chance to give himself; and after a while he'll begin to dislike himself for being so selfish.

We can put it another way. Water has a tendency, because it gives so much on a feeling level, to generate a lot of guilt in other people. And the list is very long, of water signs who are hurt by 'cold and unfeeling' children, lovers, husbands and wives who simply cannot endure the guilt any longer. It's known in the trade as emotional blackmail. Water is a master of the art.

Although he will always be there to help if you are in need, water sometimes feels rejected if you aren't in need. It's a perverse and difficult situation. If water isn't needed, his lifeblood isn't reaching him. What can he do? He may leave the relationship himself, because of the 'coldness' with which he's being treated. So it's into the arms of another lover – only to find with sadness that the new one has the same face as the old. Water signs tend to be fascinated and attracted, as well as irritated, by the air signs. Water admires air's detachment, his coolness, his urbanity, his distance, his aloofness. Many water people have a fantasy that this cool, detached airy partner is secretly an emotional child who really just needs a lot of love. True enough. But it can be pretty offensive if you are thirty or forty and your partner is still mothering you.

Without water, there would be no human relationship, no affection, no love. Too much of it drowns. Perhaps we could use a little drowning at this time in history, since we have been made to feel so ashamed of our own needs and feelings that we are guilty simply if we are inconsistent. Perhaps a little of the 'art of the small' is needed by everybody. And so the water signs have an important message to teach. A brain without a heart, like the tin man in the Wizard of Oz, either rusts into rigid paralysis, or destroys the world.

—

Cancer

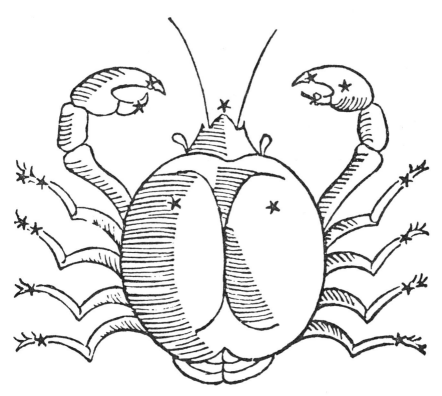

*D*on't throw out that old plastic bottle,' said a Cancer friend to me once. 'It might come in useful some time.' This piece of advice is a paradigm (a miniature replica of a much larger reality) of Cancer. Whether it's an old plastic bottle, an old lover, an old house, an old belief, an old bit of string, an old memory ... Hang on to it, says Cancer. You never know when you might need it again. Not that Cancer is a particularly 'practical' sign in the way we have met practicality in the element of earth. Cancer is much too imaginative, too immersed in a world of dreams and

longings and subtle currents of emotion, to treat everything in the literal terms of how much it's worth. But
one of the strongest urges in this watery sign is the urge
for security. For what's known and familiar, comforting
and safe. It is an emotional motivation, not a practical
one. I once knew a Cancer man who kept an old
shoebox locked in a desk drawer. In it was the most
bizarre assortment of objects gathered together that I
have ever seen: old chewing-gum wrappers (thankfully
the gum was missing), pieces of rope, old photographs,
bits of lace, nuts and screws and used bent nails,
fragments of magazine articles, a dried flower of
unknown origin, and most difficult to believe, an old
(and used) French letter. At this point, being familiar
with astrology, I didn't even bother to ask why. I knew
the answer.

Now this rather extreme example of Cancer's penchant for saving things is a little pathological. But you
can be sure that every Cancer has a metaphorical
shoebox somewhere, where things from the past linger.
Beneath the Crab's peculiar and often disconcerting
penchant for not letting go – of anything – lies one of
the most sensitive and vulnerable of all the zodiacal
signs. Cancer is ruled by the moon, and the moon's
phases, constantly shifting and changing, are an apt
image for the constant ebb and flow of moods, desires,
feelings, fears and intuitions that wash through this
apparently solid and conservative temperament. Yes,
conservative. Think about what the word means. Cancer
knows all about conservation. Waste not, want not.
With all the canniness of a Scot (Scotland, in fact, is
said to be ruled by Cancer), the Cancerian will carefully
nurture and protect those tender feelings beneath a
bristling fortified wall of souvenirs, mementoes, stock
certificates, insurance policies, old photographs, family
support, tradition, and a strong tendency toward pre-

serving the *status quo*. That is, as long as the *status quo* protects 'me and mine'.

Cancer is traditionally the sign of the family. This doesn't necessarily mean that every Cancer wants, or should have, a family in the conventional sense. Lots of Cancers, contrary to popular conception, are not domestic. They needn't have ties of blood. But the feeling of continuity with the past is terribly important to Cancer. The past is often more real to Cancer than the present, because it's known and therefore safe. Cancer's roots sink deep into the earth. Where there is a past, there can be a secure future. With his roots firm in the ground, Cancer can indulge in his love of exploration, his wandering instinct, his changeability. He knows there's something to come back to. Cancer can be a little dynastic in his attitudes. He's aware of descending from something, and also aware of the responsibility of himself producing descendants. The love of history typical to this sign is part of the need for continuity. A Cancer who is cut off from his roots is a sorry creature – until he learns to grow new roots, either a new family or a group of friends or a work project. Something. Without these things, the Crab withdraws ever more tightly into his shell, until he is imprisoned by his own fear of the future and his terror of the unknown.

The Crab is an instructive animal to watch if you want to learn about Cancer. Firstly, it never moves directly toward something it wants. It always circumambulates, to make it look as though it is actually heading off into a completely different direction. 'What, me? Interested in that? Don't be silly. It's the last thing on my mind.' But when it grabs for the prize, and those pincers close, you have to virtually kill it to get it to let go. It won't fight; crabs are non-aggressive animals. It will take pummelling, pushing, shoving, any treatment you care to give it. It simply hangs on, until you get tired and go away.

Watch a Cancer woman at a party, when she spots a man she is attracted to. Move straight in and begin a conversation? Never. She will circle around the room, studiously ignoring the desired object. She will chat brightly to everyone within range. She will somehow contrive to join a group standing nearby. She might succeed in spilling her drink an inch from his trouser leg, and probably not even be aware of what she is doing, in any calculating way. Cancer is an instinctive sign, doesn't like to analyse its own motives. But take the initiative directly? Never. That exposes her to possible rejection, humiliation or looking ridiculous. If you really want to see a Cancer terrified, threaten him with those things: rejection, humiliation, loss of face. Cancer is so sensitive, so vulnerable to other people's opinions of himself, so paralysed by public image, that he will rarely leave himself in a situation of exposure if he can possibly avoid it. Hence the often misread coolness. Cancer is not cool. But he is intensely self-protective. It's never the Cancer who gets drunk with the lampshade on his head, making an exhibition of himself. That is, unless he absolutely trusts everyone present. Then anything might happen.

It's been said that Cancers are manipulative. This is absolutely true. But let's explore this trait of manipulativeness. It has some rather complex sources. Cancer is a water sign. His great gift is his capacity to subtly work with feeling – his own and those of others. He doesn't plan this out, as a strategy, the way an air sign would. He operates with a marvellous instinctual grace that adapts itself to the immediate situation. Rather than go after a goal aggressively and in the open – remember that fear of rejection and humiliation – he would rather work on the atmosphere and on the feelings of other people, to orientate them toward his own objectives. Whatever one may think of President Jimmy Carter's political or religious sympathies, one must concede that he is a good conciliator. He is a Cancer. This facility for working to smooth quarrels and bring people together is a wonderful gift when dealing with children. Cancer will never bully a child, or use unjustified 'heavy authority'. The 'do it because I say so' approach isn't one of Cancer's tools, as it is of Scorpio and Aries and Leo. Cancer gently guides, so that half the time you think the idea came from you. Subtlety is one of the chief qualities of Cancer.

This, like every other gift in human nature, is double-edged. The nastier edge appears when the Cancer applies the gentle pressure of emotional blackmail to get you to do things his way. Most people in our culture are terribly vulnerable to guilt. It's ingrained in our Judeo-Christian heritage. Being selfish is a sin, almost as bad as Original Sin. And Cancer is a past master at the art of stimulating a sense of guilt. An insecure Cancer, anxious to hang on to the person or situation which gives him his safety, will often use this deadly implement to get his way. We might call this role the Martyr. It goes something like this:

ADOLESCENT TO CANCER MOTHER: Well, Mum, I've finally decided what I'm going to do next year. I'm going to travel abroad, go to Paris, and study languages at the Sorbonne.

CANCER MOTHER: (*after some silence, during which she digests (a) that her child is 'leaving her', (b) what she can do to stop him.*) Paris? Yes, I suppose Paris is a lovely place. I've never been to Paris myself. I never had the time, or the money. (*A sad, martyred look crosses her face. The suffering of the world is upon her.*) That will be wonderful for you. I wish I could have gone to Paris when I was your age. But I had to bring up all you children, and work a job at the same time. And your father never made much money, and wouldn't take me anywhere. I worked my fingers to the bone, supporting you children and taking care of the house. Then there was the war, and all that. I would have loved to go to Paris.

CHILD: (*beginning to feel vaguely guilty about being happy and having a future, although unsure just why*): Well, when I'm settled over there, I'll have you come for a visit.

CANCER MOTHER: Visit Paris? Oh, no, I couldn't. I have nothing to wear, and I'm so tired these days, keeping the house in order and washing and ironing the clothes . . . Of course, if you waited another year, Julie would be old enough to get a job . . . But of course you must go next year. Still, it would have been nice. But I'll stay here and take care of your father. (*Long sigh, recognizable as the Cancer Sigh.*) It'll be terribly lonely here. But I suppose life is all about sacrifice, isn't it? If you really love, then you have to sacrifice.

CHILD (*feeling even guiltier*): Don't you want me to go?

CANCER MOTHER: (*in great protest*) Of course I do! How can you ask me that? I think it's wonderful that you young people can have the freedom and the money to do what you like, it isn't like it was when I was young and your parents came first . . . I suppose people are just more selfish these days . . . I was just thinking of those lonely evenings at home, you know the phone always rings for you these days, all my friends have moved out of town, and I never have time to see them, being so busy with the cleaning and shopping . . .

Needless to say, the end of this scenario is not a trip to Paris. Not next year, or even the year after that. If foiled yet again, this kind of Cancer will not hesitate to develop a bad heart, migraine headaches, or the old time-honoured phrase, 'Do you want to kill me?' Once upon a time this was also known as the Jewish Mother Syndrome. Now perceptive people will have noticed that you don't have to be either Jewish or a mother to play this game. Husbands play it, children play it, wives play it, boyfriends and girlfriends play it, even employers play it. When Cancers are threatened with isolation or the loss of loved ones – through independence, distance, or any other means – they will often resort to the martyr. Not a pretty device.

The thing is, Cancer does need to be needed. And to love and nurture and cherish. And to play the role of Mother, in some shape or form. (This means Cancer men as well.) The important thing is to find the Child on levels other than the purely biological one. Once the children have grown, Cancer needs other outlets, preferably creative ones. The sensitivity, the gentleness, the delicate touch of this deep and subtle sign can be as usefully and productively placed on a project, a business, a home, a work of art, a piece of poetry, an animal, a garden. If it is all poured wholly into the beloved person, it is pretty natural for that person to either rebel or to turn inward in seething resentment, without fully understanding why. Cancer pays a tragic price for his emotional blackmail: the enmity of the loved one, in the end.

We should observe two more things about the crab, to complete our initial portrait of Cancer. The crab develops in a cyclical way. This is true too of Cancer people. I once had a pair of hermit crabs as pets. These creatures are particularly fascinating because, rather than having hard shells of their own, they wear the shells of dead molluscs, and camouflage them. There is a kind of Cancer whose shell is culled from others, as well as a kind who grows his own. Now when a hermit crab outgrows his shell – which he inevitably does – he must find a bigger one, and make the move in total safety. Underneath the shell, the crab is a defenceless, completely vulnerable creature. There is a period of time when crabs must hide in the sand while the new shell grows hard. They have to remain hidden, or they will be instant dinner for the nearest seagull without so much as a by-your-leave. Cancer people too have these cycles, where they must withdraw after a change and a period of new growth. Surprise them or intrude upon them when they are going through their quiet private time, and you can damage them irrevocably. Damage them in childhood, and they will retreat into a too-small shell, sometimes never to emerge. It takes a long time for the Crab to forget, once he has been wounded.

Finally – and perhaps most importantly, since it leads into our discussion of Cancer myth – is the Crab's natural environment. He is neither a creature of water, nor of land; he inhabits the border between the two. Let's translate this into human terms. On one side is the dry land of the real world – bills, real estate, responsibilities, commitments, facts. That's one of Cancer's needs. The other is the fathomless depths of the ocean of his imagination. Cancer belongs to both worlds. He must have time to give to each – time to nurture his secret dreams and longings in the shifting waters of his deep inner nature, and time to build a place of shelter and security in the world. A complex sign, Cancer. And a complex personality. It is almost impossible to get a Cancer to analyse himself, or to trot out his deepest secrets. Popular astrology usually considers Scorpio to be the most secretive of the signs. But Scorpio is secretive on purpose. He knows his safety lies in smokescreens. Cancer is secretive by second nature. He is full of half-germinated seeds that need the darkness and the safety of quiet and privacy. His retreat is natural, not thought out. It must be respected. The creative fruit he brings forth is worth waiting for.

♋ The Myth

We can sum up the Cancer myth in a word. Mother. And what a complex word! Mother is not only the woman who bore you, nurtured you, raised you. It is also what depth psychology calls an archetype – that is, a symbol of an innate life experience common to everybody. Mother means different things to different people. It can mean the safety and pleasure and warmth of a secure childhood. It can mean the devouring, possessing emotion which threatens to suffocate. It can be strong and sustaining. It can be destructive and dark. But we all have come from mothers. For Cancer, the experience of Mother in all its forms is rooted in his inner life. He never wholly escapes Mother, for he must learn to become Mother. At the beginning and the end of his life stands this powerful figure – representing the feelings, the past, the childhood, and the security he strives for so intensely. Mother is always an enigma for Cancer. You can find Cancers who seem to have no family feeling at all – 'family' is an embarrassment to them, not at all something they cling to. You can be pretty sure, in these cases, that childhood holds some memories that Cancer would rather forget. Many Cancers are perpetual wanderers, always seeking roots somewhere else. Often they are running away – from the past, from childhood, from Mother.

Let's look a little more closely at the ancient myths that deal with the Mother. Before there were ever gods on Mount Olympus, or heroes to fight the Trojan War, there was the Mother Goddess. The most ancient religions of the world begin with the worship of the Mother. To these archaic peoples, Mother meant Mother Earth. It meant the fruits of the harvest, and

land itself from which men drew sustenance. Throughout all the countries of the Mediterranean, and the
Near East, from which our western civilization has
sprung, the worship of the Mother was the worship of
the power of the earth to give and withhold life.

We tend now to be a little arrogant about the
'superstition' with which our ancestors worshipped the
earth and prayed for rich crops and a good harvest. We
have a vast and imposing array of modern technology
with which we believe we control the earth. We no
longer placate the Mother by elaborate mystery rites.
Man believes he is supreme; the earth is there for the
taking, and the heavens too. Yet think about childhood.
Mother is as powerful to a child as Mother Earth once
was to our ancestors. She is huge, vast, mysterious – the
source of food and life, the giver or withholder of love
and comfort. Nothing a man meets will ever be so big
again as Mother was when he was a baby at the breast.
Do you think we so easily forget? And if that child is a
Cancer – sensitive, open, aware of all the secret currents
of feeling that pass back and forth between himself and
his family – he will certainly not forget. He may
obliterate recall of it, because it frightens him that
anything should have that much power. But deep down,
Mother remains a mystery, as powerful as the mystery
of the growing crops. These are things we cannot really
tackle with our well-trained, rational minds.

Now there are some interesting sidelights to the
myths about the Great Mother. First of all, she always
had a consort. That consort was both her son and her
lover. In ancient mythology, incest themes abound. If
we take them symbolically, rather than literally, this
means that the Goddess and her Lover stem from the
same source, the same origin. And this son-lover is
often represented in myths as the creative life of nature
– the artist, the beautiful young god who infuses his
breath into the growing plants, the sun-god who brings

light to the world in the spring. Easter, our great Christian religious festival to celebrate the Resurrection of Christ, has its roots in an older past: the celebrations of the resurrection of the young god, returned to bring life back into the land after the cold winter. In the autumn, according to the myth, he dies – and the earth grows barren, and nothing grows, and the world is shrouded in barren cold. All over the Mediterranean the festivals of the death of the god were celebrated by thousands of women mourning his passing, weeping and offering sacrifices. In the spring they rejoiced.

What does this mean, when we consider that it is a myth closely bound up with Cancer? First of all, it is a myth of cycles. Whether myths were devised to explain nature or were deeper and more profound in meaning, is a matter of debate among archaeologists and psychologists. But here we have a myth about an eternal waning and waxing of life – like the moon, which rules Cancer. Cancer is a sign of phases, of cycles. The Cancer individual experiences these ebbs and flows of life-force, of creativity, of joy and sorrow, perpetually through his life. He is closer to the natural processes of Mother Earth than any other sign; many Cancers are in fact extremely vulnerable to the changes in climate and season, and go into a kind of hibernation during the winter. They may be slightly depressed, or listless, or lacking energy. Then, when the spring comes, they come to life again.

There is another, deeper meaning to the myth. The Mother and the young god who symbolizes creative life: here you have a picture of the way in which artistic creativity works. Many Cancers are highly imaginative, creative people. Writers like Proust, Hesse, *et al.* fill up the ranks of creative Cancerians – painters like Van Gogh (Cancer rising), etc. In some way, the creative Cancer is a kind of midwife: he creates something, drawing from depths which he can scarcely understand, making something from the fabric of his dreams and visions and fantasies and feelings. When it has been created in form, the phase is over. For a period of time he may feel depressed, empty. That is the winter. Then, he is ready to create again. The thing he is drawing from is a mystery. No true artist can really explain where the source of his inspiration lies. It's like the ocean – huge, fathomless. He, like the crab, inhabits the patch of sand midway between the mysterious ocean and the dry land of ordinary life. Ideas and images come to him, and he gives birth to them. Then the tide recedes, and for a time he is stranded. Then the process begins again.

Cancer is a sign of great complexity and depth. On the surface, you may catch the Cancer playing any role – he is a born actor, and his sense of camouflage and self-protection always compels him to play a part in any social situation. He may be giddy, giggly, moody, whining, sullen and sulky, affectionate, passionate, withdrawn, ecstatic. You can never be sure how he's going to wake up in the morning. But beneath the kaleidoscope of shifting feelings and moods, beneath the hard carapace shown to an unfriendly world, there is this perpetual cycle of death and rebirth, of winter and spring and summer and autumn. This is why it is important for Cancer to be creative, to express himself emotionally in some way. For, if we take this myth on its deepest level, Cancer is both the Mother and the son, and is not likely to be able to explain to anybody the mysterious rhythm he follows – the rhythm of the sea, of the moon, of the tides. Don't expect Cancer to be consistent. He's not likely to be, unless he's chosen consistency as a mask because he feels the pressure of others' opinions. The true Cancerian is a moody crea-ture, unable to explain always why he feels as he does. But, then, why should he explain? Nature owes us no explanations. We either appreciate her, or we lose something very precious.

♋ The Shadow

It's time to take a look at the less pleasant side of the crab. We have already had a peep at some of Cancer's tricks to sustain relationships. But most Cancers are aware, however dimly, that they play emotional games at times. They may not admit it, or discuss it. One of Cancer's favourite expressions is, 'Must we talk about everything? Some things are better left unsaid.' But Cancer isn't blind. With sure-footed instinct, Cancer can read emotional currents very well – even his own.

The unknown side of any sign, as we have seen, lies in the element which is antithetical to it. Water signs, being feeling-orientated, have a secret side which resembles the air signs. Cancer's gentle, sensitive, sympathetic quality – the loveliest aspect of the sign – carries a strange shadow behind it. We can sum it up in one term: destructive criticism.

Listen, some time, to the ordinary everyday conversation of a truly Cancerian person. Ordinarily they are full of sympathy – oh, don't be too hard on the poor man, he can't help it; how can you turn away such a pathetic stray kitten? Yes, I know she's taking advantage, but she's old and lonely . . . etc. Cancer is quick to excuse the more difficult behaviour traits of others, especially family, because of that sympathy and sense of recognizing other people's needs. But listen, some time, to a Cancer having a good gossip. Some of the nastiest, bitchiest things you'll ever hear come streaming out. Little, snippy things – not disagreements of opinion, or honest debates, or recognized dislikes – for this side of Cancer is epitomized by the bridge club ladies who get together and slash the friend to pieces behind her back and then smile sweetly when next they see her, wondering why in the world she should be offended when, after all, they didn't really mean it . . . the Cancer father who, without attempting to be snappish, tells his child how to be. 'Why can't you be like little Johnny down the street, he doesn't show his father disrespect' . . . the Cancer mother who, a little jealous of her daughter, says before the important dance, 'Yes, you look lovely, dear . . . as lovely as possible, all things considered . . .' This is the veiled insult, the disguised criticism, designed to strike below the belt, to demean, to hurt, to goad. Cancer's shadow might be pictured as a gnat, a wasp with a little sting. And most of the time they are completely unaware of it. Criticize? Never. Many Cancers, displaying this shadow to others, will protest. They like to think of themselves as kind, sympathetic, understanding. But the shadow side of any water sign is ruthless. And can be cruel. Or cold. This is true of all three water signs. With Cancer, the shadow speaks through the mouth.

What are the true motives behind this? Since we are wading through murky waters here, let's have a close, honest look. Remember what we said about water signs. Most important to them is their relationships with others. Water signs do not like to be alone; they cannot bear isolation or rejection. Cancer, a sign of intense feeling needs, has a strong tendency to live through his loved ones. Eternal fidelity. Cancer is a possessive sign – as possessive as Scorpio is traditionally. But Cancer is more subtle about it. So, to sum up, we might say that Cancer often finds his entire meaning in life through those people close to him. And something in him, deep down, rebels.

Resentment – quiet, seething, unobtrusive, silent resentment – is one of the greatest emotional problems of all the water signs. In Cancer, resentment can reach a fine art. Somewhere, deep down among all the loving, sympathetic emotions, is the nagging feeling that you are not really living your own life. This is especially true when Cancer gives and sacrifices and gives and sacrifices, and the loved one isn't prepared to come when the string is pulled at last. That resentment turns into negative criticism. It's an act of vengeance. Remember the tendency water signs have to have fixed ideas buried deep down in their minds? Well, the idea here is: I've given him (or her) everything. Now he owes me something back. And if the gift isn't returned, well, then, he deserves a little knocking back into place.

This may sound a little ugly. It is. But if Cancer can reach the root of his resentment, and act on it – act positively, not with negative criticism – his relationships will remain much healthier and more secure. And acting positively means, not too much martyrdom. Not everyone is a child that needs to be ferociously protected. Some people – perhaps all people – need to be let go once in a while. And Cancer needs to learn to nurture himself, his own needs, his own wishes. The more he does this, the less resentment he'll carry. And then the shadow stays in the basement where it belongs.

Another peculiar facet of the shadow that Cancer can turn against himself is the way in which Cancers eat up popular opinions without checking their facts. Give them one or two pertinent bits of information and they will bring to bear the full weight of their own feelings and prejudices, and pass judgment. Negative criticism also implies judgment. And Cancer's judgment, when it's based on half-digested opinions like this, is likely to be not only faulty, but destructive. It can be called opinionatedness. Listen for the 'They say' or 'Everyone knows'. It's the commonest voice of Cancer's shadow. And the real object of the exercise is: I protect me and mine. Anything outside is suspicious.

How do you deal with a Cancerian shadow, once it's

let loose? Sometimes it's best to ignore it. After all, it isn't meant with malice. Sometimes it's best to confront it, and bring a little honest truth into the discussion. But most important, it's best to notice it. Those little barbs and inferences, unnoticed, sink in. Cancer has immense emotional power, because he can read the feelings of others so well. And whatever the shadow, the light is there too – the compassion, the subtlety, the gentleness, the caringness. That's worth a lot.

♋ The Cancer Lover

In a true Cancerian, love has a lot to do with security. It also has a lot to do with affection and kindness and sympathy. And it has a lot to do with Mother.

Cancer is as capable of intense passion as Scorpio. But because it is a more vulnerable sign, Cancer tends to be more discriminating about where that passion is expressed. And very slow to commit it, because trust is terribly important for all the water signs.

Initially, people in love tend to behave in similar ways. But if Cancer becomes truly involved, the myth of the mother is likely to begin to enter. This may mean needing to be mothered – and this can apply to women as well as men. Many Cancer women look for rather maternal men – men who will be kind and gentle with them. Equally often, it means Cancer wants to do the mothering. Show your pain, your helplessness, your weakness, your need, and you have won Cancer where your strengths might interest him much less. Remember that Cancer needs to be needed. And don't expect everything to be spoken. It's a rare Cancer who wears his or her heart in full view on the sleeve. You have to learn to read signals, if you're involved with a Cancer. And become a gifted interpreter of moods. Sullen sulkiness means he feels rejected. Clinginess means he needs reassurance. Whining means he's feeling sorry for himself today. Crabbiness means he's feeling unappreciated. And so on. But try to confront the issue, and the Crab will slide away from you. Usually he doesn't understand himself what's going on. It's just a stray mood.

Cancer tends to be loyal in relationships. This is because security is important. But it is a changeable sign; and that loyalty may take a lot of buffeting on the surface. Cancer is notorious for keeping the home base and collecting thrills on the journey. On the other hand, if he is sufficiently secure, he will usually be aware of his priorities. Anything that jeopardizes the security of the relationship isn't on.

Divorce is often a horrific experience for Cancer. Many Cancers will remain uncommitted because they sense the gruelling experience a separation would entail. The disruption of the nest is a true trauma for Cancer, where a Sagittarian might happily pack one bag and go, or a Virgo wrap up the financial affairs tidily before exiting. No separation is easy for Cancer, even if he deeply longs for freedom. Once again, you must learn to read the signs. Gradual withdrawal emotionally, sexual coolness or impotence, are Cancer's way of saying, 'Get me out of here.' But Cancer will rarely be the one to make the decision to go. First of all, the emotional confrontation is too terrifying. Secondly, other people's opinions are too terrifying. Cancer would much rather become quietly, progressively, more unpleasant until you're the one to throw him out. Then he doesn't have to feel guilty.

It does take a lot, though. It takes trampling on his feelings, being insensitive or cold, shattering his dreams, bullying him, expecting him to be strong when his strength lies in camouflage and tenacity. Betrayal of trust goes deep with the water signs. Rationally they may excuse it. Emotionally, they never do.

The nest is naturally important to Cancer. It is a sign of habit. Even an unsettled Cancer, maintaining a casual affair, will usually collapse in the same chair in the living room, and indulge in the same rituals of food and drink. Permanent the liaison may not be; but that need for roots and security can give the feeling of continuity to even the briefest, most casual of Cancerian relationships.

It is very easy to love Cancer for his gentleness, his sensitivity, his imagination, his subtlety, his peculiar brand of courage when what he loves is threatened. It is more difficult to endure the moods, and the innate egocentricity of the child which is always present in this complex sign. Whether mother or child, whichever role the Cancer plays – or both – the constant need for affection and reassurance is always present. If you have one of those emotional natures which is coolly self-sufficient and resents giving affection – particularly when it might not be returned due to a mood – then it's best to stay away from Cancer. If you have a warm heart, and an understanding of what life is like from the inside of this alternately fragile and tough dreamer, you may be surprised. Cancer's greatest offering in relationships is his profound, instinctual understanding of human nature and human pain. And that isn't often to be found in the marketplace these days.

♋ The Cancer Man

'Never think,' wrote the poet Rainer Maria Rilke, 'that there is more in life than can be packed into childhood.' We might say, with more accuracy for Cancer, that there is not more in life than can be packed into Mother.

And here you have the greatest strength and also the greatest weakness of the Cancer man in love relationships. This man is tied, one way or another – in love or in hate, and often in both – to Mother.

It may sound simplistic to say that all Cancer men are mother-bound. But it would come close to the truth. Remember what we said about the myths connected with Cancer? And in particular the myth of the Great Mother? Well, there is a test that confronts every Cancer man, and he runs up against it sooner or later in life. He can either embody the Mother himself – which doesn't necessarily mean changing nappies – or he can look for a mother all his life. Our world being what it is, with so little attention paid to people's inner lives and motivations, most Cancer men take the latter road.

If you think about it, you'll see it's natural. Cancer is a sign of feeling and of deep emotional needs and often dependency. It clings. It doesn't like to stand alone. In childhood, this need for attachment and warmth will naturally focus on the mother. The trouble is that once adult, Cancer men are often still looking for that nurturing, protecting women who will always forgive them, always understand them, care for them, shelter them. You might say, Why not? But Cancer, which is a feminine sign, gels oddly with the masculine psyche. In each man's unconscious, buried deep within him, is the myth of the Hero. How can a hero keep running back to Mummy for comfort and understanding? Psychology postulates that the mother-son tie is one of the most difficult things a man must contend with in life. If he doesn't deal with it – as many Cancer men don't – then his relationships will suffer for it.

There is usually a scenario which follows this theme, and which is pretty common in Cancer marriages. For one thing, Cancer men usually marry young. That is, if they aren't mother-haters. The mother-haters usually marry very late, if at all. They don't know they hate their mothers. They're afraid of women – hence the lack of commitment. But this is a distorted kind of Cancer, a Cancer on the run from his own emotional dependency. You can see a lot of those running about with extra-hard shells on, never really letting you see the vulnerable person underneath. If you probe, they snap at you like good crabs.

The more open Cancer man will, then, usually have a family by the time he's twenty-five. Because of their gentleness, they make excellent fathers, so long as they're not jealous of the mothering their own children receive. But later on, in the thirties or perhaps forties, the pattern that Cancer sets tends to go awry. He will usually be attracted to a strong woman – one of those capable types, often intellectual, who either overtly or subtly must carry the emotional strength for the relationship. His moodiness, changeability, snappishness, fears – all must be understood and coddled. But it is natural for any adolescent boy to kick out against mother. It's part of the growing-up process. Eventually Cancer must too, because he's a man. You can imagine what happens then. Who gets kicked? Well, the surrogate mother, of course. If that happens to you, it's not pleasant. Although Cancer is not a divorce-prone sign – after all, marriage is a form of security, isn't it? – Cancer men can be wanderers *par excellence*. They always come back again. But the question is whether you want them when they do.

This is a sign with a lot of inbuilt conflict for a man. For one thing, the sensitivity and imagination don't mix well with society's macho expectations of men. Did I hear you say times have changed, women are liberated, etc.? Maybe in London, Paris, Amsterdam, New York. But most of the rest of the world lies between. Sophisticated cosmopolitan cities excluded, it's still a little difficult for a moody, sensitive, introverted, imaginative man to get away with being himself. He must learn camouflage. Cancer's two most common camouflages, as we have seen, are the hard shell and the 'good drinking companion' jolly extrovert face. But these things take their toll on the person inside, unless he's pretty confident in himself. How many people you know are that?

For another thing, the mother problem isn't an easy one to solve. Motherhood is both sacred and profane; it is both a biological fact, with little glamour attached, and an archetypal experience. To toe the line between berating woman – and the maternal side of woman – and overglamourizing it so your mother can do no wrong, is a hard task. To live within the shadow of the Mother, so in touch with the forces and currents that wash the shores of ordinary life, is a great and harrowing task psychologically for a Cancer man. Most would rather not even think about it. But the deep creativity of this sign cannot really emerge without some understanding of its myth and its task. The Cancer man is never an easy lover or husband. For one thing, he's too complex, and defies the stereotyped image of the masculine with which our society is embued. For another, he's evasive and indirect, and the deeper the feeling or the problem, the less likely you are to hear about it. He can be sulky and crabby one moment, effusively sentimental and affectionate the next. But most of all he has feeling, and he's alive. Curious about just about everything, he will rarely be rigidly intellectual, but will more likely store what interests him in his extraordinarily attentive memory and draw it out to tell an anecdote or illustrate a point.

Donald Sutherland is a typical Cancerian actor. He is notorious for disliking interviews, for his evasiveness, his versatility, his moodiness. Yet he is extremely masculine, in his own fashion. Not the Burt Reynolds type, maybe. But the loveliest quality in the Cancer man is tenderness and gentleness. They are short-changed these days. Invest your trust, and you draw it out. Who wants Burt Reynolds, anyway?

♋ The Cancer Woman

There are two types of Cancer women. Those who are Mothers. And those who are Eternal Children. Often they cross, and you find both in one. Cancer is often the epitome of the feminine – moody, non-rational, alternately loving and cruel, unpredictable, gentle, soft, capable of surprising ruthlessness, and ultimately enigmatic and full of mystery.

Don't think, because she can cook, that she's domesticated. Or that, because she likes children, she's docile and has no ambitions of her own. Cancer women can be intensely possessive, driving, ambitious people. It's just that they tend to live it through someone else: the husband, the lover, or the child.

Many Cancer women choose deliberately to play the role of Mother. They have a wonderful gift for making a home, for creating a warm, loving atmosphere, for dealing with gentleness with all the bruises – physical or emotional – which their loved ones incur. But don't forget that the Mother Goddess, in the myth, has more than one face. Her domestic face heals, nurtures, supports. Her dark face is wild like the maenads who dance the sacred dance of Dionysus on the mountaintop and dismember the faun they catch. There are secret depths of emotional storms and a strange, matriarchal consciousness in the Cancer woman. Some Cancer women show this archaic attitude by seeing men essentially as sources to beget children. They hark back to the old days when the Mother ruled and the king was sacrificed every five years. For this kind of Cancer, all men are essentially children, to be cosseted, loved, and made pregnant by.

A relationship with this kind of Cancer is both frightening and a great challenge. Frightening because it can castrate a man. If you are always treated like a boy, you remain one; and if you weren't before, you become one. On the other hand, meeting it with a challenge of masculinity can lead to a wonderfully dynamic, passionate, constantly stimulating love. In the ancient myths, it is the hero who challenges the power of the Mother – not by demeaning or subjugation or denial of her rights, but simply by affirmation of his manhood and his own destiny – who is truly the hero. There is a fascinating quality about many Cancer women because of this dark aspect to the sign, which is much in evidence in Cancer women. It beckons, it fascinates, it attracts, it repels. But safe and domesticated, it isn't. Think again. The cooking may be great. But you need to understand the woman.

The Cancer woman, too, must create. Usually her creativity is expressed through the bearing of children. But at mid-life, when the children have begun to grow away and need a friend more than a Mother, many Cancerian women suffer a deep crisis of identity. Who am I? What is my own life about? This is the greatest challenge that can befall a Cancer woman. In a sense, Cancer women's real life doesn't begin until this stage of the journey. The first part of life is often bound up with the home and family, the natural and right and instinctual expression of all the femininity and creativity of the sign. But later on the world must become larger, and the family bigger – the reason, perhaps, why many Cancer women make such excellent teachers, counsellors, and therapists. The creativity must be shifted on to levels other than the biological – perhaps why so many Cancer women make such excellent painters, novelists, actresses with depth and subtlety in mid-life.

The depth and richness of the Cancer woman shows itself most truly after thirty-five. It is a slow-maturing sign. Crabs don't race like greyhounds. But the Cancer woman, often more oyster-like than crablike, may take half a lifetime to grow her pearl – her wisdom about human nature, and the depth of her love for people and life. Perhaps this is the most mysterious of all the faces of the Mother: Sophia, which means, in Greek, wisdom. And wisdom comes from the heart, not the intellect.

Scorpio

*I*t's said that you can recognize a Scorpio by his stare. That famous stare has become downright notorious in general astrology textbooks and sun-sign columns. Enigmatic, penetrating, probing while revealing nothing, apparently hostile or ruthless. The man with the x-ray vision. This little cameo, along with the infamous passion which is usually attributed to the sign, has gone a long way toward making life pretty difficult for Scorpio people. After all, when someone asks you at a party what sign you are, and you look at them (penetratingly) and reply, 'Scorpio', and they give a little gasp and back away in fright, or instantly inquire what you're doing later, well, it can get a little ... difficult.

Scorpio is without doubt the most perplexing and perhaps the least understood of all the signs of the zodiac. Scorpios themselves do not help this problem, since they are indeed prone to playing the enigmatic, mysterious type when they are unsure of a situation and are checking out the currents. Let's abandon preconceptions and start from the beginning. What is it about the eighth sign that seems to provoke so much confusion, fascination and dread? Open a medieval astrological text and, if you're strongly Scorpio – sun, moon or ascendant – you may as well take a flying leap off the Golden Gate Bridge, or turn yourself in to the police right away before you perpetrate violence or sexual assault on someone. The descriptions are that bad. Power-driven, sex-crazed, violent, warlike, vindictive, cunning: the image is a pretty horrific one. The modern equivalent isn't much better. It's a real nuisance having to live up to Mata Hari (who was a Scorpio) or Don Juan. Tiring, you might say. What is Scorpio really like?

Like Cancer and Pisces, this is a water sign. Earlier, we talked about water as the element which is most connected with the feeling side of life. This means that Scorpio, regardless of his habitual smokescreens – and make no mistake about it, Scorpio has the best smokescreens of any of the signs – is a sign of profound feeling and sensitivity, easily affected by the emotional currents inside him and around him, susceptible to the feelings of others, easily hurt, sympathetic, compassionate, often intensely lonely, and driven by an almost voracious need for relationship. Never mind that 'loner' business that has been tacked onto the sign. Scorpio is no loner at heart. Just the opposite. He longs for a really profound, close union. It's just that he's rather discriminating about whom he allows into his psychic field, being so intensely sensitive. And also, he's, well, you might say a little mistrustful of people.

Let's talk about the mistrust. Scorpio might prefer to call it realistic caution. Like all water signs, Scorpio has no illusions about the goods in the shop window necessarily matching those in the shop. Scorpio has an uncanny way of perceiving what other people don't wish to be known. Often they don't know it themselves, which makes things even more uncomfortable. It is very unnerving to feel that somebody knows something about you that you don't know yourself. From early childhood on, Scorpio sees through hypocrisy and sham with his curiously tuned nose for undercurrents. Being watery, he will often not be able to formulate these perceptions. More likely, he'll have strong, immediate gut reactions to people. And you can be pretty sure that when he smells brimstone, he's liable to be dead right. The trouble is that he smells brimstone just about everywhere.

Scorpio, you see, is privy to one of the most profound and disturbing secrets of human nature: all individuals carry within them a dark side. Scorpio cannot afford to be romantic, because he knows perfectly well that alongside mankind's nobility and greatness he is also still an animal, and a not very attractive one at that. We mentioned that the element of air is idealistic. In principle, man is fundamentally good. The element of water is more realistic. Principles are lovely, but life is different. No wonder Scorpio sometimes seems deeply cynical. How could he be otherwise, when he is constantly barraged with the unwelcome and unoffered sight of everyone's dirty linen, including his own?

One of Scorpio's greatest difficulties in life is to learn tolerance. Compassion he's got in plenty, although he will be ruthless when necessary and, unlike his Piscean and Cancerian fellows, is far less likely to be swayed by a sad story when the teller has made no effort to help himself. But even with all that compassion, you usually find that Scorpio is intolerant of weakness. Suffering he responds to; he has the deepest sympathy for pain and loneliness. A great number of Scorpios may be found in the helping professions, both medicine and psychology, because they are so keyed in to people's pain and the struggle of those trapped in their own darkness. But laziness and weakness Scorpio will not abide. His attitude is that no matter what sort of mess you are in, you can do something about it, and make of your life what you will. By the time he is ready to leave this life, Scorpio will usually have found the secret to performing this little act of self-transformation himself. Why, then, he reasons, can't others? What he fails to realize is that people are made differently, and not everyone has his capacity for ruthless self-discipline. Also, it just isn't everyone's path in life. Scorpio's famous Luciferian pride – the cut-off-your-nose-to-spite-your-face variety – keeps him from recognizing that it's sometimes necessary, even courageous, to yield.

Which brings us to another important facet of Scorpio's nature. We'll discuss it in more detail further on. Suffice it to say here that Scorpio has a great problem relinquishing control. This means control on a lot of levels. It may be controlling spontaneous expression of emotion outward – we all know the character that, even after a couple of bottles of wine and a fifth of whisky, still maintains his iron grip on himself, and will never, *never* allow himself to appear foolish or sloppy in front of others. It may be controlling other people – and this is a real problem in Scorpio's close relationships. It may be controlling life itself – where you find the arch-manipulators who pull the puppet strings all around themselves to keep the world in its place. Whatever the nature of it, somewhere in his life every Scorpio has a large key which fits a large iron door behind which lies . . .

Well, you wouldn't really want to know, would you? Take all that insight and immense sensitivity, add a liberal dash of the fierce pride and determination to carve his own path through life, throw in a dose of general mistrust of people's motives and you don't exactly come up with what is colloquially known as a 'laid back' person. Sometimes this produces an attractive and fascinating smouldering quality – hints of fathomless depths. Lucky you if you can plumb them. Sometimes it produces a downright paranoiac.

It has often been said that Scorpio, because of his great will-power, patience, persistence and insight, can succeed at anything he puts his mind to. This is generally true. Scorpio is hard to beat once he decides he's going to achieve something. Because this is a sign of feeling, Scorpio commits himself emotionally to everything he does. Otherwise he can't be bothered. Whether it's becoming a nation's leader (like Charles de Gaulle, a famous Scorpio) or changing a lightbulb, if it interests him, then it will never be just a lukewarm job. It will be done with heart, soul and body thrown in. When you are really emotionally committed to something, you're going to put all of your talents and resources into it. Mountains are effortlessly moved in this way. Insight makes it possible for Scorpio to sidestep, avoid or outsmart – or, if necessary, bludgeon – those who might wish to pull him down, long before anybody else realizes a confrontation is coming. Martin Luther was a Scorpio. Who but a Scorpio could defy the whole Catholic Church? Teddy Roosevelt, another famous Scorpio, had a favourite expression which was his formula for success:

Walk softly and carry a big stick.

And the steady control of this fixed sign, which allows Scorpio to wait for years if necessary to achieve his goal,

misses nothing, forgets nothing. It's a remarkable formula for success.

The thing is, success is not usually what motivates
Scorpio. Certainly there are those born under the sign
who, frustrated in their emotional lives, make absolute
power their ultimate goal. But that's a pathological
expression of the sign, not a genuine one. Twist anybody
painfully enough and you will find they seek power to
compensate. The real key to Scorpio's enormous determination to make something of himself lies deep within
his own secret soul. His heart is always a battleground,
for the masculine and feminine elements war within him
constantly, forcing him to delve into his own motivations far more deeply than our extroverted society
considers healthy. He has all the feminine sensitivity
and feeling of the water signs; yet he is ruled by Mars,
the god of war, and Pluto, the lord of death. We are
taught very early in western culture that Scorpio's brand
of introspection is 'brooding', and that to indulge in it
is basically neurotic or egotistical. But Scorpio sees it
differently. And, after all, he's probably right, at least
as far as his own path is concerned. For him it's not
neurotic brooding. It's a way of trying to find the truth
about himself and about life. To Scorpio, skimming
along the surface is offensive. He loathes superficiality
almost as much as he loathes weakness of character. He
must understand why he feels as he does, why he acts
as he does, why others act and feel as they do. He delves
and probes into regions which would send the other
signs scurrying to the beaches and discothèques. Scorpio
must ultimately understand himself, and come to some
kind of truce with the warring forces of his nature which
allow him no peace.

Every Scorpio carries within him a wound of some
kind, an emotional or sexual problem or conflict or
frustration which – no matter how hard he tries –
refuses to be solved. He usually creates this problem

himself. He has a penchant after all, for creating crises and then pitting himself against the enemy in grand dramatic style. There is more than a touch of the theatre about Scorpio. This is the secret of Scorpio's self-destructive tendency. This is why he really injures himself, goads himself with something that he cannot overcome. It spurs him to achieve something within himself, which is ultimately much more important to him than outer achievements. He can perhaps recite for himself the lines of William Ernest Henley's poem:

> I am the master of my fate,
> I am the captain of my soul.

♏ The Myth

Let's look first at the figure which symbolizes Scorpio. In very ancient astrology – Egyptian, Chaldean and Hebrew – Scorpio was represented not by the familiar scorpion, but by the serpent. This is a profound symbol which tells us a lot about Scorpio. Firstly, the serpent sheds his skin cyclically, and was thought by the ancients to be immortal and capable of constant self-renewal. Now this pattern of outgrowing a skin, sloughing it and growing a new one runs through Scorpio's life. Often his life breaks up into distinct chapters, as he moves through one cycle after another. All come to ultimate destruction. Then he rebuilds and starts again.

The serpent is also, in ancient mythology, a symbol of the wisdom of the earth itself – timeless, ancient, knowing the secret life of all things. He moves close to the ground, and hears the secrets of the roots of things. In Biblical lore the serpent is the Devil, the Father of Lies, who tempted Eve in the Garden. He is Lucifer, the fallen angel. You can see that he has a double face.

You can take him as dark or light, good or evil, for he contains both. And so does Scorpio. He has equally great power for good or evil, healing or destruction. Goethe (who had Scorpio rising) created a typically Scorpionic figure in Faust, caught between the extremes of heaven and hell.

The scorpion, a more recent development traceable to Greek astrology, is in some ways a less descriptive animal. But he can give us some valuable clues about the Scorpio temperament. Firstly, he is an isolated animal. You don't find herds of scorpions roving the desert munching flies together. Scorpio, the human being, is also not a collective creature. He usually dislikes crowds, mistrusts loud extroverted parties, and prefers a small circle of trustworthy friends or a single lover. Secondly, although the scorpion is a deadly creature (not all varieties have a fatal sting, but they all give nasty bites), he is completely nonaggressive. Scorpions will not attack other animals. On the other hand, if you are silly enough to step on one, well, it's your problem, isn't it? You should have watched what you were walking on. Attack this tiny creature and he will move in for the kill no matter how much bigger you are. Scorpio people have an acute sense of justice. They don't believe for a minute in all that sentimental stuff about turning the other cheek. You give back as good as you get, for it's the only way to survive. Scorpios make bad martyrs – unless, of course, like Ghandi, this posture is necessary to prove a point.

There is a fascinating legend about the scorpion: if you corner him, and give him no avenue for escape, he will sting himself to death. This sounds a little apocryphal. But I have seen it happen. Once in the south of France I watched a group of children surround a small brown scorpion with sticks, so that it was completely trapped. It committed suicide. The message here is that Scorpio would rather destroy himself, and go down in flames by his own hand – literally or psychologically – than submit to another's ultimatum or control. It's that damnable pride again. 'Better to reign in hell,' as Lucifer says in Milton's *Paradise Lost* (Milton had Scorpio rising), 'than to serve in heaven.' If Scorpio ever truly bows his head, he has learned one of the most valuable lessons of his life. More likely he'll go through the sham of bowing, and pay you back threefold later. He will usually, in the end, only submit to whatever he understands as his gods. And he sometimes has some pretty peculiar gods, this enigmatic fellow. Find a Scorpio who has gone apathetic and outwardly submissive and you'll see someone eaten up from within with furious resentment and jealousy. Often this is unknown even to himself. Then you'll come up against real destructiveness, of the worst kind – like in those 'happy' families where the wife quietly sabotages her husband's masculinity and loads her children with guilt in revenge for her unlived life. Repressed Scorpionic rage isn't pretty. Nobody promised it would be. But every Scorpio has the courage to face whatever is in him, and transform it. As we said earlier, Scorpio has no illusions about life.

There is one famous myth which is particularly fitting for Scorpio. It's one of the twelve labours of Hercules. In this particular labour he is told to slay the Lernean Hydra. Beneath the outward success and power, this myth describes Scorpio's real destiny. Hercules is sent to destroy a large, deadly creature called a Hydra, which inhabits a dark cave in a swamp and preys upon the folk of the countryside. The Hydra is a serpent-like beast with nine snake heads, each of which is equipped with deadly poison fangs. A sort of multiple cobra, you might say. And it has a very nasty propensity: cut off one of its heads, and it sprouts three new ones in return.

Hercules at first attempts to club the Hydra to death, then to slice its heads off. He is about finished, since this results in a proliferation of heads. Then he remembers a piece of advice given to him by a wise teacher. The Hydra cannot stand the light. So Hercules gets down on his knees and lifts the creature up into the sunlight. It shrivels up and begins to die. Only one head remains, for that one is immortal, and buried within it is a precious jewel. But one head is easy for Hercules to handle. He simply buries it under a rock.

The explanation of this myth isn't really necessary for Scorpio. They usually come, sooner or later, to that place in life where they discover the hydra within themselves. But some explanation might be of value to the less introspective signs. We can say that the hydra can mean many things: jealousy, vengeance, resentment, anger, frustrated sexuality, violence. Scorpio is a sign of intense desire; and the hydra's many heads can mean the many desires of the uncivilized human heart. Left to grow in the darkness, they can become poisonous, and begin to destroy others. But they cannot be dealt with by repression. They must be understood, held up to the light, respected as part of oneself. And although vanquished, it is a good idea to remember that one immortal head. For Scorpio, all human beings carry within them the seeds of good and evil. Evil is not an abstract thing, or somebody else's fault; it is in everyone. Human brutality cannot be blamed on society, but ultimately only on oneself. It is relevant to realize that Freud, the great founder of modern depth psychology, had Scorpio rising. Therein lies the deepest meaning of Scorpio's myth: come to terms with the hydra in yourself, and you redeem the world.

♏ The Shadow

What can we say about the dark side of Scorpio, when he is already so well acquainted with his own darkness? This is a water sign: full of feeling, subjective in approaching life and people. Scorpio has the courage to face all manner of things, but these usually lie on the emotional plane. What he often can't face is the degree to which his reactions are governed by his opinions. We said earlier that the water signs as a group tend to opinionatedness, because they are so often unaware of their own thought processes. Being so subjective and concerned for their own personal values, it is difficult to see the clear, fair, bird's-eye view of things. And here is one of Scorpio's greatest blind spots. He can be downright fanatical in his views about people and life. And this fanaticism can, in the wrong place and at the wrong time, spur him into some pretty unpleasant actions based on biased or distorted judgment.

Let's take an example of this in everyday life. Let's look at the Scorpio woman who has been hurt in a succession of relationships. For all her insight and sensitivity, you will find that a lot of Scorpio women have formed fixed, crystallized opinions about the opposite sex. Big, blanket generalizations. Like, 'All men are bastards', or, 'No man can be trusted', or 'All men are unfaithful'.

Here is a typical scenario. We might call it the Othello syndrome.

SCORPIO WOMAN: Where were you tonight? You said you'd be back at eight. It's midnight.
(*This is invariably said in an accusing tone of voice,*

*making it perfectly clear that whatever explanation is
offered, only one will be believed.*)

AIR MAN: Sorry, dear. I had a frenetic day at the
office. Then the car broke down, and I spent two
hours trying to fix a leaking radiator. It's just been
one of those days.

(*A note of defence creeps in. Resentment about being
mistrusted. Preparation for becoming cagey if pressed.*)

SCORPIO WOMAN: (*Silence. The atmosphere becomes
visibly chilly. Icicles form around the dinner dishes.
When he tries to touch her affectionately, she recoils.
She is thinking to herself: He's cheating on me.
Bastard, they all do it in the end. I'll be damned if I'll
let him use me like that. Right. No sex for a month.*)

AIR MAN: What's wrong, dear? I told you, I couldn't
help it.

SCORPIO WOMAN: Nothing's wrong, dear. (*Stony
glare. She imagines he knows she knows, and is trying
to make him feel suitably ashamed. He hasn't the
vaguest idea what is running through her mind.*)

Give one of these a week, a year, ten years, and you
have a real horror show, straight out of *Who's Afraid of
Virginia Woolf?* Scorpio can ravage a marriage, a love
affair, a home, with this kind of behaviour. It isn't
sufficient to just say it's a jealous sign. There are many
kinds of jealousy. Possessive, yes, but all water signs
are possessive; they all need relationships, and all fear
aloneness. But Scorpio's pathological jealousy isn't
simply fear of losing a loved one. We all fear that.
Underneath you will find some bitter little vision of life,
some black belief about the fundamental rottenness of
men/women or whatever. Scorpio's shadow is his nega-
tivity, couched in rigid opinions which lurk below the
surface and often torment him at the moments when he
should feel happiest.

It takes a long time for Scorpio to learn to trust and

to forgive. Usually he's learned that mistrust early in life, from seeing the dark shadows standing behind his parents and his religious upbringing and his education. And the wound takes a long time to heal.

It isn't the vindictiveness in these classical situations that is really the problem. Although we're taught that it's un-Christian, a little honest revenge is often healthier than the outward show of acquiescence and the inner, repressed anger that spews out through indirect channels that so many of us call being 'good'. Besides, sometimes it does the world of good for someone to get back what he's just dished out; it might stop him from doing it again. What's really wrong here is that Scorpio never gives the other person the benefit of the doubt. The opinion is already formed, prepackaged like frozen vegetables, ready to be trotted out and tacked onto the offender regardless of whether it's true or not, and without knowing the facts of the situation. Water signs are uncomfortable with facts. Facts confuse the issue, which for water is primarily how it feels, not what really happened. Scorpio's shadow side completely ignores the other person's viewpoint.

This is a pretty hard thing to live with. You can see its traces not only in individuals, but in political and religious ideologies as well. Certain astrologers have considered that Germany is traditionally ruled by Scorpio. Where else but in a Scorpio country could you have a single fanatical idea – antisemitism – arise with such force to take complete possession of a nation with such destruction following in its wake? The Scorpio who cannot deal with the hydra within himself will project it onto the world and see it in others. Then you have the persecutors who believe it their mission to redeem humanity at gun-point. St Paul was said to have been a Scorpio. Much of the bloodshed committed in the name of Christ throughout the ages stems from his interpretation of Christianity. Never forget that Scorpio is a sign of great power – for good or ill. No Scorpio, however apparently insignificant, is without influence over those close to him. See that mild little man over there in the grey suit, reading the *Wall Street Journal*? He may not think about things like witch-hunts and the paradox of violence in the name of Jesus. He may not have read *Faust*, or *Paradise Lost*. But he's a Scorpio. He has insight and power, however repressed. And he can make of his life anything he wishes.

♏ The Scorpio Lover

Enough has been written about Scorpio's famous sensuality and erotic inclinations to make further descriptions redundant. Not only redundant: they're not strictly accurate either. Passion, Scorpio possesses in abundance. But that passion may not necessarily come out in the obvious way. Sexuality for Scorpio is more a matter of emotion – a symbol, a way of reaching a different order of experience. It isn't just a physical release. Taurus is really the sign of pure earthy sensuality, not Scorpio. Many Scorpios have a deep mystical feeling about sex, and sex and love are bound up with a longing for some kind of experience which the ordinary relationship can never provide. Call it what you like – a mystical experience, a taste of the depths, a surrender, or whatever. It has less to do with the body, and more to do with the soul.

You might call Scorpio erotic, rather than sensual. There is a world of difference. Pick up a copy of any *Playboy* magazine and you will see crude sexuality at its most rampant. It's the body which is the turn-on. Eroticism is different; it's the tone, the colour, the atmosphere, the underlying feeling. Watch a film like the Japanese *Empire of the Senses*. Sexual it isn't; erotic

it is. When you understand the difference, you'll understand Scorpio's sexuality. Sometimes there are darker
undercurrents to it – a trace of cruelty, a touch of
masochism, some fantasies that involve things our
grandmothers pretended didn't exist. Experimentation
is something Scorpio will happily pursue – provided it's
erotic, not mechanical. 'How to' journals bore him. He
doesn't need to learn how to. His curiosity is usually
alive from the age of three onwards. It's something else
he's after.

Because Scorpio is a fixed sign, it possesses a capacity
for enduring loyalty and love. This can sometimes
amount to an act of great self-sacrifice. That same
fanaticism that we sometimes see in Scorpio's religious
and political views can permeate his relationships as
well. On the negative side, his fixity can amount to
absolute possession. Either way, there isn't anything
lukewarm about the Scorpio lover. That is, if he is in
love. If he isn't, and the magic gateway into the upper
(or lower) realms isn't visible, you are liable to be
confronted with that chilly quality which all water signs
possess when their feelings aren't engaged. Sorry.
Nobody home.

Scorpio's biggest problem as a lover – male or female
– is, you guessed it, his need to maintain control. This
includes the famous jealousy, as it does the deep and
enduring love. But he must, at all times, be master of
the game. Sometimes this can show in some pretty petty
ways. Like having too much pride to apologize when he
has done something really stupid, because it means
you've one-upped him. Or finding little malicious ways
to test you, so that you always have the feeling you're
the dispensable one. On the other hand, paradoxically,
Scorpio has little respect for someone who won't fight
him. That, after all, is weakness. So you're caught in a
bind. He has to win, but he resents it if you don't give
him a little flack for it. Fights are fairly common in

Scorpio relationships. That is, if you haven't got one of the repressed Scorpios where everything seethes inside, like a hot volcano boiling, but all you see is an occasional puff of steam out the top. If you've got one of those, beware. Send your Scorpio to an encounter group to release the pressure. It isn't much fun when it blows at you.

Crises and blow-ups are fairly common games within Scorpio relationships. Implacable resentment, and making you pay for any insult – real or imagined – are other bonuses on the less pleasant side. What about the advantages?

What is really rare about Scorpio as a lover is that he has a real capacity for understanding the other person. Since he misses very little, he will usually know an awful lot about you very quickly. For those who don't like this kind of honesty, choose some other sign. But if relationship means something more than hanging about at discothèques together, try a Scorpio. His way of conducting relationships – if it becomes a relationship, rather than a one-night experiment – always has depth. He knows how to read another person's needs – and, if not threatened, will do his utmost to meet them. All water signs thrive on being needed. Scorpio is no exception.

Granted, you might not like the amount he or she knows about you. But probing is Scorpio's business. You can't expect this sign to play with veneers. He may keep his secrets, but you won't be allowed to keep yours. Scorpio is not above scanning the telephone numbers in your little black book while you're in the bath, or checking the receipts in your wallet. Both Scorpio men and women do this. Yet this primitive attitude of 'You're mine and that's that' can be immensely flattering. Scorpio is said – particularly by air signs – to be too 'heavy'. But that kind of heaviness is a matter of taste. Whatever else is going, you know that the relationship is terribly important to a Scorpio. The job, the in-laws, the boys at the club don't come first. And there's a great deal to be said for someone who considers a relationship something current and important, rather than something which can be placed on the shelf while he gets on with something else.

There are a lot of current opinions and definitions of jealousy. From *Cosmopolitan* magazine to erudite psychology books, jealousy is one of the most perplexing and ever-present of human emotions. Some people believe that jealousy is a natural accompaniment to life, the sour with the sweet. Others think it's pathological, a sign of insecurity. Others believe it has something to do with older standards of morality. Still others believe that it's morally wrong, and not part of the idealized state of self-abnegating love which says, 'Whatever makes you happy makes me happy.'

You won't hear a Scorpio mouthing that sort of drivel. More likely he'll tell you, 'Whatever makes you happy without me, you'll pay for.' Jealousy is undoubtedly, in some people, a symptom of deep insecurity and mistrust. Like the beautiful model who once came to me for a horoscope, who was certain her boyfriend fancied everybody else because she didn't think she was worth anything at all. Possessiveness, in some degree, on the other hand, is pretty natural. No one likes to lose what they have become attached to. To Scorpio, possessiveness is as natural as breathing. His feelings are intense. They don't let go easily. It's simply how he's built. Unless a Scorpio has deliberately hardened his feelings because of fear of involvement, you won't find many Scorpio swingers. If you do find one, you can be pretty sure they are running away from their own deep capacity for love, for fear it will hurt.

Double standards are often part of Scorpio's game – male or female. What's good for him, he won't tolerate in you. Many Scorpios believe – with all the emotional fixity of which they are capable – that they have the prerogative to flirt, or have affairs – but not you. 'It's different,' they say blithely. And it's not male chauvinism either; I've heard this from Scorpio women as well. If you want equal standards, you have to train your Scorpio. This means wearing armour, helmet, arquebus, and lance. It also means being prepared for some god-awful rows, many tears, some rather spicy words, and quite a few hurts – with only the chance of eventual understanding. Otherwise, accept the *status quo*. Is it worth it? I once knew a woman married to a Scorpio man who had to put up with all of it – the jealousy, the double standards, the little barbs, the moodiness – the works. I asked her why she stayed with him. She replied, 'Because he's exceptional. He's himself. He's also true to himself. Of course he's a bastard sometimes. But he's an individual. I respect that.' There you have it. For many people, complain as you like, Scorpio's fierce individuality can only inspire respect – and often love.

No one experiences a relationship with a Scorpio without changing. They come out of it more self-aware, sometimes a little scarred, but looking at life a lot more deeply. Don't expect fair play and sweetness and light. Remember Milton's Lucifer – better to reign in hell than serve in heaven. But it is said, by some very wise people over many ages, that life is made up of light and dark both, and that only the fool believes it to be otherwise. And Scorpio is no fool.

♏ The Scorpio Man

Let's strip away the glamour and see what's underneath. Remember that this is a water sign. For all its great strength and courage, the emotional needs of the Scorpio man are much similar to those of the Piscean and the Cancerian. Affection, acceptance, reassurance, love, companionship. In large quantities. Undiluted by criticism. As a water sign, Scorpio cannot bear coldness. They are terribly sensitive. That mask of nonchalant nonreaction is a mask. Remember that. No Scorpio will advertise the fact that he is hurt or feeling neglected. You have to train as a telepath. But remember that this is a watery, feminine, vulnerable sign. Feminine, you ask? How could this creature be feminine? But there is a curious paradox about Scorpio. The opposite sexual element is very strong in people of both sexes. The moodiness, emotionalism, eroticism, and subjectivity are typical sides of the female face of Scorpio. So is the possessiveness. Many Scorpio men are acutely embarrassed by the presence of so much emotion in themselves. That's when they become the hard-driving, ruthless, ambitious Scorpios of the text books. But think of what it took to get them that way. Can you unbend them? Maybe, maybe not. Probably, in the end, it rests with the Scorpio himself.

This is not an easy man to live with. For one thing, you won't get straight answers if you ask pertinent questions like 'Do you love me?' On the other hand, you'll get brutal scrapings of the bottom of the barrel when you least want it – like a vicious hour-long analysis of your motives in flirting with Mr AQ. at the party, and why it stems from your sexual inadequacies and your rejection by your father. He can cut deep when he wants, and then honesty precludes compassion. That's the straight answer you don't want to hear – especially when he's got destructive, and decides he's going to hit back at you for some hurt you've inflicted on him without your even realizing it. Tell you you hurt his feelings? Not likely. And often he won't apologize either. To live with this man, you must understand him; and to truly understand him, you must like him. Yes, I mean like him. And respect him – what he's made of, what drives him, what his loneliness means, what the depth of feeling does to him in a society which requires men to be detached, what his sensitivity means in a world which does not value it. If you can't like him, then leave him alone; for you'll never, never change him. Only a Scorpio can change himself. And very likely, if you ask, he'll do the opposite.

If you are the type who minds having to acquiesce – or to give the impression of it – then stay away. This man is not for independent women of the more vociferous kind. On the other hand he respects strength; and if you make allowance for his pride, which won't permit him to admit a wrong or lose a battle, no lover is more devoted, compassionate, insightful or gentle. Show your pain to a Scorpio and they will do anything for you. Show your arrogance, treat them with shallowness, attack them, and you have no chance of receiving anything at all – except their unpleasantness, which can be pretty unpleasant. And don't trifle. A Scorpio who thinks he's being mocked can be the most difficult person in the world. His pride will not allow it.

What about the jealousy? Well, let's be realistic. It's not going to go away. Nor is his feeling that he has the prerogative – for flirtation, for affairs, for whatever he feels he wants – while you don't since you're his. If you must have other relationships, be extremely clever and extremely discreet. Otherwise you're in for a hellish time; for it is difficult for this man to forgive a betrayal. It's the worst thing you can do to him. The best is to believe in him – and to side with him when he's going through one of his the-world-doesn't-understand-me phases. Scorpio trusts few people because few people trust him. This begins in childhood, for he is never truly a child – yet is treated like one, often far beyond a reasonable point.

♏ The Scorpio Woman

There are two keywords you should remember about the Scorpio woman: depth – meaning that hers is a subtle, complex, and never obvious temperament, and will – meaning that this woman is not about to bow her head to anyone or anything, unless it's temporarily necessary to achieve an end. You might also keep in mind other Scorpio qualities: the famous possessiveness, intensity, pride, loyalty. No Scorpio is either easy to understand, or easy to live with; but then, if you wanted something light and frothy and unobtrusive, you'd be with someone else, wouldn't you?

Let's consider the business of depth. Scorpio is a sign which never takes a superficial view of life; it's almost impossible for the Scorpio woman to accept something at face value. This can span a pretty broad range, from the caricature Scorpio who, when you say 'Good morning', wonders exactly what you mean by it, to the Scorpio whose motivation and deepest need is to understand – both herself and the people around her. In short, this is a woman who expects something more from a relationship than surface tokens. Love, to Scorpio, is more than demonstration of affection or security or sexual gratification, or even intellectual camaraderie. It's a bond which – hopefully, from her point of view – touches to the soul, and means no secrets. No secrets doesn't mean the superficial way of interpreting it, either, like where were you at five o'clock on Thursday afternoon. It means that she expects honesty of character. Scorpio, being a water sign, has a lot of compassion, which usually comes from her own propensity to torment herself. The Scorpio woman is probably more capable than any other of both understanding and accepting human weaknesses and human darkness. She's not afraid of ugliness, internal or external, because to Scorpio dark and light make life interesting. What she can't stand is the hypocrite, the person who lives in pretence. If you need your masks and your props, stay away from this woman, because that x-ray eye will see through the lot; and she won't stop at seeing, either. There's a strong tendency to try to remake others in Scorpio, and the Scorpio woman will often take it upon herself, consciously or unconsciously, to help transform you – especially if you've got a lot to hide.

Unfortunately for her, there are a great many men roaming the world to whom the idea of being emotionally honest, or straightforward in revealing their own motives, is absolute horror.

Not that that's such a reprehensible thing. It isn't easy to face the mirror, not to the degree Scorpio thinks you should face it. But this is the one area where the Scorpio woman shows her intolerance. She can accept anything in anybody except what she considers to be weakness of character – that is, the person who hasn't the strength to face himself. And she can be pretty scornful, and pretty scathing, if she feels let down.

That propensity for depth is a double-edged sword. On the one hand, it makes her a rare woman, because she's capable of not only seeing but also sharing your pain and your dreams and your burdens; and her enormous strength of will and loyalty are unshakable even when yours are flagging a little. But her expectations are high; and it isn't easy to live up to them. Basically, she expects that you, like her, should want to be constantly engaged in the great alchemical work of transformation, nothing less. If you happen to prefer sailing and cowboy films to introspection, you might have to explain yourself. Your only chance is in convincing her of the justice of your right to be yourself.

Justice is a thing the Scorpio woman understands. Her sense of justice is so keen and so sensitive that it's virtually inflexible. If she thinks you're in the right, then she's capable of sacrificing completely her own desires and opinions. If she thinks you're in the wrong, and you don't apologize or change your viewpoint, she'll retaliate.

Let's talk about retaliation, since, if you're involved with a Scorpio, you'll have to get used to the concept. Scorpio's sense of justice, as we mentioned, is pretty acute. It isn't an intellectually based judgmental faculty like Libra's either; it's a powerful, gut-level, emotional reaction to any situation where she feels she's been abused or treated wrongly. This can range from being rejected or insulted – which in the case of the more paranoid Scorpio may mean an imaginary rejection or insult – to betrayal. Betrayal is perhaps the thing she fears and hates the most. And if she feels betrayed, she's more likely to strike back than to turn the other cheek. Nice Christian patience and mildness are not, repeat not, qualities which you should be trying to find in Scorpio. It's good basic primitive stuff – eye for an eye, and all that. Never maliciously, or with cruelty. Just enough to teach you a lesson.

Does it sound a little hair-raising? Well, it depends on how you look at it. The Scorpio woman's feelings run deep and intense, and she doesn't like them to be taken lightly. She's hurt easily because of this intensity and sensitivity, although she can't really be hurt by people in general – only those few she really cares about. Scorpio is extremely selective in love and friendship. Everybody else can go to hell. She isn't intimidated by either public disapproval or snide comments or gossip behind her back. Only from those people whom she loves and respects can a criticism or a rejection wound. But then it really wounds. And whether you argue philosophically about the rightness or wrongness of it, that's her stance. Injure her and she'll injure you back, if at all possible. Unless, of course, you did it accidentally. Then she'll forget about it immediately, because that isn't the same thing.

Scorpio has a long memory for both good and ill. Help her, show her encouragement, and she'll always remember it. Betray her and she'll never trust you again. In fact, very likely she doesn't really trust you in the first place, or anybody for that matter, because her sensitive and virtually psychic perception of human character tells her that nobody, but nobody, is really a saint. She's always on her guard, against life and against the shadowy side of others, and against the more convoluted fears and desires in herself. It takes a long time before Scorpio settles into a relationship. She may seem to. But she'll watch for a long time to make sure you're what you say you are.

Of what use, you may well ask, is this kind of hypersensitivity? Why not just go out and enjoy life and take the bitter with the sweet? Fine if you're a Sagittarian or a Gemini, but not if you're a Scorpio. And the use of it – if 'use' is the word we want – is that spending any time around a Scorpio teaches you to be more aware. Aware of yourself, aware of your motives, aware of your own needs, aware of what drives others, aware of the whole invisible realm of the psyche which we ordinarily, in our extroverted blundering western culture, overlook. Why be aware? Well, if you aren't, then you get nasty things happening – like inadvertently being hurtful and destructive to other people and yourself, and on a broader, collective level, being destructive to whole cultural groups and societies. If we all had Scorpio's insight, we very likely wouldn't have much in the way of human cruelty, because we'd catch it first in ourselves.

But for this kind of depth the Scorpio woman pays a price; and the price is that it's hard for her to be frivolous and carefree. Here she needs the help of a partner, and a lot of tenderness and understanding. She'll always have secrets; all Scorpios do. But to watch Scorpio come out of its tangled brooding into a little sunshine is a lovely thing to watch, because then the real warmth and generosity of the element of water is available to other people.

There was that other word, will. It's wise to remember, in dealings with Scorpios of either sex, that you ask, rather than order. This is important to remember if you have a Scorpio child; if you have a Scorpio employee; and if you have a Scorpio woman as well, because (a gentle reminder) the two planetary rulers of Scorpio are Pluto, lord of the underworld, and Mars, god of war.

Not that Scorpio isn't a feminine sign. Remember Mata Hari? She was a classic Scorpio. There's a mysterious and often fascinating quality about Scorpio women; they often exude a sensuality and a thinly veiled and lightly controlled passion which can be intensely magnetic. They also often inspire fear and mistrust, because you're never quite sure what's going on behind those eyes. But those two powerful planetary rulers point out that, along with the intensely female quality of the sign, there's also a lot of fire and a lot of courage and a lot of pride. Don't try to crush the pride. You'll get almightily stung if you do. Scorpio demands respect, and this applies to the Scorpio woman as well as the Scorpio man. She's a person unto herself, not anybody's mate, servant, or property. if allowed to offer herself freely, she's capable of devoting her life. But if you demand or take for granted, you'll meet either with a cold, frosty glare and a deliberate reverse of what you asked for, or you'll suddenly get a screaming, ranting Valkyrie running at you with a spear. She can be temperamental.

The Scorpio woman needs an arena where she can

release the fighting qualities of Mars. Releasing them in a relationship isn't always very pleasant, and she does need to have a good fight on occasions. The warrior quality of the sign tends to take to causes, and to other people's fights; the Scorpio woman may often be seen championing the weak or the abused, whether it's in a political arena or a medical or psychological one. But she does need a theatre to work in; and because she thrives on crises, she needs space to promote them, to accomplish her thirst for transformation and change. Otherwise, guess who bears the brunt of it. Scorpio doesn't like things placid for too long; she mistrusts too much contentment. She's always looking for the worm in the apple, and if things are quiet for too long she'll begin to suspect something's going on underneath. Then she'll upend the whole apple cart, and start a quarrel or a scene, or provoke you into one, in order to find the worm. Never mind. When it turns out that there isn't any worm after all, she's not the least bit chagrined. She accomplished what she was really after: a change in the relationship, a deeper look, a new expression of emotion. She'd rather have you furious than bland and uninvolved.

The airy signs find her fascinating but a torment, because she seems to contain all those depths they're so fascinated by but terrified of; and she pulls them into their emotions, which is the most difficult place in the world for the element of air to be. The other watery signs generally understand her, but they too are likely to be afraid of the probing eye that sees too much. Earth, stolid and realistic, often doesn't understand her; earthy people may love her depth and shrewdness, but miss the fundamental point, and suddenly find themselves upheaved and staring at a reality they didn't know existed. And fire responds to her innate theatricality, but often flies into really dramatic scenes and conflagrations. No other sign can really subdue or tame the Scorpion; all you can do is decide whether this is someone you can understand and love, and if so, then go along for the ride, because it's bound to take you into some pretty strange quarters. One thing it will never be: shallow or boring.

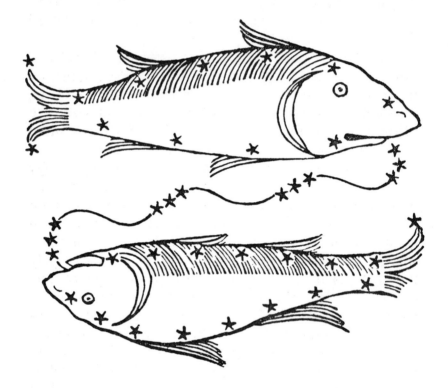

Pisces

7he range from Einstein to the ranks of junkies queueing at midnight in Piccadilly Circus for their weekly methadone is a pretty broad range. So is the range from the Fish, that for two thousand years has symbolized the mystery of Christ, to the sad, scruffy, ineffectual figure which Vivian Robson once described in an astrology text as 'the dustbin of the zodiac'. But this bizarre combination of paradoxical things is typical of Pisces.

In an attempt to understand the real motivations of the Piscean (a thing which is impossible right from the outset, but which one must, irresistibly, try anyway), I once asked a Pisces friend what he thought about it.

'Well,' he replied with a perfectly straight face, 'it's a well-known fact that every Pisces secretly longs to be given the fishing rights to all the dustbins in Oxford Street.'

And there you have it. Take the dustbin literally or symbolically as you please. What the rest of humanity discards, disdains, ignores or cannot comprehend, Pisces pursues. In the midst of the waste and wreckage of human dreams and the heights of disappointed fantasies, he will fish . . . and fish . . . and fish.

Pisces is ruled by Neptune, who in ancient mythology is represented as the god of the oceans and the underground waterways of the earth. Dripping with seaweed, brandishing his trident, he is unpredictable in behaviour: sometimes friendly to sailors, offering them smooth seas and a calm wind, other times strangely inimical, raising destructive storms and calling monsters out of the depths. The figure of Neptune tells us something about Pisces right away. This sign is connected with a realm that has no boundaries, no measurable depths. 'From water all life comes,' the Koran tells us. And nothing less than the source of life itself is the real secret for which Pisces fishes. No wonder, if he fails, that he reverts to the disillusioned, deluded escapist.

It is sometimes said that Pisces, the last sign of the zodiac, contains a little bit of each of all the others. And watching a typical Piscean, this certainly seems to be true. No one is as much a chameleon as Pisces, a natural actor. The theatre and the film industry are full of fishes, playing their parts. There is a marvellous fluidity and complexity in Pisces people which can be alternatively enchanting and irritating, for they are so many people that you begin to wonder when the real Pisces will stand up. The secret is that there is no 'real' Piscean.

He actually is everybody. And if you think it's easy to live with that kind of empathy and identification with the human race, think again.

It is also said that Pisces incarnates either to serve or to suffer. This, too, seems to be true in its fashion, although it is a little extreme. But the tendency Pisceans have to become the people with whom they are strongly involved causes many of them to be subsumed. Sometimes texts refer to Pisces as 'wishy-washy', because there is a passivity, a kind of inertia in these people that shows most clearly when a crisis is upon them. Watch a Pisces in a dilemma that calls for quick decision and action. You'll go grey waiting for that positive move. Decision, if it is to be quick, means you have to exclude one choice for another. To Pisces, the problem is that so many choices are available; and if you look at all of them carefully, why, they all contain some truth. How do you choose when every choice is a right – and a wrong – one?

This is one of the keys to Pisces' often enigmatic behaviour: everything is relative. Like all the other zodiacal traits we have explored, this one is double-edged. Seeing the relativity of truth is a great gift, because it breeds tolerance. If man throughout history had possessed a few more truly Piscean traits, there would have been no Spanish Inquisition, no Nazi holocaust, no Salem witch hunts, no bigotry and persecution. If everything is relative, then you can't condemn others for their viewpoints. The problem with this attitude is that it can be incredibly lax. Pisces has sometimes been accused of immorality. But that isn't strictly true; to be immoral, you have to have morals to break. And the calm wise indifference with which Pisces greets human transgressions not only applies to his own. He will sit quietly while his wife leaves, his children insult him, his employer heaps abuse upon his head, the taxman takes half his income, and his landlord throws

him out of his flat. It can drive you to frenzy – watching
the complete blank acceptance with which so many
Pisceans accept misfortune – as though they were born
to it, expect it, welcome it. And maybe they know
something the other signs don't – that all this suffering,
all this misfortune, means little if you are not attached
too strongly to life.

Pisces is the sign of the mystic. And this mystical
streak means several things. For one thing, many
Pisceans are deeply religious – although not necessarily
in an orthodox way. But they have a longing for, and a
sense of, some other reality, something transcendant,
magical, elusive, that makes ordinary life seem drab
and meaningless. Truly a vale of tears. For another
thing, Pisces has a deep wisdom about the futility of so
many human desires. Intense ambition, powerful passion, covetousness, greed – the ordinary human motives
that drive us all – pass through him and pass out again,
for none of them have that much power over him. He
is as capable of these emotions as any other sign. But
somehow, somewhere deep down, he doesn't really
take them all that seriously. After all, it's only *maya*, as
they say in the East – only illusion.

Pisceans seem to have this strange and cynical wisdom
about life and people even from childhood. Pisces
belongs to the element of water, and, like Cancer and
Scorpio, is deeply sensitive to the secret undercurrents
that lie behind the mask of ordinary human behaviour.
It's hard to fool a Pisces. But the difference between
the Fish and his two watery fellows is that Cancer and
Scorpio, being more strongly attached to their own
emotions, will act on their reactions. Cancer, sensing
that someone is a little untrustworthy, will move to
protect himself and his loved ones. Scorpio, sensing the
same thing, will usually attack the enemy, to teach him
a lesson, or withdraw in strong disgust. Pisces will look,
see, feel saddened, and forgive. And will generally let

himself be taken advantage of or cheated despite his insight. Why? Well, I've asked Pisces people that, when they've got into the classic Pisces bind of being the sucker. 'It doesn't really matter that much,' they say. Or, 'Well, he needed it more than I do.' Or some other remark which reminds you once again that this world is not the real one for the Fish. He hears a different drumbeat.

The Fish is a creature which lives underwater. And Pisces does too. He moves in the depths of a world which is difficult to fathom if you are an airy, earthy, rational type. Everything is seen double, or in quadruplicate; nothing is ever simple or clear. Every thought and action has thousands of associations which ripple out into infinity. Pisces does not understand boundaries. You can see this in the habits of the ordinary Pisces. He will frequently eat until he makes himself sick, or drink until he collapses, or get so loud and extroverted that he offends everybody, or go so quiet and withdrawn that he terrifies everyone. Everything to excess. It's because he doesn't really understand how to discriminate, how to limit, how to choose. If you have ever kept a tank of tropical fish, you will know that you cannot just leave a week's worth of food and go away on holiday. A fish will simply eat and eat what's in front of him until he kills himself. There's no sense of moderation in Pisces. How could there be? He's a creature from another world, unsure of and unused to the laws by which the clear, cold world of matter and facts operates.

What he has to compensate for this rather disturbing failing is a boundless imagination. For here too, the Pisces has no limits. He can envision anything. Einstein was a Pisces, and a good example of where a brilliant intellect can go when it is not hidebound by conventions and dogmas. Many great musicians and painters have been Pisceans; their imaginations know no bounds

Anything is possible. Pisces holds the secret to the source of life, the realm of dreams and fantasies. Psychology calls this the unconscious. Pisces has a key to this world – one given him at birth, as a gift. He can come and go as he pleases. The trouble is, he often finds it difficult to come back.

Pisces has a real problem coping with reality. That is, with the one bound by time and space and structure and facts. Although his intuition may be lightning-quick, and his intellect brilliant, he will often overlook something simple, like the electricity bill. Pisces has a bad reputation with money. It's not that he is 'impractical' in the ordinary sense. He may even display bouts of meanness, and have some pretty shrewd, canny ideas about how money might be made. It's more that he can't – and won't – bear limitations. The whole concept of being limited by time, space, and other people is intensely irritating to Pisces. His mind is on larger things.

This can be infuriating to more earthy types, or airy types who like everything planned, structured, and explained. Although Pisces, as a water sign, often finds himself in relationships with the air signs, they see reality in very different ways. For Pisces, these things are not important. He would rather decide on the spur of the moment to take a quick plane to Tahiti, or to suddenly buy a Porsche, than he would plan six months in advance a package Thompson holiday and a good, sensible Mini which uses less petrol and a smaller insurance premium. All this has led to Pisces being called childishly irresponsible. This is rather unfair. He's responsible enough with the things he cares about. It's just that his conception of what's real may differ from that of other people's. Quite radically.

Pisces is also an incurable romantic. He may have many defences to hide this innate tendency, but romantic he was born and romantic he will die. And romance doesn't just mean about love affairs. It means about everything. The house he lives in must be a castle, with moat and drawbridge; the car must be exotic, the bed revolving with platforms and coloured lights ... well, you get the idea. He lives in his imagination. In his imagination, everything is not only like a set piece out of *Star Wars*, but it also changes constantly. Pisces gets bored more easily than any other sign. The constantly changing landscape of the depths is not easily replaced by the unchanging banality of life on dry land. Pisces needs a little theatre in his life. If you can't provide it, he'll create it. Often to his own destruction. But that too has a dramatic ring.

If you like safe, solid people who always mean what they say and also mean it next week and the week after, stay away from Pisces. The only thing which is truly consistent about him is his love for, and longing for, change. That and the closeness he has to the world of dreams, which is far more important to him than the 'realities' of the welfare state where food, shelter and free medical care plus a visit to the local every two nights means happiness. Not for Pisces. Give him hyacinths for the soul anytime. He is remarkably adaptable, and can manage in a garret; but garrets are romantic. Council estates aren't.

♓ The Myth

In many fairy tales there is a peculiar and enchanting figure, sometimes called an ondine or melusine, sometimes called a mermaid, who lives in the depths of the sea or a vast lake, and falls in love with a mortal man. This legend may also be seen in the legend of the Swan Prince – although here the creature from the 'other realm' bears feathers rather than scales. And these ancient stories, in all their various forms, have the same basic theme: the union of a mortal, an ordinary flesh-and-blood human, with something from another level of reality. This meeting is fraught with difficulties. There are always conditions attached. And it usually ends in disaster or difficulty, not because it is doomed from the start, but because of the ineptitude of the mortal who attempts to impose his own laws or values on his mysterious, other-worldly partner.

Usually the melusine agrees to live on dry land, and inhabit a mortal body, so long as her mate observes one special condition. He must not ask her a particular question, or look in a particular box, or enter a particular room at a particular time. In other words, there must be respect for the mysteries of this other realm. And the mortal, driven by ordinary human curiosity and lack of respect for this magical dimension, inevitably asks the question or opens the box. So the bond is broken, the melusine disappears into the depths again, and he is left to sorrow. Or, sometimes, she drags him down with her, drowning him in her embrace.

This motif, which we can find in several myths and fairy tales, is a story which has special meaning for Pisces. As we have seen, Pisces is the last sign, the completion of the cycle. Every sign leaves its trace in Pisces; there is not so much a particular Piscean dilemma as that Pisces embodies the human dilemma. In this last of the zodiacal signs is represented all of man's helplessness, his longings, his dreams, his needs, his powerlessness in the face of the universe, his delusions of grandeur, his longing for love, his sense of a mystery or a divine source which he strives for yet cannot wholly reach without great sacrifice.

You might say that in every Pisces, symbolized by the two fish trying to swim in opposite directions yet bound together by a golden cord, there is this dilemma of a meeting of two dimensions. There is the ordinary

mortal side, which is used to facts and realities of a
tangible kind. Eat, sleep, make love, and die – or bread
and circuses, as the Romans used to say. And there is
also a melusine – or, in the case of Pisces women, the
masculine equivalent – which inhabits the dark depths,
and which occasionally flashes its tail above the water,
catching the sunlight, entrancing the mortal on the
shore. How this meeting is dealt with is the story of
each Piscean life. Some Pisceans simply follow the
mermaid down, forgetting that human lungs cannot
survive underwater. Here we have the derelicts of
humanity, the lines of the junkies and the chronic
alcoholics and the hopeless, the wasted, the despairing,
the abject. It is these whom Christ, in Christian
mythology, declared blessed, for they had sacrificed
everything of ordinary life and for their suffering had
earned the key to another realm.

For other Pisceans, the fairy tale has a different
ending. It is here that we can see the genius of men such
as Einstein – where the melusine, the glimpse of other
realms and of a universe barely comprehensible to the
ordinary mind in its majesty and infinity – is translated
through the human brain, offering to the world a
charting of the unknown waters.

Obviously, not every Piscean is an Einstein or a
drunkard. But perhaps the task of every Piscean is to
come to terms in some way with the transpersonal
realm, and to have the courage to be its mouthpiece.
Here we find the poets and musicians, the great actors
and playwrights, the visionaries and mystics who
attempt to bring to ordinary life a glimpse of something
else. This can be through a work of art, or it can exist
in the humblest expressions of human love.

It is not easy, perhaps, to be born as Pisces. Many
Pisceans simply cannot accept the size of the challenge.
And, after all, who can blame them? It is not easy to
make peace with a melusine; and our education does

not help us, since it tends to emphasize that anybody with the secret life of the Pisces must be at best a lazy daydreamer, and at worst emotionally disturbed. The fairy-tale world in which many Pisces children live is criticized, bludgeoned, mocked or argued out of them very early. And it's important to remember here that Pisces is a mutable – that is, a changeable – sign, malleable, easily influenced, often hungry to please. Pisces is more easily distorted, more easily pressured by a hostile environment, than any other sign. So the melusine calls unheard from the depths of the soul, and the average Piscean disguises himself from himself by a rationalistic attitude toward life.

Another important mythological motif that tells us something about the Fish is the Christian myth itself. When I use the word 'myth' here I do not mean to imply something true or untrue, but mean it in the sense that all myths are apertures into another world. If one is a Christian, then the New Testament is truth while the religious symbols of other faiths are myth; if one is either non-Christian or open-minded, one can see that all myths describe God. So let's look at the Christian myth.

The Christian era is sometimes known as the Age of Pisces. Without going into lengthy explanations about precessions of the equinoxes and other astronomical phenomena, let's just say that about every two thousand years a new zodiacal sign colours man's history and culture. You can see the traces of this sign at work particularly in the religious symbols that emerge during the time it is in power. The Fish is one of the great symbols of Christianity; and in this symbol can be found many important themes that pertain to Pisces, both in this broad way and in the individual life of the person born under the sign.

Firstly, there is the aspiration. Before the coming of Christianity, man and God were two different things;

there could be communication between them, there could be enmity or friendship; but man was not like God and God was not like man, and never the twain could meet. But one of the essential meanings of the Christian myth is that God incarnates as man; that there is a halfway point, an intermediary, a bridging of the two worlds. We are back to our friend the melusine here. But, instead of melusine, read soul or spirit. So we can, if we want to consider the religious aspect of Pisces, say that there is a strong awareness in many Pisceans, especially the more mystical ones, of themselves – and the whole of mankind – being some kind of halfway house between animal and divine.

You can imagine that this creates problems. Being aware of two dimensions like this is pretty confusing, especially when the one tends to pop up when the other should be operating. No wonder Pisces is said to be confused a lot of the time.

Second to the aspiration is the urge toward self-sacrifice. Now this can be of the noblest kind, and one of the characteristic renditions of this can be found in the lives of the Saints. These figures – whether one believes in Saints or not – are in a sense the epitome of this side of Pisces. Everything devoted to the ideal – whether it is God, a country, a people, the poor, the suffering, or whatever. Pisces may often be found searching desperately for a cause to which he can devote himself, even sacrifice himself. It is an ecstasy which the other signs want no part of, since they all still have left some shred of a personal sense of their own 'I'ness. Pisces doesn't. It's the completion of the cycle, the end. And there's a very strong tendency to want to give up everything, offer it up, disintegrate, disappear.

Compassion and love of an impersonal, unbiased kind are also Piscean virtues extolled in this last era. Love thy neighbour as thyself, turn the other cheek – these are Piscean aspirations. Of course you have to remember that there's another fish to the pair, too. But much of the history of religion in the last two thousand years has forgotten about that second fish. It's locked down in the basement, and popularly referred to as the Devil.

You get the picture. We can look objectively at the myths of the Greeks, Romans, Egyptians, or whomever, and see how some of these mythical heroes and motifs fit particular zodiac signs. If we can strip ourselves of our prejudices, and remember that every age has considered its teaching the only true one, we can perceive that in the figure of Christ we have a model of Pisces – as the sign would like to be. And in the figure of the Devil, we have the dark fish, the other fish, which we must now consider.

♓ The Shadow

You might know, of course, that nothing is all light. With all those beautiful aspirations and longings for purity, devotion, goodness, mercy, compassion and self-sacrifice, there's bound to be a pretty big wallop of a shadow downstairs. It's always like that, of course. And this basic law of life – that everything comes in opposites – is nowhere truer than of the sign of Pisces.

Remember that we said Pisces knew no limitations? This is certainly true of his aspiration. Nothing less than union with the divine, the source of life, will suit. Whether this is achieved through religious longing, creative expression, or heroin is not so important as the experience itself. Right? Right for Pisces, at any rate. And the dark fish knows no limits either. His name is Power.

In ordinary situations, Pisces tends to be the victim. We can meet this figure in many Pisceans – they are the ones who are taken advantage of, used, bled white for money and sympathy, held in bondage through their sympathy, made to feel obligated through their tendency to feel guilty for everybody else's sins. It is almost inevitably the Pisces who stays with the violent husband, nurses the schizophrenic wife, raises the retarded child, supports the ailing mother, gives up this, that or the other thing to help somebody else. It is sometimes very hard to tell whether these are the noblest or the silliest of human beings; and whether they are truly saints, or wield a tremendous power through making the other guy feel hopelessly obliged. Nobody has quite as much power as a martyr. Maybe it's a little of both.

In *The Iceman Cometh* by Eugene O'Neill there is a character named Harry: an ordinary sort of man with the usual array of vices and virtues. And Harry has a wife who, although we don't know whether Eugene O'Neill practised astrology, must surely be a Pisces. Harry's wife forgives him for everything. No matter how abusive he is, no matter how badly he treats her, she never raises her voice in anger, or rebels, or shows a little bitchiness herself. She always, always forgives. And of course it makes Harry worse. If you make anybody feel guilty, then they will resent you, and if they resent you, then they're going to treat you even more badly the next time. So Harry's treatment of his wife goes downhill, from bad to abominable. Soon he is beating her, bringing other women into the house, and other favourite pastimes of the Right Bastard. And Harry's wife does the natural Piscean thing: she forgives. She understands. She has compassion. She makes Harry feel so guilty, so terrible, that of course at the end he has to kill her. He simply has to. That's why saints are always martyred. Saints they may be; but they make the rest of us feel blacker. And anyone who poses as a saint is shirking his share of common evil, and reaps it triplefold.

There is an interesting moral in Harry's story about

Pisces. For one thing, it shows how much power this 'powerless' sign can wield. For another thing, it shows how much power Pisces often wants. Outward passivity is a dangerous animal, since the will has to go someplace. And every so often you see it break out, and encounter strange Pisceans like Attaturk and Julius Caesar, who, unlimited as always, must conquer the world.

Many Pisceans have this kind of secret fantasy. Feeling as though they are the most powerless of mortals, they secretly envision themselves as rulers over all. It's understandable enough. It's troublesone and even dangerous if it goes unnoticed and unchecked. Attaturk, when he took over the rulership of Turkey in 1930, massacred an entire nation of Armenians who stood in his path. This kind of universal emperor, who sees fit to wipe out masses of people, is the opposite extreme to the Christian eaten by the lion in the arena. Sometimes the roles reverse, and the lion is actually the Christian.

If a sensitive Pisces is brutalized enough – and they often are, for people tend to see in them the reflections of their own feared weaknesses and vulnerability – then he may turn to cruelty for an outlet. This is a perplexing quality in some Pisceans which is never discussed in textbooks, for the simple reason that it is too disturbing. Yet it is common enough, from the small example of the schoolchild who torments his fellows, or animals, to the large example of the psychotic. But what is this kind of cruelty? Once again, we must remember that Pisces represents not so much a type of person as a rendition of human nature. The Pisces is all of us. That's why he's so often the victim. It's exaggerated; but it's there. Watch the pattern of a Pisces' life, and you will see the reflection of any man's, distorted, exaggerated, but a true mirror. It's said that Pisceans make wonderful healers, priests, physicians, counsellors. This is undoubtedly true, for they have the innate compassion

and wisdom and insight. They can also heal because
they have been wounded, and because there isn't much
in human nature that they haven't already glimpsed in
themselves.

But a too passive Pisces is a dangerous creature. The
dark fish is bound to break out sooner or later, either
in a genuine psychosis, or in self-destruction – whether
quick or the slow kind like drug addiction or alcoholism
– or in subtle, unnoticed destruction of another, like
Harry's wife in *The Iceman Cometh*. It's rarely overt;
unless that Pisces has a more aggressive ascendant like
Aries or Leo, or a strong Mars, it's all under the surface,
for Pisces is a genius at undercurrents.

There's another side to the Pisces shadow, which is
connected to the first. We can call this syndrome the
Misunderstood Genius.

FRIEND TO PISCES: So what are you doing lately?
Haven't seen you in a couple of years.
PISCES: Well, I'm working on a really great novel.
I've just got the first twenty pages done, but I can
envision the whole thing in my mind. It's going to be
the greatest literary work of the century. I always
knew I had it in me to write a great novel.
FRIEND: But didn't you have about three others
started when I last saw you? I thought . . .
PISCES: (*embarrassed and beginning to feel as though
Friend is accusing him of something*) Oh, those were
only trial runs. This one is the real thing. I'd probably
have it finished now, if it weren't for that damned
part-time job I've got, in the library. I get so tired
that I can't write at night.
FRIEND: How often do you work there?
PISCES: Oh, only a day a week. But, you know,
there's so much to do around the flat, and my reading,
I mean, you can't write a novel without reading other
people's work, and I watch TV a lot, and films, and . . .

FRIEND: (*beginning not to believe*) Well, good luck with it.

PISCES: (*on the defensive*) You don't think I'll finish it, do you? I suppose you think I have no talent. But I do, you know. Just wait. Nobody understands. I wrote a few pieces for magazines, but the editors are these typical fools, they only publish rubbish, they don't know a good thing when they see it. Just wait You'll hear of me one day. Then you'll be sorry.

FRIEND: Sure, man, I didn't mean . . . Well, anyway, good luck.

The Misunderstood Genius, often a Pisces or a Pisces ascendant, most emphatically doesn't lack talent. What he lacks is realism. Pisces, with such a rich, abundant, limitless imagination, often bitterly resents the ordinary limitations of time and space. And those brilliant ideas that flash through his mind like the flash of a fish in the water are often truly brilliant. What he lacks is staying power, discipline, continuity, and the ordinary respect for hard work and good craftsmanship that has propelled many a mediocre writer of far less ability into fame and fortune. Pisces often presents himself as the new Poet, the new Writer, the new Film-maker, the new Prophet. One day . . . when the world understands him . . . But the world is so annoying sometimes. It expects him, HIM . . . to hustle like ordinary folk, work ordinary jobs, pay ordinary rent bills and electricity bills and national health stamps and car insurance, when it should all be made easy, after all, if they only knew what talent he had, what he could do for the world . . . A familiar story, and a sad one. And the saddest part of all is that, often, the Pisces won't be able to find the happy middle, the balance point between valuing his dreams and taking the time to craft them into shape. He simply becomes embittered, disillusioned, and gives up in disgust. So the visionary becomes the most prosaic and most cynical of men, and never writes a line again, or scorns that paintbox that lays in the attic gathering dust. And he can say to his grandchildren, 'Yes, once I dreamt of being a painter . . . But . . . but . . . something went wrong.' What? The confrontation with reality, the meeting of the melusine with the mortal. Either extreme is failure: drowning underwater, or losing the dream because it's exposed too soon, without faith.

Pisces is sometimes called the sign of self-undoing. And it is important to remember that it's truly self-undoing with Pisces, never the undoing of others. Pisces often has such a wealth of talent and vision that he is one of the most blessed of men. Yet so often his life is a failure. And this is because of his shadow: his visions of self-aggrandisement are so often too large, much too immense to ever be fulfilled, so he's doomed to self-disappointment and self-disgust. And his bitterness at life can erode him, because he feels betrayed by it. If he can begin to understand that he is it, that there isn't any 'world' that is inimical to him, that he must simply understand both the divine and the mortal sides of himself and care for them both, then he's truly unlimited. And what strange children marriage with a melusine can produce!

♓ The Pisces Lover

You might expect that all the qualities we have mentioned about Pisces would be in abundant display in his love-life, for Pisces is usually in love. If not with a human being, then with a cause, or with God, but he is usually in love. It is in his nature to give; and since this is a water sign, a sign of feeling, it is impossible for Pisces to conceive of a life alone – unless it is the kind of aloneness which the monk or the nun elects in exchange for union of a different kind.

You may see the sensitivity, the gentleness, the tendency to devotedness in abundance. You may also see the overcompensation of many Pisceans to their own need for people, exhibited in coolness and a deliberately forced detachment. You may see the Piscean tendency always to put the other person's wishes first, and to blossom under any show of affection or tenderness. Or you may see the shadow side take over, where the partner must always be in the position of the servant catering to the lord's whims. Either way, the root is the same. If Pisces can trust, he will give everything. Not necessarily tomorrow, or next year. Fidelity and structure are not part of his nature. But today, now, in this moment. And if you string together a long string of moments, you may discover that it's been a lifetime.

One of the more disturbing qualities about Pisces is that he is so ready to enter into a relationship with just about anybody on a certain superficial level that people misunderstand his motives. He's not really coming on; he's listening with sympathy. He's also easily seduced, not necessarily only literally. You can't cage Pisces; his extroverted side flows out so easily to other people that you may as well get used to it. But this is, remember, a wise soul. He sees through people very quickly. And although he's led often one way or the next out of sympathy or flattery or a stronger personality, he has the capacity to recognize what's really of value to him.

This is not likely to be a lover who only notices one man, or one woman. That's impossible for Pisces; he's not only interested in everybody, he's often attracted to everybody. His morals are his own; better find out what they are first, so you aren't surprised later. Don't take them for granted. But the curious detachment in this sign is in evidence even in these highly fraught situations; when he says it meant nothing, it probably meant nothing, and it would be better if it meant nothing to you too. If you're the really possessive type, you're in a little trouble. He may be technically faithful; his imagination certainly isn't, and never will be. Not likely that he'll be either. But it depends upon whether you value technical fidelity, or a depth of understanding and tacit communion which no other sign can offer.

There is also a quality in Pisces, like Virgo – the opposite sign – which is essentially untouched and unpossessable, no matter how formal the contract is, no matter how long you've known him. Some part of Pisces will always belong to the cosmos, to his own inner self, and not to you. Unlike the simpler signs such as Aries or Taurus, Pisces is simply not capable of saying, 'Here I am, a simple soul at heart, I'm yours.' He may give you forty-five of the sixty-eight selves he's discovered that week. Don't expect all of them. There will be dreams, visions, that he can never communicate. If you keep asking a Pisces what he's thinking about every time he gets that vague, dreamy look in his eye, you'll drive him and yourself crazy, and never get any satisfactory answers. The real truth is that he probably doesn't know; he just went off, and if left alone, will undoubtedly come back again. Many of Pisces' ways of communicating are nonverbal; it's not a sign that excels at debate and defence. Many Pisceans are completely inept at explaining themselves or their feelings. They rely on touch, atmosphere, a subtle communion that is almost telepathic. Try to force them into rigid explanations and definitions and it's like holding a handful of water; it slides through your fingers and is gone.

Evasiveness is a word often used to describe Pisces. Deceptiveness is as well. But it isn't the calculated statesmanship of the Capricorn, or the deliberate secretiveness of the Scorpio, or the mental gymnastics of the Gemini. When you see thirty different things, how can you explain one? Expecially when the chances are that the other person can't even comprehend what it's like to see thirty? And ambivalent emotion – well, that's equally difficult. How to explain when you love and hate someone, when they're ugly and beautiful, when everything shifts and changes and takes a new shape faster than you can say chameleon? For all these reasons and more, Pisces is an elusive partner. You take the feelings as they come, and let them go as they go. Attempting to define and freeze them into structures is a futile exercise. Many people are badly hurt by Pisces, not because the sign is cold and unfeeling, but because the other person expects a conventional linear expression of love, like 'I love you, I always will, and that's it,' when a phrase like that is downright ridiculous to the Piscean who knows that love is a very varied state, that it has many meanings all of which change all the time, that everything is relative, that you can't plan the future, etc., etc.

But if you know enough of the world and yourself to allow for motion rather than stasis, basking in the flow of a Piscean's feelings can be the most healing and regenerative relationship you'll ever have. The trick, perhaps, is not to ever trample on his dreams, nor ever think you understand him completely. Just when you do, he'll change on you. If you dislike change, pick a Taurean or a Leo. But if you like unexplored regions, and unclimbed mountains, and futures that are shrouded in mist and beckon, and magic castles with unexplored treasures, then don't fear Pisces. Only don't think you've got only one person. You've got everybody. A cast of thousands. What better way is there to learn about life?

♓ The Pisces Man

You may have observed that Pisces is a strongly feminine sign. Feminine, that is, in terms of its feeling bias, its imagination, its softness, its compassion. Many Pisces men are extremely masculine, and perfectly capable of what Jung calls, Knowing what you want and doing what you have to do to get it. But all in all, the combination of being a man and being a Pisces is a slightly uneasy one. Largely, once again, because of collective pressures and social expectations.

There are a great many turntypes among Pisces men. They compensate in a thousand ways for being Pisceans. Some of them run in terror from the depths of their underwater visions, into an extreme and brittle kind of rationality which calls for statistics, definitions, and proofs. They are the dogmatic material scientists, attempting to stamp out in others what they fear in themselves. They have no tolerance for what they call 'emotionality', and cannot abide moodiness in others because their own threatens to overwhelm them.

But if a Pisces man has the courage to face his own vulnerability, and to see that it can live happily side by side with his manhood, then you have a rare creature. And if he's able to maintain his manhood without disappearing underwater into the realms of escape, that is. This is the hero of so many books and films, the antihero, the gentle fighter, the sensitive lover. It's perhaps closer to our modern myth of man than any other, since it's a peculiar marriage of male and female. The Pisces man who has accomplished this has a rare charisma, a drama about him that makes him endlessly fascinating both to men and women alike.

Sadly, many more Pisces men hit the extremes. We've

mentioned the rationalist, the Pisces who hates being a Pisces and wants desperately to protect his own sensitivity. The opposite kind is also common enough. He's the fellow who loves strong women, especially women who can support him financially; who can take care of him while he's writing the eternal half-finished novel, while he's contemplating the job he'll never take. He's the passive victim, abused and betrayed by a cold, brutal wife, looking for pity and sympathy and playing for all its worth to the maternal instinct of some poor foolish woman who thinks all his romanticism is true tenderness and feeling. These are pathetic Pisceans, and their wives and lovers are frustrated women who have to be men most of the time and chafe violently against it. Many Piscean men of this type gravitate toward the powerful signs in women: Leo, Aries, Scorpio, Capricorn. They have no strength of their own, and seek it in a partnership.

As you might guess, Pisces tends to run to extremes. It's rare that you get a neutral Pisces. It's generally one extreme or the other.

The Pisces man generally needs to feel 'understood' more than anything else. This isn't so much a sign of strong physical passion as it is a sensuous sign, a sybaritic sign. Dragging the woman off by the hair to the cave isn't generally Pisces' style. Allowing himself to strike up a warm, sympathetic conversation and then allowing himself to be seduced by good wine, soft music, satin sheets and erotic underwear is much more his style. Pisces is as happy being passive as a lover as he is being, literally or figuratively, the one on top. It's his particular brand of masculinity. Often he will make himself the buffoon, the clown, the victim, for he works a lot from sympathy and empathy. Women love to protect him. He can protect himself perfectly well. But it isn't always in his interests to let you know that.

Trust him and you'll bring the best out of him. See

only the shadowy side of him and he'll have a devil of a time trusting himself. He never trusts himself anyway; he's brutally realistic, beneath all those visions. He needs the trust and loyalty of another person to bring out his own – the realistic trust, that is. Accuse him of something, and he'll happily go out and do it, just to please. His way of fighting is not to fight; it's to bend so far backwards that you fall on your face. Impotence is also his way of fighting. In this, you'll see the feminine side of the sign in strong colours. Passive resistance is a technique dear to the Piscean heart.

You might think he can be easily dominated. Think again. In fact his world doesn't include dominant or submissive. He'll play pliant on the surface because it's easier, because it's not that often important enough to draw blood. Beneath that pliant surface, it isn't that he needs to control; he just wants to be left alone. Try to dominate, and you'll discover you're empty-handed. He's simply drifted away, without a fuss.

If you are the type who likes to have all your decisions made for you, don't choose a Pisces. On the other hand, if you want someone to henpeck, pass on this one too. Now you see him, now you don't. No promise or marriage contract means anything to him if the fundamental values of the relationship have been abused. And he'll see through all games pretty quickly. He just won't be there the next morning. No note, no phone call. Just gone. Like the fish.

But if you want a relationship which is more nearly like the ideal vision of what the so-called 'liberated' woman seeks (and these are rare animals as well), you will find that Pisces is not one of your diehard male chauvinists. Being strongly emotional himself, he usually has immense empathy for women. He generally gets on with them better than men. And with his profound understanding of human nature, you're not likely either to be the housekeeper or the sex object. You get to be a person. And that's worth quite a lot.

♓ The Pisces Woman

Many paeans have been written to the Pisces woman, for her mystery, her gentleness, her compassion, her elusive charm, her pregnant silences. And she may be, indeed, the archetypal feminine. The lovely, gracious princess of the fairy-tale castle, waiting for the suitor to rescue her and cherish and protect her, is modelled on Pisces. The Pisces woman has a unique ability to make a man feel terribly masculine, because she seems so often to need protecting, cherishing, and tenderness. Because she has such a changeable range and depth of feeling, she often gives the impression of being slightly unformed. It brings out the Pygmalion tendencies in any would-be artisans. Many men think they can shape her into what they choose. In part, it's true. The qualities of devotion and gentleness and softness are in abundance in many Pisces women. But blank slate she's not.

Like the Pisces man, she's unfathomable, and possesses a soul which no one can ultimately reach. Although eager to please and rarely argumentative, she also has the gift of defence through submergence. Now you see her, now you don't. She may physically disappear, usually with a lover; but more likely she'll be physically present and simply psychologically disappear, gone to the underwater realms or to someone else in fantasy. It's a very peculiar feeling when she's gone. No one home.

Romanticism runs very high in the Pisces woman. She expects, and needs, the poetry and tenderness and style that any fairy-tale princess merits. Starve her of these and you will drive her either to another lover or into herself, where she may transform into the martyr.

Provide them, and your princess becomes a queen. Simple. Yet astonishingly difficult for many men, since Pisces, as a watery sign, seems to attract airy types who believe they can impress her with their sparkling intellects and long for the exhibitions of feeling she herself provides without realizing they must give in exchange.

And make no mistake, the Pisces woman, if she is disappointed, will not hesitate to deceive. Remember Elizabeth Taylor and Richard Burton? Being good to her isn't enough. You must enter her dreams with her. Ignore them, patronize them, and you do so at your own risk. There is a strongly theatrical element in the Pisces woman. She has a unique gift for getting herself into the most dreadful dilemmas and crises which no one could possibly sort out, and then going about among her friends asking for advice which is never taken since her need to suffer and sacrifice is fed by the dilemma. A perplexing creature.

But meet her in later life, and all the compassion and wisdom which come from having seen the seamy side of just about everything yield a glow and a richness which is far more meaningful than the unshaped marble which Pygmalion sees in her late teens and early twenties. In this, the last of the signs, the Wise Woman emerges – with all the instinctual wisdom of her sex and all the human insights of her sign. Often she is almost mediumistic, preferring to shelter herself from life because this gift is so dubious and so difficult to bear. There is also more than a touch of the witch in Pisces; whether it is white or black depends on whether she has been badly bruised, and how badly. A Pisces woman gone wrong is a vampire, playing on the fantasy life of others, and draining their strength. Never underestimate her, because she may be inarticulate or reluctant to explain herself. Neptune is an enigmatic god; to love him is to love the ocean, for all its moods and changes, its anger and its peacefulness, its destruction and its beauty.

Some Further Last Words...

*L*et's look now at a typical scenario of air and water relationships. We can call it the Intellectual and the Loyal Helpmeet.

It usually begins, like all good romances, with lots of promise. The Intellectual generally has a pretty good opinion of himself because the rest of the world keeps telling him it's wonderful to be an intellectual. He may have learned to control or repress his innate loneliness and his inability to relate to people. He has learned – say at about age twenty-five – to live primarily in his head. And what an impressive head it is! He may be a lecturer at a good university. He may be an economist, or a politician. What he does is Important. At least, that's what everyone has told him, all along the way. His parents did, because it made them feel important to have such a Bright Boy in the family. His teachers did, because they were taught that Intelligence was the same as Intellectuality. He is totally inept in human relationships – in a word, grossly insensitive. He doesn't know how to pay a compliment to save his life. He's shy, awkward and clumsy with women, so he compensates by being arrogant and assuming they're stupid. Besides, he has Important Work to do.

Not an attractive animal, you might say. In fact, you might not know many of these. They are not usually the ones who come to your Saturday night dinner party. They are busy running the government, making the laws of the country in which you live, determining educational policy, setting up medical programmes, and generally controlling everything in the world around you. As I said, they have Important Work to do. The fact that our Bright Boy doesn't know a flying pilchard's worth about how people feel is beside the point. He has fourteen university degrees and can prove anything by statistical analysis. God help us.

Well, one day our bright boy meets a Suitable Match. She is usually someone his family has arranged for him to meet, although sometimes Bright Boys marry 'out of their class', which means somebody *not* arranged by the family. Now the Suitable Match is usually warm, sweet, sympathetic and charming. She, because she is primarily a feeling type, has not been encouraged to make anything of her life. After all, only Bright Boys and Bright Girls should pursue careers. The Suitable Match is generally expected to marry well, be a good wife and mother, and sacrifice her own wishes and individuality to keep the home together while hubby goes off to his Important Work.

Because our Suitable Match usually underestimates her own intelligence – a characteristic of the water signs, who are quick to absorb popular opinion about what makes an intelligent person – she will settle for this kind of drivel without much question. Besides, she's only nineteen, and what can you expect? Also, because her feelings are so important to her, she will do virtually anything to keep a relationship together. She is usually fairly devoted to her family. She hates to hurt anyone. She's wonderful with stray cats. She once thought of doing something in the helping professions – nursing, say, or social work, or maybe even a degree in psychology. Degree, did I hear you say? She's perfectly capable of it. But usually the watery types are impressed with their own lack of intellectual acumen. 'Oh, no,' you'll hear her say, 'I'm sure I would never have been able to do it. All that academic work seems so difficult.'

Anyhow, they marry. He, because he has the idea that she's the perfect match. Firstly, she's attractive; secondly, she's suitable; thirdly, she so obviously idealizes his brilliant intelligence and listens, really listens, to everything he says. And what he says is so Important. Their conversations consist generally of his views on how the world can be changed, or the chemical formulae that produce mutations in fruit flies, or the political theories of J. D. Smith reinterpreted. Hers consist of fond, 'Really? Oh, how wonderful!' and a strong inner feeling that he's just a large overgrown child playing adult. Well, he is. She's full of tenderness and ideal love.

Look at them a few years later. Many years later. She has had the obligatory 2·5 children – partially because she really likes children, they're so helpless and lovely, and they need her. She's begun to learn that Bright Boy doesn't. At least, not in any recognizable way. His Important Work keeps him working long hours, and this is his excuse for being tired, insensitive, boorish and inconsiderate when he comes home. When he arrives, he expects her to always be warm, sweet and charming, just as she was when they first met, along with a well-prepared meal, a wonderful warm atmosphere, attentive and well-disciplined children that don't demand too much of him and are always neat and presentable; and he expects her to be available when and if he's sexually interested. (Bright Boys aren't known for their passion, which tends to be regulated to Saturday nights except before elections and football matches.)

And she? Well, she's seething, positively boiling with resentment. It's so hot and explosive that her hands shake. Does she know it? Probably not. Firstly, it would be too painful to recognize that there is something seriously wrong with this relationship. Her own feeling needs have in no way been met; she has the security, materially, but no affection. That would mean leaving; and the severing of relationships, especially old, established ones, is a positive agony for the watery type. Better to endure it and make the sacrifices. Secondly, it would involve a confrontation. And water signs are not very good at arguments and confrontations, largely because their sensitivity to atmosphere and their need for harmony makes it a nightmare. Even a small argument is an anguish.

So a little more time goes by. Bright Boy's friends are almost exclusively involved with his Important Work; he only brings them home for Important Dinners, where she is relegated to the role of Good Hostess. Her friends are usually other married women, with whom she discusses the children, clothes, gossip and his Important Work (which she has never really taken the time to understand, any more than he has taken the time to explain it to her).

Wouldn't you know it. The outcome is predictable. She has the requisite Affair.

Bright Boy, on his side, hasn't had any 'affairs'. He has had what is known fondly as an 'occasional screw' – usually while travelling on business, and usually a meaningless, sad scenario with an unknown face on the pillow in the morning and the usual curt insensitivity as he leaves. He has no room for emotion – only sentiment. Loyal Helpmeets, on the other hand, tend to get heavily entangled with people like the Neighbour, or the girlfriend's Husband. It's because they're so under-standing – known, familiar, sympathetic. The Neighbour is over one day (to borrow a cup of sugar?) and she breaks down in tears, and it all comes out, how badly he treats her, how cold he is, how unfeeling toward the children, and the next thing is that somehow they're in the bedroom, and you know the rest. Neighbour, however, is usually married himself. But that's a whole other scenario.

If he's unmarried, it's the long, agonizing process of How Can I Leave Him? What About the Children? It's suffering and sacrifice all the way. The truth of it – the cold, brutal truth – is that she doesn't want to leave our Bright Boy. She wants him to give her what she needs, which he's incapable of doing. Unless he opens his eyes, that is. Generally his eyes are opened by the discovery of the affair, or the elopement. Then he plays Betrayed. Betrayed has known all along that women were basically untrustworthy creatures, demanding, possessive, etc. Really he's talking about the woman in himself – the repressed, trampled feeling nature he has never really dealt with. She's Wronged Wife – and he becomes the scapegoat for all she hasn't done in her own life. Then follows the Settlement, Maintenance Payments and Child Support scenario, which is too unpleasant even to write about.

Sounds cynical? How right you are. An awful lot of marriages end this way, between air and water types. Is there any alternative? Of course there is. As follows.

Bright Boy, in the first place, can take a good honest look at himself along the way, from a perspective other than the one in which he has been brought up. Is his excellent intellect really an excuse for the complete lopsidedness of his nature? No, it isn't. It may be socially acceptable, but it's psychologically very unhealthy, and sooner or later the price is paid for such a violation of nature. He can try, and trying means a lot, to understand his own feelings as well as those of other people; to become more aware of the feeling level of life; and to respect what he doesn't understand, if they aren't his own values. He can learn to recognize that a need for affection over the breakfast coffee is as Important Work as whatever it is he's going to do to save the world. Important because what is the world, except what we see through our own eyes? And he can make an effort to like and understand women as friends, and even as intellectual companions, without the usual contempt so characteristic of this type.

Loyal Helpmeet can, on her side, discover that she's a person too, and that she can be an interesting person with an interesting life. She doesn't have to justify her life by the fact that she loves; she can also think, work, create, travel, and discover her own individuality. She can also do something about her own mental laziness, instead of expecting everyone else to do it for her. Like finding out what she thinks about things, rather than disgorging half-digested meals of other people's opinions. She can make an effort to see that Bright Boy, whatever his faults, has ideals which are really important to him; that he's something more than a large overgrown infant who needs regular meals. He needs friendship and companionship, not mothering.

Simple things. But difficult, because they mean that each of these two people needs to understand something of the reality of the other. What can they then give each other? Water can give air healing and love, warmth and affection, human relationship and human reality, to balance the crystal-clear intellect with human values and a heart. Air can give water objectivity, a vision of the larger world, the stimulus of ideas and discussion, and a realization that people are different and think differently and have different needs. If you looked at them in a few years, you wouldn't find them polarized, but meeting somewhere in the middle, having enriched each others' lives. Why must it be so hard? Probably because most of us can't be bothered to take the time.

Conclusion

This little astrological survey has not always been kind. It has in many places been deeply cynical and, I hope, disillusioning. There isn't a great deal of time these days for the luxury of entertaining sacred cows – particularly when two thousand years of blindness have pushed us to the point where the rate of mental illness, emotional disturbance, marital and sexual crises is so enormously high. It's pretty useless to blame the times, the government, or the society. As Jung once wrote,

> If there is something wrong with society, there is something wrong with the individual. And if there is something wrong with the individual, there is something wrong with me.

But the cynicism with which the astrological types have been portrayed is not a true cynicism. It is meant as a prod, a goad to look.

Astrology is, as we have seen, a guideline, a pointer to human behaviour. We don't enter the world as blank slates ready to be written on by parents, society, education. We come in as individuals – however small the spark. Something in each person is especially him, unique, and not like anybody else. Something in each person is also, if you like, divine – or, if you prefer the more prosaic way of looking at it, each person's life has a meaning or purpose which it is up to him to explore and discover. Working from the outside in has never helped much in seven or eight thousand years of history.

Working from the inside out hasn't really been tried. Maybe it's the only solution we've got left.

And astrology also has no morals. It isn't either good or bad to be an Aries or a Taurus, an air sign or a water sign. Each of them has a piece of the truth, a piece of reality. Each of them is incomplete. Whatever you start with, where you finish is up to you. Some of the typical patterns, the sad scenarios described, aren't fated. They're what we do with what we have when we're blind, stupid, and human. They can all be rewritten, a little or a lot. Why are we so afraid to recognize that we play a part in the cosmos, and the cosmos plays a part in us?

One of the axioms of modern depth psychology is that each individual has in him an innate need to be whole, to be complete. It's also quite apparent if you look at people that we aren't whole or complete. We live in an age of specialization – the Renaissance Universal Man was an ideal which died quickly in the midst of the dubiously named Age of Enlightenment.

We're also educated not to be whole. Instead, we increase the natural lopsidedness with which we're born by aggravating what we do well, and pretending to ignore what we do badly. And we fall in love, most of the time, with people who might just possibly replace what's missing. Opposites, as the old saying goes, attract. You'd think this would make a marriage made in heaven. It would, if it weren't for the little overlooked fact that opposites also repel. When confronted with an opposite, there is just as strong a desire to convert it as there is to merge with it. Change that person, we say, to make him see life more like I do.

Maybe the way through isn't either to make oneself over (like the Loyal Helpmeet) to please the opposite, or to patronize the opposite because it's too stupid to be like oneself. And maybe it's not such a good idea, either, to expect the opposite to clean up our own mess, (like the Eternal Youth) or to believe our one and only meaning in life is to take care of somebody else (like the Earth Mother). Ambrose Bierce once wrote:

An egotist is somebody who has the audacity to think he's more important than I am.

Maybe the way through is to find a place in the middle to meet. And even if you don't succeed in any ideal way – for fairy tales don't come true in the complexities of human relationships in any obvious way – your life is enriched that much more by trying.

Other people are a mystery. They behave as they do because of their own inner logic, not yours. Their realities are different, their hearts are different, their ideals are different. Some are, naturally, more congenial. We can't really love everybody. But we can understand, and here astrology has a very loud and important voice. More than anything else, it aids in understanding, and from understanding comes genuine (not patronizing) tolerance. And also compassion, which is one of the basic building blocks of love. Know something about the other signs, the other elements, and you discover that the world is much larger than you thought, and much more interesting.

And for those who don't want it larger, who want to keep it small and exclusive so that there is only one truth, one reality – well, don't blame fate for what happens. I wish you luck. But life itself is against you.